The Garland Library of the History of Western Music

One hundred eighty-five articles in fourteen volumes

General Editor
Ellen Rosand
Rutgers University

Contents
of
the
Set

Volume Fourteen

*Approaches
to
Tonal
Analysis*

*Garland Publishing, Inc.
New York & London
1985*

Library of Congress Cataloging-in-Publication Data
Main entry under title:
Approaches to tonal music.

  (The Garland library of the history of western music ; v. 14)
  1. Musical analysis—Addresses, essays, lectures.   I. Series.
MT6.A67   1985   781   85-16825
ISBN 0-8240-7463-7 (alk. paper)

The volumes in this series have been printed on acid-free,
250-year-life paper.

Printed in the United States of America

Contents

Acknowledgments

Cone, Edward T. "Three Ways of Reading a Detective Story—or a Brahms Intermezzo," *Georgia Review*, XXXI (1977), 554–74. Copyright © 1977 by the University of Georgia, reprinted by permission

Forte, Allen. "Motive and Rhythmic Contour in the Alto Rhapsody," *Journal of Music Theory*, XXVII (1983), 255–71. Copyright © 1983 by the *Journal of Music Theory*, reprinted by permission

Imbrie, Andrew W. " 'Extra' Measures and Metrical Ambiguity in Beethoven," in *Beethoven Studies*, I, ed. Alan Tyson (New York: W. W. Norton, 1973), pp. 45–66. Copyright © 1973 by W. W. Norton, Inc., reprinted by permission

Keller, Hans. "K. 503: The Unity of Contrasting Themes and Movements," *The Music Review*, XVII (1956), 48–58, 120–29. Copyright © 1956 by *The Music Review*, reprinted by permission

LaRue, Jan. "A System of Symbols for Formal Analysis," *Journal of the American Musicological Society*, X (1957), 25–28. Copyright © 1957 by the American Musicological Society, reprinted by permission

Meyer, Leonard B. "Grammatical Simplicity and Relational Richness: The Trio of Mozart's G minor Symphony," *Critical Inquiry*, II (1975–76), 693–761. Copyright © 1976 by The University of Chicago, reprinted by permission

Mitchell, William J. "The Tristan Prelude: Techniques and Structure," *The Music Forum*, I, ed. William J. Mitchell and Felix Salzer (New York: Columbia University Press, 1967), pp. 162–203. Copyright © 1967 by Columbia University Press, reprinted by permission

Réti, Rudolph. "The Thematic Plan of the Ninth Symphony," in Réti, *The Thematic Process in Music* (New York: Macmillan, 1951), pp. 11–30. Copyright © 1951 by Rudolph Réti, reprinted by permission

Schachter, Carl. "Rhythm and Linear Analysis: Durational Reduction," *The Music Forum*, V, ed. Felix Salzer (New York: Columbia

Preface

The Garland Library of the History of Western Music, in fourteen volumes, is a collection of outstanding articles in musicology that have been reprinted from a variety of sources: periodicals, *Festschriften*, and other collections of essays. The articles were selected from a list provided by a panel of eminent musicologists, named below, who represent the full range of the discipline.

Originally conceived in general terms as a collection of outstanding articles whose reprinting would serve the needs of students of musicology at the graduate and advanced undergraduate level, the series took clearer shape during the process of selecting articles for inclusion. While volumes covering the conventional chronological divisions of music history had been projected from the very beginning, several other kinds of volumes cutting across those traditional divisions and representing the interests of large numbers of scholars eventually suggested themselves: the volumes on opera, source studies, criticism, and analysis.

Indeed, although the general objective of excellence remained standard for the entire series, the specific criteria for selection varied somewhat according to the focus of the individual volumes. In the two on opera, for example, chronological coverage of the history of the genre was of primary importance; in those on source studies, criticism, and analysis the chief aim was the representation of different points of view; and in the volumes devoted to chronological periods selection was guided by an effort to cover the various geographical centers, genres, and individual composers essential to the understanding of a historical era.

The articles themselves were written over a period spanning more than a half century of modern musicological scholarship. Some are "classic" statements by scholars of the past or early formulations by scholars still active today, in which musicological method, intellectual vision, or significance for their time rather than any specific factual information is most worthy of appreciation. Others represent the most recent research, by younger scholars as well as more established ones. No general attempt has been made to bring the articles up to date, although some authors have included addenda and misprints have been corrected where possible.

Since no single reader could be fully satisfied by the selection of articles in his own field, the aims of this collection, by necessity, have had to be considerably broader: to provide not only a wide range of articles on a large number of topics by a variety of authors but to offer the student some sense of the history and development of individual fields of study as well as of the discipline as a whole. The value of these volumes derives from the material they contain as well as from the overview they provide of the field of musicology; but the series will fulfill its function only if it leads the student back into the library, to immerse himself in all the materials necessary to a fuller understanding of any single topic.

Ellen Rosand

Panel of Advisors

Richard J. Agee, The Colorado College
James R. Anthony, University of Arizona
William W. Austin, Cornell University
Lawrence F. Bernstein, University of Pennsylvania
Bathia Churgin, Bar-Ilan University
Edward T. Cone, Princeton University
John Deathridge, King's College, Cambridge
Walter Frisch, Columbia University
Sarah Ann Fuller, SUNY at Stony Brook
James Haar, University of North Carolina at Chapel Hill
Ellen Harris, University of Chicago
D. Kern Holoman, University of California at Davis
Robert Holzer, University of Pennsylvania
Philip Gossett, University of Chicago
Douglas Johnson, Rutgers University
Jeffrey Kallberg, University of Pennsylvania
Janet Levy, New York, New York
Kenneth Levy, Princeton University
Lowell Lindgren, Massachusetts Institute of Technology
Robert Marshall, Brandeis University
Leonard B. Meyer, University of Pennsylvania
Robert P. Morgan, University of Chicago
John Nádas, University of North Carolina at Chapel Hill
Jessie Ann Owens, Brandeis University
Roger Parker, Cornell University
Martin Picker, Rutgers University
Alejandro Planchart, University of California at Santa Barbara
Harold Powers, Princeton University
Joshua Rifkin, Cambridge, Massachusetts
John Roberts, University of Pennsylvania

Stanley Sadie, Editor, *The New Grove Dictionary of Music and Musicians*

Norman E. Smith, University of Pennsylvania

Howard E. Smither, University of North Carolina at Chapel Hill

Ruth Solie, Smith College

Maynard Solomon, New York, New York

Ruth Steiner, The Catholic University of America

Gary Tomlinson, University of Pennsylvania

Leo Treitler, SUNY at Stony Brook

James Webster, Cornell University

Piero Weiss, Peabody Conservatory

Eugene K. Wolf, University of Pennsylvania

Volume Fourteen

*Approaches
to
Tonal
Analysis*

Edward T. Cone

THREE WAYS OF READING A DETECTIVE STORY— OR A BRAHMS INTERMEZZO

O NE of the reasons we like to read stories is to find out what happens. It is certainly not the only reason, and for some of us it may even be a minor one; but for others it is all-important. Obviously, then, an essential element of a narrative writer's technique is his control of the reader's awareness of events. The skillful author makes sure that we learn what has happened, what is happening, and what is going to happen, exactly when he wants us to know it, and not earlier or later.

From the writer of a mystery, in particular, we expect a high degree of precision in this regard. To be sure, we must avoid traps of the kind that Dickens laid for the unwary in *Our Mutual Friend*. As he wrote in the Postscript to that novel, "I foresaw the likelihood that a class of readers and commentators would suppose that I was at great pains to conceal exactly what I was at great pains to suggest. . ." (namely, the identity of his hero). But in the typical detective story, to allow the average reader to deduce or guess the solution too early on—before the actual dénouement—would be a major flaw revealing gross technical deficiency. For most of us, indeed, the nagging suspicion that we have already solved the riddle makes it almost impossible to continue to read a mystery with much pleasure. But if that is the case, how can we ever read a mystery for a second or even a third time—unless we have almost completely forgotten it? How can *The Moonstone* and the Sherlock Holmes canon achieve the status of classics of a sort, when classical status, if it means anything, implies that the work in question rewards close and repeated scrutiny?

The usual answer that we reread the mystery classics not for story but for style, for portrayal of character, for comment on society, is insufficient. If that were all, we should be content to browse through the Sherlock Holmes tales, savoring appropriate passages here and there. We may occasionally enjoy such selective study, but it does not satisfy the aficionado. He likes to reread these stories as stories, and the reading-for-atmosphere theory adduces no motive for him to do so. Why, to take a specific and personal example, do I take such pleasure in yet another perusal of "The Adventure of the Speckled Band"? One probable reason is that I now appreciate it, at least to a limited extent, as a work of art. This must mean, among other things, that I apprehend it as a structure; but what kind of structure?

The plot of "The Speckled Band" is comparatively simple. An English physician, Dr. Roylott, has lived for some years in India, gaining there a reputation for violence and cruelty. On his return to England, he marries a wealthy widow with twin daughters. When his wife dies, her will stipulates that he is to enjoy her estate so long as the daughters remain single; when they marry, the money is to be divided. Subsequently one of the twins becomes engaged. Not wishing to give up her share of the estate, the doctor plots to murder his stepdaughter. He contrives each night to introduce, from his own bedroom into hers, a poisonous Indian snake, a speckled swamp adder. Eventually, as he has planned, it fatally bites the young woman. The cause of her death remains a mystery; for the dying girl's only words refer wildly to a "speckled band," and the poison is one that evades normal medical analysis. Two years later the remaining sister, Helen Stoner, becomes engaged. When certain suspicious occurrences remind her of her twin's death, she is frightened, and she applies for help to Sherlock Holmes. In answer to her appeal, the detective surreptitiously visits Dr. Roylott's house, where his investigations enable him to guess the truth. Hiding at night in Helen's room, he attacks the snake when it appears and drives it away. Returning to its master, the enraged adder inflicts on him the fatal bite intended for his stepdaughter.

This version of the tale—call it Version A—does, it is true, reveal a simple and satisfying structure: a pattern of crime and detection, of villainy and retribution, of the malefactor hoist with his own petard. But Version A is not the story as we read it. The order of events as revealed by Conan Doyle (or Dr. Watson) is quite different. Watson, after promising to reveal the truth about the strange death of Dr. Roylott, begins his narrative with Helen Stoner's call upon Sherlock Holmes. She recounts her family history, dwelling on the circumstances of her sister's death, and she describes the recent events that have driven her to seek Holmes's aid. He agrees to help her and she departs. Holmes begins to speculate on the case—misguidedly, as it will turn out—but is interrupted by the abrupt appearance of Dr. Roylott himself, whose actions in trying to avert investigation merely confirm Helen's description of his violent nature. Undeterred by threats, Holmes, together with Watson, visits the doctor's house, where, as we know, he soon deduces the correct solution to the mystery. Watson, however— and therefore, presumably, the reader—is left for a time in ignorance. Although he accompanies Holmes on his nocturnal vigil and is present during his attack on the snake, Watson remains both literally and figuratively in the dark until the moment when he sees the speckled band coiled around the head of the dead doctor. Only then does Holmes reveal to his friend, and to us, the chain of inference that has led him to the truth.

That is the story as we read it—or more specifically, as we read it for the first time, without prior knowledge of its outcome. As opposed to Version A, which recounted the events in their natural chronological order, Version B, as we may call it, arranges them artfully and purposefully. In the present case the purposes are to mystify and to create mounting suspense until a dénouement simultaneously relieves the suspense and convincingly explains the mystery. The first responsibility of a detective story is to achieve success on this First-Reading level.

A First Reading need not, of course, be literally that. The phrase refers to any reading based on total or partial ignorance of the events narrated, whether one is actually reading a story for the first time, or is making a renewed attempt to "get" a story previously read but imperfectly comprehended (perhaps found impenetrable), or is returning to a story read long ago and since forgotten. In each case, one important motivation is a desire to find out what happens—or, in the case of a mystery, to understand what has already happened.

Once one has glimpsed the structure underlying a recounted series of events—the pattern of their causes, their interrelationships, their outcome—one's consciousness of that pattern is bound to inform subsequent readings of the narrative. What I call the Second Reading (whether it is actually one's second, third, . . . or tenth) is controlled by that consciousness. It is a reading, that is to say, in which one's mental reconstruction of Version A serves as a continual gloss on Version B. As each detail occurs in the narrative (essentially Version B) it is considered in the light of its position in the plot-structure (essentially Version A). B is thus regarded as the vehicle for the realization of the pattern defined by A. Mystery and suspense are banished from this reading, which admits of no emotional involvement on the part of the reader—except perhaps that resulting from his admiration of the writer's technique. In one way the Second Reading is not a true reading, or certainly not just a reading; for the reader, far from concentrating on the text before him, is constantly comparing what he is being told with what he knows from his previous encounter. His mental activity can thus be more accurately described as thinking about the story while using the text as a means of ensuring accuracy. In a word, the Second Reading aims at an analysis—not necessarily a conscious analysis, formally constructed, but at least one implied by a synoptic overview. This synoptic analysis treats the story, not as a work of art that owes its effect to progress through time, but as an object abstracted or inferred from the work of art, a static art-object that can be contemplated timelessly. Paradoxically, the Second Reading achieves its goal when it ceases to be a reading at all—when it becomes the pure contemplation of structure.

The First Reading, then, is completely innocent of analysis, and the Second Reading is for the sake of analysis, explicit or

5

implicit. That analysis is put to use in the service of yet another reading—the Third. Like the First, this one is temporally oriented: it accepts the story as narrated. Again like the First, it aims at enjoyment; but now, guided by the synoptic comprehension of the Second Reading, it can replace naive pleasure with intelligent and informed appreciation. Yet at the same time this reading requires an intentional "forgetting." For if one is really to appreciate a narrative as such, one must concentrate on each event as it comes, trying to suppress from consciousness those elements meant to be concealed until some later point in the story. The pattern of Version A revealed by the Second Reading still exerts its control, but it must do so invisibly and silently. To be sure, it can never really be forgotten, but in the Third Reading it must remain hidden—a concealed motivation behind the actual narrative structure determined by Version B.

To put the distinction somewhat differently, one can say that the First Reading is purely experiential: one knows only what one experiences (i. e., is being told). The trajectory of the reader's thought is one-dimensional, moving along the path laid out by the author. In the Second Reading one knows much more than one is being told; the trajectory of thought is zigzag, or even discontinuous, constantly shifting back and forth between the planes of memory and experience, until at last one is able to achieve a comprehensive bird's-eye view of the narrative path. In the Third Reading there is a double trajectory. Thought moves simultaneously on two levels, one fully conscious and one at least partly suppressed. The primary, open level is once more that of experience, as the reader follows the actual narration; but this time he is in a position fully to enjoy the journey, for he is now both confident of his direction and aware of the relative importance of each event along the way. He cannot fully suppress what he already knows, for he travels at the same time on the plane of memory; but he tries to ration what he knows in such a way as to make the path of experience as vivid and as exciting as possible.

To be sure, we cannot really ration what we know. Our subconscious minds contain no selective filter to strain our memories—no sieve that allows only those memories useful for a given purpose to penetrate our overt consciousness, while retaining the rest. But we often find it necessary or convenient to pretend that this is the case and to act as if it were so. When we play games, even though no prestige or money is involved, we assume that a great deal is at stake. (People who really love a game have no need of a material risk to make the contest realistic; their imaginations are sufficient for the task.) When we go to the theater, we pretend that the actors are not actors and that the stage-set is not a set. Children, of course, often create imaginary lives for themselves that are almost as vivid to them as their real lives; many adults retain something of this power in their capacity for daydreaming. It is the same faculty, or a closely related one, that enables us to respond emotionally to what we know is only fiction, and especially to experience during a Third Reading something of the excitement characteristic of the First.

For the Third Reading is an ideal First Reading. Or simply: the Third Reading is the ideal reading. It is the only one that fully accepts the story as a work of temporal art and tries to appreciate it as such. And when the Third Reading, in its turn, engenders an analysis, it is an analysis, not of an abstract structure or art-object, but of the concrete work of art itself. It is not a synoptic but a diachronic analysis, one that deals with the events of the tale in their narrated order. Although it cannot avoid attending to the overall pattern investigated by synoptic analysis, it will allow itself to recognize that pattern only as a gradually emerging one, and it will concentrate on the strategies of concealment and disclosure by which the author controls the process.

Let me illustrate the differences between the three readings by reference to a specific passage in "The Speckled Band": Dr. Roylott's sudden appearance at Holmes's flat, hard on the heels of his stepdaughter's visit. The incident is obviously meant to astonish a First Reader, who, like Holmes and Watson, is utterly unprepared for the intrusion. As the situation develops, the same reader, if at all sophisticated, will begin to wonder whether Dr. Roylott is being introduced as a red herring: he is so unprepossessing, so threatening and violent, that he is much too obviously a villain. The truth must be otherwise than one has been led to suspect.

7

That is not the case, however: Dr. Roylott is just the villain he appears to be. The Second Reading thus entails a reconsideration of the episode. From his new vantage point the Second Reader discerns a certain symmetry: at the outset, Watson promises to reveal the true circumstances surrounding Dr. Roylott's death; at the end of the story that death is described; in between Dr. Roylott himself appears in one revealing episode. The passage is not essential to the plot, but it is necessary if the doctor is to be anything other than a shadowy figure evoked by Helen's narrative and Holmes's deductions. Without such an opportunity of meeting the villain face to face, so to speak, the reader can never fully appreciate the justice of the retribution that eventually overtakes him.

The Third Reader, too, will recognize the symmetry, but he will let himself realize it—or, if you prefer, he will pretend to realize it—only gradually, as the tale unfolds. Unlike the average First Reader, who probably fails to notice or to remember Watson's initial indication of the direction the story will take, the Third Reader will not allow the significance of the opening reference to Dr. Roylott's death to escape him. He will therefore not make the mistake of assuming that he is reading a conventional mystery in which the crime is committed by the most unlikely person. He will understand, as he is meant to, that Helen Stoner's narrative is to be taken as veridical and that her description of her stepfather is, as Holmes gets her to admit, understated rather than exaggerated. He will dutifully draw the correct conclusion that Dr. Roylott engineered one death and is now plotting another. He will realize, in other words, that the mystery is not one of Who but of How. And so, when Dr. Roylott appears on the scene, the Third Reader will find in his wild behavior confirmation of this interpretation of his character. The reader, moreover, will allow himself to luxuriate in the antipathy he is obviously meant to feel, so that he will eventually enjoy all the more thoroughly the horrid spectacle of Dr. Roylott's head encompassed by the speckled adder. But unlike the Second Reader, he must not look forward to this delicious moment. He must resolutely try to keep himself in the dark about the nature of the "band"—speculating, perhaps, like Holmes himself, on the possibility that the dying sister's

words referred to a band of gypsies. Later, when Holmes and
Watson visit the Roylott estate, he will depend only on the
information revealed by their observations. He may permit himself to be a bit more perspicacious than Watson, whose myopia,
I believe, is cunningly devised by the author to give the reader
a slight sense of superiority; but he will keep the actual solution
of the mystery waiting in the wings of his consciousness until
Holmes is ready to bring it center stage. At that point his
realization of the identity of the speckled band will remind
him of Watson's original promise to explain how Roylott really
died, and at the same time it will enable him to grasp the extent
of the doctor's wickedness. So he will rejoice in the poetic
justice of the outcome, at seeing "violence. . . recoil upon the
violent," to use Holmes's phrase.

This coincidence of the fulfillment of a narrative promise,
the solution of a mystery, and the execution of justice is essential to the artistic effect of the dénouement. Theoretically, it
could be apprehended by a First Reader; practically, its complete
appreciation must await a Third Reading. That is why I have
called the Third Reading an ideal First Reading. But the effect,
in any event, is unavailable to the Second Reader, for it depends
on the appraisal of each event in exact narrative sequence; that
is why I insist that only a diachronic Third-Reading analysis
treats the story as a work of art. Such an analysis, along the
lines I have sketched, would, I believe, explain the endless
fascination of this much-anthologized tale: it derives primarily
from the power of the narrative to control the emotional reactions of the reader in such a way as to afford him maximum
satisfaction at the final revelation. At that point his emotional
release coincides with his discovery of the truth. The narrative
structure is not an abstract, static design but a temporal progression of events carefully arranged with a view toward their effect
on a willing, sensitive reader. Hence the superiority of "The
Speckled Band" over such a story as "The Adventure of the
Lion's Mane." There, too, a dying man's words afford a clue
to his mysterious death, which turns out again to have been
caused by the sting of a poisonous animal (a huge jellyfish).
But that tale is dominated by detective-story clichés: rival lovers,
one of whom is killed; an obvious suspect—the surviving lover—

9

who refuses to explain his odd behavior; a detective who keeps most of his knowledge to himself; and a solution that exonerates the suspect. The narrative structure arouses no patterned sequence of emotions stronger than that of curiosity followed by satisfaction.

It would be incorrect to generalize to the point of claiming that a Second-Reading analysis never treats a story as a work of art. Joseph Frank's seminal essay "Spatial Form in Modern Literature"* points out the difference between traditional novels, which are properly apprehended in narrative order, and those by writers like Proust, Joyce, and Djuna Barnes, who "ideally intend the reader to apprehend their work spatially, in a moment of time, rather than as a sequence" (p. 9). In the case of a book like *Nightwood*, the distinction between art-object and work of art no longer applies. To appreciate this novel as a work of art is precisely to apprehend it as a timeless object. Here Frank's quip about *Ulysses* is apt: "Joyce cannot be read—he can only be reread" (p. 19). For novels like these, the Third Reading is not an ideal First Reading but a more efficient Second Reading. More correctly, perhaps, one should say that there is no Third Reading but only a series of ever more thorough Second Readings.

It is thus important to distinguish between narratives for which the Third Reading is appropriate and those for which it is not. True, the claims of most detective stories to be works of art are at best modest, and they will suffer no great harm even if never subjected to a Third Reading. But gross misinterpretations of important works of literature have resulted from a confusion between readings and the levels of analysis pertaining to them. The popular conception of *Oedipus the King* as a tragedy of fate, demonstrating the helplessness of men in the grip of an inexorable destiny, depends on a Second-Reading analysis that arranges both the events enacted and those recounted to form a pattern of prophecy and fulfillment. But this is really an analysis of the underlying mythic structure, not of Sophocles' play. The motivation of the tragedy is Oedipus' determination

---

*Joseph Frank, *The Widening Gyre* (Bloomington: Indiana University Press, 1968), pp. 3-62. Subsequent quotations from Frank are from this edition.

to do his kingly duty and discover the truth despite all warnings. Indeed, Third-Reading analysis reveals a structure something like that of a modern mystery melodrama—the kind in which the audience is privy to the solution, but not the detective.*

The suppression of information that I have described as essential to a successful Third Reading may not always be possible, even as a game of pretense. On the other hand, the principle involved has some general validity that extends beyond the realm of pure prose fiction. There is, in fact, a progression among the genres and media of temporal art, leading from those in which the suppression required for the Third Reading (or Watching, or Hearing) is difficult, if not impossible, to those in which it is easy or even unavoidable. For example, a story told in the first person by an attractive and sympathetic character, whom the reader can imagine as a close friend or even as himself, offers more opportunities of success in this direction than one narrated by an omniscient author; and if the information thus imparted is further restricted to the contents of letters or diaries, the reader often finds himself sharing the limited vision of the supposed writer. A well-performed play, no matter how familiar, can rivet one's attention on the fictitious present of the action. And according to some theories, at least, a good actor is an ideal Third Reader, who really experiences the succession of emotions he is supposed to be feigning. The progression thus depends on the degree to which one can imaginatively participate in the fictitiously depicted life. And here at last we come to my real subject—music; for if what I have suggested elsewhere is correct, what I call "identification" is essential to the understanding and appreciation of a work of musical art: "an active participation in the life of the music by following its progress, attentively and imaginatively, through the course of one's own thoughts, and by adapting the tempo and direction of one's own psychic energies to the tempo and direction of the music."**

---

*See. for example, A. E. Haigh, *The Tragic Drama of the Greeks* (Oxford: Clarendon Press, 1896), p. 193. For a startlingly unorthodox interpretation of the play, see Philip Vellacott, *Sophocles and Oedipus* (Ann Arbor: University of Michigan Press, 1971).

**Edward T. Cone, *The Composer's Voice* (Berkeley: University of California Press, 1974), p. 118. The subsequent quotation from Cone is from this edition.

The listener, and even more the performer, must experience music by living through it.

Except in the case of a simple and unproblematic composition in a well-known style, satisfactory participation is hardly possible for a First Hearing—or Reading: the difference is not essential because reading music requires (or should require) intense listening, either actual or imagined. Whichever mode of approach is employed, the purpose of one's first contact with an unfamiliar composition is to find out what the music has to say—or, in other words, what happens. So long as that is one's primary motivation for listening, one receives the music as something entirely external to oneself, and is consequently engaged in the activity of First Hearing—which may in fact extend through a number of actual hearings or readings. Only when the listener is reasonably confident of what is coming, to the extent that he can expectantly follow the course of the composition, is he ready for the Second Hearing.

At this stage identification, rare enough in the case of the First Hearing, is completely out of the question. The Second Hearing must probably be, in point of fact, a Reading; for its aim is to arrive at a spatially-oriented view of the composition as a whole, and its method is atemporal study. The Second Reader examines the composition at his own speed—even in his own order, for he may have to separate adjacent ideas and juxtapose distant ones in his attempt to uncover all the relationships governing the musical structure.

It is the Third Reader for whom identification is possible and, if I am right, crucial. Like the First Hearing, the Third is temporal and experiential; but it is characterized by an enriched perception of the temporal flow, and it realizes a controlled and appreciated experience. Fortunately, to achieve this level of perception is easier in performing or listening to music than in reading fiction. One reason for the obtrusiveness of our memories during a Third Reading of literature is the natural difficulty most of us experience in trying to concentrate exclusively on a single train of verbal thought. Concepts and images of all kinds are constantly impinging on our consciousness. It is no wonder, then, that when we read a familiar story it is hard to prevent remembered ideas and images from interpenetrating those actually before us at the moment, sometimes even replacing and contradicting them. But when we listen intently to music, the immediacy of what we are hearing makes it difficult or impossible for us to entertain other *musical* ideas at the same time. Thus our memories of the Second Hearing are more likely to be verbal, or diagrammatic, or even mathematical. These concepts can direct, or modify, or occasionally correct what we actually hear, but they can never replace or contradict it—not, that is, so long as we are fully participating in the actual music itself.

For this reason it is dismaying that so much analysis—so much of the best analysis—not only begins but remains firmly planted in Second-Hearing ground. Synoptic and atemporal, it proceeds from an initial assumption of omniscience; it is based on the premise that comprehension of the whole is prerequisite for appreciation of the part. In one sense, of course, this is true. That is why a First-Hearing analysis, except perhaps at the most superficial level, is a contradiction in terms. But the Second-Hearing analysis, even at the hands of a master like Schenker, does scant justice to our experience of hearing a composition in real time. It accepts as the goal what should be only a stage—albeit an important one—of musical comprehension. That is the thrust of Schoenberg's reported complaint that he could not find his favorite passages in Schenker's analysis of the *Eroica*: "Oh, here they are, in these tiny notes!" he is supposed to have exclaimed. And I insist that if anyone boasts, on the basis of synoptic analysis, that he hears the opening chord of Beethoven's First Symphony as a tonic, and the initial tremolo of the Ninth as a dominant, he is probably deceiving himself and is certainly missing the point of the music. He is confusing what he is hearing with what he has learned.

Of course, from the omniscient point of view the opening harmony of the Ninth *is* the dominant, but even from this perspective it would be more accurate to say that it *becomes* the dominant. A single chord can have no function. Functions emerge only during the course of a progression, and our identification of them can shift according to what the progression reveals. Composers play with the resulting ambiguities, and one of the great joys of the Third Hearing is to become fully aware of them. A complete account of these effects is the task of diachronic

13

analysis, for they lie beyond the scope of the purely synoptic.

Thus I applaud Tovey when he writes: "Half the musical miseducation in the world comes from people who know that the Ninth Symphony begins on the dominant of D minor, when the fact is that its opening bare fifth may mean anything within D major, D minor, A major, A minor, E major, E minor, C sharp minor, G major, C major, and F major, until the bass descends to D and settles most (but not all) of the question. A true analysis takes the standpoint of a listener who knows nothing beforehand, but hears and remembers everything."* Tovey's "true analysis" is of course none other than my Third-Hearing analysis, and his characteristically emphatic language explains vividly what I mean when I describe a Third Hearing as an ideal First Hearing.

Tovey goes too far in his insistence on the listener's total ignorance. I should prefer to limit that to ignorance of the specific musical content of the composition in question. For the serious music-lover takes advantage of all relevant information—historical, biographical, music-theoretical—that may prepare him to receive that content. His aim, after all, is to make every hearing—even the First—as rich as possible. Thus he knows that Beethoven was counting on a contemporary audience conditioned by familiarity not only with the tonal language in general, but also with the conventions of the classical style; therefore, as a sensitive and intelligent listener today, he tries to approach the composer's work in a similar frame of mind. When hearing the First Symphony, he imaginatively sets himself to expect the tonic consonance with which the typical classical symphony began. Only in that way can he ever experience the delight that accompanies the transformation of puzzled wonder (Is it a dominant? Can it be a tonic?) into satisfied relief. (It was both: a tonic treated as the dominant of its own subdominant.) This is the insight of the Third Hearing that should eventually replace both a naive First-Hearing reaction (It is clearly a dominant seventh) and a sly Second-Reading interpretation (It may sound like a dominant but I know better).

In his Intermezzo Op. 118 No. 1, Brahms has developed

---

*Donald Francis Tovey, *Essays in Musical Analysis*, Vol. I, *Symphonies* (London: Oxford University Press, 1935), p. 68.

Beethoven's opening incident into a full-fledged mystery story.*
The mystery, of course, concerns the identification of the tonic.
Probably none of us can completely recapture the flavor of
his first encounter with this problematic piece, but I still recall
my surprise on discovering that the key is neither the F major
suggested by the opening sonority, nor the C major of the
first cadence and of the reprise, but—A minor! A First Hearing
(or Reading) must, I think, take the opening as V^7-I^6. Even
a listener sharp enough to construe the B^b of m. 1 as a passing
tone will be influenced by its color and hence construe the
chord as a dominant substitute, III^6. Accordingly the C-major
cadence at the end of the first part will be accepted as the
usual tonicization of V. The development then elaborates a
chain of applied dominants, VII-III-VI, the last deceptively or
elliptically skipping its resolution to II and moving to V. Here,
at the recapitulation, occurs the first event to give the unprepared listener serious pause: the V^7 (or III^6), instead of resolving
as before to the presumed tonic F, moves to a climactic C.
Like the expected F, it is only a first inversion; but its register
(the highest so far, followed by a precipitous descent), its unique
variation of the opening motif, its cancellation of F (by sharping
it as a neighbor to G)—these factors dispose one to accept C
as the tonic after all. But then the ensuing A minor must be
construed as VI—an odd cadence for a reprise, but one that
might lead to a new development. Instead, a literal repetition of
the second half now raises the suspicion that perhaps A minor
was the goal all along—a surmise that becomes a certainty on
the return of the cadence in that key, expanded and fully
confirmed.

If my account is approximately correct, the First Hearing
turns out to be a peculiarly unsatisfactory affair. The listener
is unaware of the tonal problem until late in the piece, when his
perception of the key relations requires an unexpected reorien-
tation. Only in retrospect does he realize that there was a mystery
to be cleared up. If he now investigates the nature of that mystery

15

---

*For much of my discussion of this piece, I am greatly indebted to Mr.
Jonathan Dunsby, whose ideas about it, expounded to me in conversation,
have stimulated and interpenetrated my own.

and tries to impose some kind of unitary pattern on his fluctuating tonal impression, he will arrive at a Second Reading informed by a synoptic analysis. Schenker has shown how the entire Intermezzo can be reduced to one concise progression: III-V#-I in A minor.* This formulation, kept in mind as a background for following the course of the piece, certainly obviates the disconcerting shifts in perspective that punctuate the First Hearing. But it spoils the fun. Whereas a First Hearing becomes aware of the tonal problem too late, a Second Hearing of this kind is conscious of its solution too soon. Puzzlement has been replaced by confidence from the outset that the opening section prolongs neither a dominant nor a tonic but a mediant.

Perhaps that is how the piece should really be understood. Perhaps no mystery is intended, and Schenker is right when he maintains, of similar progressions, "The tones of the [subsidiary] degrees are connected only through their relation with the coming tonic; they point the way only to it" (p. 138). If that is so, it implies that the Intermezzo and pieces like it can be comprehended only spatially, like the novels discussed by Frank. This is, to be sure, a tempting position, especially with reference to certain contemporary compositions, serial or otherwise, whose organization is abstract and complex. With regard to such works it is probably the correct position. But one surrenders too much if one adopts it unnecessarily. I am convinced, for example, that standard analyses do violence to Berg's Violin Concerto in this respect. They assume the basic twelve-tone set as independent factor, preexisting our experience of the composition; and they tell us, accordingly, that at the outset we are hearing alternate notes of this row. From a synoptic, spatially-oriented point of view that is true; but surely the effect of the introduction, considered as a temporal event, depends on the fact that the row has not yet been defined, and that it can only dimly and fragmentarily be discerned.

In the case of the Brahms Intermezzo, I find that I cannot even rehear it as Schenker's spatial interpretation would wish. In actual performance, as opposed to abstract conceptualization,

---

*Heinrich Schenker, *Der Freie Satz*, 2d. ed. (Vienna, 1956), *Anhang*, p. 63, Ex. 110, d3. The subsequent quotation from Schenker is from this edition.

the piece stubbornly resists all my efforts in that direction. Why should Brahms be so negligent in offering me clues along the way to guide my listening, and so diligent in misleading and side-tracking me? I conclude that he intends to puzzle me. I have only to glance at the Intermezzo Op. 76 No. 4 to realize that he is perfectly capable of composing a piece that postpones the arrival of the tonic until the latest possible moment, yet never permits the slightest doubt as to the identity of that tonic. There the suspense is due to uncertainty as to when and how the tonic will arrive; here, I submit, the suspense is, or ought to be, due to the more fundamental uncertainty as to what the tonic is.

A successful Third Reading of Op. 118 No. 1, then, will accept neither the deceptive shifting of the First Reading nor the structurally precise but empirically unrealistic unity of the Second. Yet the Third Reading can never totally forget the other two. To a certain extent, in the present case, it is their synthesis, translating the shifting into tonal ambiguity, and the structural unity into a process whereby that ambiguity gives way to final clarity.

A Third-Hearing analysis of the Intermezzo tries to do justice to the complexity of this synthesis. Instead of determining the tonic ahead of time, it recognizes in the opening of the piece a marshalling of three "suspects," C, A, and F. Each appears as the bass of a characteristically ambiguous chord of the sixth—ambiguous because its function wavers between those of its theoretical root and of its actual bass. Thus the opening progression, literally a succession of first inversions (Ex. 1), conceals a series of abortive attempts to complete a root position by a 6-5 resolution, each one defeated at the crucial moment by the entrance of a fresh bass note that converts the fifth into a dissonance against the next chord (Ex. 2). Were these harmonies allowed to complete themselves, they would stand revealed as the three candidates for the key of the piece: F, A, and C. But they are not granted completion, and we must accept the B♭, G, and E of the soprano as the lengthened passing-notes that Brahms's careful phrasing (by descending thirds) suggests. This means in particular that the first chord, despite its strong flavor, is not a true dominant seventh: the opening must be heard and played

17

as in Ex. 3, not as in Ex. 4. Furthermore the D# of m. 5 is not a mere passing note but at least momentarily a resolution (as Brahms indicates by writing it thus and not as E♭). The descending fourth of the opening melodic motif has here been compressed into a simultaneous interval—an augmented fourth that converts the governing harmony of the measure into a French sixth on F. Due emphasis on that chord will give an acute listener his first hint of the possibility of an ultimate resolution into A minor (Ex. 5)—a hope to be dashed by the turn of the next measure toward C. And so the Third Hearing fastens neither on the F suggested by the initial pseudo-seventh, nor on the C established at the cadence, but keeps an open mind among the three options presented.

The foregoing has dealt only with the opening section of the Intermezzo, and only superficially at that: it has not touched, for example, on the interesting role of doublings. Yet I hope it has suggested how one might carry out a complete and thorough Third-Reading analysis. One point should certainly be clear: the close relationship between a Third Reading and a performance. Indeed, a performance is, or should be, the projection of a Third Reading. For the performer, as opposed to the mere sight-reader, is intimately familiar with the entire composition. Like the synoptic analyst, he puts to work his knowledge of the whole in order to shape his conception; but unlike the analyst he must then suppress that knowledge. He must relegate it to the background of his consciousness, where it continues to influence, even to determine, his interpretation; but he has internalized it to the point where he need no longer be aware of it. His attention is focused instead on the vivid reconstruction of the actual temporal flow of the music.

This view of performance may in turn help with our earlier problem concerning the successful Third Reading of a work of fiction. One who actually performs a story—i. e., reads it aloud—must concentrate on its temporal flow; in his absorption he may even "forget" what is coming next. And the more closely a silent reader, of a novel as of a musical score, approaches in imagination the simulated conditions of an actual performance, the closer he will come to an ideal Third Reading.

Just how much a performer should allow himself to draw

Example 1

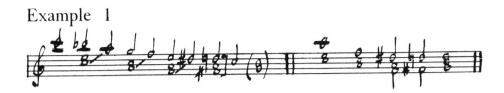

Example 2

Example 3

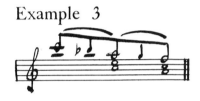

Example 4

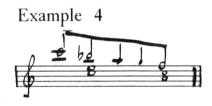

Example 5

Example 6

Example 7

20

on his store of memory varies from work to work, even from moment to moment within the work. When Mozart, in the Adagio of his Piano Sonata K. 332, states a phrase in B♭ major and immediately starts to repeat it in B♭ minor, it would be absurdly literalistic to insist that the change occurs only with the arrival of the diagnostic D♭ on the second half of the first beat of the measure (Ex. 6). Clearly the contrast is between the two phrases as a whole, and it is up to the pianist, by rhythmic articulation and adjustment of dynamic, to ensure that the minor coloration is already perceived at the beginning of the measure. But this reversal of mode, like the sudden return to major a few measures later (Ex. 7) raises a problem of performance in wider context. Should the pianist anticipate such deceptive resolutions, or should he try so far as possible to let them take him unawares? Is his dramatic role that of a Dr. Watson, who is surprised by every new turn of events, or of a Dr. Roylott, who engineers them? Is he sharing his astonishment with his auditors or is he trying to spring a trap on them? Or is he perhaps playing a subtler part—that of a Sherlock Holmes, who deduces the course that events must take and is hence prepared for whatever happens?

Such distinctions are not always easy to make, but some cases, at least, ought to be obvious. When Tristan and Isolde are interrupted at the height of their passion by the return of the King and his retinue, the music is equally caught off guard; but the orchestra (like Brangäne) reacts before the lovers do, substituting an anguished dissonance for the expected resolution.

A related effect, in a purely instrumental context, can be found in the Andante Cantabile of Tchaikovsky's Fifth Symphony. When the motto-theme, which once before has tried unsuccessfully to take over the course of the movement, returns for a second time (m. 158), it is obviously launching a surprise attack. The trombones and bassoons, which carry the motto, know what is coming, but not the suddenly interrupted violins.

Similarly, in Chopin's Fantasy Op. 49, when a sforzato diminished seventh rudely shatters the dreamy atmosphere of the central B-major section, the pianist should try to convey a sense of his own shock. The musical persona he portrays comprises at least two implicit agents, of which the one suddenly

21

and devastatingly interrupts the other's revery. (I am using here a vocabulary developed in *The Composer's Voice*.)

On the other hand, when I wrote that ". . . the players of Haydn's 'Surprise' Symphony must somehow surprise themselves," (p. 127) I was wrong. The players are not surprising themselves, or one another (for the strings join in the chord that interrupts their own quiet theme). They are all playing a joke on the audience, as Haydn himself is supposed to have pointed out.

The Mozart examples previously cited are typically subtle. The shifts of mode, if not actually willed by the musical persona, are at least anticipated: witness the careful textural preparation of the minor, and the asymmetrical but balancing return to major. The pianist should find ways to convey these effects in performance, leading his auditors, as well, to expect the shifts, or at least to accept them as appropriate. Here as elsewhere, although the version of the composition projected by the player cannot (and should not) be identical with the one realized by the listener, the power of the interpretation can be measured by the extent to which it guides that listener's First Hearing, or modifies and enriches his Third.

22

MOTIVE AND RHYTHMIC CONTOUR

IN THE ALTO RHAPSODY

Allen Forte

This essay presents an introductory study of the harmonic and melodic motives of the Alto Rhapsody and their rhythmic contours. It interprets the relations among the motives and discusses some of their extraordinary manifestations in the foreground and middleground of the tonal structure.

This eloquent and profound work has a recondite character corresponding to that of the unusual poem chosen by its composer. Only slowly, after much patient study, does it reveal some (but not all) of its mysteries.

Indeed, so elaborate is the concealed structure of this extraordinary composition—at various levels—that the present essay can only deal with a limited number of aspects. It is hoped, however, that these will indicate the intricacy of the musical fabric in its entirety, providing a basis for further study and perhaps suggesting analytical procedures that might prove to be fruitful in studying other works of the master.

The essay begins with a discussion of several of the primary motives in the music and the ways in which they are expressed in rhythmic contours. It then presents some ideas about the significance of these motives as they occur throughout the work at various levels of structure.[1]

The motives of the Alto Rhapsody. Example 1 provides, in ordinary music notation, an analysis of the primary motivic material of the opening music. As will be shown, virtually all of the remaining melodic as well as harmonic configurations derive from these components, either singly or in combination. The initial rhythmic shape of the motive is also significant.

Let us consider, first, the opening musical segment. This consists of eight motives. Those formed in the bass are assigned the letter a, with an identifying numerical superscript, while those formed in the upper voice are labelled b and also have superscripts. The Greek letter alpha is assigned to the first three sounding pitches, which comprise a very special motive in the music: the augmented triad B-E$\flat$-G, symbolizing, perhaps, the fundamental dichotomy presented in the poem. We shall see, in a moment, some of the wondrous and mysterious ways in which the alpha motive appears in the music.

Motive a^2 is made up of the first three pitches in the bass, B-C-E$\flat$, and contains two additional important motives: a^1, the dyad B-C, and a^5, the linear minor third, C-E$\flat$. The final motivic component of the bass that is of interest in this context is motive a^3, which descends stepwise from E$\flat$ to A to form the interval of a diminished fifth (tritone).

In the upper parts, motives b^1 and b^2 appear in succession, presenting, respectively, a vertical major third and a vertical minor third. The upper parts relate directly to the bass, however, in the following ways. First, the uppermost voice of the upper part comprises the dyad G-G$\flat$, the inversion of motive a^1. This relation is symbolized by the bar above the a, and the bar is read "inversion of." The most remarkable of the relations between the upper and lower parts, however, is the formation of the inversion of a^2 ($\bar{a}^2$) as the combination of b^1 and b^2.

Finally, motives b^1 and a^1 combine to form the tetrachordal sonority B-C-E$\flat$-G, which is labelled β (beta). The significance of this will become evident in due course.

This reading of the motivic components of the opening music of the Alto Rhapsody as distinct entities is fully substantiated in the music. It is not the product of an arbitrary atomization, for it is consequential. Since Brahms composes the transformations of the motives with the utmost delicacy and subtlety, they are sometimes difficult to understand. It is hoped that the explanations that follow will be both lucid and convincing.

Even a cursory examination reveals that each of the motives is in some way distinct from the others with respect to rhythmic pattern. Yet the relations among the patterns serve to unify them. Thus, the dotted quarter/eighth figure of motive a^3 is a contraction of the pattern of motive a^2 by exactly half, while the pattern of b^2 almost replicates that of b^1, with attacks falling in corresponding places in the measure

Example 1. Measures 1-2: the basic motives

Example 2. Measure 5: motive a¹ and its inversion

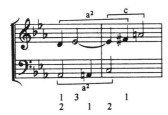

Example 3. Measures 9-10: motives a² and c in combination

Example 4. Measures 18-20: beginning of contralto aria

Example 5. Measures 113-115: reference to alpha

(beats two and four). And motive beta is delineated by the simultaneous attacks in upper and lower parts, the only such simultaneity in the opening segment.

The interpenetration of the motives apparent in the opening music continues to develop in the sequel. For example, in m. 5 (Example 2) the bass carries the last of the sequential statements of a^1 (as G-A$\flat$), while above it in the uppermost part the inversion of a^1 is brought in with the *rhythm* of motive b^1. Here rhythm binds the two motives together in a distinctive way.

At m. 9 (Example 3) two forms of the a^2 motive are counterpointed to form a rhythmic structure consisting of two interlocking symmetries: the pattern (in quarters) 1 3 1 against the pattern 2 1 2. Here the lower form of a^2 has the rhythm of b^1, while the upper form begins with the reverse of the rhythm of the a^1 motive: quarter/dotted-half for dotted half/quarter. At the same moment, the eighth triplet (not shown) is introduced for the first time, creating an association of triplet rhythm and motive a^2. This pattern hints at the 6/4 of the contralto aria that begins in m. 48, foreshadows the accompanimental syncopated pattern eighth/quarter/quarter . . . /eighth introduced in m. 55, and is a preparation for the more remote triplet pattern which pervades the choral section from m. 116 on.

The interpenetration of the motives and the introduction of new motives is composed in an organic way throughout the work. This is strikingly evident in the upper voice of m. 10 (Example 3). Just as motive a^2 is completed in the bass the E$\flat$ of the upper voice form of a^2 extends upward in an arpeggiation of the diminished triad, E$\flat$-F$\sharp$-A. This motive, labelled c, has not yet been discussed. Clearly it is associated with motive a^3, since it traverses the tritone. Not only does it span the same interval, but it has the same boundary pitches (E$\flat$ and A) as the original form of a^3. What is the meaning of this motive, the ascending triadic arpeggiation, introduced here so dramatically? The answer: It is the way in which Brahms prepares the entrance of the contralto in m. 18 (Example 4). [We will return to the opening contralto phrase later on. Suffice it to remark here that it contains b^i in its original register (Examples 1 and 4).] This is not the only occurrence of the diminished triad form of motive c in the orchestral introduction. An earlier and especially beautiful passage is discussed in connection with Example 9.

There are subtle reflections of the alpha motive throughout the work. For example, just before the chorus enters at m. 116 (Example 5) the bass ascends to B, recalling the first pitch of the orchestral introduction, and just for a moment the three pitches B-G-E are sounding. Although not literally the augmented triad of the alpha motive, this is quite sufficient to recall the opening gesture of the orchestral introduction and to suggest (which proves to be the case) that the apparently contrasting music of the choral section is related to that of the introduction in very specific ways. Here again, elemental rhythm plays a crucial role in the association: the duration of the B-G-E sonority is the same as that of the alpha motive in the first measure.

However, the most interesting occurrences of the alpha motive are those which are somewhat concealed in some ingenious way. The first of these is in the first phrase sung by contralto, to which it was promised we would return. Concealed within the ostensibly diatonic configuration is the alpha motive, beamed in Example 6 for greater visibility. This concealed or indirect form of alpha is followed immediately by the direct form, the first return to the initial sonority of the introduction, so that the indirect form is replicated by the direct form, becoming more audible in retrospect.

Example 7 displays another concealed form of the alpha motive and permits a tentative generalization—that is, that these occurrences are delineators of form throughout the work, serving to demarcate sections and always referring back to the initial sonority of the orchestral introduction. Measure 128 (Example 9) is another case.

In Example 7 special attention is drawn to the pitch B, which is highlighted since it is the only new pitch in the context. It is also the key pitch in the vertical form of the alpha motive at that point and completes the linear form beamed in the example.

And once again the interpenetration of the basic motives is apparent here, for motive a^1 occurs in the contralto line just after the dual statement of the alpha motive. The central pitch B in the two forms of a^1 here is in the lowest register of the contralto part and occurs in the same register as the B in the orchestra (violin II) at m. 41. Notice also that the bass presents the inversion of the a^1 motive and that the voice in mm. 39 and 40 outlines the b^1 motive, the major third E♭-G in the same register as the initial form of that motive (Example 1).

Over a somewhat larger span of music, motive alpha appears in the contralto line at the beginning of the aria, m. 48 (Example 8). There the rest in m. 50 serves not only to allow the singer to breathe, but also to articulate the alpha motive. This is beamed on the lower stave of Example 8, which is an analytical interpretation, using Schenkerian symbols, of the music represented in ordinary notation on the upper stave of the example. The alpha motive shown in Example 8 will receive further attention along with other aspects of the music there (Example 18). For the present, it will suffice to observe that it is formed within the major sixth E♭-C designated by the Schenkerian unfolding symbol (the incomplete beam attached to stems in reverse directions). This sixth is the intervallic expansion (by tonal inversion) of motive a^5 (Example 1), a derivation which is made clear when, with the com-

Example 6. Measures 18-20: the alpha motive

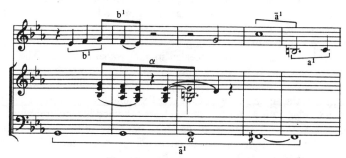

Example 7. Measures 39-43: the alpha motive with a¹ and b¹

Example 8. Measures 48-53: the alpha motive with a¹ and a⁵

Example 9. Measures 128-141: the alpha motive as middleground

Example 10. Measures 6-9: motive c in the middleground

pletion of the ascending sixth E♭-C, the descending third E♭-C enters as the head motive of the consequent phrase. In addition, the graph in Example 8 shows that the ascending line incorporates the motive ā¹, highlighting the second and third components of the alpha motive.

It should also be pointed out that the reading of the alpha motive within the ascending sixth, as shown in Example 8, is substantiated by the integral unfolding of that motive in the upper voice of a parallel passage in mm. 86–89, which terminates on the pitch B over the dominant and is followed directly by the return of the sixth of m. 48, thus providing a contextual clarification of the relation between the sixth and the augmented triad.

Of all the occurrences of the alpha motive, however, perhaps the most extraordinary is the large-scale motion which begins in m. 128 and extends to m. 141. While the passage in all its detail is quite refractory, the essential outline emerges as translucent, and is shown in Example 9.

Specifically, the alpha motive in Example 9 consists of the large-scale bass progression represented in beamed half notes: E♭-B-G. Each of these bass notes supports a key area and each is approached by a modulatory progression, with the exception of the first. The upper voice also presents a large-scale form of the alpha motive, again represented in beamed half notes on Example 9: G–D♯-B. The point of departure for the progression is the tonic C, the cadence at m. 127, while the point of arrival of the progression is the dominant in m. 141, with the special pitch B in the soprano. Thus, the large-scale progression from C to G encompasses the bass notes C-E♭-B-G, and this is motive beta (Example 1).

Example 9 is a complete Schenkerian graph of the passage from m. 128 through m. 141 and contains information that will not be discussed in this essay. However, the three forms of motive a^2 deserve attention. The first is a component of the bass line of the first modulation. The second also partakes in the modulation but in the upper voice and in inverted form. The third, also in inversion, begins on E♭, one of the pitches of alpha, and leads to B, the melodic goal of the passage.

I turn now to interesting and significant occurrences of the other basic motives, both singly and in combination.

It will be recalled that motive a^1 in its basic form is the dyad B-C (Example 1). In Example 10 we see this motive combined with its inversion and stretched out, yielding the *erquicke* motive (motive f), which will be discussed at greater length below, a motive that characterizes the music beginning with the choral section.

In Example 10 the bass beginning with G at the end of m. 7 and ending with A♭ on the first beat of m. 9 also presents a form of a^1, here enlarged by the stepwise motion down to C in m. 8, which should be regarded not as a progression to C minor, but as an arpeggiation below G, prolonging it and the motion from G to A♭.

Example 11 summarizes the rhythmic shapes associated with the multiple forms of a^1 and its inversion as shown in Example 10. It will be recalled from Example 2 that the pitch content of motive a^1 was associated early on in the music with the rhythmic pattern of motive b^1. The same feature is evident in the rhythmic patterns of this passage. In the bass of m. 6 a^1 has its original pattern of dotted half/quarter, while counterpointed against it is its inversion, with the rhythm of b^1. When a^1 and its inversion are combined to form the *erquicke* motive in mm. 7-8 the rhythmic patterns are reversed, as shown in Example 11a. There the motion D♭-B reduces to dotted half/quarter, the rhythm of a^1, while the motion B-C has the pattern half/quarter, the rhythm of b^1, providing a firm rhythmic origin of the components of the concealed *erquicke* motive. The final two forms of a^1 and its inversion in the upper voice have the same pattern, representing successive contraction (acceleration) from dotted half/quarter (a^1) to half/quarter (b^1) to quarter/quarter.

In the bass, a^1 and its inversion merge on G, with the resulting pattern as shown in Example 11b: The A♭ has the value dotted half, followed by G as a quarter, the original pattern of motive a^1. However, this G is then expanded through the next measure by means of arpeggiation down to C so that it has the total value of quarter/whole. G then resolves to A♭, which has the duration dotted half. The numbers below Example 11b show the relation between the two interlocking rhythmic patterns associated with the motives. The components of the second pattern 5 3 are greater than their counterparts in the first pattern by exactly two quarter notes, the duration of the upper-voice motives in m. 8 (Example 11). In this specific rhythmic sense the passage is organically developed and unified, temporally articulating the pitch-motive components.

At its original pitch level (B-C) motive a^1 appears directly and unconcealed in the contralto solo line at dramatic moments: for example, at m. 43 and in mm. 65-66. Throughout the work, because of its association with the motive a^1, as well as its other motivic associations, the appearance of the pitch B is an event of great significance. Thus, the 7-8 suspension in Tenor 1 at mm. 156-157, shown in Example 12, represents motive a^1, not only in its original pitch form, but also in its original rhythmic contour (dotted half/quarter). And what might otherwise be construed as a routine musical formation is, in fact, a very special one in this unique composition.

The motive a^2, it will be recalled, is the succession B-C-E♭ in the bass of the orchestral introduction (Example 1). It contains motive a^1. In its most explicit and perhaps most striking occurrence motive a^2 has the

30

Example 11. Measures 6-9: rhythmic structure

Example 12. Measures 156-157: motive a^1 as suspension

Example 13. Measures 55-56: motives a^1, a^2, and beta

Example 14. Measures 60-62: motives a^1 and a^3 combined

Example 15. Measures 97-103: motivic structures   263

form D♭-E-F, the inversion. This is in the contralto solo at mm. 55–56 (*Menschenhass*), shown in Example 13.[2] It is evident that the rhythmic shape is proportionately and precisely related to the original contour of a^2. In quarter notes the original is 3 1 1, while here the succession is 4 2 2—the latter an enlargement of the former by exactly one quarter.

Example 13 also displays the beta motive, which is played by flute following the contralto statement of a^2. Motive beta also contains motive a^2, and this is bracketed in Example 13. The two motives are joined by motive a^1, as E-F here, emphasizing once again that there is an extraordinary interaction of the basic motives of the Alto Rhapsody.

Motive a^3 occurs throughout the work and is associated with motive c in its diminished-triad arpeggiation form, since both outline the tritone. However, explicit and unconcealed forms of a^3 are not plentiful. Measures 60–61 present the most striking examples (Example 14). The first of these is pitch-identical to the original outline in the bass of the orchestral introduction: from E♭ down to A. The second ends on the special pitch B, which then resolves to C, creating motive a^1 in its original pitch-form, but with a retrograde of its original rhythmic pattern.

With the exception of the music presented in Example 9 for mm. 128 through 141, the discussion thus far has dealt mainly with shorter excerpts. Let us now consider a longer passage, one in which motives a^2, a^3, and β are combined.

In Schenkerian notation, Example 15 shows the passage that extends from m. 97 through m. 103, where the tonic harmony with raised third is regained. The upper voice projects motive a^2 in its inverted form over a span of five measures, and this is represented as the beamed structure D♭-E-F in the example. (Compare Example 13, where a^2 has the same pitch components.)

This large-scale expression of the motive is remarkable enough in itself, but what follows is even more extraordinary with respect to the motivic design of the music: When F is reached in the upper voice at m. 101 it then becomes the head note of motive a^3, shown here as the unfolding from F down to B, the latter, of course, being the sentient pitch nucleus of the composition. The unfolding of motive a^3 within the dominant 7th harmony does not conclude the passage however. This occurs in m. 103 when the oboes bring in the double appoggiatura D♯ over B, resolving to E over C against the tonic bass. The upper notes of this figure are then understood as the completion of the *erquicke* motive which F in m. 101 initiated. Further, the motion from F down to C, which then leads to B, introduces another form of the dyadic motive $\bar{a}^1$.

One additional feature of the passage requires attention: the two occurrences of motive beta which are attached to the first two elements of the large-scale projection of a^2. Thus, the melodic configurations of the passage are composed motivically in a most eloquent and artistic way, one that seems to be characteristically and perhaps uniquely Brahmsian.

The bass, too, is motivic, presenting a large-scale unfolding sixth, the major version of the upper voice of mm. 90–93 (and 48–51). Within this sixth is the diminished triad form of motive c, the beamed structure F♯-A-C.

Example 16 displays the rhythmic organization of the motives a^2, a^3, and a^1 given in Schenkerian notation in Example 15. In this expansive setting, the elements of motive a^2 have equal durational value, the breve, summarizing the two-measure pattern that is apparent in the score. The last of these two-measure patterns, however, differs from the first two, because motive a^3 enters and is somewhat concealed by the diminutions above it (in oboes), which prepare the completion of the *erquicke* motive, as explained earlier. Thus, the equal duration assigned to each element of motive a^2 is of fundamental importance here, for in this way the motive is articulated over the long span. The composer takes care to assure that the final pitch, F, in m. 101 is heard for its full breve value by repeating it in oboes as the voice part skips down to C of the a^1 motive in m. 101.

Example 16 also shows the symmetrical rhythmic pattern created by the motivic succession $a^3 a^1$, represented numerically as 3 6 6 3. This can be interpreted as a structure developed from the durational proportions of the opening music: half/quarter.

A motivically based configuration of still larger scale is shown in Example 17, a Schenkerian graph of mm. 30 through 41. There in the top voice we see a large-scale projection of motive b^1, composed out with a connective passing tone as E♭-F-G. Each component of this motion has the same duration, as did motive a^2 in Example 16. Attached to the first component, E♭, is the linear progression E♭-D-C, a large-scale repetition of the diminution in m. 30. In m. 33, when C is approached by B, there is more than a hint of the *erquicke* motive. In mm. 34 and 35 the second component, F, of the long ascending line has attached to it the descending arpeggiation F-D♭-A♭, complementing the ascending arpeggiation A♭-D♭-F, which is the basis of the voice part here. A descending arpeggiation is also associated with the third component of the long line, G, in mm. 38 and 39. This is then followed in the upper voice of mm. 39 through 41 by the descending version of motive b^1, G-F-E♭. Just as E♭ is reached, B is brought in by second violins, to form motive alpha as a vertical sonority and to complete the somewhat concealed form of alpha that began at the end of m. 39 and which is beamed in Example 17. This B prepares the same nucleus pitch —in the same register—sung by the contralto in m. 43.

Example 16. Measures 97–103: rhythmic articulation of motives

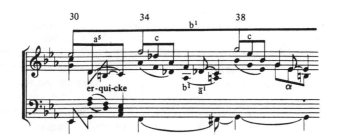

Example 17. Measures 30–41: motive b¹ in the middleground

34

Example 18. Measures 48–53: motive e in context

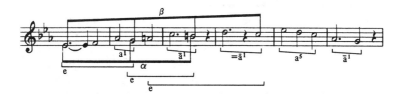

Example 19. Rhythm of e motives

In sum, Example 17 presents an analysis which reveals the motivic unity of a long passage and also illustrates the fact that in this work (and in Brahms's music in general) a significant motive may penetrate the middleground level and is not necessarily restricted to foreground statements.

In Example 10 the *erquicke* motive was shown. The same example also includes a beautiful occurrence of motive c, the first vocal configuration, as the beamed ascending arpeggiation of the diminished triad A♭-B-D, a particularly exalted expression of c, both because of the traditional expressive quality of the diminished triad itself and also because of the dramatic ascent to the high register by flutes and oboes, with a supporting crescendo. This diminished triad differs by only one pitch from the *Aber abseits* form of motive c; namely, G in the latter replaces A♭ in the former. Indeed, it is perhaps not far-fetched to place some emphasis upon the half-step relation between the two as it suggests motive a^1.

Motive e (Example 18), although plausibly regarded as a separate component of the music of the Alto Rhapsody, has a number of strong associations with motives introduced earlier. Perhaps most obvious of these is its contour replication of the opening bass tetrad in the orchestral introduction. This relation is made explicit in the music and will be pointed out in a moment. The relation of motive e to motive alpha within the ascending sixth can be seen in Example 8.

Motive e as it occurs in mm. 48-51 (and mm. 90-93) presents a many-faceted surface. As shown in Example 18, the initial form of e is followed by three interlocking forms, each apparently with a different rhythmic shape. The initial and terminal points of the first two forms coincide exactly with the pitches of the alpha motive: E♭-G and G-B. The third form overlaps the second form, beginning on A in m. 49 and extending through to the final note of the long ascending sixth. Its last two components are D and C (the *ein Ton* motive of m. 120).

A comparison of the rhythmic shapes of the three occurrences of e is informative (Example 19). The first or primary form begins with a whole note and continues with three notes of equal value. The opening dyad thus has the rhythmic proportions of motive b^1, and, indeed, b^1 in its original pitch form is contained within motive e here, as E♭-F-G. The second form begins with three notes of the same duration, but the third of these is enlarged by one quarter note, the value by which this form differs in total duration from the first form. The final occurrence of e is not quite identical to the other two in pitch structure, for the final dyad is not the semitone motive $\bar{a}^1$, but the whole step D-C. Also the final form is stretched out, and contiguous formation of its components is interrupted, first by the C on the first half note of m. 50, then by two interpolated rests. However, and remarkably, the actual

267

duration of the pitches that belong to this e create a rhythmic pattern which is the same as the pattern of the second occurrence of e. Thus, rhythm associates and articulates the relation between the two pitch formations. And, on this basis, the motive D-C of m. 51 must be regarded as the analogue of C-B of m. 50, hence as a variant of motive $\bar{a}^1$. (In the choral section this motive sets the key words *ein Ton* (m. 120) and *Herz* (m. 127). In both instances the rhythm is that of motive b.)

Finally, the relation of motive e to the opening tetrad and to motive a^2 is made explicit in mm. 108-111. This is shown in Example 20, where motive e is brought in in inverted form, so that the initial dyad is motive a^1 and comprises the special pitches C and B. In the next phrase E is changed to E♭, creating a different tetrad, one that resembles the opening tetrad of the orchestral introduction, but is not identical to it. However, not only does this new tetrad contain two manifestations of a^1, the second inverted, but it also contains two forms of a^2, as shown in graphic notation at the bottom of Example 20, thus making explicit the relation of motive e to the motives of the opening music. The rhythm of the initial a^1 motive in both tetrads in Example 20 is, of course, whole/half, the rhythm of the first dyad of e in m. 48, the beginning of the contralto solo. Thus, rhythm articulates a formal connection as well, since m. 108 is the onset of the closing music of the aria. Also, and obviously, the two tetrads in m. 20 have identical rhythmic contours.

If there is any single motive in the Alto Rhapsody that stays in the memory as especially characteristic of the work, surely it is the *erquicke* motive, motive f. Example 21 shows its first occurrence in the choral section and indicates, in analytical notation, the context in which it arises: namely, as the final dyad in the descending sixth from C to E, motive a^5. In negotiating this sixth, the composer does not permit the upper voice to proceed in a direct stepwise manner, but skips away from A, avoiding G, which is bracketed in Example 21 as a substitution.

The F-D♯-E form of motive f is always followed by the B♭-G♯-A form in the choral section. As a result of their temporal intersection (for example, in m. 122) the interval of a tritone is formed either as E over B♭ or B♭ over E. Is it far-fetched to regard this as yet another appearance of the tritone motive a^3? A convincing interpretation, one which supports a negative response to the question, will be shown in a moment.

The explicit statement of the *erquicke* motive in m. 122 of the choral section is not, however, its first statement. This has already been demonstrated in connection with Example 10. It remains to locate the first and last statements of this motive, which is so crucial to the music and to the text which is set by the music.

Example 22, the last illustration for this essay, shows the first occurrence of motive f, *erquicke*, in the bass line of motive a^3 just at

Example 20. Measures 108-111: relation between e and a²

Example 21. Measures 120-123: the *erquicke* motive in context

Example 22. Measures 2-3: first occurrence of the *erquicke* motive

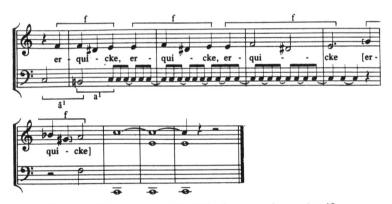

Example 23. Measures 168-175: the *erquicke* motive (f)

the beginning of the orchestral introduction. Since the *erquicke* motive originates within the tritone motive a^3 it is not illogical to find an allusion to motive a^3 in the interpretation mentioned earlier.

The rhythmic relations among the components of the first *erquicke* motive (Example 22) are shown on the upper staff of Example 22. The motion from A to B♭ has, of course, the rhythm of a^1, while the literal duration of the motion C♭-B♭ is the rhythm of b^1. In this indirect way the component rhythms of the opening motives are expressed.

The final occurrence of the *erquicke* motive is entirely conceptual. Beginning in m. 167 are three successive statements of that motive in the form F-D♯-E (Example 23), the first two presented by first tenors, the third by the contralto solo. It will be recalled that in the choral section the F-D♯-E form of the motive is always answered by the B♭-G♯-A form. Therefore, in the silence immediately preceding the final cadential succession, it is not difficult to imagine the definitive unfolding of the motive B♭-G♯-A (bracketed in Example 23), for A is, indeed, the penultimate melodic note in the plagal cadence. Moreover, this final virtual form of the motive has the rhythmic contour of the F-D♯-E form in mm. 167-169.

Example 23 also displays the organic rhythmic deceleration in the subordinate parts which ultimately resolves into the half-note duration in the middle of measure 171, a process which explicates the origin of the eighth-note triplet figure in measure 9 (associated with motive a^2) and the way in which it prepares the syncopated figure first introduced in the setting of the core word *Menschenhass* in m. 55 of the aria. That is, *Menschenhass* is finally resolved, in the most complete musical way, in the motivic and rhythmic structure at the close of this masterwork.

* * *

From the musical evidence it seems clear that Brahms composed the Alto Rhapsody in a very special way, using a small number of highly charged and interrelated melodic and harmonic motives. These motives, which are sometimes concealed in the foreground of the music, recur in subtle ways throughout the composition, extending to structural levels beyond the foreground. Each transformation of a motive, as well as the interrelations of motives, is articulated by rhythmic shapes, and the processes that are engaged, although complex, become more accessible when it is realized that motive and rhythm are inseparable in Brahms's music.

Although no deep structural levels have been discussed nor, indeed, has the overall structure of the work been considered in any detail, it is hoped that this introductory presentation provides some insight into Brahms's way of composing in general and that the analytical procedures given both implicitly (in the analytical sketches) and explicitly (in the comments) may contribute to a more effective approach to the study of his music.

NOTES

1. The reference to levels of structure invokes, of course, Schenkerian concepts. However, the present study examines foreground and lower middleground strata only and extends neither to middleground structures of longer span nor to the highest, or background, level.
2. Two pages of sketch-draft for the Rhapsody are in the possession of the Gesellschaft der Musikfreunde, Vienna. On the first of these pages, at the bottom, is inserted a sketch for the music at mm. 97–99, which corresponds to that at m. 55. This inset is keyed (by an x) to the sketch for m. 55. Thus, as Brahms composed the earlier passage he conceived the later one. Motivic considerations were probably paramount, for the latter passage consists of an expansion of motive $\bar{a}^2$, heightening the special significance of that motive in the music.

"Extra" Measures
and Metrical Ambiguity
in Beethoven

Andrew Imbrie

✳ THE EXISTENCE OF "strong" and "weak" measures in Beethoven's music has long aroused the curiosity of theorists and performers. Beethoven himself explicitly pointed the way to our investigation of still higher units of metrical organization through his famous indications "ritmo di tre battute" and "ritmo di quattro battute." A certain amount of ink has been spilled over the "correct" metrical interpretation of various passages; yet the proper study of these matters has often been hampered by a persistent confusion, not only over appropriate criteria, but over the nature of rhythm and meter. The problem is further complicated by an apparent reluctance on the part of theorists to think in terms of the formal and expressive possibilities inherent in metrical ambiguity itself.[1]

In the present essay I shall attempt to explore these issues through two examples from Beethoven's work. In each of these, there is an "extra" measure that does not fit into an otherwise tidy metrical scheme. In each case, a theorist has taken note of the problem.

I

The first example comes from the first movement of the Sonata in D Major, Op. 10, no. 3. Sir Donald Tovey, in his discussion of the first group of the exposition,[2] subdivides it into phrases, calling them the "four-bar unison theme" and three "six-bar phrases."

---

[1] A notable exception is the discussion of the performer's options by Edward T. Cone, *Musical Form and Musical Performance* (New York, 1968); particularly

pp. 45 ff.

[2] Donald Francis Tovey, *A Companion to Beethoven's Pianoforte Sonatas* (London, 1947), pp. 60 ff.

Tovey quite rightly distinguishes this phrase structure from the metric structure that determines which points are strong or weak. His judgment of the metric structure is expressed by the statement: "The rhythm dates its main accent from bar 2." Although he gives no supporting arguments, we might supply two reasons for the plausibility of this interpretation. First, it places all four phrase endings, both fermate and both sforzandi at metrically accented points. Second, it presupposes a two-measure module, which can easily be heard as governing the harmonic flow. We can, without undue strain, perceive the first group as consisting of a dominant preparation (extending through measure 1) followed by two measures of I, six of V, two of I, four of V, and six of I—each harmonic change taking place at the beginning of an even-numbered measure.

Ex. 1

Example 1 illustrates this interpretation by means of metric reduction. Each quarter note of the diagram represents a full measure of music; the bar lines represent the division into two-measure units, each beginning with a metric accent on the first beat of an even-numbered measure. The heavy bar lines represent a higher grouping by multiples of these two-measure units, according to the perceived harmonic changes. A primary metric accent occurs after each heavy bar line. There is one such downbeat for each phrase, with the exception of the third, which has two. Each phrase ends with such a downbeat accent, and is, therefore, perceived as being masculine.

The first irregularity takes place at measure 22; for as Tovey states, in his analysis of the subsequent transition, "the accentuation of the whole paragraph must be dated from bar 23. To shift the accent elsewhere leads only to confusion." Measure 22, then, must be perceived as an isolated "extra" measure intruding upon the even flow of the two-measure units or their multiples. Here we may choose to regard the span of time between accents as having been foreshortened—an effect somewhat mitigated by the presence of the fermata, which lengthens the measure to a size comparable, if not equal, to that of the two-measure module already established. Or we may choose to hear the fermata as "standing for" a full two measures, but as specifying a relaxation in the rigidity of the metronomic count. Whichever way we hear it, however, the fermata must presumably be perceived, and hence performed, differently from the fermata at measure 4, which occurs without any accompanying change in the prevailing module.

Tovey's interpretation gives rise to another discrepancy between two similar events—this time thematic events. The sforzando at measure 4, when treated not only as a dynamic but also as a metric accent, creates a sense of decisive shift from the tonic to the dominant, which then prevails (as we have seen) for six measures. In a similar manner, the tonic chord at measure 10, when perceived as a strong masculine cadence, shifts the prevailing harmony back to I, which lasts until challenged by the entrance of the A in the bass just before measure 12. But although measures 5 and 11 are thematically parallel, the first is dominant in effect and the second tonic, as a result of the influence of the accents that precede them. This discrepancy, in turn, tends retroactively to weaken the effect of the masculine cadence at measure 10 and to raise the question of whether, indeed, it should have been perceived as a primary metric accent. Our suspicions are increased by the sudden forte at the upbeat to measure 11.

Finally, Tovey himself acknowledges what seems to be a serious difficulty in his own analysis, without resolving it. At the end of the exposition, he remarks, "the rhythm has changed step; nobody knows when." He is apparently referring to the fact that, starting with measure 113, a series of low A's in the bass has confirmed the meter beyond doubt by placing the accents at the beginnings of odd-numbered measures. When the repeat is taken, the continuation of this clear meter brings the music out with an accent, not at measure 2 but at measure 1.

Is Tovey's analysis simply erroneous? Before taking up this question, let us consider the alternative. Suppose that the end of the exposition, instead of failing to connect with the repeat, serves rather to clarify it. This hypothesis entails a radical revision of our analysis of the first group,

43

though the notion of a two-measure module does not have to be abandoned. A simple reversal of the strong-weak relationship between the first beats of adjacent measures leaves all thematic correspondences undisturbed. It is the harmonic aspect of things that becomes a little more complicated. The new placement of accents (on the first beats of odd-numbered measures) is out of phase with the most obvious perceptible pattern of harmonic change. Besides, the sforzandi now occur at weak points and must, therefore, be felt as offbeat accents. And the cadences are now feminine.

Moreover, to make the situation still more precarious, it appears that the location of the *primary* accents must be moved away from the cadences entirely. Our predilection, of course, is always to place the chief accent of weight as close as possible to the end of a phrase in order to produce a sense of closure. This sense is progressively weakened the closer the accent is shifted toward the beginning. Thus, for example, a primary downbeat at the beginning of measure 9 or 15 would produce a feminine cadence, yet the phrase as a whole would still be perceived as weighted at the end. All other things being equal, our predilection for closure would cause us to locate accents here as our second choice. But let us look again at the end of the exposition (since we are already relying on its connection with the repeat to clarify the metrical scheme). Beginning with measure 93, a succession of emphatic accents on A in the bass establishes an unmistakable meter, this time at the level of four-measure groups. The accents occur at the beginnings of measures 93, 97, 101, 105, 109, and 113. Only after measure 113 does the bass then begin to subdivide four into two (which does not materially weaken our sense of the higher organization). If we now take the repeat, the continuation of the meter at this higher level will require us to place the *primary* accents at the beginnings of measures 1, 5, 11, 17, and 23. (The four-measure unit becomes stretched to six by the corresponding expansion of the second, third, and fourth phrases.)

Example 2 illustrates this interpretation. It will be seen at once that our apprehension of the musical events must undergo significant changes. If it be assumed that metric accents on all levels exert an attractive influence on what *precedes* them—i.e. that they indicate goals of motion—then it becomes immediately apparent that the relationship between phrases must now be heard in a new way. Instead of behaving like a series of formal statements, each ending with a period or at least a semicolon, the phrases now become linked to one another, each preparing the next.[3]

---

[3] For a straightforward example of linked-phrase construction, see the rondo of the Sonata in C Minor, Op. 13, mm. 79–82, 83–86 ff. The structural downbeat is deferred to m. 107.

Ex. 2

The primary accents at measures 5, 11, 17, and 23 release a part of the pent-up energy left over from the preceding phrases. The silences between phrases, rather than being felt as "dead time," now become active and rhetorical. The phrases end with question marks—or at least dashes. The fermate, instead of adding emphasis to events that have already taken place, now serve the opposite purpose of maintaining the pressure of unresolved tension. What Tovey took to be tonic cadences (measures 9–10 and 15–16) become weightless formulas, whose real function is to provide sufficient relief from the prevailing dominant harmony so that the next downbeat may bring with it the requisite degree of contrast. The tonic harmony has been divested of its formal authority and relegated to the humble role of an inflection. What strikes our ear particularly, now that the accents are placed in this new position, is the insistent reiteration of the motive D–C♯, which occurs across every "heavy" bar line from 1 to 17; and the large-scale melodic outcome of this motion becomes, for the first time, a matter of concern.

How, then, are we to choose between these two contradictory readings? The first has the advantage of directness: a cadence is a cadence; and those tones in the melody that are loudest, longest, or most cleanly articulated are downbeats. The harmonies change on cue. Yet there is that embarrassing "extra" measure 22, along with the other discrepancies already mentioned. The second reading has the advantage of fitting perfectly with the end of the exposition when the repeat is taken. It is unnecessary to postulate an extra measure, either at the repeat sign or at measure 22. Finally, the second reading has another advantage not yet alluded to. It regulates the musical flow on a much larger scale. Not only does it turn a succession of suspiciously pat and formalistic statements into a series of incomplete gestures, building one upon another to a point of crisis, but it provides, through this accumulation, sufficient and appropriate energy for the modulatory process that follows. The first coincidence of cadential accent with structural downbeat is deferred to measure 53, the point at which such a coincidence can be most effective.

Yet this second reading raises some questions too. First, there is the objection that the listener can have no foreknowledge of future subtleties and must, therefore, accept at face value the simplest interpretation of events as they occur. This familiar argument, if carried to its logical extreme, leads to an atomistic theory of musical perception, according to which music is assimilated as a stream of raw data by a simple cumulative process; such a theory leaves out of account the listener's ability both to anticipate probabilities and to revise former impressions. However, the question still remains, as a practical matter, whether in the present instance the listener is given sufficient opportunity to perceive the music at all according to the second, more "precarious" interpretation. Of course, the performer can do much to encourage such an interpretation, by stressing, in a number of possible ways, the suspenseful character of the fermate, by boldly attacking each new phrase, and by underplaying the cadential formulas. Yet the fact remains that these formulas *do* sound like cadences; the arrivals of tonic harmony *are* strongly marked; the pauses between phrases *do* separate those phrases. It may be observed, in addition, that the sense of closure at the tonic cadences is enhanced by the thematic structure: the second phrase has all the earmarks of the classical "consequent" phrase, completing and balancing the first, "antecedent," phrase. The third is a varied repetition or confirmation.

Tovey could have brought still another argument in favor of his interpretation. Although he could not ignore the difficulty of relating the end of the exposition to the repeat of the beginning, he could have supported his case by pointing to the recapitulation.

The dominant preparation for the recapitulation begins at measure 167, and establishes a clear meter at the four-measure level, with downbeats at the beginnings of measures 167, 171, 175, 179, and 183. Assuming that the fermata here does not upset this basic meter, the next downbeat —by continuation—comes at the first beat of measure 187, which corresponds to measure 4 of the exposition! The cadence of the six-measure consequent phrase comes on the next downbeat (measure 193, corresponding to measure 10), and when the new transition arrives, there is no longer any extra measure: we come out effortlessly in six measures on the downbeat of measure 205, corresponding to measure 23. Even the sudden forte that disturbed our serene acceptance of the importance of the first beat of measure 10 has been replaced at measure 193 by a mere crescendo.

Although these facts do not invalidate the second interpretation, they make it impossible to dismiss the first—at least as far as the recapitulation is concerned. It would appear that we are to hear the exposition in one way and the recapitulation in another. Or, to put it more exactly, the ambiguity exists from the start. Our initial predilection to hear the music Tovey's way is somewhat compromised at the outset by the metrical imbalance at measure 22, and still more by the eccentricity of phrase divisions that appear to be overarticulated in a context of almost explosive forward thrust. But we probably cannot supply, in retrospect, any viable alternative until the metrical situation is clarified for us by the end of the exposition and its connection with the repeat. At the recapitulation, on the other hand, the need for tonic harmony is greater, while the need for explosive forward thrust is much less—such thrust having largely spent itself by now. The time is ripe for resolution and reminiscence in measured phrases. And because of our original predilection, the simple structure of the recapitulation strikes us, paradoxically, not as a new in-.terpretation, but as the return of an old one.

47

II

I have chosen to open with this example because it seems to offer a preliminary demonstration of Beethoven's technique of metrical ambiguity. In Op. 10, no. 3, the ambiguity appears not merely as a characteristic detail but as a creative force, and the strategy of its deployment affects the psychological impact of the whole movement. I am suggesting that we accept the following notions: that two contradictory metrical interpretations of the same event can be simultaneously entertained in the mind of the performer and listener; that the subjective "color" of that event is partly attributable to this contradiction; and that the composer can, wherever the event recurs, favor one or the other side of the contradiction, thereby helping to satisfy the dramatic or formal requirements of the music.

Since the appreciation of metrical ambiguity presupposes a clear definition of accent and its relation to meter, it may be well at this point to set forth a few of the guiding principles that underlie the present discussion of Beethoven's music. These principles are, I believe, close to those tacitly assumed by Tovey and Schenker, theorists whose work provides the stepping-off points for the analyses in sections I and III of this essay. These analyses are predicated on the concept of accent as a concrete meter-defining agent rather than as an abstract element on a vague prosodic model—an alternative concept that has come to the fore in certain recent writings on rhythmic theory, notably those of Cooper and

Meyer.[4] Among other difficulties that many have felt with the Cooper-Meyer theory is its difficulty of application to actual musical performance. The present analyses are predicated on a return to a more traditional method of inquiry; I hope they may serve to reaffirm for the theorist a concept whose practical usefulness to the conductor and performer remains undiminished.

"Accent means contrast, and vice-versa."[5] The structural role of accent is to fix or mark off those points in time which either establish, confirm, challenge, or overthrow the meter. Sessions's definition implies that accent has no duration. It is the fact of contrast or change that constitutes accent. A harmonic change per se has no duration; only the constituent harmonies have it. A dynamic change must be instantaneous if it is to create accent; dynamic changes involving duration (crescendo or diminuendo) have the effect of deferring accent until some decisive *point* is reached. The species of melodic accent called agogic—whereby a tone receives accent by virtue of its longer duration—is only an apparent exception to the rule, for our perception of the longer duration has the effect of causing us retroactively to place the accent at the point of attack. The same thing can be said for the accentual effect of placing a dynamic "swell" on a given tone.

Meter is established in the mind of the listener by those patterns of accentual recurrence that allow him to perceive a higher order. We have seen that two different kinds of recurrence can produce two alternative meters, especially on higher levels of organization. And especially at these higher levels, the recurrence need not be absolutely regular. It is perhaps necessary to emphasize this point, in view of a common and widespread assumption to the contrary. As has just been observed, the test for meter is simply that the sense of recurrence is present, and that such recurrence allows us to perceive a higher order. Regularity of recurrence is, of course, the surest way in which accents can be metrically oriented. But regularity on lower levels inevitably (at least in Beethoven) gives way to flexibility at higher levels of structure.

According to Edward Cone in *Musical Form and Musical Performance* (page 26, my italics):

> The classical phrase has often been analyzed as an alternation of
> strong and weak measures, on an analogy with strong and weak beats

---

[4] Grosvenor W. Cooper and Leonard B. Meyer, *The Rhythmic Structure of Music* (Chicago, 1960). See, for example, the discussion of accent on pp. 7–8, and such statements as: "Unaccent is an as-pect of accent, and a rhythmic group is an accented shape" (p. 119).

[5] Roger Sessions, *Harmonic Practice* (New York, 1968), p. 83.

within a measure. In other words, the larger rhythmic structure is treated simply as metric structure on a higher level. Now, I do not deny that such an alternation often occurs, especially in the case of short, fast measures; but I insist that on some level this *metric* principle of parallel balance must give way to a more organic *rhythmic* principle that supports the melodic and harmonic shape of the phrase and justifies its acceptance as a formal unit.

This insight into flexibility at higher levels is achieved at the expense of a blurring of the distinction between meter and rhythm. The idea that once an organization in time becomes flexible rather than mechanical it thereby becomes rhythmic rather than metrical stems from the notion that meter has to be absolutely regular. In my opinion, the distinction between meter and rhythm lies elsewhere, and we should now try to define it.

In the foregoing discussion of the opening of Op. 10, no. 3, the attempt was made to show that all accents are to be heard as occurring on specific beats—regardless of whether these accents are of local or of general significance. It was never claimed that an entire measure or group of measures was accented with respect to any other comparable unit. It is easy—and, therefore, tempting—to speak of "accented measures" rather than to use clumsy expressions like "measures on whose first beats the primary metric accents fall": yet the difference in meaning is important. The same semantic confusion exists in musicians' everyday use of the word "beat." Sometimes we treat it as if it meant a unit of duration, as in the expression "the second half of the beat." At other times we treat it as if it meant simply a point in time, as in "off the beat."

It is this distinction that I believe to be crucial to our understanding of the difference between rhythm and meter. For the present analysis, I shall stipulate that rhythm is the patterning or proportional arrangement of sounds and silences with respect to their durations, while meter is the measurement of the distances between points in time. Distance and duration are not synonymous: the former is the measure of the latter. (Compare the spatial distance between two points in geometry with an actual line drawn between or through them.) In studying a composer's manipulation of metric structure, it is important to be able to treat accent as the specific agent responsible for the fixing of instants, or points, in time; and to keep this function clearly separated from the essentially motivic function of a rhythmic, or durational, pattern, which may be placed in various positions with respect to such points in time. It is true that the motivic pattern may be one of the elements whose accentual content helps to establish the meter, but many other accentual factors (e.g. harmonic, linear) must also be taken into account.

Cone remarks that "there is a sense in which a phrase can be heard as an upbeat to its own cadence," and that "larger and larger sections can also be so apprehended." [6] In my opinion, this statement describes our apprehension of musical phrases and sections very well, provided that the term *upbeat* is understood as referring to a *durational* unit, and *cadence* as the *point* in time at which the primary metric accent occurs. *Upbeat*, in this context, would mean a *rhythmic* element characterized by a sense of preparation for a forthcoming *metrical* event.

It might be nice to have a terminology that could distinguish an *upbeat* (in the sense of a relatively lightly accented point) from, let us say, an *anacrusis* (in the sense of a passage of music perceived as building toward an imminent downbeat). Cone is using *upbeat* for *anacrusis*, as hypothetically defined here. In similar fashion, theorists sometimes refer to durational units (motives, phrases) as being *accented*. Since it is true that an important downbeat accent may impart a generalized sense of greater heaviness to an entire rhythmic unit, perhaps this phenomenon could be described by some such term as *weighting*, to distinguish it from accentuation itself. *Weighting* would then be the opposite of the "upbeat quality" (*Auftaktigkeit*) attributable to what we have just called *anacrusis*.

Let us return now to the question of regularity and flexibility. It has already been proposed that our sense of metrical organization depends not upon regularity as such, but more generally upon a sense of recurrence. The importance of recurrence lies in its ability to establish and to distinguish hierarchical levels of structure. The degree to which, and the levels at which, an approach to regularity will be felt as necessary in order to bring about the effect of recurrence will vary greatly among composers, among individual works according to the relative complexity of their formal requirements, and, of course, among styles and eras. Having said this much, I believe that it is only fair to acknowledge that meter acts as a conservative force. It is the principle that attempts to reduce to "law and order" the protean rhythmic complexities of the musical surface. It is the frame of reference by which we try to measure and judge the relative values of the changes taking place in the music. Our desire for security prompts us to accept the simplest, most nearly regular interpretation of events, unless and until they force us to seek the next simplest. And our desire for order leads us to seek as many higher levels of metrical organization as our powers of attention and synthesis will allow.

---

[6] Cone, *op. cit.*, p. 26.

III

These observations should help to throw light on problems such as that of the "extra" measure. The laws of "conservation of simplicity" and "separation of levels" should account for the fact that, for example, a $\frac{1}{4}$ measure occurring in a prevailing metrical context of $\frac{4}{4}$, tends to be understood as an elongation of the measure preceding or following it, rather than as a measure in its own right. Perceived in this way, the departure from regular metric reccurence is much less extreme, and the separation between the levels of organization (quarter-note level and measure level) remains undisturbed. To state it another way, if two strong metric accents succeed one another at an uncharacteristically close interval of time, we attempt to hear one as taking precedence over the other (i.e. as occurring at a higher level).

Heinrich Schenker, in his discussion of the development of the first movement of the Fifth Symphony,[7] asks us, in effect, to accept measure 208 as an "extra" measure. Up to this point, his analysis of the entire movement has clearly shown the operation not only of a two-measure module, but in addition, of a norm of four measures that is indispensable to the proper understanding and performance of the principal rhythmic motive. In Schenker's analysis, compound groupings of eight or twelve measures are common, and departures from the four-measure module occur in multiples of two to form occasional extended groupings of six, ten, or fourteen. The only exceptions, so far, occur at measures 6 and 25, which are treated as independent anacruses and are not counted. The justification for this is that both of these measures are immediately preceded by fermate, which in turn, by lengthening the end of the motive, dramatize its independent character at the outset, and hence facilitate its later recognition as a unit. In fact it is this very independence, in the case of the first four measures, that provides Schenker with a strong argument in favor of the metric as well as rhythmic importance of the four-measure unit throughout.

Measure 208, however, he regards as the fifth (relatively accented)

51

---

[7] Heinrich Schenker, "Beethoven V Sinfonie," *Der Tonwille*, I (1921). The bulk of the chapter on the first movement has just been reprinted in translation in Elliot Forbes, ed., *Beethoven: Symphony No. 5 in C Minor*, Norton Critical Scores (New York, 1971). This excerpt leaves out, among other things, some pieces of advice to the performer and some rebuttals of statements by other theorists. I shall quote the Forbes-Adams translation wherever possible, but for the quotations from the latter part of the chapter I shall be obliged to rely on my own translation.

measure of a six-measure group which then *overlaps* by one measure
with the beginning of another six-measure group at measure 209. His
diagram shows it in this manner:

Ex. 3

Measure 209 is treated as simultaneously weak and strong, depending
on which of the two overlapping groups is being considered.

Assuming the validity of the rule proposed above, requiring the
precedence of one of any two closely contiguous strong accents, we
would be obliged to assign precedence to the downbeat of measure 209,
since it initiates the subsequent metrical grouping (just as the first beat
of a measure is, metrically, the strongest of that measure). Thus measure
208 would be "extra," and would become, in fact, the last of a five-
measure group. Example 4 shows this by metric reduction.

Ex. 4

Schenker's diagram, as we have seen, portrays the groupings as though
they were six-measure units. These, then, intersect at a junction that
marks off the melodic completion of the outline of the fourth, F–B♮:

By reinterpreting m. 209 as a strong measure (although it was originally weak) followed by a weak m. 210, the nodal point becomes
especially underlined, so that from here on there is no longer any
difficulty in recognizing that only the winds have the strong measures.

. . . When Beethoven places the diminuendo for the strings already at Bb in measure 210 as against Cb in the following measure for the winds, he thereby establishes the character of that measure as weak with respect to 209—what a profound stroke of genius! [8]

The question arises, however, whether the reinterpretation of a single measure provides explanation enough for the effect of this passage as perceived from the metric point of view. That a metrical shift takes place there can be no doubt. Unlike the "extra" measures of Op. 10, no. 3, the one in the Fifth Symphony cannot be even provisionally explained out of existence through regrouping. It can only be relocated—and, as Schenker has shown, this has been attempted (Müller-Reuter, for instance, places it at measure 216 [9]). The problem is that there is an odd number of measures separating the downbeat of measure 126 (the beginning of the development) from that of measure 249 (the recapitulation), and this fact must be explained somehow in metrical terms. But relying on any single measure to account for the phenomenon is a little like putting an excessive number of rather delicate eggs in one basket.

The listener's intuitive response to the passage in question is that of one who has been led step by step into a precarious position. The motives have been liquidated; the texture has been radically simplified and now consists of the raw alternation of chords between winds and strings; the harmonies seem to have traveled far from the home tonic. (The actual logic of their relation to the basic key has, of course, been thoroughly demonstrated by Schenker.) The rhythms, too, I believe, have been deployed throughout the preceding measures in such a way as to prepare the ear gradually for the metrical dislocation. Both preparation and dislocation are accomplished through metrical ambiguity on a large scale.

To demonstrate this, it will be necessary first to allude briefly to the exposition, and to examine a simpler ambiguity. Schenker's analysis establishes the four-measure module as the metric basis for all the music from measure 44 through measure 79, after which he postulates a fourteen-measure unit, to bring the music to the clear downbeat at the beginning of measure 94.

An advantage of this reading is that by placing the downbeat of a four-measure unit on the Eb of the horn call (measure 60), it emphasizes the motivic resemblance between this and the opening subject. For the two can then be shown to be identical not only in general contour and in length, but also in placement with regard to the metric accent. This

53

---

[8] Schenker, *op. cit.*, pp. 13 (= Forbes, *op. cit.*, pp. 178–79), 18.

[9] T. Müller-Reuter, *Lexikon der deut-* *schen Konzertliteratur, Nachtrag* (Leipzig, 1921), pp. 22–23.

Ex. 5

consideration weighs heavily with Schenker.[10] But he also makes much of the fourteen-measure extension that follows (measures 80–93), stating that its cumulative power partly depends on its having exceeded what he regards as the eight-measure span of the preceding groups. One could mention another reason why the listener might be disposed to hear the passage according to Schenker's interpretation: the inherent resistance to change in every listener will cause him to cling to the four-measure module as long as possible; thus the end of the fourteen-measure unit is the latest point at which a change can be made in recognition of the primacy of the structural downbeat at the beginning of measure 94.

Of course, this is not the first time that the four-measure module has been violated: the ten-measure extension (measures 34–43) has already provided a prototype. Furthermore, the distortions and rhythmic displacements of the motive that immediately follow (measures 44 ff.), and that are associated with the modulation, increase the sense of stress, as Schenker has shown. He regards the E♭ at measure 60 as the point at which all this tension is released: "The introductory motto of the second subject, with its emphatic expression, re-establishes contact with the metrical scheme that had been broken during the modulation: the half notes E♭ and B♭ appear again in the first and third measures of the group."[11]

But is it not possible also to hear the second subject in another way? The stresses developed in the course of the modulation may just possibly prove too powerful to admit of an instant resolution on the tonic of the new key, falling within a re-established four-measure scheme. Consider, then, the alternative of a six-measure group preceding a structural downbeat on the B♭ at measure 62.

Ex. 6

This, by the way, is also Riemann's interpretation, to which Schenker objects only on the ground that it does not reflect any awareness of a motivic correspondence with measures 1 through 4.

---

[10] Tovey also scans the passage in this way: see his essay on the Fifth Symphony in *Essays in Musical Analysis* (London, 1935), I, 38–44, reprinted in Forbes (cf. especially p. 146, ex. 2).

[11] Schenker, *op. cit.*, p. 9 (= Forbes, p. 173).

One effect of this interpretation is to change the cadence in E♭ from full to half—which, in my opinion at least, is more consistent not only with an effective dramatic deployment of the resources of tonality (the deferment of a decisive cadence in the new key until a later point) but even with Schenker's own linear analysis, which reveals the crucial importance of B♭ at this moment. Besides, the B♭ is strongly emphasized by the fact that it initiates a thirteen-measure pedal point. The B♭ is also clearly favored by Beethoven's dynamics: the *ff* marking at measure 59 applies to the entire horn solo; the *sf* on all three half-notes assures their equality of emphasis, except that the sudden diminuendo after the attack on the B♭ marks it off as more "interesting," an impression confirmed by the contrast of the subsequent *p, dolce, legato* in the strings. In this connection it is curious to note that here, and only here, Schenker recommends to the performer a distortion of Beethoven's dynamics: "If the meaning of measures 63 ff is to be rendered, the following articulation must be applied: $\overset{\frown}{4}\;|\;1\;2\;\overset{\frown}{3}\;4\;|\;\overset{\frown}{1}$ in measures 63–74, and $\overset{\frown}{4}\;|\;1\;\overset{\frown}{2}\;3\;4\;|\;\overset{\frown}{1}$ in measures 75–82." [12] By stressing the first (weak) measure of the violin melody, he not only contradicts the spirit of Beethoven's *dolce* but cancels out the effect of the horn diminuendo, which places the accent at a point unacceptable to Schenker.

As a final argument in favor of this interpretation, one might add that the placement of the principal metric accent on the last note of the motive does not really conceal its correspondence with the original motive of measures 1–5. In fact, one could regard it as an exploitation of a metrical ambiguity already inherent in the original motive—an ambiguity enhanced rather than destroyed by the lengthening of the second fermata (measures 4 and 5). And the distortions of the motive beginning at measure 44, far from merely providing tension to be released all at once, can be explained as helping to prepare the ear for a transfer of accent to the last note.

If this interpretation is accepted, it will have the further effect of nullifying the irregularity of Schenker's fourteen-measure extension (measures 80–93), and bringing it into line with the four-measure module. The sense of broadening is still present, however, to the extent that three fairly distinct four-measure units (measures 70 ff.) are followed by a homogeneous twelve-measure unit (measures 82 ff.).

The point of the comparison of these two readings is, once again, not to make a final decision as to which is correct, but to show that both are

---

[12] *Ibid.*, p. 18.

Ex. 7

possible. The ambiguity raised in the exposition has its consequences in the development, to which we should now return. Upon the reappearance of the horn-call motive, this time in the violins, Schenker places his structural downbeat at the beginning of measure 180. This is consistent with his earlier decision, and plausible in its context. It is made possible, among other things, by the previous foreshortening of the last member of a sequence of large-scale anticipations, beginning at measure 158 and leading to a downbeat at measure 168. Schenker has shrewdly drawn attention to the increase in velocity of the downward bass movement at measure 167, which has the effect of precipitating this downbeat and inhibiting us from accepting it as the beginning of another two-measure anticipation. Thus the group ends up containing fourteen rather than sixteen measures, and is followed by a twelve-measure group leading into measure 180.

Once the primary metric accent of the motive has been unequivocally assigned to its first measure (180), the consequences drawn by Schenker are inescapable: motivic and metric consistency demand equivalent downbeats at the beginnings of measures 188 and 196. By continuation of this logic, the succeeding patterns of paired chords must then be perceived as having accents at the beginning of each pair. Thus we are led to the confrontation that must be resolved before the end of the development, by which time the accents clearly fall at the beginnings of odd-numbered measures. Schenker's solution, already described, has at least the virtue of locating the reversal of accent at the most inconspicuous possible place.

Let us now entertain the other alternative, suggested for the horn-call motive in the exposition, by placing the primary accent at measure 182. This has one immediate and perhaps surprising consequence: it removes the need for Schenker's foreshortening of the two-measure anticipation. The four-measure module, firmly established from the beginning of the development, may be clung to with relative impunity until it brings us to our downbeat at measure 182. I mention this only in order to suggest that there may be a deeply buried, ultraconservative layer of our consciousness as listeners which will persist in interpreting our experience for us as long as possible within an established framework, even in the face of increasingly disturbing events. If this is so, it can perhaps be said to contribute, somewhat obscurely, to our predilection for an accent at measure 182.

Not that Schenker's argument for an accent at measure 168 can be dismissed; this metrical shift of two measures is only the first of that series of disturbing events which, in my opinion, prepare the ear to accept the still more disturbing disruption of the two-measure module itself.

The accent at measure 168 is separated from our downbeat at measure 182 by another fourteen measures, the first eight of which form a separable part by virtue of their divisibility into two rhythmically identical subunits of four each.

Ex. 8

The remaining six measures would then be analogous to our six-measure group beginning at measure 56 in the exposition, in its function of introducing the horn-call motive. In the present instance, the metrical situation *within* the group (measures 176–181) has become unstable as a result of the liquidation of the preceding rhythmic figure, so that we can imagine it as either three groups of two or two groups of three measures. The former interpretation is, of course, the conservative one; but the latter is crucial to the eventual absorption of the "extra" measure into the metrical scheme. One indication of the plausibility of this grouping is the accent created by the bass when it cuts off at the F♯ in measure 179 (note that the analogous D of measure 58 occurs at the third measure of the group, whereas the present F♯ initiates the fourth measure of the group). Another factor that adds to the importance of measure 179 is the melodic completion of the double-neighboring-note motion around D. (There are emphatic Ds in the melody at measures 176, 179, and 182, a fact that encourages still more our hearing groups of three measures.)

So far the primacy of the accent at measure 182 has not been questioned. If we do not do so, we shall be obliged by reason of consistency to supply a similar accent at measure 190 and, by analogy, at measure 198. We would then find ourselves, as Schenker did, with the accent on the first of each pair of chords, and would face the same dilemma in trying to sense some subsequent one-measure shift.

If, however, instead of counting from measure 182 we count from measure 179, everything comes out smoothly. The analogous accents at measures 187 and 195 confirm us in our choice by marking strong cadences, and the subsequent grouping of the chords into end-accented pairs proceeds without further difficulty.

What is proposed, then, is the metrical reinterpretation, not of a single measure, but of a three-measure group: measures 179–181. This group

59

should be understood, simultaneously, as the last half of a six-measure group and the first part of an eight-measure group. Such an interpretation, if acceptable on other grounds, would be desirable because of its greater smoothness and its more organic integration into the larger metrical scheme. Smoother because it has a less disrupting effect on the listener's perception of the periodicity of metric accents, and more organic because the listener's acceptance of the three-measure group in question

Ex. 9

has been prepared in advance and confirmed by subsequent reiteration. The advance preparation consists, in part, of the matching of the two three-measure groups within the ambiguous six-measure unit, measures 176–181, which resembles the matching of the two four-measure groups of measures 168–175. (The shift from fours to threes is reflected in the rhythmic condensation at measures 176–179.) Confirmation by subsequent reiteration is achieved through matching the two eight-measure groups, subdivided each into three plus five (measures 179–194). The acceptance of all these odd-numbered groupings is facilitated by just such parallelisms, on the principle that two odd numbers add up to a larger even number. (Compare the two seven-measure groups in the first movement of Op. 10, no. 3: measures 53–59 and 60–66.) The entire operation is summarized in the following diagram:

Ex. 10

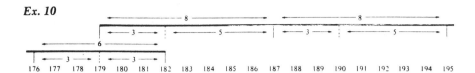

Two final observations may be of interest. First, the grouping of the chords into end-accented pairs (measures 196 ff.) seems, to this listener at least, intuitively more satisfying in itself than the opposite grouping. Among a number of possible reasons for this is, perhaps, a "subliminal" association with the pattern of the accompaniment to the *dolce* violin melody (measures 63 ff.), which also occurs immediately following the horn-call motive.

Second, just as an attempt has been made here to push the "conservative" interpretation of events as far forward as possible in order to see how long one could cling to an established pattern, it might be interesting to see how far back one could push a "radical" interpretation in order to see how soon one could adopt a new pattern. It might be possible, then, to group measures 168–178 in this way:

61

Ex. 11

The acceptance of an isolated three-measure group at measures 168-170 is encouraged by the change of harmony on the (syncopated) downbeat of measure 171: note that here, for the first time, the initial pattern of three short notes is identical, both melodically and harmonically, with what follows. Although this interpretation may be difficult to accept per se as the vehicle for the accomplishment of the metrical shift, it may at least contribute to the preparation of the ear for the acceptance of the "real" shift soon to follow. There have been times when I have found myself hearing the passage in this way.

It is my belief, however, that when the experienced listener is at his peak of alertness and receptivity, he is capable of responding on several simultaneous metric levels. It is not so much that he consciously and systematically keeps track of the various metrical interpretations of events, but rather that he responds directly and intuitively to the tensions between or among them—just as he responds directly to both the local and the more general structural significance of a harmony or, on occasion, to its pivotal role. Beethoven, more than any other composer, produced masterworks that engage our sensibilities in this way.

62

Addendum

The reader of this article may well feel justified in concluding that in my discussion of the development section of the Fifth Symphony I have actually repeated Schenker's error on a larger scale. Schenker asks the listener to interpret the downbeat of a single measure (209) as both weak and strong (at the same level of metrical organization). I seem to be asking the listener to do the same thing with a three-measure group (179–181) (see ex. 10). To be consistent with my own ground-rules I must, clearly, decide which downbeat is stronger at this level: that of measure 179 or that of 176 or 182. I declare for 179, because of the clear harmonic and linear arrival there, supported by the dynamics (see ex. 11) and the clear structural importance of the two eight-measure groups initiated there. Thus the metrical accents at this level of the hierarchy would have to be placed at the beginnings of measures 168, 179, 187, 195, etc. This declaration of mine should not weaken the rôle of the three-measure unit at 176 in preparing the listener's acceptance of the 3 plus 5 pattern within the eight-measure groups. The relation between the downbeats at 176 and 179 should simply be perceived as weak to strong. The decision for 179 rather than 182 has the effect of somewhat diminishing the metric importance of the last note of the motive, which first appeared at measure 62. I would regard this as acceptable, especially in view of the progressive liquidation that immediately follows. I refer the reader to ex. 9, where the note in question is preceded by *dotted* bar-lines at 182 and 190, and by none at 198.

K.503: The Unity of contrasting Themes and Movements—I

BY

HANS KELLER

> It is certain that . . . one can get beyond the instinctive faith in the great masters and account for one's finding something beautiful; this is doubtless necessary nowadays, if we consider how terribly arbitrary and superficial evaluations have become.
>
> . . . my colours follow from each other as of their own accord, and when I take a certain colour for my starting-point, I am quite clear in my mind about what to derive from it, and how to get life into it.
>
> . . . *Much*, indeed *everything* depends on my feeling for *the infinite variety* of tones *of the same family*.—VINCENT VAN GOGH, from the 418th letter to his brother (his italics).

TAUTOLOGY is the greatest insult to the dignity of human thought. Yet most so-called "analytical" writings about music, from the humble programme-noter who has absolutely nothing up his record-sleeve to the great Tovey who may or may not have withheld a lot, boil down to mere tautological descriptions. I maintain that if you want to open your mouth or typewriter in order to enlarge upon music, you must have a special excuse. Mere "sensitivity", receptivity, and literacy will not do, for it will merely land you in describing the musical listener's own *perception* of the music, as distinct from promoting his *understanding*—whereupon, to be sure, he will consider you "an excellent critic".

> "A succession of majestic chords in which the whole orchestra takes part opens the first movement. Built upon the triad of C major, they descend with slow stateliness from realms above, hastening a little as they draw near us, then rise again to beyond their starting-point."

Thus the much-praised Girdlestone (1)* on the beginning of K.503. This sort of "criticism" or "analysis" has two aspects, the descriptive and the metaphorical. The descriptive is senseless, the metaphorical usually nonsense. If you are so deaf that you don't hear that these C major chords (they aren't "built upon the triad of C major", but simply C major triads) "hasten" in the third bar (and not so "little" either!), I don't see that you will profit much by Girdlestone's assertion that they do so. And if you believe his metaphor that the chords "draw near you", "descending from realms above", you are so utterly stupid harmonically that, frankly, you aren't worth bothering about. The chords move away from home, and if "you" are anything, you are at home in the tonic triad: it is on the assumption of your capacity for *harmonic nostalgia* that the whole composition develops, and since the C major chords move the music away from the C major triad, they don't "draw near us". Not that all

---

* Numbers in brackets refer to the references at the end of this first part of our analysis.

metaphors are of this kind.   But in order to arrive at a psychologically valid metaphor, your musical understanding must be more, not less complete than it need be for some detailed technical observation, for only if you are omniscient about a particular passage can you ensure your metaphor against wrong implications in which any right point it may possess may be submerged.   However, if you do know all that much, at any rate by way of your emotions, why not articulate your knowledge technically and thus save both yourself and the reader the trouble of analysing your metaphors instead of the music, in order to find out whether they mislead?   What Girdlestone did, on the other hand, was, to feel terribly sensitive and submit to the first wrong images that occurred to him, and to my knowledge everybody has submitted to his innumerable fallacies ever since.   Once he got himself into the literary swing, of course, he could not get out of it: ". . . then rise again to beyond their starting-point". A musical child of six can see that this is absolute rubbish, but we nod our cultured heads in refined agreement.   Who rises?   The C major chords? But they are past and gone.   Does, in fact, anything "rise"?   "Then rise again" implies a motion corresponding to the previous "descent, with slow stateliness, from realms above", and there is no such motion.   "Starting a tone higher, the same thing is repeated on the chord of the dominant seventh" would at least be a faultless description, if not so readable as Girdlestone's style.

Faultless descriptions are Tovey's speciality: his "analyses" are misnomers, even though there are occasional flashes of profound analytical insight.   Otherwise, there is much eminently professional tautology.   I have no doubt that Tovey was a great musician.   His writings are a symptom of a social tragedy, for they are both a function of the stupidity of his audiences, the musical *nouveaux riches*, and too much of a mere reaction against the unmusicality of his academic forbears.   "A new rhythmic figure rises quietly in the violins". Thus Tovey (6) on Ex. 4 (x[1]) below, in what has become a classical essay to which Hutchings refers as "a more penetrating analysis than will be found" in his own book (2).   But this isn't analysis; it is pure pleonastic description. Anybody who has to be told this new rhythmic figure is a new rhythmic figure cannot possibly understand a bar of the Concerto, with or without Tovey's help.

"After dwelling on this new dominant with sufficient breadth, the pianoforte settles down into the second subject.   This will come as a surprise to orthodox believers in text-books, for it has nothing whatever to do with Ex. [7], which seemed so like a possible second subject."

Is this analysis?   Has anything been explained which we don't hear as a matter of course?   According to the *Oxford English Dictionary*, to analyse means "to ascertain the elements of".   Where are the elements of these new rhythmic and thematic entities?   Where do they come from?   How can they possibly be entirely new and yet be the inevitable consequences of what precedes them and the inevitable premises of what succeeds them?   If structural "analysis" does not show that, in a masterpiece, the new is not new, if it

65

describes contrasts instead of analysing their unity, it is sailing under a black flag, pirating the music without paying anything in return.   It is ultimately designed for the typical journalist's reader, who doesn't want to hear anything but what has been present in his own mind in the first place.

The analysis which here follows is based on the tenet that a great work can be *demonstrated* to grow from an all-embracing basic idea, and that the essential, if never-asked questions of why contrasting motifs and themes belong together, why a particular second subject necessarily belongs to a particular first, why a contrasting middle section belongs to its principal section, why a slow movement belongs to a first movement, and so forth, must be answered if an "analysis" is to deserve its name.   During my work (3) on Mozart's chamber music as well as in the course of previous analyses, I have developed, first a method of analysis, and then, on a purely practical basis, a theory of unity, which I hope to formulate in full in a book on criticism.   Frankly, I am in no hurry to systematize my abstractions: practice should precede theory.   That, at the same time, I continuously demand theoretical justification from myself goes without saying.   But basically, my method is as intuitive passively as the creative process is actively, and from the reader I require nothing but an unprejudiced musician's *ear* which, as Schönberg has said, is the musician's sole brain.   My analysis, then, aims at ascertaining the *latent* elements of the unity of *manifest* contrasts.   Within the given space it cannot hope to be complete; I shall concentrate on the most difficult questions.   I have not chosen the work to suit my own purposes; it was the Editor's choice.   While I hope that my new approach is a proper way of paying homage to Mozart's genius, I hasten to qualify its newness and to draw attention to previous investigators and musicians to whom I feel indebted in some way or other— above all, to Oskar Adler and Arnold Schönberg; also, with certain reservations, to Heinrich Schenker and Rudolph Reti.   I have detailed these acknowledgments in (3).

At the outset, I must ask the reader to keep the score at hand; my music examples are chiefly references: otherwise they would have to cover most of the work.   The harmonic structure of melodic quotations must always be kept in mind.   It will be convenient to regard the first movement's bars 1–7/1 as the basic idea.   I say "convenient" because strictly speaking, we ought to start from the opening, basic motif of the movement, but the derivation of what I call the basic idea from the basic motif is obvious.   The first problem is the contrast of Ex. 1 (bars 7 *f*.):

It is here that mainly conjunct melody takes over from the chordal arpeggio line of the basic idea.   The contrast is thus twofold, melodic and rhythmic; it is thrown into relief by the texture, *i.e.* the contrasting orchestration, as well as by the dynamics and phrasing.   Now, the melodic unity is afforded by the chordal progression from bar 4 to bar 5 which produces the central conjunct moment in the basic idea. Stripped of their respective rhythms, the violin (a) and flute (b) motifs containing this step reveal their antecedental significance for the bassoon and oboe phrases (c) of Ex. 1:

The derivation is one of "interversion" (Reti: (5)) *cum* transposition within a sequential frame: re-grouped and rhythmically standardized, the notes of (a) and (b) on the one hand, and (c) on the other, form a tonal sequence.

The rhythmic contrast is unified not only by the implications of the basic idea, but also by those of its background. On the one hand, that is to say, the dotted rhythm is already given by the basic motif, becoming more explicit in the timpani motif of bar 4 (diminution) and the first-oboe motif of bars 5–6 (augmentation), but these elements only establish a basis for the rhythm of Ex. 1, not the actual and specific unifying factor. On the other hand, however, it is easy to hear how a mediocre eighteenth-century composer would have constructed the opening passage rhythmically:

67

The unity of the contrast would thus have been more manifest, but the contrast itself would have been weaker. Mozart says: "Ex. 3 goes without saying, therefore, don't let's say it, but vary it immediately". I submit that this principle of composition, *i.e.* the simultaneous suppression and definite implication of the self-evident, pervades the music of every great master and, incidentally, makes the understanding of Schönberg's music difficult—because what was self-evident to him was not self-evident to everyone. For obvious historical reasons, Mozart's terms of reference for suppressed backgrounds were more generally known.

The pulse of three quavers which, with the dotted notes of Ex. 1, becomes near-manifest, will prove a supremely important determinant of the entire movement's unity. So far we have only been concerned with continuity which, as an aspect of unity, is comparatively easy to analyse, because the composer must always make continuity immediately convincing, at any rate on the emotional level, if the unfolding of his music is to be understood at all. As soon as we arrive at Tovey's "new rhythmic figure",* however, the question

---

* At a later stage, he suddenly calls it a "Beethovenish rhythmic figure"—another deplorable instance of un-self-critically accepting the first association that springs to one's mind (compare Girdlestone on p. 48). Mozart used the figure far more often than Beethoven, and if Beethoven "had it" from anywhere, he had it from Mozart.

why the new is not really new becomes far more complicated; in fact, this contrast is perhaps one of the two most difficult to solve in the entire Concerto:

Its less difficult aspect is, of course, again that of continuity: I have added the preceding half-bar in Ex. 4 in order to make the transition from one motif (*cf.* Ex. 1) to the next, contrasting one more easily comprehensible. Melodically, the basic contrapuntal 2-bar sequence x^1 is an augmentation of x, derhythmicized to an extent which, to those who take a superficial view of classical music, seems characteristic of twelve-tone technique alone. However, the sequences continue up to G and then return to the tonic. Why up to G? Because the outline thus filled in, *i.e.* tonic-dominant, is but an "octave-transposed" version (to put it serially) of the basic tonic-dominant motif of the work.

Not that these factors would in themselves be strong enough to determine and define the unity: there must again be rhythmic and—since a "new" and surprising C minor has emerged—harmonic forces operating on a latent level. Once more from the standpoint of continuity, the latent rhythmic unity can be made manifest with comparative ease: the implied three-quaver pulse of Ex. 1 and of the first note in Ex. 4 comes to the fore in the upbeat of the "new rhythmic figure". The dotted crotchet is split up into its constituent units: it is no chance that the three quavers remain on the same note. Again, a mediocre eighteenth-century composer would no doubt only have been capable of a lesser contrast, interposing between Ex. 1 and Ex. 4 this kind of phrase:

Natural enough in itself, this phrase (whose rhythm is implied in the first bar of Ex. 4) would have amounted, in its context, to an obviosity. As I have tried to indicate in (3), all masterly composition is compression: we may regard Ex. 5 as another suppressed background.

But it would be cheating to suggest that the rhythm of Ex. 4 has herewith been solved. Its three-quaver pulse is, after all, very different from that implied in Ex. 1: it has become an upbeat. In terms of continuity, to be sure, the new rhythm is implied by the implication of Ex. 5's rhythm at the beginning of Ex. 4, but this would again be too weak a determinant for so drastic a thematic contrast. Does the basic idea itself contain any implication of this upbeat?

The diminution of the basic motif's rhythm starts with the upbeat to bar 3, but this circumstance is only retrospectively realized, for when we hear the beginning of bar 3, the diminution has not fully established itself: it is defined by the middle of bar 3. In other words, rhythmic model and diminution overlap. Now, if we straighten out the rhythm of the diminution from where it is established, we arrive at the rhythm of Ex. 6:

Ex. 6

In the subsequent bar, this straightening process does in fact emerge to the surface, and it is again on the second beat of the bar that the new crotchet rhythm is established. Consequently, the second, third, and fourth crotchets are invested with the significance of a three-crotchet upbeat to the inverted seventh on the supertonic, and this three-crotchet unit is confirmed, by way of counter-balance, by the first oboe's dotted minim in bar 6. There is, then, the implication of a three-crotchet upbeat in the basic idea, and the three-quaver upbeat of Tovey's "new rhythmic figure" is a straight diminution of it.

Even the C minor tonality, finally, which like the rhythmic figure itself proves of the greatest significance for the further development of the structure, is latent in the basic idea, *i.e.* in the flat sixth of bar 6.

"The only way to prepare the mind for G major after this grand opening", says Tovey, "would be to go to *its* dominant and pause on that". And he goes on to give his famous explanation that since this does not happen, the close in G is "*on* the dominant, not *in* it". What he overlooks is that contrary to his description, the *Wechseldominante* is in fact reached for a moment in bar 36, with the result that the close "on" the dominant is more "in" the dominant than it could otherwise be. In other words, the greatest possible harmonic contrast is established within the unity given by the close on the dominant and the ensuing, pre-determined C minor (see Ex. 4 and its harmonic derivation from the basic idea):

69

Ex. 7

The "new rhythmic figure" now appears in the shape of a chordal inversion or retrograde version (a) of the work's basic motif (tonic-dominant), but resumes the melodic line of its own first appearance (compare x^2 in Ex. 7 with x^1 in Ex. 4). The march character of this theme has been determined by the march character of the basic idea: note the extreme contrast which Mozart achieves within the *alla marcia* frame by a double-dotted march rhythm on the one hand and an entirely un-dotted march rhythm on the other. Soon, however, another dotted rhythm emerges as a counter-melody in the flute, not march-like in itself, but, on the contrary, an almost lyrical *legato* syncopation—

Ex. 8

—whose rhythmic pattern proves to be a displacement of the rhythmic scheme of the basic idea's third bar,

the syncopation itself being given by the basic idea's fourth bar (*et seqq.*),

so that this seemingly new idea represents a compression of two successive aspects of the basic idea. The ensuing march figure, again "new" on the surface level,

is based on the suppressed background of the basic idea (see Ex. 3) and, by way of straightening diminution, on the basic timpani motif (bar 4); while Ex. 12

proves a varied interversion of the harmonic degrees that make up Ex. 8's first seven notes. Motif (a) once more confirms the three-quaver pulse (upbeat) which had gone underground in Ex. 8, while motif (b) turns out to be a compression, harmonically varied, of the melodic corner-stones of the basic idea.

With the piano entry, the second of the Concerto's two most difficult problems of unity presents itself:

"The pianoforte enters", reports Tovey, "at first with scattered phrases. These quickly settle into a stream of florid melody . . .". But why are they scattered? How are they scattered? Why are they scattered in the way they are scattered? What, in short, is the compositorial cause of these absolutely unprecedented, utterly "new" triplets?

We have seen that various aspects of the three-quaver pulse have so far been exploited (Exs. 1, 4, 7, 8, 12); the triplet is its last and newest aspect.

This circumstance makes the piano entry possible; it does not, however, necessitate it.   There is only one conceivable *causa efficiens* for this drastically new rhythmic pattern: it must be a sharply implied variation of something which is the very opposite of new, *i.e.* something so self-evident that it has, again, been suppressed:

This is the background continuity, more manifest two bars further along (*cf.* the rhythm of x in Ex. 13 and x^1 in Ex. 14).   The shake is an extra-rhythmic device; the only possibility of defining it in the very process of its suppression is to vary it by another device which, in the manifest context, is "extra-rhythmic" too, inasmuch as it is without overt rhythmic precedent.   The triplet alone fulfils this function.

The rhythmic reintegration with the three-quaver pulse must, of course, be all the more stringent.   The basic manifest form of the three-quaver pulse is Tovey's "new rhythmic figure" (x^1 in Ex. 4)—in other words, a three-quaver upbeat implying a preceding quaver rest.   We observe that the crucial triplets (Ex. 13, bar 2) start likewise with a (triplet) quaver rest, though for the moment a seemingly unrelated one.   However, the next—and only other—triplets (built, of course on the rhythmic pattern of the 2nd bar of Ex. 13) retain the quaver rest Ex. 15 which,

meanwhile, has explained its latent significance, for Ex. 15 is, at the same time, a manifest variation of Ex. 16,

whose derivation from the "new rhythmic figure" (x^1 in Ex. 4) is equally obvious and has indeed been consolidated as early as the *ritornello*, a few bars after Ex. 4:

Melodically, the piano entry is of course based on the triadic opening of the basic idea, but what about the orchestral bar which introduces it?   "Then

71

the strings seem to *listen*, for one moment of happy anticipation''. Tovey's perceptive metaphor, though completely valid psychologically, does not get us far below the descriptive level. A glance at Ex. 2 (a) and (b), however, does. We are again confronted with a motif consisting of the three conjunct degrees, mediant, subdominant, and dominant, that constitute the central entity of the basic idea. And now, in view of Ex. 2's own structural context, we realize how the opening of the solo exposition springs from the opening of the *ritornello* not only melodically, but also in its rhythmic-harmonic structure. Juxtaposing, that is to say, the suppressed background exposed in Ex. 14 with the foreground of the basic idea's continuation quoted in Ex. 1,

Ex. 18

we not merely hear the rhythmic origin of the piano entry, but actually detect a latent antecedent-consequent relationship between the two phrases. I have come to regard this principle of postponed complementation as a fundamental factor of unity in extended master structures (3). For the rest, it may prove useful to remember that the way to a mysterious unity may easily lead over a hidden continuity.

According to Tovey, the theme of the bridge passage is again ''a new theme'', as indeed is its key, modulation to which would have been ''a mistake in [the] ritornello because of its symphonic character'':

Ex. 19

However true descriptively, Tovey's approach again fails to answer the most important creative questions. The point about this E flat major is that it *has* been reached early on in the *ritornello* (Ex. 20), as central, relative-major consequence of a C minor (Ex. 7) which, in its turn, we have heard to derive from the basic idea:

Ex. 20

Rhythmically, the theme derives, by manifest continuity, from the rhythmic figure of Ex. 4 (x^1), the three-quaver pulse remaining operative throughout until, in the cadential phrase y^1, it confirms the relation of the theme with the opening of the solo exposition (see y in Ex. 13) on what one might call the pre-manifest level (on the analogy of Freud's pre-conscious system): upon reconsideration, Tovey could hardly maintain that y^1 was new, even in his restricted sense of the term; transposedly speaking, Ex. 13 (z) and Ex. 19 (z^1) are in fact identical.   There are strong reasons for the theme's cadential re-emergence towards manifest unity with the solo opening; the melodic motif in question is once again that of the central entity of the basic idea (third to fifth degrees) (see Ex. 2 (a) and (b)) which, in the second part of this article, we shall hear playing a decisive part in the unity of the movement's principal contrast, formed by the second subject.   Meanwhile, diving beneath the continuity of the three-quaver upbeat and pulse, we find that the $4+4$-quaver pattern (second bar of Ex. 19) lies itself dormant in Ex. 4 (x^1), the change of notes on the latter halves of the first and third beats of the bar corresponding to Ex. 4's textural (imitational) change-overs at the identical metrical points. For the rest, the four-quaver unit is of course predetermined by the *ritornello*'s four-quaver implication which I have made explicit in Ex. 5.

This predetermination assumes prime importance as soon as we come to examine the melodic-rhythmic derivation of the transition theme (Ex. 19). So far, we have traced back only the cadential phrase y^1—by far the easiest task.   The preceding melody needs explanation, as does indeed the fact why the three-quaver pulse expresses itself in this particular way, why, for instance, the three-quaver upbeat assumes the melodic form of a group of two semiquavers and two quavers in bar 3.   The answer can virtually be given without words.   It is again a case of deferred complementation, and a little re-constructive re-composition will make the unity immediately clear (*cf.* Exs. 1 and 5):

Behind this latent derivation, based again on the principle of the postponed consequent, there now looms the first-oboe (and violin) motif of the basic idea which proceeds from the submediant to the dominant,

touching on the way the very note which, as we have shown, is the ultimate source of the key of the present theme (Ex. 19), *i.e.* the flattened submediant. More "in front" of the creative causal chain are Exs. 8 and 12 with their rhythmic constituents.

By way of concluding this first part of our analysis, I would put forward a more tentative suggestion.   I do not think that our interpretation of Ex. 19 (y^1) represents its ultimate reduction.   It is, in fact, "too easy", too easily tangible. It may seem absurd to submit that something is implausible because it is too

73

plausible, but the psychologist will understand my paradox, while the artist will at least be prepared to consider the proposition that in a composition which we call both masterly and "deep", every single contrast has as deep as possible a root of unity—deep enough, and therefore sufficiently concealed, to invest the contrast itself with the greatest possible intensity. The melodic outline of the basic idea's first phrase is given in Ex. 23 (*a*). Transposed to C major, the outline of Ex. 19 (y[1]) is Ex. 23 (*b*), which turns out to be an inter-version of Ex. 23 (*a*)'s notes (degrees), as well as containing, once again, the harmonic force of a postponed consequent.

If this reduction is true, it applies of course equally to Ex. 13 (y) and indeed to the first bar of Ex. 13 which, we must not forget, is preceded by the C of the *ritornello*'s C major close. Particularly in view of the fact that a highly perfect cadence, emphasized by a three crotchets' general pause, separates this C from what, according to our analysis, would be its background continuation as a melodic motif, we again have to assume, as (*inter alia*) in the case of Ex. 4, (x) and (x[1]), that quasi-dodecaphonic de-rhythmicizations operate in classical music as latent unifying factors. I have tried to show in (3) and (4) that this is in fact the case: background serialism is, in my submission, a principle of classical unity.

The ultimate aim of the present method of analysis is to get at the heart of the music by dispensing with verbal accounts altogether. As soon as the principles of unity implied in the method are accepted, it will be possible to analyse unities simply by way of music examples (or, in lectures, by playing), with hardly a word in between. There will be no more metaphors, no more pleonasms which, by their very nature, are always "sensitive": if you talk of a "false lie", you are sensitive to the fact that a lie is false.

(To be concluded.)

REFERENCES

(1)   C. M. Girdlestone: *Mozart's Piano Concertos*, London, 1948.
(2)   Arthur Hutchings: *A Companion to Mozart's Piano Concertos*, London, 1948.
(3)   Hans Keller: "The Chamber Music", in *The Mozart Companion*, ed. H. C. Robbins Landon and Donald Mitchell, London, 1956. (To be published in March.)
(4)   Hans Keller: "Strict Serial Technique in Classical Music", *Tempo*, Autumn, 1955. (The date of publication is misleading: (4) was written after (3) and represents in some respects an advance on it.)
(5)   Rudolph Reti: *The Thematic Process in Music*, New York, 1951.
(6)   Donald Francis Tovey: "The Classical Concerto" (1903), in *Essays in Musical Analysis*, vol. iii, London, 1936 (sixth impression: London, 1946).

K.503: The Unity of contrasting Themes and Movements—II

BY

HANS KELLER

(Continued from p. 58.)

BETWEEN the publication of the first part of this article and the writing of the second, H. C. Robbins Landon's essay on the musical origin and development of the Mozart concertos (4a)* has appeared. It contains a description and partial analysis of K.503's first movement, which, despite one or two serious faults, seem to me to amount to the best investigation into this "essence of Mozart's approach to the sonata form: unity within diversity" (Landon) in our entire literature, so far as I am familiar with it. Landon repeatedly dives from the descriptive down to analytic level, and although he does not dive deep enough, he does, in more than one instance, bring into sight the latent unitive forces behind the manifest music. I was particularly fascinated by his reminder that the *Terzverwandschaften* (or, as he translates the term, "tertian modulations"†) that form such an important element in the harmonic unity of the movement "are presaged by the modulation C minor → E flat in the ritornello", which even earlier on shows a "definite trend from C minor to E flat", thus laying "the ground for the later mediant relationships". It will be remembered that in the first part of this article, we reduced the tonic (C) minor of Exs. 4 and 7 as well as its ensuing relative (E♭) major (Ex. 20) and, of course, the E♭ major of the theme of the bridge passage (Ex. 19) to the basic idea's first-oboe (and violin) motif (bars 5–7, Ex. 22) with its flattened submediant. Landon does not trace the tertian harmonic structure as far back as all that, but we, in our turn, omitted one important link in the causal chain of tonalities which is not perhaps sufficiently manifest to excuse our neglect, *i.e.* the "mere suggestion" of an E♭ major growing from C minor as early as bars 17*ff.*, whereto Landon very perceptively draws attention.

The theme of the bridge passage (bars 146*ff.*, Ex. 19), on the other hand, Landon describes less perceptively as "sliding from a G major cadence into E flat (the flattened submediant)", calling it, moreover, "the first theme of the second subject". Let us take these two errors in turn.

His harmonic error has in fact an immeasurably graver precedent in Girdlestone (1): "A cadential figure concludes the passage [preceding the bridge passage's theme]; wavering between C minor and G major, it chooses the latter key but is uncertain of the mode, and a tutti phrase, on the incisive

---

* Numbers in brackets refer to the bibliography at the end of this article, which covers both Part I and Part II. In order to preserve the alphabetical order already established at the end of Part I (see MR, XVII/1), Landon's work has been given the number 4a. (See, likewise, no. 2a.)

† I suggest "tertian relationships" instead, since these are not always a matter of modulations.

three quaver rhythm thrown thrice from first violins to the rest of the orchestra and back, remains in the same undecided frame of mind". Confounded by the mystery of nothing more than an *Italian sixth upon the submediant of C minor*, Girdlestone rolls two elementary blunders into one: there is no wavering of either key or mode; what the Italian sixth produces is simply a half close in C minor, naturally with a dominant tinge. One should have thought that Tovey (6) had described the passage quite clearly for Girdlestone's reference: ". . . culminates on the dominant of C minor, which the full orchestra sternly emphasizes with the rhythmic [three-quaver] figure". Landon's interpretation is, of course, less catastrophic than Girdlestone's, but since not even the latter's description has, to my knowledge, ever been challenged, let it be said once and for all that the postulate of a "G major cadence" is absolutely inadmissible: Landon has driven his mediant relationships rather too far into "a new guise" (4a).

I say "postulate" instead of "proposition" because Landon's thematic error may be partly based on his harmonic one: with the key of G major in his mind, which according to him introduces the theme of the bridge passage (Ex. 19), he may have had fewer qualms about assigning the latter to the "second subject" stage than he would have had if he had got his harmony straight in the first place. This question of what to call the theme is not a petty terminological squabble, but a decisive formal issue. If, as we are no doubt all agreed, Ex. 25 (*b*) below is the second (dominant) subject, Ex. 19, the theme starting in E flat, cannot possibly be part of it, can't be its "first theme" while Ex. 25 (*b*) is its "second"; for what have the two in common that welds them into one of the characteristic unities upon which every sonata structure is based—into a "subject"? Nothing. Landon may well have reacted against the general reluctance to give this theme any sort of structural place and name: for Tovey it simply is, as we have seen in Part I, a "new theme", while Girdlestone, who invents his terms as he floats along, calls it "the solo theme"; and Hutchings (2) doesn't mention it at all. "Bridge passages" are not the fashion nowadays, especially when they are themes rather than passages, because the term sounds academic and does not indeed give a very happy idea of those weighty and well-defined themes which go to form certain transitions, especially some of Mozart's.* Nevertheless, there always is a bridge between the first- and second-subject stages, and the nameless theme in K.503's solo exposition fulfils this function. It is, be it remembered, a modulating theme driving up to the dominant's dominant, which is the harmonic springboard for the second subject. In a way, the discrepancy between the term "bridge passage" and the beautiful melody which Mozart composed as a transitional theme may even be considered fortunate, for the tune throws Mozart's originality into relief against the conventional sonata scheme. But the scheme is there although the text-books say so; it exists even in the background of this movement, and if we wince at the phrase "theme of the bridge passage", "transitional theme" is the only alternative that is structurally justified.

---

* The most outstanding example is the "bridge passage" of the "Prussian" D major Quartet's slow movement—a lyrical melody which, by successive solos, leads the structure through vi to V.

77

As we have seen at the outset of Part I, the solo exposition's real second subject (Ex. 25 (b) below) presents what one might call the climax of Tovey's triumph over the text-books, "for it has nothing whatever to do with bars 51ff. [i.e. Ex. 7], which seemed so like a possible second subject".* Ironically enough, the stupidest text-books are somewhat rehabilitated by our depth analysis. For so far as its unity with this C minor (later major) theme is concerned, the second subject illustrates once again our principle of postponed complementation. It would be cumbersome, though not difficult, to show why y in Ex. 25 (b) is a natural consequence of x in Ex. 25 (a) (which theme is, of course, immediately restated in the major), how the dotted mediant in Ex. 25 (b) is necessitated not only by the harmony, but also by the rhythm of Ex. 25 (a), including the upbeat and the quaver movement in the second violin. Fortunately, Mozart has done most of the job for us in a practical fashion. For once, that is to say, the latent compositorial background is, at the same time, a manifest historical background. In the second act finale (Ex. 24) of *Figaro*, which opera was completed on 29th April, 1786, *i.e.* about seven months before the completion of the present Concerto, Mozart confirmed our analysis by way of anticipation (see x° and y° in Ex. 24),

78

---

* It did not seem so; it was. The second subject does in fact consist of two themes, although they aren't Landon's two: their exposition is split between the *tutti* and the solo expositions. The second-subject status of Ex. 7, that is to say, is structurally confirmed by the development and by the recapitulation, where the two themes are united at the second-subject level, in reverse order. The following analysis proves that this uniting is really a reuniting process; as will be seen in Exs. 24–25, the manifest split between the themes corresponds to a latent split between their basic motifs which form a close background unity.

even going to the extent of showing that the melodic quaver movement of Ex. 25 (*b*) is an implied diminution of the crotchet movement in Ex. 25 (*a*): see "*E nol desti a Don Basilio? per recarlo . . .*" in Ex. 24.   Still further behind than Ex. 25 (*a*), there looms of course the suppressed background diminution brought to the fore in Ex. 5; in fact, the first thematic contrast of the piece (bars 7*f*., *cf*. also Exs. 1, 18, and 21) forms the antecedent for another deferred consequent:

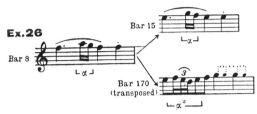

Ex. 26 even explains part of the determination of the second subject's motivic turn (α^2) as a developing variation of the two semiquavers on the off-beat of the dotted rhythm (α).   We have seen that bars 7*f*. derive from the central conjunct moment in the basic idea (bars 4–5, first violin on the one hand and flute on the other: see Ex. 2).   So does, indeed, the basic phrase of the second subject (*y* in Ex. 25 (*b*)), which now furnishes the three conjunct degrees of both (a) and (b) in Ex. 2 in their proper scalic order (mediant, subdominant, dominant), thus reversing, at the same time, the orchestral bar (see Ex. 13) that introduces the piano entry; Ex. 27 takes the liberty of combining the two phrases:

"R" means, of course, retrograde motion.   But there is another element of reversal here: we note that while the two phrases can go round in circles *ad infinitum*, the second subject's makes a better unprepared beginning than the first's, *inter alia* because it is in fact an untransitional opening phrase upon the tonic root position with little of an "open" start, whereas the first's might be called an "interrupting cadence" which, if it is used for a start, *prepares for*, rather than *defines the beginning of*, a rhythmic structure: hear its introduction of the solo entry, where it hides the seams between *tutti* and solo.*   The *later* (second subject) phrase, then, is more of an *ante*cedent, the earlier (first subject) one more of a consequent.   The principle of postponed complementation thus manifests itself here by way of reversal—a process which I have often found to

---

* It will be noticed that on rhythmic-harmonic grounds and for simplicity's sake, this analysis treats the beginning of the piano part as coinciding with the resumed first-subject stage.   In precise reality, matters are, of course, far more complex: "the hiding of the seams", the transition between the first and the second exposition, is an extended process which includes the piano's first paragraph and ends with the *tutti* resumption of the principal theme proper in bar 112. This circumstance should be quite obvious on the descriptive level and need not detain us.

obtain in master structures, and which seems to me to contribute essentially
to the build-up of background tensions over a wide musical space (3).   If,
with my submission in mind, the reader will now cast his ear back to Exs. 8
and 12, requoted and reversed in Ex. 28 (B and A respectively), he will observe
a pure and simple instance of this *"principle of reversed and postponed antecedents and consequents"* (3):

In the movement itself, A is of course the earlier phrase, B the later one.

As for the second subject's turn (α^2 in Exs. 26 and 27) which, on the surface
level, has emerged as an entirely new rhythmic element, Ex. 27 proves that it
has a further determinant on top of α in Ex. 26, namely, Ex. 27's α^1—the very
shake which, as we have noted in Part I, is also the determinant of the only
previous rhythmic pattern of radical manifest "newness", *i.e.* the triplets in
the piano entry (see Exs. 13–14).

How close is the integration of first and second subjects can be illustrated
by once again reconstructing a suppressed background.   Ex. 29 (*a*) gives the
opening of the solo exposition, while Ex. 29 (*b*) recomposes it in the manner of
a mediocre eighteenth-century musician (who has benefited from Mozart's art
of transition), replacing the first- by the second-subject phrase; it will be
observed that nothing else need be changed:

So far, however, we have not analysed the unity of first and second subjects
beyond the latter's first bar (y in Ex. 25 (*b*)) which, based as it is on the tonic
triad alone, does not yet show all the theme's distinguishing characteristics.
The great surprise, in fact, comes with the second bar, both melodically and
harmonically.   The cadential leap from the submediant to the supertonic is
something absolutely unique which removes the melody far from the "type"

of which Girdlestone (p. 427) considers it "the representative": the sudden disjunct motion arises out of the underlying function of a half-close—"quarter-close" would be the word!—to which the resolution of the third inversion of the chord of the seventh upon the supertonic is made subservient. It may indeed be said that the theme changes from the "melodic (conjunct) melody" of the first bar to the "harmonic melody" of the ensuing bars up to the imperfect cadence proper (end of Ex. 25 (*b*)): together with the opening turn, the basically harmonic, cadential skip at the end of the first two-bar phrase determines the entire melodic structure of the foreshortened second. But where do the harmonic determinants of this leap to the resolution's pivotal A come from in their turn? What, in fact, is the source of the second subject's harmonic structure?

When we turn to the authorities in order to find out what they have to say on the harmony of the first subject, we encounter a curious conspiracy of insensitivity on the purely descriptive plane; even the two leading writers, Tovey and Landon, are here thoroughly disappointing. The latter breezily talks of the beginning as of "a straightforward chordal alternation of I and V (or rather V⁷)", and for Tovey, too, it is no more than "a majestic assertion of [Mozart's] key, C major, by the whole orchestra", "little more than a vigorous assertion of the tonic and dominant chords", even though a few lines further on we hear that the opening is "mysterious and profound in its very first line", that "it shows at once a boldness and richness of style which is only to be found in Mozart's most advanced work". But he does not explain this richness; what is less, his music example omits the C in the harmony of bars 4*ff.*, thus treating it as if it were a mere pedal. In Part I, it may be remembered, we have been careful to talk "of a three-crotchet upbeat to the inverted seventh on the supertonic". The significance of what may have seemed a pedantic description should now become clear, for the ground-plan of the second subject's basic harmony—I–II$_2^4$–V$_5^6$–I—is identical with that of the first's, though the second compresses into two bars and a beat what the first subject had developed in no fewer than 16 bars: we have already indicated in Part I that all masterly composition is compression. For the more detailed textural relations between the two subjects within this common harmonic scheme, the reader is referred to the score.

In his preface to the Eulenburg pocket score, Friedrich Blume* remarks that

> one passage in the first movement remains obscure: bar 175 [second bar of Ex. 30], . . . 5th note, and bar 183, Flute and Oboe I, 5th note. In both cases the autograph reads a″ instead of a‴ (Oboe: a′ instead of a″). It might be that Mozart, with regard for the normal compass of piano and flute at the time, deflected the motif in bar 175 downwards from sheer necessity (Beethoven did so frequently, but with Mozart cases of this kind do not seem to be known). But then there remains the question why he chose the lower octave also in the oboe. The parallel passage, bar 350, contains the motif (in lower position) in the piano part with the upward form† whilst in bars 358 seq. the

---

* The somewhat idiosyncratic translation, which is faithfully reproduced, is anonymous.
† "upward *from*" in the actual translation: I hope I have resolved the misprint to the translator's satisfaction.

81

flute and the oboe with the bassoon exchange both the upward and the downward
version. Hence it is not by all means [*sic*] necessary to regard the downward turn
in bars 175 and 183 as a makeshift which modern interpretation should avoid, and it is
not cogent when older editions contain the higher note in this instance. Nevertheless
the passage remains questionable. For this reason the upper note was given in small
print in the present edition.

Musicologically, the passage is "questionable"; musically, perhaps, it need
not be. First of all, we observe that the second bar of Ex. 30

is not a mere variation of the second bar in Ex. 25 (*b*), but actually clinches
the second subject's harmonic unity with the basic idea: the one harmonic
element of the first subject which, since it does not occur in Ex. 25 (*b*), has been
excluded from our above-defined ground-plan, *i.e.* the flat sixth of bar 6/4
(Ex. 22), now reappears in a progression and compression strictly predetermined
by the first subject itself. Now the quasi-serial octave transposition on which
Blume ruminates is, of course, like all octave transpositions, a chordal inversion
and therefore stresses the vertical aspect of our "harmonic melody" at what
in any case is a crucial inflection, and what according to our analysis emerges
as the conclusive point of definition of the harmonic unity between the two
contrasting subjects of this sonata form. But Mozart wouldn't be Mozart if
he neglected the melodic aspect of a principal motif while stressing its harmonic implications: as a matter of genius' natural course, he has composed
himself into the only position where this *harmonic* inversion is identical with
the *melodic* inversion, *i.e.* into an harmonic context where the octave transposition required is that of a tritone. In the recapitulation, this call to harmonic attention (which has been repeated in bar 183) is no longer necessary,
so that Mozart can allow himself the characteristically paradoxical procedure
of introducing the *straight* form of the motif *by way of variation*. Professor
Blume's solution, then, is musically justified, whereas his doubts, expressed in
the smaller-type note in Ex. 30, are not: the old editions are wrong.

    The rest of the movement does not contain any further problem of thematic
or harmonic unity; we can safely leave it to the descriptive artists of musical
criticism.

    Nor do the other two movements show anything like the structural com-
plexity of the first. I suppose this is what Professor Hutchings means when he
says (2) that "had [the] second and third movements been as fine as [the] first,
the whole work would have been a greater example of Mozart as a concertist
than the so-called 'Emperor' Concerto is of Beethoven". But it is not legitimate critical method to turn the comparative complexity of successive movements with different functions into a criterion of evaluation; criticism's original
sin is the lack of a *tertium comparationis*.

The principal theme of the *andante* grows from the basic idea and the second subject of the first movement, again by way of compression: the upbeat-bar, a descending tonic triad *arpeggio*, is melodically identical with bars 1/4–3/3, whence the phrase proceeds straight across to the other pillar of the basic idea and first subject, which made Landon speak of "a straightforward chordal alternation of I and V", *i.e.* the dominant seventh. And it is the leading-note in the treble that includes the second (solo) subject in this process of compression, for if you apply the parallel condensation of harmonic structure there and jump across to the dominant in root position (concluding half-close in Ex. 25 (*b*)), you hear the leading-note preceded by the tonic in the melody. In other words, the third note of the present theme is over-determined by the first and second subjects because it forms the pivot of their compression: we are dealing, as it were, with a background "modulation" from one melody into another.

The most difficult problem of unity in this movement is, not unnaturally, the main second-subject phrase, Ex. 31 (*b*), here quoted in the tonic version of its orchestral exposition. Both the minor-seventh and the quartal skip from the third down to the seventh degree seem absolutely new thematically. As soon as we listen to the phrase serially, however, it emerges as but a variation of the first subject's first consequent (bar 3, Ex. 31 (*a*)).

83

Ex.31

Serial listening means being prepared for de- and re-rhythmicizing and octave transpositions. By way of octave transposition, x^1 derives from x. Why now does y^1 skip two notes of y? Because the variation, whose construction is horizontally harmonic, only includes harmonic notes. Once again we see how octave transposition serves to stress the vertical aspect of a "harmonic melody" at the crucial point of harmonic variation: in Ex. 31 (*a*), the conjunct C and B♮ form part of the same (dominant) chord, but in Ex. 31 (*b*), these two notes, now sharply distinguished and articulated by the minor seventh, mark the progression from tonic to dominant. In both instances, there then follows tonic-dominant-tonic; the f′ of Ex. 31 (*a*) has, for the moment, receded into the position of an ornamentation (shake) which, on the manifest level, is retro-determined by the cadence initiated by the ornamented note; it is rhythmically required owing to the paradoxical, melodic and harmonic need for a sustained, yet fast-moving leading-note. The cadence of Ex. 31 (*a*), finally, is harmonically retained in Ex. 31 (*b*); the melodic variation y^2 is a sequential consequence of y^1.

The piano's own contribution to the second subject (Ex. 32) contains a triplet which is *not* an augmentation of the demisemiquaver triplet in Ex. 31 (*a*)'s cadence (z), but an augmentation of the very first (upbeat) bar, whose triadic 3/4 crotchets form the proper rhythmic model. Nevertheless, from the standpoint of continuity as distinct from that of large-scale unity, the triplet does, at the same time, form a variation (by diminution) of a differently accented three-note pattern, *i.e.* the three-quaver upbeat at the corresponding juncture of the preceding bar (beginning of Ex. 32):

I call this principle of developing variegation, with which the text-books do not acquaint us, that of *"polyrhythmic diminution"* (3). For the rest, the thematic evolution taking place between the opening of the movement and Ex. 32, as well as the three-quaver upbeat following Ex. 32, does not leave us in any doubt about the fact that the penultimate source of these upbeating three-note rhythms is the three-quaver upbeat that plays such a basic rôle in the first movement (see, for instance, Ex. 4), while their ultimate source is the three-crotchet upbeat which, in Part I, we have shown to be implied in the basic idea of the work.

What, on the other hand, *is* a "polyrhythmic augmentation" of z in Ex. 31 (*a*) is z^1 in Ex. 32: as in the case of the first movement, the two contrasting subjects emerge as two aspects of the same thought. At the same time, again from the point of view of continuity, the descending fourth with which Ex. 32 (as indeed the Concerto) opens proves basic throughout the melody: z^1 is a sequential diminution of z^0 which, in its turn, applies the process of polyrhythmic diminution to the preceding bar. Ex. 33, then, extracts the fate of the fourth right to the end of the theme,

which is followed by Ex. 31 (*b*) (in the dominant, of course), whose y^1 and y^2 emerge as the natural consequence of Ex. 33 as well as being, by dint of the orchestral exposition, one of its causes. Thus does continuity lead us back to the virtuous circle of unity.

In a previous MUSIC REVIEW (*2a*), I have already analysed the unity of the finale's chief thematic contrasts, including, of course, the central, subdominant episode. This analysis would have to be inserted in a complete version of our essay at the present stage, but readers of this journal would not, I feel sure, want me to waste their time and my space on what they have read before. It thus remains to solve the most difficult problem of the movement's unity with the basic idea of the work. The derivation of the *rondo* theme from the opening movement's first subject will not prove unfathomable, nor will many attentive musicians fail to notice that the new middle section which Mozart inserts instead of the *Idomeneo* Gavotte's reveals a further facet of the *alla marcia* element in the first movement (see the latter's basic idea on the one hand, and Ex. 7 on the other), while the lavishly modified return of the principal section reproduces the basic idea's flat sixth (Ex. 22) as well as its consequence, the tonic minor. The real problem is the central episode itself: it is such an extreme manifest contrast to every preceding theme that its indirect derivation from the rondo theme (*2a*) hardly suffices for establishing its relation to the whole work's basic idea. Ex. 34, then, proposes to elicit the strongest direct connection with the first movement.

The unity between Ex. 34 (*a*) (*cf*. Ex. 4) and the basic idea has been analysed in Part I.

REFERENCES

(1) C. M. Girdlestone: *Mozart's Piano Concertos*, London, 1948.
(2) Arthur Hutchings: *A Companion to Mozart's Piano Concertos*, London, 1948.
(2a) Hans Keller: "The *Idomeneo* Gavotte's Vicissitude", MR, XIV/2, 1953.
(3) Hans Keller: "The Chamber Music", in *The Mozart Companion*, ed. H. C. Robbins Landon and Donald Mitchell, London, 1956.
(4) Hans Keller: "Strict Serial Technique in Classical Music", *Tempo*, Autumn, 1955 (but written after (3)).
(4a) H. C. Robbins Landon: "The Concertos: Their Musical Origin and Development", *op. cit.* (3).
(5) Rudolph Reti: *The Thematic Process in Music*, New York, 1951.
(6) Donald Francis Tovey: "The Classical Concerto" (1903), in *Essays in Musical Analysis*, vol. iii, London, 1936 (sixth impression: London, 1946).

A System of Symbols for Formal Analysis

By JAN LaRUE

Anyone studying the music of the 18th century must develop some form of shorthand to represent musical procedures concisely so that comparisons can be made broadly as well as from measure to measure. The present system evolved during the analysis of several hundred classical symphonies, particularly those of Haydn, in which thematic interrelationships challenge any system severely. Shorthand methods usually reflect idiosyncrasies of the analyst: what one finds workable may not prove satisfactory in the hands of another. Thus the present system of symbols, although the writer has found it workable and convenient, will not necessarily answer all requirements. It furnishes a stockpile of suggestions rather than a total solution.

In the choosing of symbols the ordinary alphabet and numerals offer the most direct and obvious code, with the great advantage that by careful selection they can be made nearly self-explanatory. Esoteric symbols and exotic alphabets require an additional step of explanation. The following application of the alphabet to functions of musical form represents an effort to combine mnemonic virtues with the need to save certain letter series for later purposes:

P—Primary themes
M—Modulatory or bridge themes
S—Secondary themes, *i.e.*, in the secondary tonality
K—Closing or cadential themes
V—Introductions
N—New material, *i.e.*, appearing after the exposition

R—Rhythm of a theme
H—Harmony, including accompaniment figures, texture, etc.

Various combinations of these letters can indicate modifications of function, the modifying elements being represented by lower-case letters: *Pnh* refers to a new accompaniment figure not present in an exposition; *Sv* indicates an introductory form of a secondary theme; *Kr* represents a rhythmic figure extracted from a closing section. Where *P* recurs in other functions, as so often in Haydn, for clarity it should be analyzed according to its immediate function, indicating the original one in parentheses: $M(P), S(Pr), K(Ph)$. Detailed interrelationships may be traced accurately by the symbols for variants and developments described below.

Often each of the sections of an exposition will contain several distinct themes. Experiments were made with systems assigning *P Q R* (or *A B C*) to primary themes, *M N O* (or *D E F*) to modulatory themes, *S T U* (or *G H I*) to secondary themes, and so on. These systems break down in the case of symphonies, and particularly concertos, with four or more primary themes and a like number in other sections. Superscripts (P^1, S^3) offer a simple solution of this problem.

Within a single theme there are often contrasted phrases that later receive separate and individual development. Lower-case *x*, *y*, and *z* are reserved to distinguish these diverse parts of a theme. Thus *Px* and

Py denote the two parts of a typical "question and answer" theme, Kz represents the final motive of a closing section, Pxx singles out the initial motive of the first part of a primary theme.

We come now to the harder task of indicating by symbol the permutations of a theme during the course of a piece. Experience has shown that one must provide for two main forms of change:

1. Minor variations of an idea may be indicated by superscripts: Px^1 refers to a slight variation in the first phrase of the primary theme.
2. Developments involving significant alteration may be shown by lower-case letters from the beginning of the alphabet (held in reserve until now for this purpose): thus Sza represents an initial development of the final motive of the secondary theme.

This method will sustain the most detailed analysis, since variations of variations and developments of developments are easily and precisely coded. For example, if Px^1, Px^2, and Px^3 represent three variants of the first phrase of a primary theme, we may indicate minor changes in the first of these variants by Px^{11}, Px^{12}, changes in the second variant by Px^{21}, Px^{22}, etc. Similarly, Sza, Szb, and Szc represent three developments of the final motive of a secondary theme, while $Szaa$, $Szab$ indicate two further stages of evolution in the first development of the motive; $Szba$, $Szbb$ indicate further evolution in the second developmental form of the motive, and so on. Indications of mixed variation and development can be made without ambiguity: thus Kx^1a represents the first development (a) of the first variant

(^{1}) of the first phrase (x) of a closing theme (K).

On first sight this may seem a bit cumbersome; however, once the logical principle behind the system becomes clear, it can be applied and deciphered with ease. In actual practice symbols as complicated as $Szab$ are rarely called for. Mozart, for example, typically substitutes a variety of themes for variety of development, and can often be analyzed by simpler means, such as the system employing "primes": A, A', etc. In Haydn, Beethoven, or Bach, however, one quickly runs out of "primes" if one wishes to indicate all of the developmental variants, and a less limited system must be devised. The present letter-number scheme is adequate even for the complex motive structure of the Brandenburg Concertos.

Symbols for ordinary theme and variation forms follow the same general principles as those just applied to sonata schemes. If a theme has two phrases, we designate these Px and Py, reserving the unused Pz for possible later cadential expansion or *codetta* effects. The first variation then takes the symbols Px^1 and Py^1, the second variation, Px^2 and Py^2, and so on. A more subtle problem appears to plague us when the second phrase of the theme is actually a variant of the first phrase. Thus if the phrases of a two-phrase theme are coded as Px and Px^1, how are we to represent the first variation? If we use Px^2 and Px^3 it will appear that the variations treat the first phrase in the same way as does the variation represented by Px^1. We must relate the variations to the theme they have in common, but indicate precisely each time the fundamental procedure changes. The proper solution lies in indicating the theme by Px^0 and Px^1, the first variation by Px^{01}

and Px^{11}, a second variation by Px^{02} and Px^{12}, and so on. This makes clear the different levels of musical relationship.

Frequently a theme will be repeated only in part. Except for important themes, one often does not trouble to differentiate the x, y, and z phrase components. Plus and minus

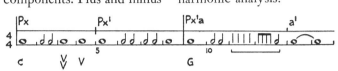

signs offer a simpler, though less precise, substitute: if the end of a theme is omitted from the repetition, this may be indicated by a minus sign: P^4-. Conversely the addition of a measure or more of related material may easily be shown by a plus sign: P^4+. For the typical end-developed phrases of Haydn, a bracket has proved handy as a symbol, $P^{4]}$ being used to indicate a developmental repetition of the last part only of a theme. $P^{4[}$ could then represent the repetition of the first part only. Two other helpful accessory symbols are the arrow to indicate inversion of a theme ($Px{\downarrow}$ or $Px{\uparrow}$) and a horizontal line to show changes of position within the texture: $\frac{P}{x}$ indicates the transfer of the theme to the bass, while $\frac{x}{P}$ indicates a change from an original bass position to an upper part.

In putting the symbols together in a final whole, the writer abandoned the usual list, sentence, pyramid-outline, and curve schemes in favor of a timeline indicating individual measures. The latter device has two important advantages. First, the proportions of the various parts to each other appear with complete graphic accuracy; second, the continuity of the timeline serves to remind us that we are dealing with a flow of ideas, not a series of static quantities. The timeline includes three levels, the upper for thematic development, the middle for harmonic rhythm indicated in conventional note values or headless stems (flagged or beamed when necessary), and the lower for tonal and harmonic analysis:

Ways of indicating harmonic analysis are doubtless just as personal as formal analysis. Wherever possible it is desirable to use familiar systems, such as the Roman numerals for chords on different scale degrees, capital letters for major keys, lower case for minor, and parentheses to indicate keys appearing briefly during the course of passing modulations. Upper ties indicate a harmony continuing over the barline ͡, while ties placed below denote chord change over a continuing root ͜. The appoggiatura cadences of V over I, I over V, and I^6_4 resolving to V appear as: $\underset{V\ \ I}{\frown}$ $\underset{I\ \ V}{\frown}$ $\underset{4\ \ 3}{\frown}$. To save space, write secondary dominants as $\underset{V}{V}$ and $\underset{ii}{V}$ rather than V of V and V of ii. Organ points in bass, middle, or upper parts may be represented as follows:

The triple level form of timeline is particularly useful for showing subtleties in phrase division. By varying the length of the vertical phrase marks, we can make punctuations of various strengths ranging from comma to period and paragraph:

For research projects the timeline

offers a final advantage: one may print up blank timelines with measure divisions already numbered, a vast saving in time and effort.

To show the system in full opera-

tion, an analysis of the first movement of Haydn's Symphony G.-A. 83 (=81a) is given below.

Wellesley College

90

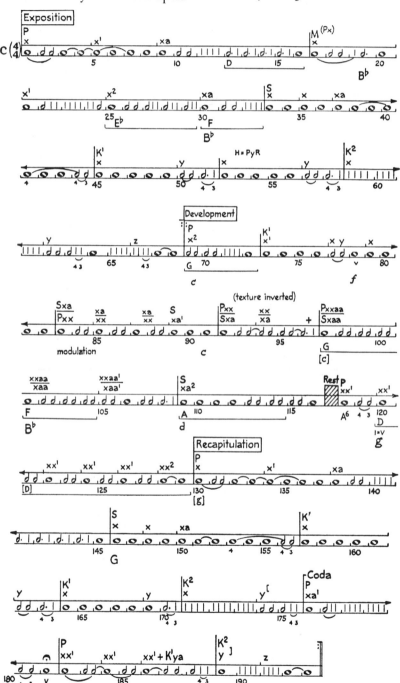

Grammatical Simplicity and Relational Richness:
The Trio of Mozart's G Minor Symphony

Leonard B. Meyer

A number of years ago I published an essay dealing with the nature of value in music.[1] It argued, among other things, that complexity was at least a necessary condition for value. The appeal of simplicity was acknowledged, but its attraction was attributed to its association with childhood remembered as untroubled and secure. This view now seems to me, if not entirely mistaken, at least somewhat confused. Schubert's song, "Das Wandern," cited in that essay as an instance of simplicity, certainly appears to be uncomplicated and straightforward.[2] It employs familiar melodic materials, regular rhythmic/metric organization, and normal harmonic progressions. But, as I have shown in a more recent study, the syntactic relationships which arise from these unassuming, conventional means are rich as well as elegant.[3]

Relational results must, then, be distinguished from material means. When this is done, it is evident that what is essential in the evaluation of music are not the foreground (note-to-note) successions of pitches, durations, harmonies, and other musical parameters but the higher-order patterns created by these palpable means. What is crucial is relational richness, and such richness (or complexity) is in no way incompatible

The suggestions and comments of several colleagues have found their way into, and improved, this essay. I am specially grateful for the help of Professors Philip Gossett, Janet M. Levy, and Barbara Herrnstein Smith.

1. "Some Remarks on Value and Greatness in Music," *Journal of Aesthetics* 17, no. 4 (June 1959); reprinted as chap. 2 of my book, *Music, the Arts and Ideas* (Chicago, 1967). Page references in this paper are to the reprinted version.

2. Ibid., p. 37.

3. *Explaining Music: Essays and Explorations* (Berkeley, 1973), pp. 152–57.

with simplicity of musical vocabulary and grammar.[4] That value is enhanced when rich relationships arise from modest means is scarcely a novel thesis.[5] Indeed, the "Value and Greatness" essay suggested it in passing: "Evidently the operation of some 'principle of psychic economy' makes us compare the ratio of musical means invested to the informational income produced by this investment. Those works are judged good which yield a high return. Those works yielding a low return are found to be pretentious and bombastic."[6] But like most writers, I failed to show how this general principle might apply to a particular piece of music. In order to demonstrate how simplicity of means gives rise to relational richness, this article will analyze a relatively brief excerpt, but one that is complete in itself, with as much precision as the present writer can command.

Few will, I think, doubt that the Trio from the Minuetto movement of Mozart's G Minor Symphony (K. 550) seems simple, direct, and lucid—even guileless.[7] Its melodies are based upon common figures such as triads and conjunct (stepwise) diatonic motion. No hemiola pattern, often encountered in triple meter, disturbs metric regularity. With the exception of a subtle ambiguity (discussed below), rhythmic structure is in no way anomalous. There are no irregular or surprising chord progressions; indeed, secondary dominants and chromatic alterations occur very infrequently. The instrumentation is quite conventional, and no unusual registers are employed. Nor, as the following prefatory "sketch" makes clear, is its structural plan strange or eccentric.

Like countless other compositions, or parts of compositions, written during the eighteenth and nineteenth centuries, Mozart's Trio is in rounded-binary form: $\dfrac{\text{Part I}}{:A:} \dfrac{\text{Part II}}{:B\text{-}A':}$ (see ex. 1). Part I, or Section A (meas. 1–18), consists of two phrases and a codetta. The first phrase

4. What the statistical methods of information theory can most readily measure are foreground successions, not extended, higher-level relationships. Consequently, the usefulness of this theory in the analysis of music is much more restricted than was suggested in my earlier essay (see n. 1).

5. See, e.g., G. D. Birkoff, *Aesthetic Measure* (Cambridge, Mass., 1933).

6. Meyer, "Some Remarks on Value and Greatness in Music," p. 37.

7. The full score of the Trio is given in the Appendix at the end of this article.

In this essay, **Leonard B. Meyer,** Benjamin Franklin Professor of music and humanities at the University of Pennsylvania, further explores and details the significance of theories advanced in his book, *Explaining Music: Essays and Explorations.* His previous contribution to *Critical Inquiry,* "Concerning the Sciences, the Arts—AND the Humanities," appeared in our first issue.

(meas. 1–6) presents the motives (labeled *m* and *n*) which are the basis for most subsequent melodic patterns. Harmonically, the phrase moves from the stability of the tonic triad (I), built on G, to the complementary tension of the triad built on the dominant (V), D. A return to tonic harmony in measure 4, as well as melodic structure, creates provisional closure, making the first four measures a subsidiary event, motive group 1, within the larger phrase. A complete cadence (ii$^6_5$–V–I^6) follows and confirms the key of G major as the tonal center of the Trio.[8]

The second phrase (meas. 6–14) builds upon and extends the patterns presented in the first[9] and modulates to the dominant (D major). After a deceptive cadence (V$^9_7$/vi–vi), which creates provisional closure and defines a subsidiary pattern (motive group 2), the second phrase closes with a traditional cadential gesture (*p*) which is related to the opening motive (*m*). Although the cadence is harmonically complete, closure is only partial: first, because it is in the "wrong" key—the dominant rather than the tonic; and, second, because as the brackets over example 1 indicate, the beginning of the codetta (meas. 14–18), marked by the entrance of the first violins, overlaps the end of the second phrase. That is, the first beat of measure 14 is a beginning as well as an end. Despite this elision, measures 14–18 are understood as an "added," concluding event—a kind of miniature coda. For they not only follow a complete cadence; they consist of the regular repetition of an authentic cadence together with a melodic motive which is familiar both because it is borrowed from the end of the first phrase and because it is an archetypal closing figure in this style.

The first phrase of Part II, the *B* section (meas. 18–26) of the rounded-binary form outlined above, is a *transition* back to the tonic. Taken as a whole, it can be considered to be a prolongation of the dominant harmony with which it both begins (meas. 18–20) and ends (meas. 26). The prolongation is elaborated by a sequential progression (meas. 22–25) through a series of harmonies whose roots are a fifth apart: E–A–D–G–(C). Though harmonic instability is minimal, the progression serves to heighten the feeling of goal-directed motion and, hence, the sense of arrival created by what follows. The melodic patterns of the transition are related to those of the second motive group of Part I and, in this way, to the opening motive: that is, *q*/∞ /*o*/∞ *m*. However, unlike *m* and *o*, motive *q* is divided into submotives *x* and *y*. This change,

8. The term "complete cadence" will be used to designate one in which a progression from the dominant to the tonic is preceded by subdominant harmony (ii or IV). Because a key or tonal center is defined by a progression from the subdominant to the dominant, rather than by one from dominant to tonic (as is often supposed), a complete cadence creates more decisive closure than one which is merely "authentic" or "full"—that is, V (or V^7)–I.

9. The symbols "*o*(/∞ /*m*)" in ex. 1 mean that "*o* is similar to *m*"

93

together with other modifications, gives rise to subtle rhythmic/metric ambiguity, making the passage less stable than harmonic analysis alone would suggest.

Section *A'* (meas. 26–42) is a *return*—both to the patterns presented in Part I and to the Trio's central tonality, G major. This "rounding out" of the binary form enhances high-level closure. Despite manifest

EXAMPLE 1

94

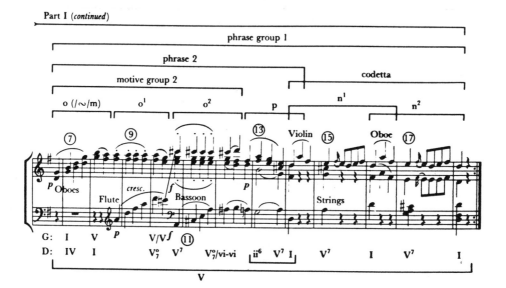

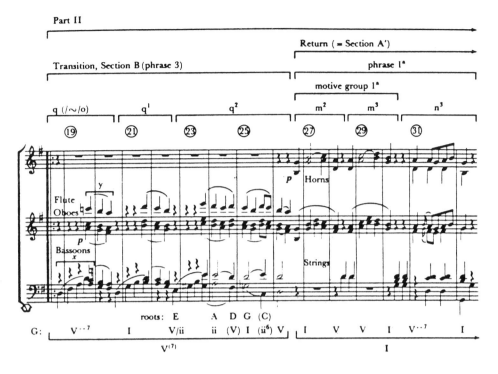

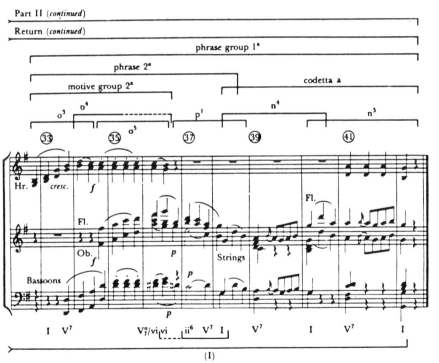

similarities, there are significant, if sometimes seemingly slight, differences between Sections A' and A. Some of these can be attributed to the fact that no modulation takes place in A'. For instance, since this section remains in G major, closure at the end of phrase 1^a (meas. 26–32) is harmonically less decisive than in Section A (meas. 4–6). The cadence is authentic, not complete. A complete cadence occurs only at the end of phrase 2^a. As though to compensate for the tension previously created by modulations (meas. 7–12), motive group 2^a (meas. 32–36) involves compression. That is, the imitative entrances of the horns (o^3), bassoons (o^4), and upper woodwinds (o^5) now occur after only three beats instead of six, as in the parallel passage in Part I. Once again an elision links the forceful cadence at the end of the second phrase to the codetta. But now closure is in the tonic.

What engages, delights, and moves us, then, is neither the novelty of the Trio's form, nor the singularity of its musical vocabulary and grammar. Rather, the competent listener[10] can comprehend and respond to its complex processes, its shadings of similarity and difference, and its structural subtleties precisely because these arise out of uncomplicated, unassuming tonal means. That the Trio's means are simple cannot be proved but will be obvious to anyone familiar with the style of classic music. That its relationships are rich can be demonstrated by exhibiting them in a scrupulous analysis of the work itself.

The analysis that follows is, alas, not only detailed but intricate and lengthy. In two respects this was unavoidable. First, because explanations are almost always longer than the phenomena they account for. A splendid sunset is over in a few minutes; a decisive battle may last little more than an hour. But a scrupulous explanation of such events is likely to be complicated and protracted. Particularly so if, as in the case of works of art, what is to be explained are not merely typical, classlike characteristics and the principles thought to govern relationships but what is peculiar—even unique—about the structure and process of the work. Second, because this essay is addressed to the interested amateur as well as the professional music theorist, terms and concepts have been defined and relationships explained which might not otherwise have been so. In addition, references to the musical examples are made as clear and explicit as possible. It is as if a literary critic felt called upon to discuss not only the relationships among action, character, and diction in a play but the fundamentals of grammar and syntax and the nature of prosody.

The analysis is difficult and extended for another reason. Every explanation must be based, whether expressly or intuitively, upon gen-

---

10. A competent listener is one who understands the style of a work not in the sense of knowing about—of conceptualizing—grammatical means, syntactic structures, or formal procedures, but in the sense that he has internalized the probabilities of the style as a set of perceptual, cognitive habits of discrimination and response.

eral principles of some sort—upon hypotheses about how the relationships latent in the work might be understood by a competent listener, including the first listener, the composer, as well as subsequent ones: performers, critics, and members of an audience. Throughout I have tried to argue, with as much care and precision as I can command, from such principles. The explication of theoretical premises and of their application is also partly responsible for the length and complexity of what follows. In this respect, the essay is doubtless somewhat self-indulgent. For it has been used to demonstrate (to myself as much as to others) that hypotheses and methods developed in my earlier studies have genuine explanatory power: that they are able to account, with considerable rigor and specificity, for the ways in which the several parameters of music interact with one another on different hierarchic levels to form the relationships peculiar to a particular composition.[11] Not infrequently it may seem that a detail—for instance, why a particular phrase mark makes sense and how it affects other relationships—has been discussed at inordinate length. Perhaps. But details are not trivialities, and subtleties may be signs of significant connections. Considered from still another point of view, the length and intricacy of this analysis are not only persuasive "evidence" for its hypothesis—that commonplace grammatical means may give rise to exceptional relational richness—but a tribute, however tedious, to the genius of Mozart's invention and the sensitivity of his judgment.

Part I

Phrase 1 (Meas. 1–6)

The patterns presented in the first phrase are the basis for much of the relational richness of the Trio. They are the main source for what follows: for motivic development, for incongruities subsequently resolved, and, above all, for implicative processes whose elaboration and realization create continuity, coherence, and closure. Though inextricably connected with what comes later, the first phrase is nevertheless patently separated from the second. All parameters—harmony, melody, rhythm, texture, and instrumentation—combine to make this separation clear.

Harmonic closure is emphatic (ex. 1). Except for the cadence in measures 37–38, that in measures 5–6 is the most complete in the Trio.[12]

11. The theoretical basis for the concepts, distinctions, and methods employed in this essay is, for the most part, contained in my *Explaining Music: Essays and Explorations.*

12. The parallel cadence in meas. 31–32 is authentic but not complete; the closure produced by the complete cadence in meas. 13–14 is only provisional because it occurs in the dominant, D major, rather than in the tonic, G major.

Nor is there any doubt about the function of motive *n*. It is a typical closing figure—a motion from the second degree of the scale, through a turn (usually ornamented by a grace note or a trill), to the tonic —encountered time and time again in the music of the period. For instance, virtually the same motive occurs in the third and fourth movements of Mozart's String Quartet in F (K. 590) (ex. 2). The characteristic shape of motive *n*, and consequently its function, is especially apparent because it is clearly differentiated from what precedes and follows (see ex. 1). It is differentiated from what precedes it by the relative coherence and partial closure of the first four measures (see below, pp. 702–3) and by a marked increase in the rate of harmonic motion—from one harmony per measure in motive group 1 to at least two harmonies per measure. Texture, too, changes. For the first time there is contrapuntal interaction among four more or less independent parts,[13] and this change in texture results in a concomitant change in sonority.

Example 2

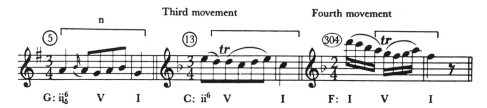

The beginning of the second phrase (ex. 1, meas. 6–14), too, helps to make the closure of the first unmistakable. Paradoxically, not only the differences between the two, but similarities, heighten the sense of disjunction. The beginning of the second phrase is distinguished from the end of the first in texture, sonority, and harmonic motion. The contrapuntal texture of measures 4–6 is followed by a return to the simplicity of parallel triadic motion with its attendant sonority, and the rate of harmonic change slows to one chord every two measures. These differences are emphasized by the change in instrumentation: the first phrase was played by the strings, the second is begun by the oboes. The contrast is especially clear because what the oboes play is related to, and derived from, what the violins played earlier.

This brings us to the disjunction created by similarity. The opening of the second phrase is related not to the closing motive (*n*) but to the

13. Until the cadential gesture begins on the second beat of meas. 4, the texture really consists of a single melodic strand, that of the first violins, doubled for the sake of harmony and sonority by the second violins. The D in meas. 2, played by the violas and celli, serves mainly to mark the beat and to complete the harmony—making manifest what was already latent.

EXAMPLE 3

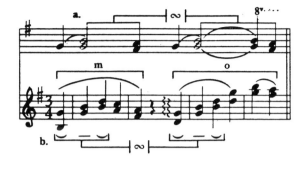

opening of the first phrase (ex. 3). Because pitch level, texture and intervals, and higher-level melodic structure (graph *a*) as well as foreground melodic/rhythmic shapes (graph *b*) are similar, motive *o* is understood as a varied repetition of motive *m*.[14] As a second "beginning," the new phrase confirms unequivocally that the preceding one is closed. For until this varied repetition takes place, it is possible that the first phrase will be extended in some way—for instance, by a repetition of the closing motive (ex. 4). Indeed, because the end of the first phrase is shorter than the initial motive group leads us to expect—that is, two measures instead of four—such extension seems not only possible but probable (see below, pp. 709–10).

EXAMPLE 4

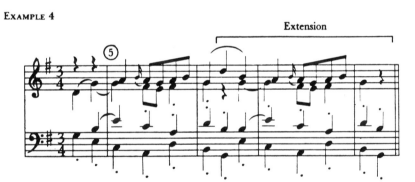

14. Repetition on the same hierarchic level creates separation; return (remote "repetition") creates coherence and closure (see pp. 717–18 below). Often modest differences between the original presentation of a pattern and its repetition act as signs that the function of the repeated passage is changed. In this case, orchestration is different: oboes replace violins; and the passage begins with a perfect fourth (D below G) between first and second oboe rather than with a minor sixth (B below G) between violins. Although the latter change may have been made because the oboe of Mozart's time could not easily play the low B, it nevertheless helps the listener recognize that this phrase has a different function—that it begins the departure from the home key.

Melodically, the tonic, G, has been strongly implied from the beginning of the first phrase, and closure is considerably enhanced by the realization of this goal in measure 6.[15]

This implication is generated by a number of interdependent melodic relationships (ex. 5).

1. The first accented, structural tone of the phrase is the third degree of the scale, B. Of the tones of the tonic triad, the third is the least stable. Its mobility implies conjunct (stepwise) motion through the second degree of the scale, A, to the tonic (graph 1a). When the second degree, A, arrives on the same structural level as the B, the implicative inference is strengthened.

2. The motion from B to A is implicative for another reason as well. Namely, it is a general rule in the formulation of implicative inferences that once an orderly process (particularly one that is stylistically established) is begun, it tends to continue until a point of stability is reached on the same structural level. The motion from B to A generates such a process and, consequently, implies continuation to a point of tonal stability, which is not realized until the G arrives in measure 6 (graph 1b).

3. The implication of descending conjunct motion is particularly strong because the structural B in measure 1 is preceded by a skip from the upbeat, G. This skip creates a *gap* which implies that the notes skipped over will eventually be presented and that the pattern will return to its initial pitch, which will function as a goal on the same level as the first structural note. In short, the gap-fill pattern represented by graph 2a also implies linear motion to the tonic, G.

But the arrival of a structural G is delayed. Instead of moving directly to G, as it might have done (see below, p. 704), motive *m* is restated (*m*¹) a step higher beginning on A. This varied repetition in turn generates implications some of which suggest continuation to G.[16]

15. An implicative relationship is one in which a musical event is patterned in such a way that reasonable inferences can be made both about its connections with preceding events and about the ways in which the event itself might be continued and reach closure and stability. "Reasonable inferences" are those which a competent listener—one familiar with, and sensitive to, the style of the composition—would make. A single event—on whatever hierarchic level: a motive, a phrase, or a period—may imply a number of alternative continuations and goals. Some of these will usually be realized proximately; others will be realized only remotely (after intervening events have taken place). Implicative relationships are often understood in prospect, as events are unfolding; sometimes, however, what was implied by an event can be comprehended only in retrospect—by discovering what the event actually led to, what it was connected with. Implications can be generated by parameters other than melody—e.g., by harmony, rhythm, instrumental timbre, texture, and so on. Frequently several parameters reinforce one another in defining a specific implicative relationship. When this is the case, the parameters are said to be *congruent*. At other times parameters are noncongruent: for instance, melody may make for closure and stability while harmony and rhythm produce continuation and mobility.

16. As we shall see (p. 716), other aspects of the higher-level patterning (*m* + *m*¹) imply continuation to D.

EXAMPLE 5

4. The fourth degree of the scale (C), which is the first structural tone of motive m^1, is even less stable than the third degree, and its mobility is enhanced not only because it functions as the seventh of a harmonically goal-directed dominant chord but because it is preceded by a gap (A–C). When the C moves to B in measure 4, the seventh is resolved, and the realization of the fill is begun. The fill is completed when A is reached in measure 5. But because the A, too, is melodically mobile and is part of a forcefully goal-directed cadential progression, the linear motion (C–B–A) generated by the gap-fill process (graph $2b$) has a tendency to continue downward to the stability of the tonic. The G in measure 6 is, thus, the goal of several complementary and converging implicative relationships, and its realization contributes significantly to the impression of closure at the end of the phrase.

Though the processes generated by motive m^1 ultimately move to G, it is important to observe that its closure on B in measure 4 is more forceful than is the parallel closure of motive *m* in measure 2. This is so because (1) as a note of the tonic triad, B is stable relative to A; (2) the B is harmonized as part of the tonic triad which functions as the resolution of mobile dominant harmony; (3) the first four measures create a familiar and relatively stable melodic pattern—namely, a changing-note figure (graph 3) in which A and C ornament a more stable B;[17] and (4) the coherence of the changing-note pattern is emphasized by the changes (already described) in texture, sonority, and rate of harmonic motion which follow it. Thus, as example 5, graph 4, indicates, the first phrase of the Trio can be understood as a prolongation of B, as part of tonic harmony, followed by a complete cadence in which A moves to G.

If the fundamental motion of the first phrase is from B through A to G, then the first motive might have moved directly from the A reached in measure 2 to the closing figure (*n*). This possibility, shown in example 6, calls attention to the relationship between motives *m* and *n* (graph *b*). For motive *m* consists essentially of a conjunct descent (B–A), preceded by a gap, and ornamented by C which is an échappée (marked E in the example). (The validity of this analysis is demonstrated by what the horns play when this music returns at the beginning of Section *A'* [ex. 6, graph *c*].) Though motive *n* is not preceded by a gap, it too consists of a conjunct descent (A–G) ornamented by an échappée (E). Thus despite manifest differences, particularly in rhythm, motives *m* and *n* are melodically similar as well as implicatively connected.

Though grammatically simple and regular, the relationships both within and between the motives of the first phrase are complicated and

17. The stability of the B in meas. 4 is probably also somewhat strengthened because it is implied by the subsidiary gap, B–D, in meas. 1. The first note filling this gap, the C, follows immediately; but return to B is delayed and, before it occurs, the implication has been generated more forcefully by the A–C of motive *m¹* (graph *a*). The comparable gap (C–E) in *m¹* begins to be filled by the D which follows. But the D does not move to C.

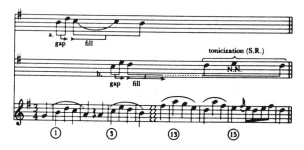

Instead, the D is transformed into a relatively stable goal when it becomes a temporary tonic in meas. 14 (graph *b*). It can function as a provisional realization because of what Professor Eugene Narmour has called "substitution by rank" ("A Theory of Tonal Melody" [Ph.D. diss., University of Chicago, 1974]). In the return (meas. 26–37), not only does the D move through C to B, but the first subsidiary gap, B–D, becomes a primary one (see pp. 749–50 below).

Example 6

in some respects even conflicting. The first motive (*m*) is related to the last (*n*) by implication (ex. 5, graphs 1*a*, 1*b*, and 2*a*) as well as by similarity of shape (ex. 6, graph *b*). The second motive (*m*^{1}) continues the first by repeating its shape on another step of the scale and, at the same time, completes it (*m*) by returning to the first structural tone (B) and the stability of tonic harmony. The second motive thus prolongs the first (ex. 5, graph 3) and, in so doing, delays the cadential figure which might have followed the first motive directly (ex. 6). Like the first motive, the second also implies motion to the tonic—not only because of its own patterning (ex. 5, graph 2*b*) and because the B in measure 4 acts as a kind of surrogate for that in measure 1 but because of the tonal tendency of the third to move conjunctly to the tonic (ex. 5, graph 4).

The relationships thus far considered have been those contributing to coherence and closure. But clearly there must be others—ones which produce mobility, involve incompleteness, and transcend the limits of the phrase. Otherwise the remainder of the Trio would not follow *from*, but would merely come after, the first six measures. As we shall see, the motives themselves, as well as the connections between them, generate patterns and implications which influence and inform later events. Before considering these, however, it should be observed that, though closure is unmistakable, it is mitigated by elements of instability and incongruity.

Harmonically, the close of motive *n* is not as stable as it might have been. Though the cadential progression (ex. 7*A*) is complete in the sense that the subdominant (ii$^6_5$) precedes the dominant, closure is mitigated

EXAMPLE 7

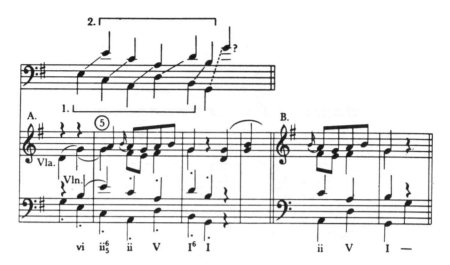

104

because the tonic chord is initially presented in first inversion (with B in the bass) rather than in root position (with G in the bass) as it might have been (ex. 7*B*). It should be observed, however, that harmonic instability is itself the result of the organization of another parameter—namely, texture.

The texture of motive *n* is compound. As a whole, it is homophonic: melody supported by accompaniment. But the accompaniment is contrapuntal. Not only does the suspension in the viola part contribute to mobility (see below, p. 707), but so does imitation between voices. The second violins begin by mimicking the rising fourth played by the violas; however, they continue by following the celli in strict canon, beginning with the E in measure 5 (graphs 1 and 2). Though the canon is scarcely audible,[18] the relationship between parts creates momentum and affects the cadence. There its consequences are audible. Because they remain canonic, the second violins have a D on the first beat of measure 6. (They could have broken the imitation and played a B, as in ex. 7*B*.) In order to complete the triad, the celli must play the third (B)—which they do.[19]

18. Because the note values are the same in both voices, harmonic progression and the melody in the upper parts tend to mask contrapuntal relationships.

19. One admittedly speculative point: The G, which begins the oboe passage on the third beat of meas. 6, might be thought of as a continuation of the canon. I.e., though displaced an octave and played by a different instrument, G is the scale tone that would have followed the B played by the second violins on beat 2 of meas. 6. There is no canon in the parallel passage in the return (ex. 1, meas. 31–32), and, as a result, the cadence can occur in root position.

EXAMPLE 8

Nor is rhythmic closure decisive. On the lowest level, the eighth-note motion at the end of measure 5 suggests that the grouping across the bar line is a closed, end-accented anapest (ex. 8). But the potential stability of this pattern is undermined by the mobility created by the weak afterbeat played by the violas and celli. Moreover, for harmonic and textural reasons, motive *n* is understood as a single composite event.

EXAMPLE 9

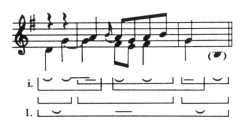

On the subprimary level (*i*), it seems to consist of a series of overlapping or pivoted groups (ex. 9). Despite its considerable ambiguity, however, the pattern is, I think, heard as a primary-level (1) amphibrach—albeit a complex one. It is so not only because of the tendency to continue the palpable amphibrach grouping[20] established by motives *m* and *m*¹

 but because the weak beats at the end of measure 4, and

especially the suspension in the viola part, make the fifth measure seem "accented" relative to the sixth. On the highest level (2), motive *n* acts as a stable goal for the preceding measures (ex. 10). However, though the phrase is end accented, its closure is not satisfactory because it is too short. The sense of morphological incongruity is the result of prior organization.

The first motive (*m*) is a structural entity on the lowest hierarchic level. But its closure is tenuous. Melodically, it ends on one of the most mobile tones of the scale, the second degree (A); harmonically, it stops on an unstable dominant chord; and rhythmically, the motive is an amphibrach which closes on a mobile weak beat (ex. 10). Thus motive *m* is defined as a formal event not primarily because it is syntactically closed but because its varied repetition (*m*¹) a step higher makes its extent clear.

20. This is a corollary of the hypothesis, mentioned earlier, that once begun a process tends to be continued to a point of stability.

EXAMPLE 10

106

Though it is a separate shape in which implicative possibilities are embedded, motive *m* is incomplete. It has no end—only a beginning and a middle. Though more closed, motive *m¹* too is incomplete. It has a middle and an end but no beginning. When the motives are combined, however, they complement one another. The result is a coherent, though low-level, syntactic structure (ex. 11, graph *a*), whose integrity and closure are not contingent but are a consequence of melodic patterning (the changing-note motion around B) and harmonic progression (the movement from tonic to dominant and back). Rhythmic relationships are quite subtle. The first four measures function both as a coherent syntactic structure and as a *sequence* of motives. Understood in the first way (ex. 11, graph *a*), the melodic return to B and the authentic cadence foster rhythmic closure, suggesting a trochee pivoted to an

EXAMPLE 11

end-accented anapest. Understood in the second way (graph *b*), motive *m*¹ functions as a mobile, ongoing event on the second rhythmic level (2). Put differently: retrospectively the structure articulated at measure 4 is relatively stable and closed; prospectively there is minimal articulation—motives *m* and *m*¹ begin a sequence which is mobile and implicative, though their implications are not realized by what immediately follows.

Whether understood in prospect or in retrospect, however, these measures establish an unambiguous morphological length of four (2 + 2) measures which acts as a standard for subsequent syntactic structures. Consequently, when the strong cadential figure of measures 5 and 6 proves to be only two measures long—and the beginning of the next phrase leaves no doubt about this—it seems aberrant. The pattern "should" have been four measures long. Two somewhat different continuations seem possible.

The phrase following motive *m*¹ might have been a single, basically undivided gesture. The result, as illustrated by the hypothetical version given in example 12, would have been a bar form of 2 + 2 + 4 measures. Because in the prospective view the sequence of motives *m* and *m*¹ is additive, it seems to suggest this possibility. Notice that closure is strengthened not only by the morphological "fit" with the first four measures but by the high-level rhythmic structure which is end accented on levels 2 and 3. In addition, the whole seems integrated because, as implied, the sequence continues to D, the relatively stable fifth of the scale, after which there is a return to the tonic. As we shall see, something similar to this sort of patterning does occur when Section *A* returns in Part II of the Trio.

EXAMPLE 12

Motive *n* might also have been lengthened by simple repetition. The result, illustrated in example 13, would have been more additive: a countercumulative pattern of 4(2 + 2) + 2 + 2. Because in the retrospective view the first four measures form a cohesive event, this sort of continuation seems appropriate. Notice that this "normalization" is more open

107

EXAMPLE 13

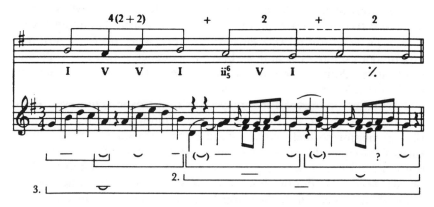

not only because the implied D is not realized but because on the second level (2) the phrase ends on a mobile weak beat. Moreover, because the morphological structure is countercumulative—that is, 4 + 2 + 2, rather than cumulative, (2 + 2) + 4—the effect is one of passive subsidence rather than of active termination.

As the reader will recognize at once, the repetition of motive *n* is precisely what concludes the first part of the Trio (meas. 15–18) in the dominant and the second part (meas. 39–42) in the tonic. In short, the discrepancy between the four-measure length established by the motive group ($m + m^1$) and the two-measure closing figure creates an incongruity—a kind of morphological "dissonance."[21] This dissonance is "resolved" in the codettas which, from this point of view, are consequences of the brevity of the phrase in relation to the structure of the motive group.

Phrase 2 (Meas. 6–14)

The closure of the first phrase is less than decisive for other reasons as well. First of all, there simply hasn't been enough music. It is not just that, given the scope and proportions of the Symphony and of the Minuetto movement of which this Trio is a part, the phrase is much too short to create convincing closure. If the six measures were played seven times (making a length of forty-two measures—that of the whole Trio, without repeats), the result would not be an enhanced sense of completeness but boredom followed by irritation. Nor is the sense of incompleteness solely a matter of familiarity with music in the classic style—a familiarity which makes the competent listener aware that trios are usu-

21. There is no incongruity on the foreground level because the motives are all the same length.

ally in rounded-binary form and that at measure 6 such form remains to be realized. What is required for convincing closure is the development and resolution of more urgent, higher-level instability: harmonic, melodic, formal, or rhythmic—or some combination of these. Such tension occurs in the second phrase and subsequently.

Second, implications generated by the opening measures remain to be actualized. One of these was generated by the very first notes of the Trio. In addition to shaping the gap-fill relationships already discussed (ex. 5, graph 2*a*), the first three notes form a familiar schema in tonal music—namely, a triad. The same principle, mentioned earlier in conjunction with linear patterns, applies to disjunct, triadic ones. That is, once an orderly process is begun, it tends to be continued as a mode of organization until a point of relative stability and closure is reached.

The nature and probability of such continuation depend upon the disposition of all the parameters involved: for instance, the position of the triad (whether it begins with the root, the third, or the fifth of the scale), the harmonization of the several pitches, the rhythmic/metric structure of the pattern, and so on. Mozart's String Quartet in F Major (K. 590) also opens with a root position triadic pattern (ex. 14). But because the fifth (C) is an accented goal—a point of relative stability—the pattern is quite closed, and further motion to a stable, structural high F is not strongly implied.[22] Notice, too, that in this case the triadic pattern is the main motive and that its metric placement is straightforward.

EXAMPLE 14

In the Trio from the G Minor Symphony, however, the relationships between the triadic pattern and the motive of which it forms a part, and between the metric and melodic structure of the triad itself, are more complicated. Although almost immediately subsumed within the larger structure of the gap-fill process of motive *m* (ex. 15*a*), the coherence and familiarity of the triad suggest—perhaps only subliminally—that it is a potentially independent shape. Given the metric designation (3/4), a kind of covert amphibrach rhythm arises (ex. 15*b*).

Though the first three notes of motive *m* are scarcely unusual, they involve a subtle incongruity. The triad begins on its most stable pitch—the root, G (ex. 16*a*, pitch). But the rhythmic group begins on a mobile

22. Nor is one presented until late in the movement (at meas. 174), and then it is a consequence of other pattern processes.

EXAMPLE 15

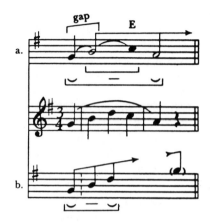

weak beat (ex. 16*a*, rhythm). The patternings are, so to speak, "out of phase." Since pitch relationships are fixed, the discrepancy can be resolved only by a change in rhythmic/metric patterning. For this reason, as well as because it is the first note of the Trio, there is a slight tendency to perceive the G as being the beginning of a metric unit—to understand it as being a virtual accent (ex. 16*b*). Put the other way around: because a stress placed on an accent ties the following weak beat to the accent, had the B (the downbeat of measure 1) been emphasized by articulation of any sort—for example, by a change in texture or harmony, dynamics or instrumentation—the following D would have been less mobile and ongoing. This helps to explain why no accompanying harmony marks the first beat of measure 1.

To the extent that such subliminal adjustments are made, the mobility both of the actual accent (B) and the following weak beat (D) is enhanced. As a result, the implication that triadic motion will continue is strengthened.[23] This implication is regenerated and realized at the beginning of the second motive group.

EXAMPLE 16

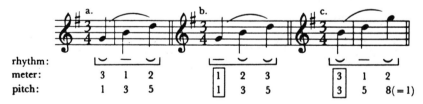

23. In the opening measures this incongruity merely enhances what was already latent in motive *m*. But when an analogous and related patterning occurs at the beginning of the transition (meas. 18–23), the ambiguity becomes manifest and significantly affects

Except for a striking change in orchestration (oboes rather than violins) and a slight change in harmony,[24] the second phrase begins like the first. But instead of being deflected down from D to C and A, the triadic motion continues upward through G to high B. Thus the implications latent in the first phrase are remotely realized (ex. 17, graph 1a), and those regenerated in the second are proximately realized (graph 1b).[25]

The high B in measure 8 is at once the goal of the extended triadic motion and a mobile appoggiatura which resolves to A on the second beat of the measure. This observation calls attention to the dual—almost punning—function of these measures. For motive o is both a realization of implications latent in motive m (graph 1a) and a variation of motive m (graph 2).[26] Both motives consist of a gap from an upbeat, G, to an accented B (prolonged through deflection in the case of motive m, and through triadic extension in the case of motive o), followed by an A which begins the fill.

But these similarities should not be allowed to obscure significant functional differences (see analysis under ex. 17). In motive m, B is a structural tone, accented on both the subprimary (i) and primary (1) levels; and A, though accented on the subprimary level, is mobile on the primary level. In motive o, however, the first B (meas. 7), though accented and structural on subprimary levels (ii and i), is part of a larger anacrustic motion to measure 8 on the primary level (1). There, transferred an octave, it becomes a mobile, nonstructural appoggiatura. Though it is unaccented, the A in measure 8 is the goal of the overall motion, and an important structural tone. Consequently, while both

111

our understanding of melodic and metric relationships (see pp. 730–31 below). Compatibility might also have resulted if the first pitch of the triad had been mobile—e.g., the third of the scale (ex. 16c). From this point of view, the discrepancy is *really* resolved through sequential motion; i.e., the sequence of motives—m, m¹, etc.—ultimately moves to o³ (meas. 32–34) and there (as well as in the main closing motive at meas. 36–38) pitch, rhythmic and metric patterns are congruent.

24, The first interval between the oboes is a perfect fourth rather than a minor sixth (see n. 14 above).

25. The equivalent triadic motion (A–C–E) at the beginning of motive m¹ does not strongly imply continuation to the upper octave. This for a number of reasons. Because it is the first event of the Trio, motive m can be understood initially *only* in terms of its own internal relationships. Its foreground, triadic patterning is, therefore, a focus of attention. (Significantly, when motive m returns at meas. 26–27, the same continuation does not follow.) Motive m¹, on the other hand, is not understood primarily as an event in its own right but rather as a varied repetition of motive m. More important, from the first it is comprehended as part of a larger process—the relationship between motives. That is, as we have seen (ex. 11, graphs a and b), motive m¹ not only complements motive m but is a sequential continuation of it. These higher-level, and more forceful, processes tend to mask foreground patterning. In short, what motive m¹ implies is the continuation of relationships *between* motives rather than those within them.

26. It will be recalled that the sign " /∾/ " means "similar to."

motives could be analyzed as amphibrach patterns, their proportions, and hence their purports, are very different. Because the primary-level accent of motive *m* is longer (three beats) than the weak beats which precede (one beat) and follow (two beats), it is rhythmically quite stable. Motive *o*, on the other hand, consists of a very short accent (one beat) preceded by a long anacrusis (four beats) and followed by a short weak beat. As a result the accent is quite mobile. The extension of the gap by an octave, the strong anacrustic motion to the high B (emphasizing its instability as an appoggiatura), and the striking change from rising disjunct to falling conjunct motion—all heighten the sense of goal direction and imply that the fill, which the A begins, will continue to descend, reaching the structural tone from which it began (the B in meas. 7), and perhaps ultimately the tonic, G.

Though complemented and even crossed by the flute part, the gap-fill process generated by the oboe—and continued by it—dominates the melodic structure (ex. 17, graph 3*a*). The linear fill descends from A to G in measure 10, and from G to F-sharp in measure 12. The oboe continues to E in measure 13, and as before this structural tone is preceded by an appoggiatura (F-sharp). But in this cadence to D, the oboe is joined by, and somewhat subservient to, the flute which plays the main melodic strand in parallel thirds above the oboe. Though the essential linear motion is never in doubt, assurance is made doubly sure. For when the oboe plays the final cadential figure (meas. 16–18), the descent from E to D is patent and unequivocal (ex. 17, graph 3*b*).

The D in measure 14 is a strong point of arrival and one of considerable stability. It is so for a number of reasons. Most obviously, because a change of tonal center has occurred (ex. 17, graph 5). When the harmony in measure 9 (first understood as the dominant of G major which preceded it) is followed by its own dominant, A major (meas. 10–11), the progression begun in measure 7 is reinterpreted in retrospect. For the harmonic progression can be more simply understood as a succession of primary harmonies in the key of D major than as one involving secondary dominants in the key of G. This interpretation is strengthened by the deceptive cadence in measure 12,[27] and is confirmed by the complete cadence (ii^6–V^7–I) in measures 13 and 14. Thus, though the linear fill begun on the A in measure 8 (ex. 17, graphs 3*a* and 3*b*) remains to be completed (it is so after the double bar, moving through C to B, then to A and ultimately to G) D is a point of provisional stability because it has been tonicized. That is, D functions as a goal by what might be called harmonic fiat.[28]

27. Were G major the tonal center, the deceptive cadence would have to be interpreted as V/iii–iii which is a very improbable progression in the harmonic syntax of classic music—at least in the major mode. The interpretation V/vi–vi in D major is much more probable.

28. See n. 17 above.

EXAMPLE 17

The D in measure 14 is, however, the intrinsic and "natural" goal of another implicative relationship established in the first phrase but mentioned only in passing (ex. 17, graph 4a). On the highest level, that of two-measure groups, the motion from B (meas. 1) to C (meas. 3) generates a linear pattern. Once begun, this pattern implies continuation to a point of relative stability. Even in the key of G major, D, the fifth of the scale, is more stable than the third (B) or the fourth (C). And, of course, the stability of this goal is enhanced because, when it arrives (meas. 14), the D is a temporary tonic. It is partly the convergence of the rising linear process (graph 4a) and the descending fill (graph 3a) in a common goal that makes the D such a strong point of arrival.

That the relationship between the process generated in the first phrase and the D in measure 14 is more than an analytic fiction is indicated by orchestration. For just at this point of arrival (the D), the violins which generated the linear process (graph 4a) return after an absence of seven measures. In other words, the instruments which began the process participate in the realization of its goal.

Throughout the Trio, the scrupulous handling of orchestration makes clear, and thereby confirms, the connection between the generation, continuation, and realization of implicative relationships. This applies not merely to the kind of instrument(s) employed but to the register they play in. The D implied by the linear process in the violins (meas. 1–4) is not only played by them but in the right octave. Similarly the extended gap-fill process, begun in measures 6–8 and provisionally stabilized on the D's in measures 14 and 18, is continued (and in the proper register) by the oboes (meas. 19–26), the instruments which generated the implicative relationship in the first place (see p. 725 and ex. 22, graph 1a).

Even the octave doubling in measures 17–18 is not simply a result of Mozart's "sense of sonority." It is a consequence of relationships established earlier. In actualizing the triadic continuation latent in the opening motive (ex. 17, graphs 1a and 1b), motive o activates a second registral region, an octave above that established by the violins (meas. 1–6).[29] Just as the oboe moves down to the D in "its octave," so the first violins, after actualizing the implied D at measure 14, move through the triad (meas. 16) to the low E and D in measures 17 and 18, playing the closing figure in octaves with the oboe.[30] Thus the bi-level registration created by the octave transfer of the oboes in measures 6–8 plays a part in

29. As in the case of "echo" repetitions, the distinctness of the registers is emphasized by the similarity between motives *m* and *o* (see graph 2).

30. In so doing, the violins continue the motion begun in the first phrase (ex. 17, graph 4b). For the linear descent presented in the first phrase is processively strong (see ex. 5, graphs 1a–1b, 2a–2b, and 4), and, since there is no explicit reversal of these processes in the first phrase, there is some tendency (despite the strong cadence in meas. 5 and 6) for the linear descent to continue.

shaping the instrumentation and registration of the cadence at the end of Part I.

The goal-directed momentum of the main melodic pattern of the second phrase (meas. 6–14)—that is, the gap-fill process begun and continued by the oboes (ex. 17, graphs 3*a* and 3*b*)—is reinforced by the organization of other musical parameters. The gradual crescendo, resulting both from the designation in the score and from the addition of instruments (first flute and then bassoons),[31] creates a sense of destination. So does the concomitant increase in richness of sonority and density of texture.

The motives (o^1 and o^2) played by the flute and the bassoons not only imitate but complement and specify relationships latent in the main melodic process. Harmonically, goal-directed motion is enhanced because the progression through a circle of fifths—IV (G major)–I (D major)–V (A major) (see ex. 17, graph 5)—suggested by the thirds in the oboes, is specified by the triads played by the flute and the bassoons. Moreover, the rising disjunct intervals in the flute and the bassoons contrast with, and thereby emphasize and make more urgent, the conjunct descent of the oboe's "fill." Though not intervallically exact, the imitation is unmistakable because melodic similarity is complemented by rhythmic identity.

Rhythmic identity contributes to the goal-directed character of the second phrase on both foreground and higher levels. On the foreground level, ongoing motion is perpetuated by the varied repetition of motive *o*. As we have seen, the relative length of that motive's anacrusis (ex. 17, level 1), as well as the mobility created by its rising triadic pattern, generates considerable momentum. As a result, the first beats of measures 8, 10, and 12 are, potentially, emphatic accents. But when these prove to be unstable appoggiaturas, the accumulated momentum is transmitted to the following weak beat. The normal mobility of the weak beat is increased not only by the momentum it acquires but by its harmonic function. For, since the circle of fifths moves upward, the first two weak beats are mobile dominants in relation to the chords which precede them, while the third (meas. 12) is a deceptive resolution. Though the impetus of each motive becomes attenuated by the prolongation of its final pitch (e.g., the repetition of the oboe's A following the closure of motive *o*), it is renewed by the momentum created by its varied repetition: that is, motive *o* is renewed by o^1, and motive o^1 is renewed by o^2.

On the next level, that of the succession of two-measure motives, rhythm is at least as mobile and goal directed (ex. 17, level 2). Because it begins the phrase, motive *o* is presumed to be stable and accented. How-

31. Moreover, not only is there a tendency for rising lines to be performed "crescendo" but for higher pitches to be perceived as being louder, even though intensity is not increased.

115

ever, when it is followed by a similar pattern (motive o^1)—one which is characterized by increasing intensity, richer texture and sonority, and ongoing harmony—motive o is understood in retrospect as unstable.[32] For when similar events (such as motives o and o^1) follow one another in a context of syntactic mobility, they do not as a rule form a single, cohesive group.[33] Rather they tend to be understood as discrete, though coordinate, events implying a more stable event to which both can be related as parts of a larger, integral pattern.[34] Both for this reason, and because it is cadential (moving from V^7 through V_7^o/vi–vi), the next event (motive o^2) is first understood as the accented goal of the preceding groups.

But it is so only initially: stability is partial and closure provisional. This, for a number of reasons. First, the cadence in measure 12 is deceptive (ex. 17, graph 5); that is, instead of continuing to the new tonic, D major, the harmony moves through an incomplete dominant seventh (V_7^o/vi) to a chord built on B (vi) which acts as a surrogate for the tonic —but one that is not conclusive. Harmonic mobility is emphasized by rhythmic instability: for the deceptive resolution occurs on a weak beat. Second, the D played by the flute in measure 12 is an octave higher than that implied by the patterns generated in the oboes (graph 3b) and in the violins (graph 4a). Last, motive o^2 is too short fully to absorb and resolve the ongoing motion of the preceding measures.

Though its stability is partial and its closure provisional, the deceptive cadence in measure 12 is nonetheless consequential. As such cadences usually do, it signals the approach of more complete harmonic closure. In addition, it provides time for the dissipation of accumulated momentum and, in so doing, prevents the complete cadence (meas. 13–14) that follows from seeming abrupt. As a result, the closure of the second phrase is more effective than it might otherwise have been.

---

32. When signs for rhythmic functions occur together, as they do under motive o (⌣), the upper sign represents the initial interpretation of the pattern, and the lower sign represents a retrospective interpretation of its function.

33. When the context is one of stability, however, repetition does not create goal-directed motion. E.g., because it follows the cadence in meas. 14, prolonging the stability it establishes, the repetition of motive n in the codetta produces relaxation and gradual subsidence.

34. The first line of Blake's "The Tyger" seems a comparable phenomenon in verse:

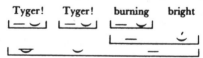

In general, the more alike two successive events are, the more separate and discrete they seem to be, and the stronger the implication that they will be followed by a differentiated event in terms of which they can be grouped. This is so because relationships (such as antecedent consequent or weak beat and accent) can arise only if there is some difference—as well as some similarity—between successive events. The ticks of a watch, e.g., provide no objective basis for rhythmic patterning.

Equally important, the momentum itself is damped by a break in the prevailing sequence. The break, or *reversal of process,* involves changes in both harmonic progression and melodic patterning (ex. 18). Harmonically, the deceptive cadence ends the progression through the circle of fifths; instead of continuing to a chord based on E, which would have been the next in the sequence (graph 1*a*), the bassoon moves, as we have seen, to a chord built on B (graph 1*b*). This change, marked and emphasized by the chromatic motion from A to A-sharp to B (the first such motion thus far), breaks the established gap-fill pattern. Observe that had the pattern been regular, the B played by the bassoon would have occurred just as it does in Mozart's music (graph 2). But this "normalized" continuation would not have reversed the process.[35] Not only would sequential continuation have been more strongly implied but the separation and integrity of the following cadential gesture would have been less apparent, and closure would, in consequence, have been somewhat less decisive.

Melodically, the flute also fails to conform to the appoggiatura figure presented by the oboes in measures 8, 10, and 12, and by the flute in measure 10. The pattern is broken; instead of falling a whole step, the flute rises a half step. In this, its motion parallels, and thereby emphasizes, the crucial chromatic motion in the bass (graph 3). Notice that the flute might easily have followed the established pattern, that is, it might have descended from C-sharp to B (graph 4*a*).[36] But had the flute moved down in this way, no reversal would have occurred; rather, continuation would have enhanced momentum.

The rhythmic structure of the second phrase is also affected by the deceptive cadence. Because harmonic and melodic closure prove to be provisional, motive o^2, at first presumed to be accented, is subsequently understood as mobile on the second rhythmic level (ex. 17, level 2). Though mitigated, goal-directed motion is not terminated. Compelling closure is still to come.

The closure created by the cadence which follows (ex. 18, motive *p*) is unequivocal—or virtually so. Its integrity and identity are assured not

35. While the parallel motion between the first oboe and the bassoon resulting from this normalization is not ideal, it is not grammatically wrong. More problematic is the lack of a leading tone, A-sharp, to make the dominant function clear. But this tone might have been played by the flute. For instance:

36. From a harmonic point of view, this would have produced a more normal doubling—that of the root of the triad rather than the third. And this suggests deliberate avoidance of the prevailing pattern.

117

EXAMPLE 18

118

only by the process reversal just discussed but by a drop in register (from the high D to F-sharp below) which, together with a marked change in dynamics from *forte* to *piano*, suggests movement toward the repose of closure. Harmonically the cadence is complete: a progression from sub-dominant (ii[6]) to dominant seventh (V[7]) to the tonic (I), here in root position.[37] The syntactic function of motive *p* is unmistakable. It is an archetypal cadential gesture in this style, as similar motives from other compositions by Mozart show (ex. 19). Even the skip from the upper tonic (8=1) down to the third (3) is not uncommon (ex. 19C).

Motive *p* is an appropriate close for the second phrase not only because it is typical but because it combines characteristic features of

37. As distinguished from the resolution of the complete cadence in meas. 6.

EXAMPLE 19

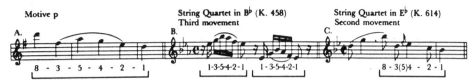

motives *m* and *o* which, as we have seen (ex. 3), are related to one another. Motive *p* is like motive *m* in intervallic structure. If the high D at the end of motive *o²* is included, the succession of scale degrees is the same (ex. 20) except that the tonic does not follow motive *m* immediately.[38] But the motives are not alike in metric placement: the tonic occurs as the second beat of motive *p*, but as the third beat of motive *m*. To make the similarity between motives unmistakable, in part *C* of example 20 the barring of motive *p* has been changed to that of motive *m*.

EXAMPLE 20

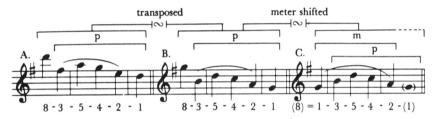

Metrically—and, consequently, in terms of melodic function —motive *p* resembles motive *o*. Both consist of a skip of a third from an upbeat to an appoggiatura whose resolution begins the fill implied by the skip (ex. 21). But instead of being an ending, as it is in motive *o*, the gap-fill pattern begins motive *p*, and, continuing beyond the rhythmically weak resolution characteristic of motive *o*, the pattern moves to closure on a tone that is melodically and rhythmically stable (ex. 17, levels i, 1, and 2).

EXAMPLE 21

38. As noted earlier, however, motive *m* strongly implies continuation to the tonic which does follow after four measures (see ex. 5, graph 2*a*, and ex. 6). From this point of view, motive *p* might be regarded as realizing a potential latent in motive *m*.

119

The relationship of the high D in measure 12 to what follows is equivocal. In terms of intervallic structure, it can be considered part of the following cadential gesture. Orchestration, too, fosters connection: the flute moves down and participates in the performance of the gesture. Nevertheless, there is an impression of incompleteness. Because of its rhythmic and harmonic mobility, yet its importance as a goal, and because of the patent change in register and dynamics, the high D seems to be "left hanging"—to be only incidentally connected with, not significantly related to, what follows. By separating the resolution of the deceptive cadence from the beginning of the complete cadence, Mozart's phrasing emphasizes disjunction. The disjunction is important because it suggests that the high D is essentially related not to the proximate gesture which follows but to processes still to come.[39]

Codetta (Meas. 14–18)

Part I closes with a codetta (ex. 17, meas. 14–18) which, though elided with the preceding cadential gesture, is nonetheless understood as a separate event. Unlike earlier phrases, however, it generates no new implicative processes. Rather, because of its own internal patterning and because of its relationships to preceding events, it facilitates closure.

Internally, a slower rate of harmonic change—compared to measures 12–14 (see ex. 17)—reduces the level of activity, while the repetition of a progression from dominant seventh to tonic not only confirms closure in D but, by prolonging the provisional stability reached in measure 14, allows time for ongoing motion to subside still further. Nor is there new melodic motion. The typical closing figure (ex. 2), borrowed from the end of the first phrase, is simply repeated with registral extension to the lower octave.[40] Texture, too, fosters closure. No contrapuntal process, such as the canon in measures 4–6 (see ex. 7), creates ongoing motion. A simple figure (melody)/ground (accompaniment) relationship enables harmonic and melodic closure to be fully effective. Differences in both texture and harmony help to explain why motives n^1 and n^2 are considered to be relatively closed, iambic groups (ex. 17, level 1), while motive *n* (meas. 5 and 6), which is melodically identical, was analyzed as a more mobile amphibrach group (see p. 707 and exx. 8–10). For in the absence of contrapuntal motion—particularly the suspension, G (meas. 4–5), which emphasized the beginning of motive *n*—the eighth-note pattern in measures 15 and 17 and the dominant-seventh harmony in

---

39. These more remote processes occur in the second part of the Trio. There, played by the same instrument and in the same register, the high D moves down through C (meas. 24) to B and A (meas. 25–26)—and eventually to G (see pp. 723–28, and ex. 22, graph 2.)

40. Because this repetition is "post-cadential" its effect is not to enhance goal-directed motion (see n. 33), but to diminish kinetic tension.

those measures suggest motion *to* the measure that follows, making the groups seem end accented. In addition, because there is no canon (ex. 7) in the codetta, the tonic chord of the new key is in stable, root position.

Relationships between the codetta and preceding events also contribute to closure. As we have seen, several implicative processes generated in the first two phrases are at least provisionally realized in the codetta: (1) The continuation of the oboe's conjunct fill (meas. 8–12) through E to D, which was masked by the flute in measures 12–14, is audibly actualized in measures 16–18 (ex. 17, graph 3*b*). (2) The D played by the first violins in measure 14—and prolonged through a neighbor-note motion (D–E–D) and an octave transfer—is the realization of a goal implied by the high-level linear motion begun by the violins in the first four measures of the Trio (ex. 17, graph 4*a*). (3) In measures 16–18 the registral relationship implicit in motives *m* and *o* is explicitly affirmed as the violins and oboes play motive n^2 in octaves (see pp. 716–17 above). (4) And the possibility that the two-measure length of motive *n* might be extended and "normalized" through repetition (see pp. 708–10 above) is actualized in the codetta. (5) Finally, and perhaps most fundamental of all, because they rhyme with the figure which closed the first phrase, motives n^1 and n^2 are understood as a "return," and the psychic satisfaction of such return considerably enhances the formal completeness and closure of the first part of the Trio.

Part II

In the second part of the Trio the processes begun in the first, and provisionally stabilized at its close, are resumed and satisfactorily completed. In what follows, the continuation of those processes in the transition and the return will be considered first. Then subsidiary relationships generated within the transition and completed in the return will be discussed. And last, the return will be analyzed, with special attention to the differences between it and Section *A* (=Part I) which it restates in modified form.

The Transition

In the prefatory "sketch" of the structural plan of the Trio, the transition was described (pp. 695–96 above) as an elaborated prolongation of dominant harmony linking the close of Section *A* with the beginning of the return (Section *A'*). But to say no more than that is both to ignore the subtle way in which the interaction among parameters shapes events within the section and to overlook important relationships between the transition and the return. At the beginning of the transition, for instance, what seems to be a continuation of the high-level melodic process (begun by the oboe in the second phrase) is artfully undermined and

121

deflected by rhythmic/metric ambiguity. A new, but subsidiary, melodic process is generated (see below, pp. 740–41 and ex. 28). This process is continued in the return. There it affects the significance of the high G in measure 36. Instead of being the mobile middle of a patterning—as the comparable high D in measure 12 was—the G is the relatively stable goal of the subsidiary patterning begun in the transition. It is only toward the end of the transition that the main melodic process is actually resumed. Its gradual emergence from the subsidiary process is a fascinating example of how the intricate interplay among melody and harmony, meter and rhythm, texture and phrasing shapes the listener's understanding of musical events.

Phrase 3 (meas. 18–26).—The relative stability achieved at the end of Part I is undermined at the very beginning of the transition (ex. 22). The C-natural of submotive y (meas. 19) transforms the D-major harmony reached in measure 18 from a stable, if temporary, tonic into a mobile dominant-seventh chord. For several reasons, motive q suggests that the gap-fill processes generated by the oboes and the flute in motive group 2 have been resumed. (1) Like motives o and o^1, motive q consists of a rising triad followed by descending conjunct motion. Because of this similarity, there is a tendency to associate the later pattern (q) with the earlier one (o) in function as well as shape. (2) The C at the start of submotive y can be understood as the continuation of two earlier descending fills; namely, that begun by the oboes in measure 8 and provisionally stabilized in measure 18 (ex. 22, graph 1a), and that begun by the flute in measure 10 but deflected and "left hanging" in measure 12 (ex. 22, graph 2). (3) Furthermore, submotive y is played by the same instruments, oboes and flute, and in the same registers as was the case earlier. (4) Last, the sonority, dominated by the thirds in the oboes, is not unlike that characteristic of the earlier descending fill.

But the resumption is provisional at best—an intimation, perhaps, of more satisfactory realization. It is so for two reasons. In motive group 2, conjunct fill occurred on the level of the measure or higher, that is, A (meas. 8–9), G (meas. 10–11), F-sharp (meas. 12), E (meas. 13), and D (meas 14). To be satisfactory, the resumption of this process must take place on the same hierarchic level, or on a higher one.[41] Submotive y does not fulfill this condition. It moves on the level of the beat (C–B–A, within the measure); and when it is restated a step higher (y^1), rather than a step lower, the provisional nature of the resumption is patent. Equally important, the appoggiatura-resolution figure so characteristic of the earlier descending fill (particularly in the oboes in measures 8, 10, 12, and 13) is missing. In short, though the C-natural in measure 18, and

41. See the discussion of the law of hierarchic equivalence in my *Explaining Music*, pp. 134–35 and passim.

submotive *y* as a whole, may serve as signals of impending realization, their main function is not the resumption of processes already begun but the generation of new, albeit subsidiary ones.

The gap-fill processes begun in motive group 2 are continued not at the beginning but toward the end of the transition (ex. 22, graphs 1*a* and 2).[42] There the oboe D of measure 18 and the flute D from measure 12 move in their respective registers through C (meas. 24) and B (meas. 25) to A (meas. 26). And this descending motion not only occurs at the level of the measure but is realized as an appoggiatura-resolution figure.

The transition ends in measure 26. As we shall see, rhythm plays an important part in this articulation: the high-level structure is a closed, end-accented group of 6 + 6 + 12 quarter notes, and, as metric placement becomes "normalized" in measures 24–26, the appoggiatura-resolution figure latent in measures 19–22 is actualized. What follows the cadence in measure 26 makes closure unmistakable. It is not merely that melody, rhythm, texture, and orchestration are significantly different, or that the patterning is more stable and regular, but that there is a *return* to relationships presented at the beginning of the Trio.

Though unmistakable, the closure of the transition is by no means definitive. Both the foreground rhythm, which ends on a weak beat, and the harmony, which cadences on an unstable dominant chord, create mobility. More important for present purposes, however, the processes resumed in measures 24–26, as well as those generated within the transition itself (meas. 19–23), are incomplete. The descending fill has reached its penultimate pitch, A, but return to the stability of the tonic—the full completion of the fill—is still to come.[43] In theoretical terms, there is a bifurcation of form and process. That is, processes generated as far back in the piece as measure 7 transcend the articulation that divides the Trio into formal entities (Section *B* followed by Section *A'*).[44]

In the return (meas. 26–42), the process begun by the oboes in motive group 2, and resumed by them in the transition, is continued and completed by the French horns. This change in the instruments performing an established process—one of the few such changes in the

123

42. Precisely how the rhythmic/metric structure of the transition moves from intimation to realization of the appoggiatura-resolution figure is discussed below, pp. 733–34.

43. Observe that the oboe's A in meas. 26 can be construed not only as part of the long descent begun by the large gap in measures 7–8 but as the fill of the smaller gap from G in meas. 6 to the structural B in meas. 7—as ex. 22, graph 1*b* shows. Looked at in this way, meas. 6–26 combine comparable processes on two registral levels into a single extended motion. From another point of view, both these gap-fill processes are analogous to that which opens the Trio. They are, so to speak, motive *m* "writ large."

44. The point seems worth making because it emphasizes that, contrary to the views of some critics and aestheticians, form and process are distinguishable and sometimes independent aspects of structure. Observe that a similar bifurcation occurred between Section *A* (of Part I) and Section *B*.

EXAMPLE 22

Trio—is probably made partly for registral reasons.[45] That is, in the relatively low register of measures 26–42, the sound of the oboes would be quite weak. The music played by the horns will be discussed in more detail later. For the present, it need only be observed that, though they begin by doubling and "clarifying" what is played by the violins (meas. 26–32), it is reasonable to regard the horns as surrogates for the oboes. For when they are given the main melodic material (meas. 32 ff.), their music is similar to that performed earlier by the oboes (meas. 6 ff.). However, while the oboes reached only partial closure (in an authentic cadence in the dominant) and provisional realization (through substitution by rank) at the end of Part I, the horns achieve both full stability and satisfactory realization. For, at the end of the Trio an authentic cadence in the tonic establishes full stability, and as they move on structural tones from A to G the horns complete both the gap-fill process they regenerate

45. The change is not inappropriate because the oboes have, from one point of view, completed part of their task. For since the B in meas. 8 is an appoggiatura, the first structural tone in the oboe's descending fill is the following A and, when it reaches the lower structural A in meas. 26, it has sounded in conjunct succession all the tones of the G-major scale. Or, to put the matter differently, the oboe part consists of a linear prolongation of A.

125

in the return and that begun by the oboes in measure 6 (ex. 22, graphs 1a and 1c).

The gap-fill process begun by the flute in measures 9–10 is also continued in the transition (ex. 22, graph 2). After provisional motion to C (meas. 19), the high D "left hanging" in measure 12 functions (appropriately) as an appoggiatura which resolves to C (meas. 24), and this pattern of descent is continued to the A in measure 26, where the flute part ends temporarily. But in the return no surrogate instrument completes its process. The flute continues; the structural A reached in measure 26 is picked up in measure 35 and, after an excursion through F-sharp and G in the upper octave (see below, pp. 740–41, moves to G (meas. 38), completing the descent from D.[46] Closure is reinforced as the flute joins in the performance of the codetta figure in the final measures of the Trio.

Before considering the larger structure of the transition, discussing the implicative processes generated within it, and following these to their realization in the return, subtle, low-level rhythmic/metric relationships must be analyzed in some detail.

To illuminate these subtleties, motive *q* will be compared with motive *o*. Their similarity was mentioned earlier: both consist of a rising triadic motion followed by conjunct descent (ex. 23, parts *A* and *B*). But there are important differences between them. Motive *o* is essentially a single gesture. Though it can be divided into parts, these are cohesive because they are functionally related as gap to beginning of fill. Melodic integrity is reinforced by harmonic progression, as tonic (meas. 6–7) moves to dominant (meas. 8). Furthermore, a single instrumental timbre, that of the oboes, connects the parts of the motive and links its two registral levels. Motive *q*, on the other hand, is made up of patently separate, almost independent, parts: submotives *x* and *y* (ex. 23, part *B*). The parts are differentiated by instrumental color, strings followed by woodwinds; and by registral contrast, bass followed by treble winds as well as bassoons.[47] Though the submotives overlap (the winds enter before the strings finish) and are related to one another in a kind of "statement / response" dialogue, no implicative melodic process welds them together. They are not understood as gap and fill. Nor does the mere addition of the seventh (C) create enough harmonic change to ensure cohesive connection.

These melodic differences have a significant effect upon rhythmic/metric organization. Motive *o*, as we have seen, consists of an

46. Although the gap has not been completely filled (the flute does not return to the structural D in meas. 9), substitution by rank here creates satisfactory closure because it occurs on the tonic. In addition, it might be argued that the horns complete this process, moving down conjunctly from D in meas. 34 to G in meas. 42.

47. Though the bassoons are not in a markedly different register, submotive *y* is nevertheless understood as separate and "high" because it is dominated by the sound of the upper winds. For the sake of convenience the bassoon part is not given in the "short" scores. The interested reader should consult the full score given in the Appendix.

extended anacrusis followed by an appoggiatura-resolution figure that function as a relatively short, but emphatic, accent (see analysis under ex. 23*A*). Motive *q* has also been analyzed as an end-accented group on the primary level (see ex. 23*B*, Perception, *R*-1). This analysis is based partly upon the prevalence of end-accented groups on the primary level at the end of Part I (see ex. 17), partly upon the tendency of rising disjunct patterns to be understood as mobile and goal directed, and partly upon the fact that the change in register and instrumentation makes the woodwind entrance seem stressed. However, even though the last two notes of motives *o* and *q* are identical in pitch and metric position (B and A on beats 1 and 2), the impression of end-accented grouping is much weaker in motive *q*.

The accent is weak because the B in measure 20 does not function as an appoggiatura. No articulation in phrasing, no change in dynamics or timbre indicates such function. No harmonic change marks the beginning of the measure, making the B into an accented dissonance—as might have been the case (ex. 23, part *C*). Put differently, the B is a "potential" appoggiatura, but its actualization *as* an appoggiatura is delayed until the very end of the transition (see ex. 24, level i). Moreover, had actualization occurred in measure 20, the continuation of the descending conjunct fill assigned to the oboes and flute (ex. 22, graphs 1*a* and 2) would have been unsatisfactory because, although the A would have been structural on the proper (equivalent) level, the preceding C and B would not (ex. 23*C*, graph).

EXAMPLE 23

Note: M = meter
R = rhythm

Though it *should* function as an appoggiatura—its metric position and its relation to previous patternings suggest this role—the B sounds more like a passing tone. It does so because, despite its notation, its metric role is ambiguous. This ambiguity is present from the beginning of motive *q*.

According to the notation, the low D which begins the transition should be understood as a mobile upbeat to the following F-sharp (ex. 23*B*, Notation). At least in retrospect, however, its metric placement is equivocal. For it seems to function partly as the accented beginning of a metric unit (ex. 23*B*, Perception). This anomaly is the result of the organization of the several parameters:

1. Since submotive *x* consists of a single ascending triad, played in unison by one group of instruments (double basses), harmony, texture, and orchestration do not articulate the first beat of measure 19. The absence of stress on this beat weakens the impression of meter.[48] To the extent that F-sharp is understood as accented, it is so because the prevalent metric organization is continued in the mind and motor behavior of the listener.

2. The triad is phrased as a single unbroken event. Put counterfactually: had Mozart written ♪ rather than ♪ , the change of bow after the D would have placed a slight stress on F-sharp, making the notated meter more palpable.

3. When a triadic pattern begins on the root, there is a tendency for the root to be perceived as the beginning of a metric unit (see pp. 711–12 and ex. 16, as well as ex. 23*B*, Perception). Because in this case no articulation is created by the other parameters (unless, of course, the conductor requires his performers to place special stress on the F-sharp which, as we shall see, would be a mistake), the D is most readily understood as an accent—as the beginning of a metric unit.[49] The relationship between melodic pattern and metric placement is more normal at the beginning of the next submotive (*x*[1]) because the first note is the fifth (D), rather than the root (G), of the triad: ♪ . But it is too late to dispel or

---

48. To see the difference that texture and harmony can make, compare the first beat of meas. 19 with the F-sharp played by the bassoons on the first beat of meas. 34. Although the triads (beginning on D in meas. 18 and 33) are the same, the F-sharp on the first beat of meas. 34 is stressed and its metric function unambiguous because the appoggiatura in the horns makes the rhythmic structure crystal clear. But nothing articulates the first beat of meas. 19.

49. From this point of view, the beginning of the transition is similar to the beginning of the Trio and may be said to intensify the ambiguity latent in the triadic pattern of motive *m*. Note, however, that in motive *m* the second violins skip up a minor sixth, from B to G, and the resulting emphasis on the note following the skip (G) probably helps to articulate the meter. So, of course, does what follows.

alter the sense of metric placement which has, in the meantime, been reinforced by the patterning of submotive *y*.

4. All parameters cooperate to suggest that the first notes of submotive *y* may be the accented beginning of a metric unit. Because it transforms the preceding triad from a provisional tonic into a dominant-seventh chord, the C renews the harmonic impulse and thereby emphasizes the beginning of the submotive. Both the change in instrumentation and the separation in register incline the listener to perceive the third beat of measure 19 as the beginning of a new metric unit. Equally important: no parametric articulation differentiates the first beat of measure 20 as the accented beginning of the meter. For instance, there is no change in phrasing at this point. In short, the simplest way to perceive the patterning of these submotives is to make the meter begin on notated third beats.

The force of the metric disturbance should not, however, be exaggerated. Because the metric placement prevalent in Part I continues to affect the listener's mental and motor behavior, and because the appoggiatura-resolution figure explicit in that placement is latent in the patterning of submotive *y*, the shift in the position of the perceived (vs. the notated) meter is not unmitigated.[50] As a result, the original metric placement could have been reestablished easily. But this does not happen. Let us consider what does take place.

A new stage in the transition begins at the end of measure 23 (ex. 24). In what follows, the rate of harmonic motion virtually quadruples: instead of two chords in twelve beats (meas. 18–22), two chords occur in only three beats (meas. 24–26). Texture, motivic pattern, and instrumentation are also altered. Instead of a dialogue between contrasting submotives played by different instrumental groups, one submotive (*y*) is the sole melodic material in a quasi-contrapuntal texture played by a single group of instruments: the woodwinds. Yet despite these manifest modifications which signal the close of the transition, rhythmic/metric changes are gradual.

The metric ambiguity established at the beginning of the transition is supported by the pattern begun by the oboes and flute on the last beat of measure 23, and, as a result, the ensuing group is beginning accented (ex. 24, level i). But the bassoons suggest the possibility of change: because it is twice as long as the note that precedes it, the half note at the beginning of measure 24 is an agogic accent, and, responding to this durational emphasis as well as to the notated meter, the bassoonists will probably place some stress on the longer note, making it seem like the beginning of a metric unit. In addition, the half-note harmony makes

50. Thus though the third beats of meas. 19 (C), 21 (D), and 23 (E) will be analyzed as structural tones (see ex. 27, graphs 3*a* and 3*b*), they are provisionally, rather than definitively, so.

129

the notes played by the upper winds into a proper appoggiatura which is properly resolved. Since appoggiaturas normally occur on the first beat of a metric unit, this also indicates that perceived and notated meter are becoming congruent.

But only "becoming." For the potential influence of the appoggiatura-resolution figure is undermined by phrasing. Instead of making the figure patent, as it might have done (ex. 24, graph *A*), the actual phrasing ties the appoggiatura/resolution both to the preceding E and to the following D. Because it begins a varied repetition of submotive *y*, the E is understood as the beginning of a metric unit. As a result, it preempts the middle-level accent (ex. 24, level i) and relegates the appoggiatura-resolution figure to a very subsidiary rhythmic level (level iii). By transcending the closure of the figure on C, the phrasing to D obscures the presence of the figure and, consequently, the accent characteristic of it.

EXAMPLE 24

130

The phrasing beyond C to D (meas. 24) is important for other reasons as well. As part *B* of example 24 shows, the motivic structure of measures 23–26 is potentially very regular. Submotive *y* is simply restated sequentially three times—though the third time (y^a) the first motivic tone (C) is preceded by a grace note (D). Had the phrasing emphasized this uniformity by repeating that in measures 19–22 (ex. 22) or one such as that given in part *A* of example 24, continuation would have been strongly implied, and the cadential closure in measure 26 would have seemed abrupt—even jolting. Mozart's phrasing ruffles this potential regularity so that, instead of being the beginning of y^{1a}, the D (meas. 24) functions as an extension of y^2. Similarly, in measure 25 phrasing disturbs uniformity and tends to obscure the presence of familiar submotives.[51]

Because the D at the end of measure 24 is phrased with what precedes it, rather than with what follows, the appoggiatura figure at the beginning of measure 25 is not subsumed within submotive y^{1a}, as it might have been (ex. 24, part *B*-1). Instead, phrase and figure begin together. By enhancing the articulation of the appoggiatura, phrasing emphasizes the rhythm of the figure and makes its function more palpable; it is now understood as an event on levels ii and i. Here perceived and notated meter become congruent again.

But the appoggiatura figure, though now manifest, is not yet fully realized as an event in its own right. It is the accented beginning of a compound rhythmic group on level i (♩ ♩ ♫), but not an integral, stable goal. It becomes so in the following measure (meas. 26). The two eighth notes at the end of measure 25 are not only a mobile afterbeat coming *from* the accented beginning of the measure (as the phrasing indicates), but, because they are separated from the second beat (B) by a skip and are shorter than the notes surrounding them, the eighth notes also function as an upbeat to the appoggiatura figure in measure 26.[52] Thus on the subprimary level (i) part, and on the primary level (1) all, of measure 25 acts as an anacrusis to measure 26 which is a stable goal. Here the integrity and function of the appoggiatura figure are fully realized.

One important consequence of the metric displacement, discussed at such length, is now apparent. It makes possible the progression, men-

51. Although they contravene the previously established, and probably more basic, motivic organization, the phrasings in meas. 24 and 25 do not create disordered patterns. Rather they give rise to a kind of substitute regularity: a neighbor-note motion of D–C–D /C–B–C (ex. 24, part *B*-2).

52. The inverted bracket in ex. 24 suggests that the upbeat is only latent—partially realized. But it is somewhat stronger than this because the eighth-note motion from D to C is itself a low-level appoggiatura figure which makes the third beat stressed (') and thereby strengthens its anacrustic function.

tioned earlier, from veiled potentiality to patent actuality. Let us briefly review this change. Though no proper appoggiatura figure is embedded in submotives y and y^1 (ex. 22), their notated metric placement and the similarity of motives q and q^1 to o and o^1 subtly intimate such patterning.[53] Submotive y^2 is the middle term, or link, in what proves to be a mirror pattern (ex. 25).[54] Appropriately, therefore, while an appoggiatura figure is unquestionably contained in y^2, its function tends to be subsumed and its identity masked by the dominance of the submotive as a whole. As the motivic patterning is weakened by the phrasing, the appoggiatura figure gains in strength and prominence until, as we have seen, it is fully actualized in measure 26. This progression is evident in the analysis of rhythmic structure (ex. 24). When the figure first appears (meas. 24), it is "buried" on subprimary levels (iii and ii); as it becomes manifest (meas. 25), it shapes the structure of the next levels: ii and i; and, finally, when it is fully realized, it participates in the organization of the highest levels (i and 1).

At the same time that it shapes events within the transition, the progression from potentiality to actuality brings about the resumption of other implicative processes—ones which, as we have seen, extend beyond the confines of the transition. For the actualization of the appoggiatura figure makes it evident (partly perhaps in retrospect, since

EXAMPLE 25

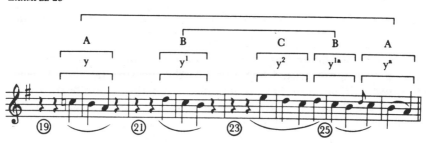

53. Performance should not, however, make this possible patterning palpable—e.g., by stressing notated accents. For then the sense of progression and of ultimate realization would be weakened.

54. The mirror structure suggests that the transition should be analyzed as a prolongation of the dominant harmony with which it begins and ends. Possibly. But it should be observed that only motivic structure is organized in this way. Harmony, rhythm, texture, and instrumentation do not exhibit this sort of symmetry. Moreover, even motivic structure is varied in reflection because submotives y^{1a} and y^a are functionally different from their earlier counterparts. More generally, some prolongations are nonprocessive; e.g., declarative and normalizing prolongations, parentheses, and those which, allowing time for respite of process, might be called "composed fermatas." (An instance of composed fermata occurs in the first movement of Beethoven's String Quartet in B-flat, Opus 130, meas. 37–40.) In the transition of Mozart's Trio, however, new processes are generated, old ones resumed, and kinetic motion enhances directionality.

actualization is gradual) that what was merely intimated in the first half of the transition (meas. 18–23) is consummated in the second (meas. 24–26). Namely, the descending fill, begun by the oboes and flute in period 1 (and completed by the horns and flute in period 2), has been resumed and continued on the proper hierarchic level (ex. 22, graphs 1*a*, 1*c*, and 2).

The end of the transition is a result of the momentary stabilization of strongly goal-directed processes. Though rhythm is most important in creating closure, modest inflections in other parameters contribute to the articulation of the cadence even as they signal its approach.[55] The regular harmonic progression through chords whose *roots* are a fifth apart—E(V⁶/ii), A(ii), D(V⁶), G(I)—is deflected in measure 25 (ex. 26, part *A* and the harmonic analysis).[56] Instead of continuing the cycle of fifths by skipping down a third to E (as the bass of a first-inversion triad built on C), there is a larger skip to C (as the bass of a triad built on A). This change produces a higher-level disjunction (ex. 26, part *B*). The fourth-species counterpoint, implicit in the relationship between bass and treble (meas. 24–25), is modified when the bass, which might have continued descending by step to F-sharp (the first beat of meas. 26), skips down to D. Melodically, the skip of a third from B to D (meas. 25) breaks the prevailing conjunct motion (ex. 26, part *C*), and the break is emphasized because eighth notes, rather than quarters, fill the gap thus created. These slight discontinuities not only damp ongoing motion and presage closure, they transform potentially uniform processes into a function-confirming gesture—an archetypal semicadence.[57]

Such changes would not have created convincing closure, however, were it not for rhythm. Although the foreground patterning ends on a mobile weak beat, middle-level rhythmic closure is unequivocal, and it is

55. The structure or form of a composition is something which the competent listener *infers* from the hierarchy of closures that it presents. The strength of any closure depends upon the degrees of closure articulated by the several parameters. Sometimes all parameters join in creating closure; then they are said to move congruently. At other times, one or two parameters will foster closure while others make for continuation of process; then they are said to be noncongruent. In the case of the close of this transition, the parameters are scarcely congruent. Rhythm, as we shall see, is relatively closed and stable, but melody, e.g., stops on one of the most mobile notes of the scale. For this reason, closure at the end of the transition is quite weak.

56. An "x" in an example signifies a disjunction or break in process.

57. As, for example, that in the fourth measure of the Theme from Mozart's A Major Piano Sonata (K. 331):

strong enough to impose upon the other parameters a stability they would not otherwise possess. Reinforced by the eighth-note motion at its close, measure 25 is, as we have seen, anacrustic to measure 26 on the primary level (ex. 24 and 26, level 1). On the next level (ex. 26, level 2), the grouping is end accented—a closed anapest. The organization is understood in this way not only because other parameters, including low-level rhythm, weld measures 23–26 into a cohesive event but because the first four measures of the transition imply this sort of structure. That is, the varied repetition of motive *q*, like that of motives *m* and *o* in Part I, make it probable that a longer group, an accent to which the essentially equivalent motives can be related (see pp. 717–18, above), will follow. When motive q^2 begins on a new step of the scale (E rather than D), it

EXAMPLE 26

134

seems the beginning of such a cohesive event. And this surmise is confirmed by what follows.

Though rhythm creates sufficient closure to articulate the end of the transition, the sense of goal-directed motion is by no means diminished. For despite the contribution to closure made by the disjunctions mentioned above, the other parameters remain open and ongoing. The harmonic progression (ii^6–I_4^6–V) at the end of the transition implies continuation to the tonic. Melodically, the descending line of appoggiatura resolutions (C–B–A), which resumes processes begun in Part I, stops on one of the most mobile notes of the scale, and the tendency to move to the tonic, G, is very strong. Moreover, melodic processes generated within the transition remain to be realized. These kinetic patternings affect the rhythmic structure of the highest level, making the whole transition function as an anacrusis to the return (ex. 26, level 3).

The sense of goal-directed motion is high not only because inhibition (resulting from rhythmically imposed closure) intensifies inclination but because an increase in psychological tempo, or pace, heightens the sense of urgency. It was pointed out earlier that by obscuring the uniformity of motivic structure, phrasing facilitates closure. Paradoxically, the same phrasing that tempers a tendency toward continuation produces a kind of composed accelerando. That is, the phrase groups at the end of the transition become progressively shorter (ex. 26, part *D*)—from four beats, to three, to two. As a result, events seem to occur more rapidly.[58]

Though the degree of closure is such that the transition is understood as a separable event, the presence of strong syntactic processes prevents it from functioning as an independent, formal entity. Rather it is a contingent one, calling for a section in which tension is resolved, stability established, and processes satisfactorily concluded. This dependence seems to be reflected in the morphology of the Trio. It will be recalled (ex. 1) that the first part of the Trio consists of two main events: the first, phrase 1, is six measures long; the second, phrase group 1, is twelve measures long. The ratio of these events (1:2) suggests that the third morphological length might be twice the second, making the succession of lengths 6–12–24.[59] A twenty-four measure unit does follow, and it proves to be not a section within but all of Part II. Moreover, since the transition is eight measures long, the proportions of Part II are the same (1:2) as those of Part I. These proportional relationships seem to indicate that (1) what is morphologically equivalent to Part I is not the return (though the return is motivically and syntactically so) but the

135

58. The change of pace itself acts as a sign of impending closure. See, e.g., the more extended "accelerando" toward the end of the development section (meas. 134–64) in the first movement of this Symphony. In both cases, pace increases because our sense of tempo depends to a considerable extent upon the rate at which differentiated events—more or less closed patterns—follow one another.

59. Another consistent succession would, of course, be 6–12–18.

whole of the second part;[60] and (2) though it is a separable entity, a cohesive bar form of $2 + 2 + 4$ measures (ex. 26, part *F*), the transition is morphologically as well as functionally subordinate.

The transition is functionally dependent—open and mobile—partly because implicative melodic processes remain to be realized. One of these, that resumed toward the end of the transition and continued in the return, has already been discussed.[61] The other, begun in the first half of the transition, is the result of the rising linear motion whose structural tones are C (meas. 19), D (meas. 21), and E (meas. 23). Once established, this pattern, too, implies continuation to a point of relative stability and closure—probably by conjunct motion through F-sharp to G (ex. 27, graphs 3*a* and 3*b*). Thus though both patterns imply continuation to the tonic, they move in opposite directions. The primary process, resumed in the second half of the transition, suggests motion *down* to G; the secondary process, generated in the first half of the transition, suggests motion *up* to G.[62]

The structure of the secondary pattern is crucially dependent upon the metric ambiguity discussed earlier. For, had there been no metric disturbance at the beginning of the transition, the C, D, and E would probably have functioned as mobile anacruses to appoggiatura figures.[63] In that case, the structural tones of the transition would have consisted of an unambiguous succession of appoggiatura resolutions—that is, a conjunct motion from A to C and back again (ex. 27, graph 2*a*); and the whole section might have been understood as little more than a prolongation of A (ex. 27, graph 2*b*). But meter is disturbed. As a result, the beginnings, at least as much as the ends, of submotives *y*, *y*¹, and *y*² are structural.[64] However, because meter is equivocal[65] the tones defining the ascending melodic line are structurally somewhat tentative. Appro-

60. The fact that the proportions of the sixteen-measure return $(6 + 10)$ cannot easily be related to others in the Trio also seems a sign of the morphological integrity of the whole second part. It might be suggested that the "stretto" in meas. 33–35 represents a compression of a more commensurate length. But if this sort of argument is allowed, anything can be made to fit—and often is. It should perhaps also be mentioned that the Trio is the same length as the Minuetto proper—i.e., forty-two measures.

61. See pp. 724–28 and 734–35, also ex. 22, graphs 1*a*, 1*c*, and 2, and ex. 27, graphs 1*a* and 1*b*.

62. The process resumed at the close of the transition is considered primary not only because it plays a central role in the melodic structuring of the Trio from meas. 6 on but because its tones are unequivocally structural—are congruent with the prevalent (and notated) meter. The process begun in meas. 19 is considered secondary both because it plays an auxiliary role in the larger structure of the Trio and because its structural tones are somewhat tentative.

63. As, e.g., in ex. 23, part *C* (treble clef).

64. Submotive *y*² acts as the common term, or link, between the different melodic processes. That is, its first note (E) belongs to the secondary ascending motion; its last note (C) is the first structural note in the resumption of the primary descending process.

65. See p. 731 above.

EXAMPLE 27

137

priately, the continuation of this process is less decisive than that of the primary one.

The continuation takes place in measure 36 of the return. There the flute, one of the instruments that generated the process, moves in the right register through F-sharp (emphasized by motion from the lower octave) to the high G (ex. 27, graph 3*a*). Even though the G is accompanied by a deceptive cadence, the realization seems satisfactory. It does so partly because it is the tonic and partly because (1) it is the goal of the secondary process, and (2) the tones generating the implicative pattern were themselves only "tentatively" structural.

Once again Mozart's phrasing is illuminating. The high G in measure 36 is comparable to the high D in measure 12 (ex. 28) but with significant differences. The D is considerably less stable than the G. It is not the tonic but part of a cadence within a modulation toward the dominant. Nor is it the goal of a process. Rather it is a transient upward deflection toward the beginning of a descending fill defined by unequivocal structural tones (ex. 28, graph 1*a*). As a result, the D in measure 12 is mobile; it seems, as mentioned earlier, to be "left hanging." It can be "left hanging" because it will be picked up and continued in the

138

EXAMPLE 28

transition where it descends through C-natural and B to A.[66] The high G in measure 36, on the other hand, is not only a more stable goal but, because it occurs in the final phrase of the Trio, remote continuation is unlikely. That is, it will not be picked up, as the D is, and move on to a further goal. Phrasing reflects these differences. Instead of ending the phrasing on the G, leaving it "hanging" and implying the possibility of continuation (as was the case with the high D), Mozart explicitly connects the G to the B which follows, fusing the deceptive cadence to the complete one that follows, and connecting high and low registers in a single gesture (ex. 28, graph 2*b*).[67]

The role of the oboes in the return is auxiliary (see ex. 27):[68] they play in octaves both with the flute (meas. 34–35) and the horns, and then rejoin the flute in the performance of the cadential gesture (meas. 36–38). Consequently, analyzing their continuation of the secondary process is problematic. However, the contrapuntal connection between the last notes (meas. 23) of their generative pattern and the final cadence of the Trio seems clear enough to make this move to closure a reasonable candidate for realization (ex. 27, graph 3*b*).[69] If this is correct, then it seems plausible to suggest that the movement from F-sharp to G (and C–B) of the complete cadence (meas. 37–38) is understood—at least in retrospect—as a preliminary realization of the process begun by the oboes in the first half of the transition.

139

The Return

The return creates high-level closure both because tonic harmony is reestablished after a relatively extended departure (meas. 6–26), and because the melodic/textural patterns of Part I are re-presented —though with significant modifications. The modifications are important because they not only insure that the whole section (*A'*) remains in the tonic but, as we have seen, make possible the realization of implications generated in preceding sections. Equally important, the changes are so designed that newly generated processes as well as those regenerated by repetition are realized within the confines of the return.

66. The deflection may even be connected in retrospect with the rising motion of the subordinate process.

67. The phrasing of the first oboe part, whose conjunct descent from B (meas. 36) through A (meas. 37) to G (meas. 38) is unmistakable, breaks as before; and the overlap of the flute and oboe phrasings assures that the motion from the last beat of meas. 34 to the first beat of meas. 38 will be understood as one pattern.

68. As we have seen, the primary process, begun by the oboes in meas. 6 and resumed by them in meas. 24, is assigned to the French horns.

69. Particularly since the oboes play the same rhythm as, and complete the harmony of, their surrogates, the French horns. For the sake of clarity, the oboe part is given in the analytic graph rather than in the short score.

Phrase 1ª (meas. 26–32).—Modifications are present from the beginning of the return (ex. 27). In the first four measures the violins restate what they played at the beginning of the Trio. But now they are reinforced by the French horns—except that the horns omit the second beats of measures 27 and 29.[70] This apparently slight qualification of tone color results in changes in syntactic emphasis. Though the implicative relationships discussed in connection with the analysis of the first phrase (pp. 702–5 and 708–10) are implicit in what the violins play, some are significantly strengthened by the addition of the horns, while others are considerably weakened.

To appreciate the ways in which the horns affect implicative relationships, the patterns generated by the violins must be briefly reviewed.[71] Though seemingly little more than a detail, the D in the violin part in measure 27—and analogically, the E in measure 29—influences the musical patterning in a number of ways. Melodically, the D (1) forms part of the triadic motion, making it unequivocal (ex. 29, graph 1); (2) creates a subsidiary gap, B–D, which the C begins to fill (ex. 29, graph 2); and (3) by forming this subsidiary gap-fill pattern, obscures the échappée function of the C (ex. 29, graph 3). Rhythmically, the D enhances the stability of the C and contributes to the mobility of the preceding B (ex. 29, graph 4). The stability of the C is enhanced because, as the goal of the subsidiary gap, it is slightly stressed (ˊ). As a result, the dactyl within the measure is a bit more closed than would otherwise be the case (ex. 29, graph 4, level i). Though it is an accent, the B has some mobility—both because it is the same length as the notes which precede and follow it (it is not agogically defined), and because, since it occurs in the middle of a coherent and familiar pattern (the triad), its stability is weakened by continuation to an ongoing afterbeat. Consequently, there is, as we have seen, a fleeting impression of amphibrach grouping (graph 4, upper bracket). Finally, if motive group 1 can be understood as a changing-note pattern (as suggested earlier), it is partly because the C (meas. 29), like the B (meas. 27), is relatively mobile (ex. 29, graph 5). For though both are accented on the primary level (1), neither is strongly stressed or markedly stable relative to the primary-level weak beats, A and B, which follow. As a result, harmonic closure—the progression from dominant to tonic (meas. 29–30)—can influence structure, making the B in measure 30 a goal of modest, though temporary, stability.

Consider now how the relationships inherent in the violin patterns

70. Note that the entrance of the horns is "prepared" by the bassoons (meas. 23–26) which not only establish the durational pattern (♩ | ♩ ♩) played by the horns but, because of similarity of tone color, are commonly associated with and act as substitutes for the horns in this period of music history.

71. For the sake of clarity and convenience, the violin and horn parts, though played together, are given in separate examples: the violins in ex. 29, the horns in ex. 30.

EXAMPLE 29

are strengthened, weakened, and even denied by what the horns play (ex. 30). The omission of the second beats in measures 27 and 29—that is, the D and the E—weakens the impression of foreground triadic motion (because only the first two notes of the triad are presented)[72] and eliminates the subsidiary gap-fill process. As a result, foreground linear motion is considerably strengthened. It is not merely that competing processes are weakened or denied. The linear pattern itself becomes more palpable and more mobile. Not only is the motion from B to C (meas. 27) and C to D (meas. 29), implicit in the first violin part, spelled out (ex. 30, graph 3), but the third beats no longer have stability, however slight, as subsidiary melodic goals. Rhythmically, too, the third beats

72. Though a structural G is presented in the upper octave toward the close of the return (meas. 40–42) orchestral as well as melodic relationships indicate that this follows not from the rising triadic motion of the violins (meas. 26–27) but, as we have seen, from the descending linear pattern of the flute (ex. 27, graph 1a).

EXAMPLE 30

142

are less stable because a weak beat that follows a note of longer duration (horns: ♩ ♪) is more mobile than one that follows notes of equal duration (violins: ♩ ♩ ♩).

The gap-fill pattern of the main motive is also strengthened. The elimination of the second beats of measures 27 and 29 makes the échappée function (E) of the third beats, which is only latent in the violin melody, manifest (ex. 30, graph 1). As a result, the fundamental structure of the motive—a gap-fill relationship ornamented by a nonchord tone—is more apparent (ex. 30, graphs 2a and 2b). Durational changes also serve to emphasize this relationship. For when a short upbeat skips to a longer downbeat, as it does in the horn parts, conjunct fill is generally implied.[73]

73. See Narmour, chap. 4.

Higher-level processes, too, are more emphatic, as well as more mobile and goal-directed. The force of the main gap-fill patterns makes the relationship generated by their succession more patent (ex. 30, graph 4*a*). As a result, sequential continuation—probably to a longer phrase that begins with a skip from B to D—is more forcefully implied than it was in Part I. Rhythm also enhances mobility and strengthens goal-directed processes. It does so by weakening the closure of the motive group at measure 30. Let me explain. If the foreground trochees

(♩ ♩) within measures 27 and 29 are to function as the accented parts

of primary-level amphibrachs— ♪♩ ♩♩♪ —creating coherent motives,

then downbeats must be slightly stressed.[74] If they are not so, then (given

the durational pattern, ♩ ♪ , and the absence of a subsidiary melodic

goal such as that which closes the dactyls in the violins somewhat) the third beat of each measure will, despite Mozart's phrasing, probably be perceived as an anacrusis, producing a series of low-level iambs:

♪ ♩ ♪ ♩ . But if the C in measure 29 is thus emphasized, then the B

(meas. 30) will seem relatively weak and mobile; as a result, it will be unable to function as a provisional goal.[75] To put the matter in another way: melodic and rhythmic mobility are so enhanced by what the horns play that the closure and stability provided by harmony (the cadence to the tonic in meas. 30) are not sufficient—as they are in the first motive group of the Trio—to make the changing-note figure an audible alternative. Finally, it should be observed that the same emphasis that weakens the closure of the motive group, and in so doing masks the changing-note figure, reinforces the impression of high-level conjunct patterning from B to C. And this pattern, which is embedded both in the foreground linear motion within measures 27 and 29 (ex. 30, graph 3) and in the sequential succession of motive *m*, implies continuation to D (ex. 30, graph 4*b*).

High-level rhythmic structure, too, is more emphatically mobile and goal-directed. In Part I, as we saw (p. 708 ff. and ex. 11), motives *m* and *m*¹ could be understood prospectively as a sequential succession implying continuation and retrospectively as a pair of complementary patterns provisionally closed by the stability of tonic harmony. In the latter case, the final B functioned as an accented goal. In the return, on the other

74. They will tend to be so both because phrasing calls for a new tonguing or attack on the downbeat and because the skip—particularly that played by the second horn—will probably cause the performer to make the first note of the measure just a bit louder. In addition, the relative length of the downbeat may make it "sound" louder.

75. Note, too, that since there is no subsidiary gap in meas. 27, the B is deprived of whatever stability it might have had as a subordinate melodic goal (ex. 29, graph 2).

hand, the force of the sequential succession is noticeably enhanced, while that of the complementary motive group is considerably diminished. The palpability of the sequential aspect of the patterning, together with the fact that the B in measure 30 is patently a mobile weak beat, calls attention to the similarity of the primary-level amphibrachs (ex. 30, level 1). Alternative ways of symbolizing the larger rhythmic structure are given in example 30. In the first, two levels are represented: the lower (2a) is analyzed as an open trochee, the higher (3) as a mobile anacrusis. In the second, only one level is represented: the first amphibrach on level 1 is symbolized as being initially understood as stable and accented and then, in retrospect, as being mobile and weak. The second amphibrach is also anacrustic. But no matter how the relationships are symbolized, what is implied is continuation—probably to a longer group which will serve as the accent in terms of which these similar groups can be patterned. The analysis indicates that such a group follows. But, as is the case with high-level melodic patterns, it does not do so immediately.

The proximate implications of the gap-fill processes are realized first (ex. 31B, graphs 1a and 1b). Though this aspect of melodic patterning is essentially the same as in Part I (compare exx. 31A and 31B, graphs 1a and 1b), the cadence is modified. The modifications, which can for the most part be attributed to subsequent changes in the return, affect the closure of the phrase, though not radically. Harmonically, the cadence (ex. 31B, meas. 31–32) is authentic (V⁷–I) but not complete. The decisive definition provided by subdominant harmony (ii§) in Part I is missing. So is the progression from the submediant (vi) through a series of harmonies whose roots are a fifth apart (ex. 31A, graph 2). Both changes are understandable in the light of what follows. Since no modulation occurs (as it did in Part I, meas. 10–14), the complete cadence in measures 37–38 is in the tonic. Had the earlier cadence (meas. 31–32) been complete, the articulative force of the later one would have been weaker by comparison. Similarly, had the progression moved through the submediant (vi), that harmony would be a bit less effective when it subsequently acts as the goal of the deceptive cadence (ex. 31B, meas. 36).[76] In one respect, however, harmonic closure is more stable than it was in Part I; that is, the tonic chord on the first beat of measure 32 is in root position rather than in first inversion (ex. 31A, meas. 6). This difference is related to the change in texture.

In the return, the texture of the first phrase (meas. 26–32) is wholly homophonic. The canon between the second violins and the celli (ex. 31A, graph 3), which led to the first-inversion triad on the downbeat of measure 6,[77] is gone, and with it the impetus of contrapuntal interaction

---

76. Because of the modulation in meas. 8–14, no anticipation occurs in Part I.
77. See p. 706 above.

and the mobility of harmonic inversion. A clear figure/ground relationship fosters stability and contributes to closure. Though probably a consequence of the harmonic considerations just described—it is difficult to say because the relation of texture to harmony is a chicken-and-egg affair—the change in texture can also be accounted for in terms of subsequent events. For immediately following the cadence (meas. 32), intensity increases as imitative entries occur at one-measure intervals (meas. 32–35) rather than following the length of the two-measure module prevalent elsewhere in the Trio. Had the cadential measures been contrapuntal, the ensuing intensification would have been less effective.

Rhythmic structure is significantly affected by these textural/harmonic changes. Because the suspension in the violas and the upbeats in the second violins and celli (ex. 31*A*, meas. 4–5) emphasize the downbeat of measure 5, the high-level rhythm of the cadence of the first phrase is an open amphibrach.[78] These are absent in Part II. As a result, the eighth notes at the end of measure 31 tend to be grouped with the accent which follows. The clearly end-accented accompaniment in

the violas and celli (♪ ♩ ♩ ♩), reinforcing this grouping, is the more em-

phatic because it "resolves" the ambiguity of the weak beats in the accompaniment figure of measures 28 and 30 (ex. 31*B*, graph 2). Are they

afterbeats in a dactyl (♩ ♪ ♪) or upbeats in an anapest (♪ ♪ ♪ ♩)?

In short, despite the tendency of the strengthened amphibrach grouping of measures 26–30 to be continued as a way of patterning events, the rhythm of the cadence is more clearly end accented—more closed—than was the analogous cadence in Part I.[79]

On balance, changes in harmony, texture, and rhythm probably strengthen cadential closure. Paradoxically, melody, the parameter which seems least altered, is very influential. And it weakens the impression of closure. Because the middleground gap-fill patterns (ex. 31*B*, graphs 1*a* and 1*b*) are patent in the return, motion to G is clearly implied, and the realization of this goal enhances stability and closure. But the effect of realization is more than offset by the increased force of the sequential and linear processes discussed earlier (ex. 31*B*, graphs 3 and 4). These higher-level processes are important not only because of *what* they imply but because their realization affects the relationship between the first and second phrases of the return, making them more cohesive than the comparable phrases in Part I.

78. See p. 707 above.
79. All symbolization, whether of harmonic, melodic, or rhythmic relationships, involves schematization and, hence, some degree of distortion. In this case, I fear, the symbolization of rhythmic relationships is even less adequate than usual.

EXAMPLE 31

146

Despite the connection created by foreground triadic motion in Part I,[80] the phrase that follows the cadence in measure 6 is in important ways a new beginning. It is not merely that it is preceded by a complete cadence. Because the opening motive (*m*) is varied (motive *o*) *at the same pitch level* (ex. 31*A*, graph 4), the separation or discreteness of the phrases, rather than their continuity, is emphasized. The sense of a "fresh start" is, needless to say, reinforced by the striking change in orchestration —from strings to oboes.

In the return, on the other hand, what follows the cadence in measure 32 is understood more as a continuation than as a new beginning. Not only are implicative patterns begun or resumed in the transition realized after the cadence (ex. 27) but the sequential and linear processes regenerated at the start of the return are continued—and by the same instruments, the horns—immediately following the cadence (ex. 31*B*, graphs 3 and 4).[81] Though the continuation begins in a register lower than that of the generative process, octave transfer through the tonic triad ensures that the implicative relationships are perceptible. For the sequential continuation, B–D, occurs in both registers, and the motion to C (meas. 34) makes it evident that the pattern is intact. Similarly, though the structural D (meas. 33) is transformed into an appoggiatura when it reaches the upper register, the clarity of the octave transfer leaves no doubt that the high-level linear motion has been properly continued.

Though by no means as forceful as in the return (note the difference made by the horns!), both these continuations were potential in the first phrase of the Trio.[82] Their delayed actualization, following regeneration, gives rise to the kind of satisfaction experienced when something only dimly discerned becomes clearly manifest.

Notice, too, that the foreground melodic/rhythmic patterns which were discrepant in motives *m* and *o* are now "in phase" (see pp. 711–12 above). That is, the first note of motive o^3 is now a mobile pitch (the third of the scale, B) as well as a mobile element in the rhythmic group. The equilibrium created by this congruence complements and enhances the sense of arrival created by the realization of melodic implications.

The continuation of high-level melodic processes calls attention to

80. See pp. 710–13 above; also ex. 17, graphs 1*a* and 2.

81. This suggests another reason why the harmonic progression in meas. 31–32 is changed in the return; namely, a complete cadence would have weakened the impression of continuity between phrases. One other, minor, point: since it suggests that the second phrase may begin on G (see n. 19 above) rather than on B, creating sequential continuation, the canon in meas. 4–6 is also inappropriate in this cadence.

82. This analysis indicates that the continuation of the first violins to D in meas. 14 (see p. 716 above) is only provisional—both because the D functions as the temporary tonic of D major rather than the fifth of G, and because it does not follow from the sequential process. I.e., though appropriate and hence satisfying, the D is in a sense the result of a happy coincidence: the violins simply "pick up" a note which really comes from a different processive relationship—the descending fill being played by the oboes.

147

another, perhaps more debatable, relationship—one probably recognized largely in retrospect. Namely, the implication, or at least the possibility, that the subsidiary will become the primary. For when the main gap-fill pattern continues sequentially, reaching B-D to C (meas. 32–34), what had been a low-level, subsidiary relationship in the violins (meas. 1 and 27) and eliminated from the horn part (meas. 27) becomes part of the main gap-fill process (ex. 31B, graph 5a).[83] The parallelism is quite apparent. Just as the C (meas. 1 or 27) implies and moves to the B (meas. 4 or 30) after two measures of dominant harmony, so the C (meas. 34) implies and moves to B (meas. 36) after the intervention of dominant harmony. The transformation of a subsidiary process into a primary one is authenticated at the cadence (meas. 36–38) where the same gap-fill pattern begins the closing gesture (ex. 31, graph 5b).

Here a hypothesis suggested earlier (pp. 720–21) is compositionally confirmed. That is, that the opening motive (*m*) of the Trio and the closing gesture of the second phrase (*p*) are related by similarity.[84] But with this qualification: the closing gesture is directly related not to the main gap-fill pattern of motive m^2, but to the subsidiary one. The change in roles is symbolized in the cadence. There what had been subsidiary (the B-D to C gap fill) is the main melody played by the flute, and what had been primary (the G-B to A gap fill) is an accompaniment played by the oboe (ex. 31B, graph 3b).

Phrase 2ª (meas. 32–38) and codetta (meas. 38–42).—The continuation of the main gap-fill process in the second phrase of the return, though unmistakable, is not exact. The size of the gap is increased and its structure modified by the appoggiatura figure in measure 34 (ex. 31B, graphs 1a–1d). As a result, the high-level processes (ex. 31B, graphs 3 and 4), which were derived from the succession of middleground gap-fill patterns, are ended—superseded by the extended fill that follows (ex. 27, graph 2c). As we have seen, the horns begin the larger gap an octave below the register in which the pattern was previously stated. Because of their range, this is unavoidable if events in the return are to parallel (rhyme with) those in Part I. It is appropriate because the register reached after the octave transfer is the one required for proper process continuation. And it is desirable because the extension of the gap by an octave strengthens the implication of descending conjunct motion and, in so doing, makes further sequential and linear patterning improbable.

Continuation of these processes is doubtful for other reasons as well. (1) Because it is the fifth of the scale, the accented D (meas. 33 and

---

83. In a sense, what was denied to the horns in the first phrase of the return is given to them in the second. Clearly it was denied not only for the reasons discussed earlier but because the horns could not have played the second subsidiary gap—the one from C to E (meas. 29).

84. The relationship between motives *m* and *o* (see p. 713) is "reconfirmed" by the sequential succession from m^2 to m^3 to o^3 (=m^4).

34) can easily function as both a termination point and a reversal point for the preceding pattern.[85] (2) The possibility of termination and reversal of direction becomes a virtual certainty when, following octave transfer (meas. 33), the D becomes an appoggiatura implying resolution to C.[86] And (3) these local patterns only corroborate what is clear from the larger relationships within the Trio; that is, the parallelism between the return and Part I makes it almost certain that an extended fill will follow the expanded gap of measures 32–34 as it did earlier in measures 6–12.

The parallelism continues as the bassoons and then the flute and oboe enter in modified imitation of the horns. But there are significant differences. The bassoons enter before the flute and first oboe (ex. 31*B*, meas. 33–35) rather than the other way around (ex. 31*A*, meas. 8–11), and imitation occurs after only three, rather than six, beats. To explain these changes, relationships between sections as well as those within the return must be considered.

1. The entrances of the bassoons and then of the flute (together with the first oboe) are explicitly connected with the end of the transition where these instruments stopped playing (ex. 27). Though in a lower register, the bassoons begin their imitation with the same pitch and interval—an octave D—which they ended on in measure 26. After moving through the deceptive cadence (meas. 36) and participating in the performance of the complete cadence (meas. 36–38), they reach satisfactory closure as they play the cadential figure with the first violins (meas. 38–40).[87]

It will be recalled that the flute is responsible for the continuation of two processes: the long-range descending fill begun in measure 10 (ex. 28*A*), and the subsidiary, rising conjunct motion generated in measures 19–23 (ex. 28*B*). The first note of its imitation, F-sharp, resumes the subsidiary process which, after an octave transfer, is completed by motion to the high G (ex. 31*B*, meas. 36).[88] The second note of the imita-

85. The fifth of the scale can be a terminal point because, since it belongs to both the dominant and the tonic triads, it is relatively stable and can function as a provisional goal. It often acts as a turning point in melodic patterns because continuing up beyond the fifth to the tonic (the next stable tone) requires special energy.

86. Moreover, insofar as motive o^3 is understood to be a sequential continuation of motives m^2 and m^3, it will probably be presumed to be the last event in the larger pattern. For sequences do not usually consist of more than three successive statements of a motive because a fourth tends to produce pairing—(2 + 2) + (2 + 2)—so that a higher-level duple pattern (4 + 4) is formed.

87. The bassoons' participation in the performance of the cadential figure in the return helps to bind the codetta to the preceding phrases. In addition, it is appropriate —perhaps even necessary—because the "early" entrance of the bassoons' imitation entails a prolongation of goal-directed, dominant harmony (meas. 35). And the increased momentum that results may not be adequately dissipated by the cadences in meas. 36 and 38.

88. Observe that since it was generated on (notated) third beats, the subsidiary process is related to the F-sharp at the end of meas. 34 by metric placement as well as by the continuation of linear patterning.

tion, the accented A, is part of the main process—the descending fill which was from the first defined by structural tones. And the same pitch (A) was last played by the same instruments (flute and first oboe) at the same interval (an octave) and in the same register where the main process "broke off"—that is, at the end of the transition.

Had the pattern played by the bassoons been given to the flute and oboe (with appropriate changes in register) and vice versa, these relationships would not have been preserved. Or, if the flute had entered a measure earlier (and the bassoons a measure later), the flute would have had to continue the high F-sharp throughout measure 35. As a result, the G in measure 36 would have been less stable because, like the D in measure 12, it would have been unable fully to accommodate the momentum and tension of the long, leading-tone anacrusis. Put the other way around: the abbreviated anacrusis in the flute/oboe part reduces the mobility of the high G. It is perhaps partly for this reason that the G can be phrased with the following B instead of being "left hanging" as the D was.[89]

2. The stability of the deceptive cadence and hence of its resolution, G, is also enhanced by the change of distance between imitative entrances. This change can probably be attributed in part to the fact that no modulation occurs in the second phrase of the return. Only two chords, tonic and dominant, precede the deceptive cadence in measure 36. To compensate for the resulting loss of motion, previously created by modulation (ex. 31A, meas. 6–14), texture is intensified through a kind of "stretto." That is, though each motive (o^3, o^4, and o^5) is basically two measures long, imitation takes place after only one measure. The piling up of overlapping entrances creates the cumulative, goal-directed tension required.

The intensification of texture not only enhances goal-directed motion, but, paradoxically, the stability and closure of both the deceptive and the complete cadences (meas. 36 and 38). This occurs because the change of distance between imitative entrances affects the morphology of motive group 2^a (meas. 32–36) as a whole. For instead of being additive (6 + 6 + 6 beats) and relatively open as was the equivalent passage in Part I (meas. 6–12), motive group 2^a is cumulative (3 + 3 + 6 beats) and somewhat closed. In rhythmic terms, the group is an end-accented anapest: ⌣ ⌣ —. The stability that results curbs the momentum developed in the preceding measures and thereby enables the closure created by other parameters to be more effective.

Harmonically, the cadences in Part II (meas. 36 and 38) are more stable than the equivalent cadences in Part I (meas. 12 and 14) because they are in the tonic.[90] Partly, stability is enhanced because textural inten-

89. The G is more stable than the D for other reasons as well (see below).

90. Perhaps, too, the cadence in meas. 36–38 seems more closed because it is complete, while the preceding cadence (meas. 31–32) is only authentic.

sity is "resolved" into congruent, homophonic motion. More important, stability and closure are strengthened because, as we have seen, melodic processes begun earlier are satisfactorily realized at these cadences. Let us review them briefly. In addition to the reasons already mentioned, the G in measure 36 is more stable than the comparable D in measure 12 because it is the goal of the subsidiary melodic process generated in measures 19–23 (ex. 28*B*). The D (meas. 12), on the other hand, is a temporary deflection of the gap-fill pattern begun by the flute in measure 8 and resumed by it toward the end of the transition (ex. 28*A*). That pattern is continued and satisfactorily completed when the structural A (left in meas. 26, picked up in measure 35, and renewed as an upbeat in meas. 37) moves to G as part of a complete cadence.

Although the tonic is reached as part of a complete cadence, the Trio cannot end here. The formal parallelism—the rhyme—with the close of Part I is incomplete, and the four-measure length latent in the morphology of the first phrase of the return ([2 + 2] + 2) remains to be actualized.[91] Nor has the main melodic process begun by the oboes in measure 6 been satisfactorily closed (ex. 22, graphs 1*a*–1*c*). For instead of moving directly through a structural A to G in measures 37–38, as they might have done (see below), the horns (the surrogates for the oboes) halt their conjunct descent at the deceptive cadence in measure 36. Because it is the structural tone with which the sequential motion of the return began, B is a plausible stopping place. That is, as example 32 (graph 1) shows, the structural tones of the sequence move from B (meas. 27) through C (meas. 29) to D (meas. 33–34) and conjunctly back to B (meas. 36). On a high level, then, it might be argued that measures 27–36 are basically a prolongation of the third of the scale ornamented by double upper neighbor-notes.[92] Though there is provisional closure

91. See the discussion (pp. 709–10) of the comparable relationships in Part I.

92. Since the B in meas. 27 is equivalent to that in meas. 1, it might seem that all that follows the first structural B is a prolongation which moves at last through A to G. And this might in turn suggest to some that the analysis given here is derived from the theories of Heinrich Schenker. However, without in any way minimizing the debt owed to Schenker, there are fundamental differences between the implication/realization model employed in this essay and the *Ursatz* model developed by Schenker and his disciples. For the Schenkerites posit the existence of a single archetypal structure (the *Ursatz*) which is realized as a specific musical composition through a set of invariant transformations. The implication/realization model, on the other hand, is pluralistic with respect to style as well as structure. It assumes the progressive generation of alternative processes within different parameters. The realization of these alternative processes, often delayed through parametric noncongruence, need not be simultaneous. In the analysis presented in this essay, for instance, implications generated by the oboes in meas. 6–8 are ultimately realized by the French horns at the close of the codetta; subsidiary processes generated by the flute and oboes in the transition are completed by the flute in meas. 36 and by the oboes in meas. 41–42. The listener's confidence in his own competence does not depend upon his comprehension of a single "deep structure." Rather, it receives periodic support from the provisional or full realization over time of a number of alternative patterns. For this reason enjoyment does not depend upon exhaustive comprehension.

on B, continuation is forcefully implied, both for reasons mentioned earlier: (1) the third of the scale is the most mobile note of the tonic triad, (2) once begun, the descending motion (D–C–B) implies continuation to a point of stability, (3) the B is harmonized by a submediant chord (vi) rather than the tonic (I)—and because at the end of the transition the main process had already moved beyond B to A.

EXAMPLE 32

The delay in the continuation of the horn pattern joins the final cadence of the Trio to the main gap-fill process and, in so doing, welds the codetta to earlier phrases.[93] It is interesting in this connection to note what Mozart does *not* do. The horns could have joined in the performance of the complete cadence (meas. 36–38), as part 2*a* of example 32 shows. But this anticipation would not only have detracted from the importance of the final cadence but would have weakened the bonding of the codetta to what precedes it. The horns might also have performed the closing figure in measures 41–42, as they did in measures 31–32 (ex. 32, graph 2*b*). But then the relationship between what the horns play at the final cadence and what they played earlier would not have been as clear. For the repeated cadential figure (ex. 32, graph 2*b*) would have been related to the earlier one (meas. 31–32) rather than to the descending fill which the horns continue and close.

The codetta of the return is more closely linked to preceding phrases than was that of Part I in other ways as well. By continuing beyond the cadence in measure 38, the bassoon, as we have seen, creates a structural and timbral coherence. The flute's participation in the final statement of the closing figure reiterates its descent from A to G and thereby reinforces the closure of the process it began in measure 8. As in Part I, there is an elision between the end of phrase 2 and the beginning of the codetta. The violins begin the closing figure at the same time that the upper woodwinds reach cadential resolution. But whereas in Part I the violins played the D implied by the sequential process of the first four measures, they need not do so in the return because the D is realized by the horns at the beginning of the second phrase. The register in which the violins play indicates that the G reached in measure 32 is their ultimate goal. In the codetta, they serve to prolong the closing figure until the morphological length implied by the first phrase of the return is reached and, at the same time, act as a common term connecting the bassoon's performance of the closing figure with that of the flute.

* * *

Mozart's Trio consists, then, of a complex network of distinguishable, but interconnected, relationships: conformant, processive, and hierarchic. Like the personae in a novel or a history, conformance —motivic, textural, or harmonic similarity—fosters coherence and provides the constancy in terms of which change can be comprehended. And, as in carefully constructed narrative, each of the alternative, yet complementary, processive strands is ultimately resolved and reaches satisfactory closure. The musical structure of the whole, however, is more formal and more patently hierarchic than is generally the case with

93. As noted earlier, the oboes complete their subsidiary pattern here (see p. 741). Since the close of the flute's primary pattern is reiterated in meas. 41–42, three alternative processes converge and are realized in the final cadence of the Trio.

most verbal narratives. This is so because, since music is not explicitly representational, pattern repetition and return are indispensable if tones are to form separable parts and parts are to combine into intelligible wholes.

Thus far nothing has been said about the emotional response elicited by these relationships. Nor has the ethos—the feeling-tone or character—of the music been considered. These have received short shrift not because they are unimportant but because it is both difficult to describe and problematic to explain the effective experiences evoked by works of art. The difficulties, and perhaps the problems as well, are compounded when, as in the case of music, the personae and processive "plots" are without semantic content and, hence, nonrepresentational. For we tend not only to classify and describe but even to recognize and comprehend affective experiences in terms of the external circumstances in which they take place and which are thought to occasion them.

The problems are not, however, due solely to the inadequacies of language or to the absence of representation. They also stem from the uncertainties and confusions which continue to plague our understanding of affective experience—whether elicited by works of art or by events in "real" life.[94] For present purposes, two different sorts of experience, often included under the general term "affective," must be distinguished. The first, "emotional response," which changes over time, is a direct result of (and consequently congruent with) cognitive activity. It involves intricate patternings of anticipation and tension, delay and denial, fulfillment and release. If we assume that cognition of the conformant, processive, and hierarchic relationships peculiar to a work of art evokes and shapes this facet of affective experience, then the analysis presented in this essay of implication and mobility, deflection and parametric noncongruence, closure and realization is analogically—or by extrapolation—an account of what a competent listener's emotional response to Mozart's Trio would be like.

94. To the best of my knowledge, there is no generally accepted theory which explains, with precision and rigor, how affective experience and the cognition of complex patterns are related to one another. As I observed in an earlier issue of this journal: "Psychology, the science upon which such a theory must ultimately be founded, has not been able satisfactorily to explain how even simple patterns are perceived, comprehended, and remembered, or how such cognitive behavior is related to intellectual and affective experience" ("Concerning the Sciences, the Arts—AND the Humanities," *Critical Inquiry* 1, no. 1 [September 1974]: 193). It should be emphasized that the relationship between cognition and affective experience is reciprocal. Affective experience—particularly emotional response—is as a rule a consequence of cognition. Tension and release, joy and sorrow are, i.e., occasioned by our understanding of events in the world. (There are, of course, feelings—e.g., exhilaration or depression—that may result from physiological causes, as when we get up in the morning feeling energetic or listless, etc.) Conversely, cognition is usually, perhaps invariably, qualified by affective experience.

Ethos refers to those aspects of affective experience which remain relatively constant over time and which are the basis for the characterization of all or part of a composition.[95] Mozart's Trio, for instance, has been characterized as a "moment of sunshine . . . calm, reposeful, pellucid, truly idyllic . . . charming . . . pure and calm . . . so Elysian a grace . . ."[96] Clearly, the ethos that Saint-Foix describes is delineated by the absence of extremes (or abrupt contrasts) of tempo and register, dynamics and sonority, together with the use of simple, even commonplace, grammatical/syntactic means—melodies made up of easily grasped intervals, flowing rhythms without marked durational differences, regular meter (with a touch of ambiguity at times), and common triads and chord progressions.

But affective experience is not, as these distinctions seem to suggest, really divided. Ethos and emotion invariably qualify one another. As a result, the foreground simplicity of Mozart's Trio is tinged with the tension of relational richness. Patent goal-directed processes prevent "calm" from being complacence and "repose" from being indolence; delay and deflection qualify "grace" and "charm" so that the former is not merely facile and the latter not merely perfunctory. Throughout, relational richness keeps the "pellucid" from being obvious, the "idyllic" from seeming fatuous.[97]

The delineation of ethos is also a matter of context. The serenity, grace, and simplicity of the Trio are especially apparent because they are in marked contrast to the dynamism, irregularity, and complexity of the Minuetto which precedes and follows. The Minuetto is in the minor mode, the Trio in the major; the Minuetto's dynamics are generally *forte*, those of the Trio, *piano;* the rhythm of the Minuetto is vigorous and syncopated, that of the Trio is smooth and flowing; the Minuetto is largely contrapuntal, the Trio homophonic—and one could continue listing differences.

But there are similarities as well. The main motive of the Minuetto (ex. 33, motive *r*), like that of the Trio (motive *m*), consists of a triad that begins on an upbeat (ex. 33, graphs 1*a*–1*c*); and, as in the Trio, part of the triad functions as a gap which is subsequently filled (ex. 33, graphs

---

95. Broadly speaking, ethos is delineated both by the disposition of relatively stable parameters (e.g., tempo and register, dynamic level and mode) and by foreground grammatical/syntactic organization (kinds of intervals, rhythmic figures, harmonies and chord progressions). Particularly when these combine to form a conventional iconic gesture—as they do, e.g., at the beginning of Chopin's famous funeral march—poignant feelings may be evoked, even though process and form have yet to shape emotional responses.

96. G. de Saint-Foix, *The Symphonies of Mozart* (London, 1947), pp. 119–20. Other writers consulted used the same or similar terms to describe the Trio.

97. In general, if ethos is to "ring true," it must be justified by the larger syntactic structure. "Empty bombast" is emphatic insistence without relational support.

EXAMPLE 33

2*a*–2*d*).[98] In both, motives move sequentially.[99] The most patent similarity is between the second statement of the Minuetto motive (*r*^{1}) and the first statement of the Trio motive (*m*); except for the difference in mode, the pitch patterns are almost identical (ex. 33, graph 4). Because the last six measures of the Minuetto are based upon the first six, a slightly varied version of motive *r*^{1} is followed directly by its counterpart in the Trio (ex. 34, graph 1). The relationship is made particularly clear because the coda of the Minuetto "prepares" the listener for the Trio through changes in dynamics, orchestration, texture, and sonority. Even the transformation of the second part of motive *r*^{1} into a cadential gesture finds its parallel in the closing figure of the first phrase of the Trio

EXAMPLE 34

98. Observe that the gap of Minuetto motive *r*^{1} (graph 2*b*) is equivalent to the subsidiary gap of Trio motive *m* (graph 2*d*). This subsidiary gap, it will be recalled, becomes the primary gap in phrase 2^a of the return (ex. 31, graph 5*a*), and this, in a sense, "prepares" for the repetition of the Minuetto.

99. But the Minuetto motive moves up disjunctly, by thirds, while the Trio motive moves up conjunctly (ex. 33, graphs 3*a* and 3*b*). Despite this difference, both patterns imply continuation to a D (in parentheses). This is so because the succession of structural tones is different; i.e., G–B-flat–D in the Minuetto, and B–C–D in the Trio.

(ex. 34, graph 2).[100] The juxtaposition of like motives emphasizes contrasts in the disposition and organization of those parameters most responsible for the delineation of ethos.[101] As a result, the ethos of the Trio is specified by its similarities to, as well as its differences from, the Minuetto.[102]

* * *

I am aware that there will be disagreements not only about particular points made in the preceding analysis but about fundamental premises. Alternative hypotheses are certainly possible, and these will undoubtedly call attention to and illuminate relationships I have failed to notice or have unwittingly neglected. Some differences will be matters of emphasis. For instance, it might be urged with some justice that matters of stylistic context should have played a more important role in my explanation of the relationships in Mozart's Trio. But whatever the basis for disagreement, what seems crucial is that premises be made explicit and arguments from them consistent. This I have tried to do.

Others will find the whole enterprise repugnant—feeling that a tedious dissection has destroyed a fragile flower of the human spirit. Though no reply will allay such reservations, I have taken the liberty of quoting a paragraph from the preface to *Explaining Music*. It seems appropriate to do so since, as noted earlier, the present essay is in part an attempt to show that concepts and methods developed in that book can account with some rigor for the ways in which musical relationships are understood by, and shape the experience of, competent listeners.

> The relationships among events within musical compositions—even seemingly simple ones—are frequently surprisingly complex and subtle. The analyses explaining them are, accordingly, often complicated and involved. I have not sought to simplify the difficult, or to gloss over intricate interactions with plausible generalities and vague poetic appeals. Rather I have tried to make my analyses as precise and specific as my abilities and the subject allow. And while I take no particular pleasure in long and sometimes difficult discussion, I know of no other way of doing justice to the wonder of music and the miracle of human intelligence which makes and comprehends it. [P. x]

100. Because the Trio ends with the first closing figure played by the flute, there is a "rhyme" with the coda of the Minuetto. There are other reminiscences of the Minuetto in the Trio. For instance, the syncopated fourth played by the viola in meas. 4–5 of the Trio seems to recall the main motive of the Minuetto (ex. 34, graph 3).

101. Although changes at its close prepare us for what is to follow, the coda of the Minuetto remains, as it were, within the hegemony of the ethos of the Minuetto, as the presence of chromatic counterpoint and harmony indicate.

102. This suggests that motivic variation and transformation are important not primarily because they "unify" compositions but because motivic constancy makes differences in ethos more palpable. If this is correct, then it is not surprising that motivic development is especially characteristic of styles, such as those of the Baroque and Romantic periods, which stress the importance of ethos.

Appendix

158

760

159

The Trio of Mozart's G Minor Symphony. Reproduced by permission from Norton Critical Scores, Wolfgang Amadeus Mozart, *Symphony in G minor, K. 550*, ed. Nathan Broder (New York: W. W. Norton & Co., 1967), pp. 44–45.

The Tristan Prelude

TECHNIQUES AND STRUCTURE

WILLIAM J. MITCHELL

RICHARD WAGNER's Einleitung or Vorspiel to *Tristan and Isolde*, completed more than one hundred years ago, remains a challenge and an enigma. A simple count of the number of analyses that have been attempted since its publication, and a superficial comparison of them, would suffice to prove this.[1] Relatively few analysts, however, have reported on the entire Prelude, or in fact on much more than the first three bars, and then only to unravel the mystery of the sonority of bar 2, the so-called "Tristan chord."

It is not the intention of this article to review these countless analyses. Suffice it to say that many of them are resoundingly vacuous, others have moments of revealing insights, and the vast majority are committed to the point of view that if all chords are properly labeled and the modulations tabulated, the result will be one Prelude analyzed. To be sure, lip service is paid to the role of linear elements, but these seem to be confined to appoggiaturas and half-step progressions.

The aim here will be, rather, to approach the work in terms of its linear-harmonic elements, and to attempt to arrive at a view of the entire work as a unified, articulated structure. The assumptions behind such an undertaking are that: (1) there are discoverable morphological meanings in the lines and harmonies; (2) these can pave the way to the comprehension of an embracing structure reaching from the beginning to the end. The validity of

---

[1] Among the more recent analyses are those by Wolfgang Fortner in *Kontrapunkte*, Band 4, p. 101 f.; P. J. Tonger, *Musikverlage* (Rhoden- kirchen/Rhein); and Ernest Ansermet, *Les fonde- ments de la musique dans la conscience humaine* (Neuchatel, Baconniere, 1961), pp. 303–8.

the assumptions must rest ultimately on the results achieved, the ways in which they are achieved, and the revitalizing view of the Prelude that they might provide.

The beginning of the Prelude is easy enough to locate; the end is another matter, since the work leads directly into Act I, Scene 1. Wagner provides us with valuable assistance in our search, for he composed a concert ending dated "Paris, December 15, 1859."[2] This ending of twenty-four bars, based on the closing pages of Act III, but clearly in A major, is dovetailed into the preceding Prelude in such a manner that bar 93 of the Prelude as usually performed is extended to two bars. In the new bar, bar 95, a plagally inflected A-chord replaces the accustomed F-chord of bar 94. There follows the remainder of the bars mentioned above. Wagner, in my view, heard the Prelude in A major-minor. The concert ending, placed by him in A, adds a substantial confirmation (see Example 1).

161

THE INCLUSIVE PLAN

IT WAS with reluctance that I decided to present a frame of reference for the entire Prelude before turning to the details. The decision was prompted by a desire to expedite as much as possible the analysis of an admittedly complex composition. The complications spring not only from the richness of detail, but also from the length of the work in terms of tempo as well as the actual number of bars. It is hoped that any seeming arbitrariness in the sketches of Example 2 will be removed by the analysis of detail to follow. Suffice it to say that in the analysis of the work, the inclusive plan was induced from the cumulative evidence of the detail, rather than the detail deduced from a preordained plan.

Example 2a presents the essential features of the outer parts in a linear-harmonic sketch. The upper part is notated in its proper register, but the bass has been assigned a register of convenience. Its proper octave registers will be indicated in the analysis of detail. Major-minor mixtures, so

---

[2] It appears in a keyboard score as an insert after p. 272 in *Richard Wagner, Wesendonk Briefe* (Leipzig, Hesse and Becker Verlag). As an orchestral ending incorporated into the Prelude, it has been published as *Vorspiel zu Tristan und Isolde* von Richard Wagner (Leipzig, Breitkopf and Härtel).

EXAMPLE I

162

EXAMPLE I (*continued*)

163

Paris 15 Dez. 59

EXAMPLE 2

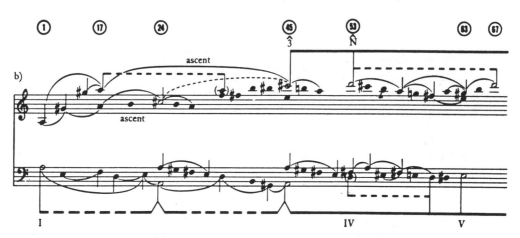

164

characteristic of the chromatic bent of the Prelude, intrude into the first sketches. Of interest in this respect is the predominance of the major mode, brought about by the long ascent to c♯³. Following the neighbor d³, c♮³ replaces the major third momentarily, but the concert ending clearly affirms A major, as do most of the details, despite the minor color of the opening bars. The bass also participates in mixed colors, asserting f¹ and b♮ (as a lowered or Phrygian second step) before the closing cadential bars.

Example 2b presents some of the detail of a higher order. Up to bar 45, the A-chord, with the help of two harmonically oriented prolongations in the bass (bars 1–24, 24–45), works toward the structurally significant c♯³. It is through a change of octave registers that this goal is achieved. Note that, after the opening a, a¹, a² have been established, an ascent to c♯² occurs (bars 1–24). Only after this (bars 24–45) is the dominating upper-

EXAMPLE 2 (*continued*)

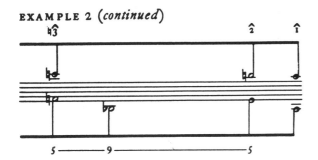

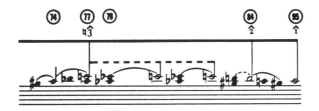

voice register attained. Bars 53–62 unroll an extended subdominant harmony as consonant support for the neighbor d³. The entry and extension of the dominant harmony (bars 63–73) presents d³ as a seventh which ultimately (bars 74–77) resolves to c³ supported by f. It is here that the delirious abandon of the music makes the case for A major momentarily dubious (bars 79–83), until in bar 84 the dominant harmony is asserted. It rules until the arrival in bar 95 of the concluding A-major–chord, plagally suspended. As suggested by the total shape of the bass and the Roman numerals, the Prelude expresses the functions, nonmodulatory, of A, albeit with a high degree of chromaticism.

THE ANALYSIS OF SECTIONS

ALTHOUGH the Prelude is essentially a continuous structure, the layout of

Example 2b suggests a convenient subdivision into seven sections. These will be bars 1–17, 17–24, 24–45 (not 44), 45–63, 63–74, 74–84, 84–96, and further. As helpful as a keyboard reduction might seem, it is imperative that the orchestral score be the main, if not the sole, reference in the discussions that follow. Only one keyboard transcription[3] of the many that have been examined retains the all-important octave registrations of bars

EXAMPLE 3

166

---

[3] *Tristan und Isolde von Richard Wagner*, Vollständiger Klavierauszug von Karl Klindworth ("Universal Edition"; B. Schott's Söhne in Mainz, 1906).

55–60 and 74–76. But even this otherwise commendable setting is occasionally slipshod with respect to Wagner's phrasing slurs.

To facilitate references to motives used by Wagner in the course of the Prelude, the principal ones and the "Tristan chord" have been quoted in Example 3 and identified by means of a letter or, in the case of the Tristan chord, by a convenient abbreviation. It is by these tags that they shall be cited in the detailed analysis. Note that motives A^2, B, C, E, F, and G have in common a terminating rhythm of an eighth note followed by a quarter note, a feature that adds to their interrelationship. Similarly, all but the first of these contain a dotted eighth note followed by a sixteenth.

Bars 1–17. Although the opening bars, particularly the sonority *Tr* of bar 2, present a continuing challenge, the inclusive structure of the bass is clear. Its broad context is formed by the initial a making its way to F in bar 17. Between these, a prolonged arpeggiation of the E-chord takes place, consisting of e (bar 3), g (bar 7), b (bar 11), and E (bar 16). Each of these is preceded by the half step above as indicated in Examples 4a and 4b. Above this bass, the upper voice moves from the opening a to a^2 of bar 17. The connection between these two points is formed by the $g\sharp^1$ of bar 3 making an ascent in a stepwise motion consisting of four groups of three notes each until the terminal a^2 is reached (Example 4b). Observe, in Examples 4a and 4b, how this complete motion opens up three octave registers and, in the octave exchanges of bars 12–15, suggests hesitantly a higher register before settling on a^2 in bar 17. The underlying sense of these seventeen bars is represented in Example 4c.

The details of the section are highly interesting. As Wagner arpeggiates the tones of the E-chord, he uses the minor third, g, with its major chord in bar 8, rather than $g\sharp$ and a thankless diminished chord. The basis of such a technique is the chordal mixture wherein the major third, $g\sharp$, replaced by the minor third, g, is reasserted in bar 16. The process of extending an overall a to F by means of an arpeggiated E-chord is unusual. A far more frequent breaking prolongation is that of Example 5 in which the basis of arpeggiation is the prevailing $F\sharp$-minor tonic harmony.[4]

Although the ultimate reading in Example 5c departs from that of

[4] F. Chopin, Mazurka, Op. 30, No. 2, bars 24–32.

167

EXAMPLE 4

a)   Bars 1–17

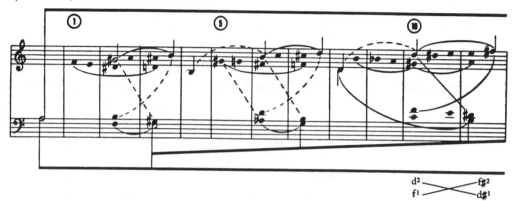

b)

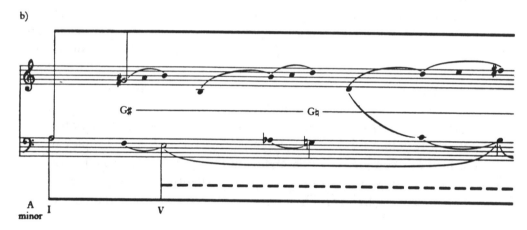

c)

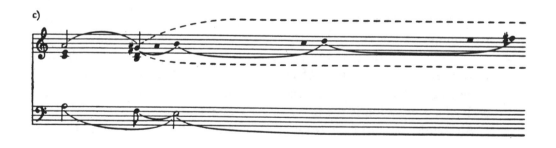

EXAMPLE 4 *(continued)*

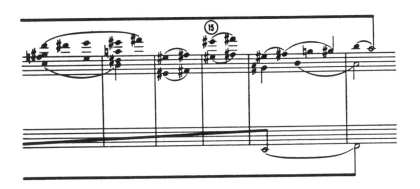

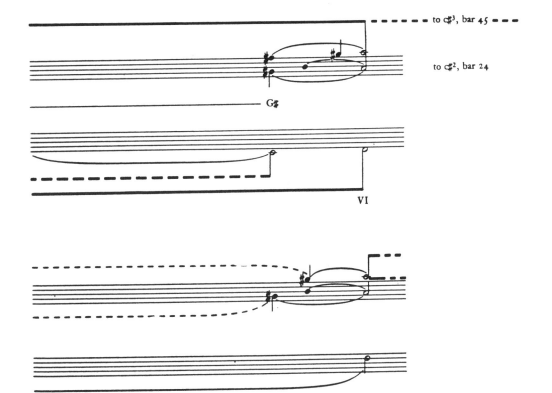

169

EXAMPLE 5

a)

170

b)

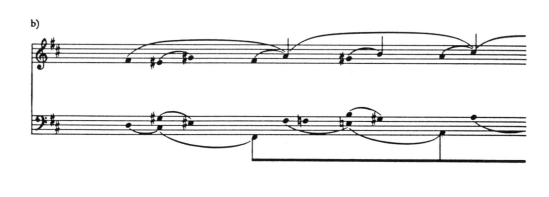

c)

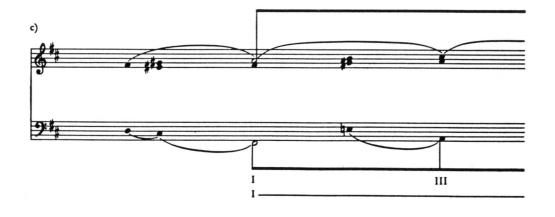

EXAMPLE 5 (*continued*)

171

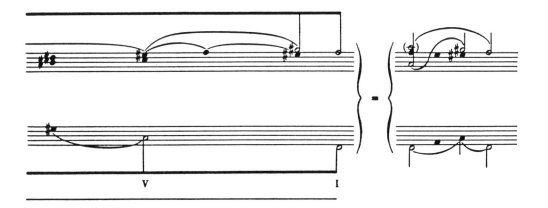

Example 4c, there are certain middle and foreground similarities that invite comparison and eventually help to arrive at an analysis of the first section of the Tristan Prelude. In both pieces, the interval of an augmented sixth appears frequently; in both pieces, likewise, the upper voice ascends in a quasi-sequential manner, the Prelude through a dominant chord arpeggiated, the Mazurka through a more usual tonic chord arpeggiated.

Let us examine the chord Tr in bar 2 of the Prelude. While Chopin's opening augmented sixth chord derives readily from a diatonic $^6_3$ (d, g♯, b, f♯[1]), by simply sharping the sixth, b, Tr does not submit so readily, for its immediate derivation is $^6_{4}$ (f, b, d[1], g♯[1]), a form of diminished seventh chord. This, in fact, is the historic derivation of the sonority.[5] In order to derive Tr from the source that provides Chopin with his chord (transposed to f, b, d[1], a[1]), g♯[1] must be regarded as a long appoggiatura, moving on the sixth beat of the bar to a[1], the 3 of $^6_3$. This is the prevailing contemporary analysis, represented by the Roman numeral II, and standing in the so-called second inversion.

Such a reading must be reassessed. Nothing that Wagner does with the chord suggests such a harmonic "functional" analysis. Note that the phrasing slur for the oboe in bars 2–3 begins on the g♯[1] under examination and carries through to b[1] (Example 6a). But this is not characteristic of the usual two-tone slur (g♯[1] to a[1]) for the indication and execution of an appoggiatura. It should also be observed that the oboe's g♯[1] to b[1] is accompanied by a very frequent kind of chordal interchange as the bassoon leaps from b to g♯ (Example 6b). Furthermore, the oboe's g♯[1], the alleged appoggiatura, rests in a much more comfortable sonority than the release, a[1], which forms part of the chord of the so-called double dissonance. Something is wrong here, for appoggiaturas, at least traditionally, move from relative stress to relative quiet (Example 6c). Closely related to the oboe's music in bars 2–3 is the initial passage of the cellos, which is transferred in bar 2 to the English horn in such a manner that, after the initial a, the cellos play

---

[5] A brief survey of the career of Tr in the hands of analysts appears in Alfred Lorenz, *Das Geheimnis der Form bei Richard Wagner* (Berlin, Max Hesses Verlag, 1926), II, 194 ff.

EXAMPLE 6

a)   The slur

b)   The interchange

c)   Tension-release?

d)   The motivic parallel

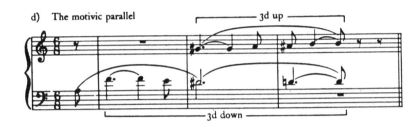

e)   The major seventh and the octaves

173

f^1–e^1–$d\sharp^1$, whereupon the English horn takes over to complete the motion from $d\sharp^1$ to d^1. Thus, a descending third, f^1–e^1–$d\sharp^1$–d^1, is answered by an ascending third, $g\sharp^1$–a^1–$a\sharp^1$–d^1 (Example 6d). Finally, the inclusive significance of $g\sharp^1$ is stressed by the fact that it stems from the opening a. This striking major seventh establishes a binding melodic connection which, considered with all of the preceding factors, must override any attempt to classify $g\sharp^1$ as an appoggiatura. Note that once the major seventh has been established, it is paralleled in bars 4–6 and 8–10 by the octaves b to b^1, d^1 to d^2 (Example 6e).

The reasons cited above seem persuasive, at least to this analyst, for regarding $g\sharp^1$ as a principal tone and a^1 as a dependent passing tone. Why is the prevailing analysis just the opposite? Probably, first, because the elevation of a^1 to the rank of a chord tone presents the analyst with a harmonic stereotype, a recurrent kind of augmented sixth chord. Probably, also because by a process of reverse harmonic expectancy, it would seem that the unmistakable dominant of bar 3 must have before it some recognizable kind of subdominant or supertonic chord. But such a mothering of the theory of harmonic functions seems excessive in the face of so many opposed textural and linear factors. Because $d\sharp^1$ of bar 2 is so clearly on the way to d^1 of bar 3, the underlying sonority of bar 2 has been represented in Example 4c as a form of diminished seventh chord, related generically to one of Beethoven's uses of it.[6]

The sonority of bar 6 has the same derivation as *Tr*, but bar 10 presents a different case. If Wagner had followed the line of least resistance and continued with the pattern established in bars 1–4 and 5–8, bar 11 would have produced a B♭-major–chord, as indicated in Example 7a. The basis of the manipulation employed to arrive at the B-major-chord, so essential an element in the broad arpeggiation of the E-chord (bars 3, 7, 11, 16), is shown in Example 7b. If additional justification of the present reading of an arpeggiated E-chord were needed, this particular summoning by Wagner of a B- rather than a B♭-chord would provide it.

A parting word must be addressed to the harmonic meaning of the opening upbeat and bar 1. The present tendency, with which I am in agreement,

[6] In Op. 13, 1st movement, *Grave*, bars 7–8, and in Op. 53, 2d movement, *Introduzione*, *Adagio molto*, bars 23–25. Attention is directed to the bass, A♭–G, in both instances.

EXAMPLE 7

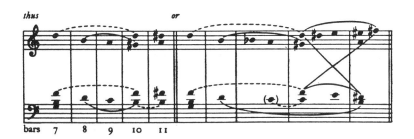

is to consider it I. In the past, the shape of the cellos' solo has been misinterpreted when the passage has been understood as an outlining of VI or IV.
The derivation is to be found less in the discipline of harmony than in that
of counterpoint. Example 8a illustrates a frequent kind of correction, in
the study of counterpoint, of the beginning of a fourth species exercise. Quite
correctly, a "license" is required, the addition of e^2 before f^2, in order to
clarify for the student the meaning of f^2 as a motion away from e^2, rather

than as a direct vertical offspring of the *cantus firmus* tone, a^1. In such didactic studies, literalness is required to derive techniques or explain meanings. In free composition, such literalness is certainly not required, nor to be expected. However, the study of counterpoint, if it has taught its lesson well, will take care of cases such as those of Example 8b, in which the fifth, though not literally present, remains nevertheless the implied linear source of the sixth.[7] In all of these cases, the harmonic meaning is uniformly i as indicated.

A highly interesting point arises when Wagner's sketches for the Prelude are consulted.[8] Originally the first note was b, and the corresponding note in bar 4 was d^1. Wagner's revisions are of critical importance. For one thing, the originally written diminished fifth b–f^1 creates a static environment, for both of these tones are contained in *Tr* which follows. Despite the tension of the diminished fifth, nothing happens. Compare this with the vital motion of a in the final version, as it moves to its successor, g♯^{1}, in *Tr*. Furthermore, the diminished fifth outlines an obvious supertonic chord, much less appropriate than the evasive minor sixth, a–f^1. As already observed, this latter interval has been variously analyzed as representing i, vi, or iv, by itself a telling indication of its suitableness to the groping, exploratory quality of the opening bars. Finally, from a broad structural point of view, a introduces the inclusive upper-voice tension of bars 1–17, consisting of a–g♯^{1}–a^2, while at the same time, as a partner in the motion, a–e–f, it contributes to the broad establishment of an enclosed A-chord in bars 1–17 and 17–24. The resultant structural balance is apparent in Example 2.

The case that follows from Wagner's decision to employ b rather than the originally sketched d^1 in bar 4 is similar to the earlier one. Aside from the superiority of b as a sequential consequent to the initial a, the resultant neutral sixth, b–g♯^{1} (bars 4–5), maintains better than d^1–g♯^{1} the tentative, searching quality of the early bars.

---

[7] Examples 8b(1) and 8b(2): J. S. Bach, opening of Praeludium XX, Book II, and opening of Praeludium XIX, Book I, *Well-Tempered Clavier*; Example 8b(3): W. A. Mozart, opening of the "Dissonance" Quartet; Example 8b(4): opening of the Tristan Prelude.

[8] Mr. Robert Bailey of Yale University who is studying the sketches has very generously in-

formed me that "the first note is a *b* in the first sketch for the piece, which extends only to the seventeenth measure. Similarly, the first note of the second phrase is a *d*. The first note of the third phrase, however, is also a *d*, as in the final version." I am indebted to Mr. Bailey and look forward to the appearance of his study of the Prelude.

EXAMPLE 8

a)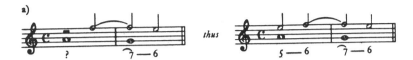

b)

b1)

b2)    b3)    177

b4)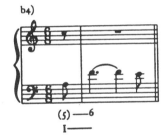

EXAMPLE 9

a)   Bars 17–24

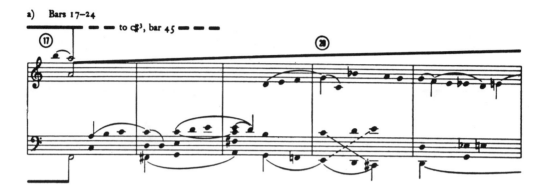

b)

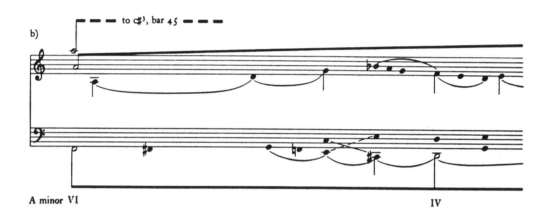

A minor VI   IV

c)

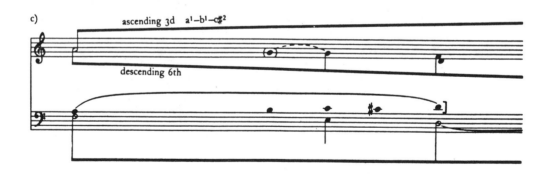

EXAMPLE 9 (*continued*)

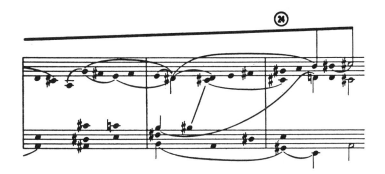

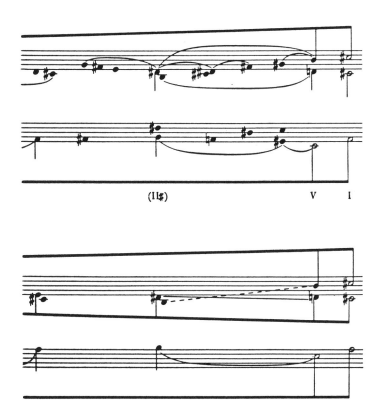

179

Bars 17–24. Bars 1–17 have, in the structural activity of the upper parts, opened up three octave registers, from a to g$\sharp^1$ and, in bar 17, a^1 and a^2. Bars 17–24 carry out a first ascent from a^1 to c$\sharp^2$ by way of b^1, as indicated in Examples 9a, 9b, and 9c. The bass of these bars brings to completion the first harmonic expression of A minor-major by picking up with F (bar 17), moving on to D (bar 21), and, after an intervening B (bar 23), concluding with E–A of bar 24. An important prolonging element is the middle-voice descent of a sixth from a^1 (bar 17) to c$\sharp^1$ (bar 24), as indicated in Example 9c. The tone a^2 and its register remain out of play until the following section.

The featured motive, motive *B*, is formed of concatenate thirds which carry out a broader connection between a–g^1–f^1 in bars 17–20–21 (Example 9a). The transitory nature of the supporting C-chord of bar 20 is explained in 9c. In bar 21, the apparent Neapolitan sixth is nothing more than a detail of the upper-voice motion from f^1 to d^1. Its accented position is characteristic of the prevailing texture of the Prelude, as has already been noted in discussing the rhythmic similarities of motives *A^2*, *B*, *C*, *E*, *F*, and *G* in connection with Example 3.

Bars 23–24 are complex. The descending sixth has, in bar 23, reached d$\sharp^1$, which stands over an inner voice b. This vertical third is inverted to become a sixth, d^1–b^1 (bar 24), in an arresting manner. The first violins, hitherto quiet, enter to span chromatically the distance from d$\sharp^1$ up to b^1, while the cellos initiate a motion from b up to d^1. After they have reached the intermediate c$\sharp^1$, the second violins intercept and complete the motion to d^1. The bass, meanwhile, breaks from B through G$\sharp$ to E before cadencing on A. These techniques and their relation to broad structure are shown in the illustrations of Example 9.

In summary, bars 1–24 form a unit, but for reasons of expository convenience they have been discussed as two subsections, 1–17 and 17–24. Over the bass, a, e, f, d, (b), e, a, three octave registers have been explored and, in the middle register, the first joining of a^1 to c$\sharp^2$ has occurred.

Bars 24–45. These bars are closely related to bars 1–24. Over the broad spread of supporting harmonies, the true register and upper voice, c$\sharp^3$, are reached, as indicated in the three graphs of Example 10.

As usual in structural analysis, the bass and harmonic frame require attention initially. Bars 24–31 are property of the A-chord. Its first expression is as a triad, but in bar 31 it acquires a minor seventh, g^1, which gives to it the color of an applied dominant to the approaching D-chord. The intervening activity is a matter of chromatic inflection rather than a modulation to E major. This becomes apparent as soon as analysis disengages itself from the chords of detail and focuses on inclusive activity, as illustrated in Examples 10a, 10b, and 10c, which should be compared with the equivalent bars in Example 2b. The D-chord prevails in bars 32–40. It is expressed first in the position of the sixth (bar 32), but eventually connects with the root (bar 37). From this point on, the minor third, f, is exchanged for the major third, f♯. The chord on B (bars 41–43) is passing by nature, for it takes its departure from the preceding D-chord and moves on to the cadential G♯- and A-chords of bars 43–44. The succession of A–D–B–G♯–A (Examples 10c and 2) offers conclusive evidence that the tonal properties of A alone are expressed in this section. Modulation plays no role.

In bars 24–31, motives C, D, and E are featured. In essence, motive C moves in parallel tenths with the bass as it courses from $c♯^2$, through b^1, to a^1. This three-tone succession is extended by suspending b^1 over F♯. As a fourth, its normal resolution should be to a third. However, before the appearance of a^1, the bass has moved on toward c♯ as shown in Example 10b, which should be compared with 10c, where the generic relationship is presented. Note in these bars, as represented in 10c, how each principal participating voice moves surely from one to another tone of the A-chord. Of particular interest is the fine parallelism to the upper voice of bars 24–28, provided by the top part as motive E in bars 29–32 moves from c^2 to a^1 and then from $c♯^2$ to a^1. Intertwined in the manner of a cambiata are ascending secondary thirds, $f♯^1$–a^1, and e^1–g^1 (Example 10a).

From bars 32 to 40, over the support of the D-chord, an arresting change of register occurs that prepares the way for the arrival of $c♯^3$ in bar 45. At first motive B is employed, much in the manner of its earlier use (bars 17–21), but an octave higher. By means of the third a^1–g^2–f^2 the upper register, last sounded in bar 17, is reopened. In bar 36 and further, motive F continues this play of registers by transferring f^1–g^1 and g^1–a^1 (bars

EXAMPLE 10

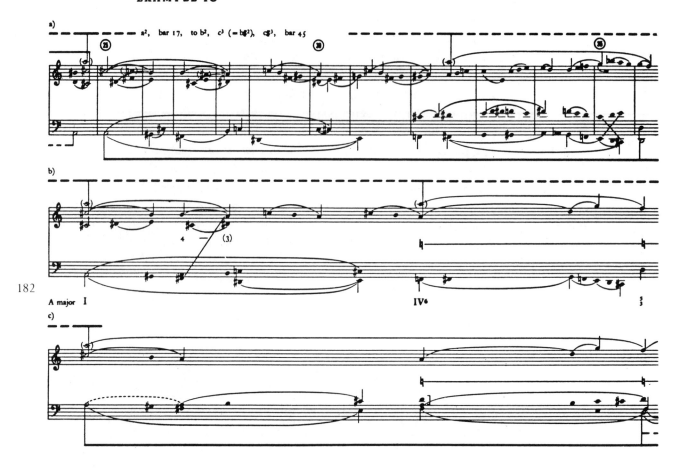

182

EXAMPLE 10 (*continued*)

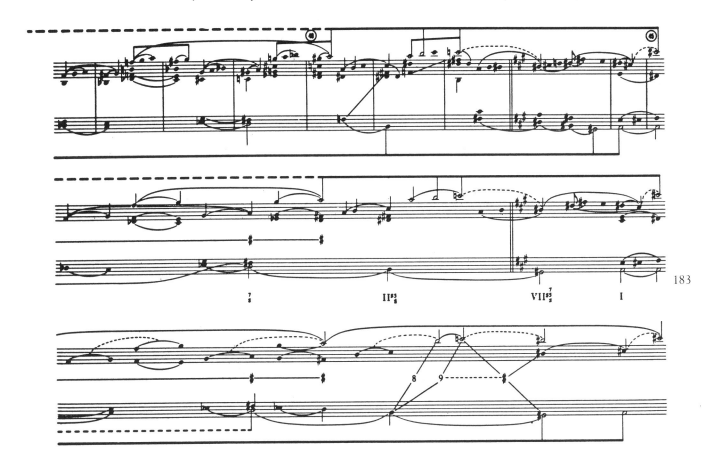

183

36–37 and 38–39) successively to f²–g² and g²–a² (Examples 10a and 10b).

As a result, the situation presented in bar 40 is a D-major–chord with a² in the top voice. The derivation of the linear-chordal relationships of bars 40 to 45 is sketched in Example 11. Under the pressure of increasing intensity and the shape of the motive, the top voice anticipates its normal accompaniment in such a way that a minor ninth, c², appears over the B-chord of bars 41–42. This is not a true chordal ninth, but an enharmonically written anticipation of the major third, b♯¹, of the G♯-chord of bar 43. It is this chord that presses on to the A-chord of bar 44 in an aroused transposition of the cadence of bars 16–17. Wagner's desired parallelism accounts for the chromatic color of the chord on G♯, rather than any putative flirtation with the key of C♯ minor.

EXAMPLE 11

184

The upper voice of the cadence of bar 44 is literally b♯¹–c♯². But it is the c♯³ in bar 45, following the cadence, that is the tone sought after and prepared for by the transposition devices of the preceding bars. Note that it, too, is reached by an octave transposition of c♯². It is characteristic of the continuous nature of the music of the Prelude that $c\sharp^3$ should arrive one bar after the cadence. In fact, it should be noted that secondary factors add to the forward impulse of the cadence bar: the double basses and third bassoon retain A^1 and A^2 into bar 45; $d\sharp^2$ in the violas delays for three beats the arrival of $c\sharp^2$; the cellos press on by means of an $e\sharp$ to the $f\sharp$ of bar 45.

In summary of bars 1–24, 24–45: over two similar successions in the bass, the structural top voice connects a^1 with $c\sharp^2$ (bars 1–24) and then a^2 with $c\sharp^3$ (bars 24–45). A different kind of action ensues.

Bars 45–63. The A-chord, well established in the earlier sections, continues through bar 52, where it gives way to the subdominant harmony that prevails through bar 63. The dominant harmony of bar 64 is then prolonged in a manner that will be described in the following section. Above these harmonies, $c\sharp^3$ gives way in bar 53 to d^3, a structural neighboring tone. From each of these tones, downward motions are generated, $c\sharp^3$ to a^2 (bars 45–48, repeated in parallel fashion in 49–50, and twice in 51–52), and d^3 to a^2 to $f\sharp^2$ (filled in, in bars 53–62). These harmonic and linear prolongations are indicated in the illustrations of Example 12.

The motive employed in bars 45–52 is motive *C*, now an octave higher than its first statement in bars 25–32. However, the different continuations in bars 32 and 53 make an important difference in identifying the retained structural tone. While in bar 32 the action, carried out by motive *B*, emphasizes a motion picked up from a^1, the entrance in bar 53 of d^3 and its subsequent prolongation indicate that $c\sharp^3$ is its linear point of departure. For the rest, the reading of details for motive *C* is virtually the same as in its first statement (cf. Example 10).

A critical point is reached in bar 55 which can be settled only by study of the orchestral score. What is the structural meaning of $c\sharp^3$ in bars 54–55? Is it the completion of a neighboring motion, $c\sharp^3$ (bar 45), d^3 (bar 53), $c\sharp^3$ (bar 54)? Or is it to be regarded as a passing tone within the D-chord, as d^3 moves through this $c\sharp^3$ and b^2 (bar 57) to a^2 (bar 58)? The bass supports the latter reading, for the entire passage occurs within the D-chord, as indicated in Example 12. Furthermore, Wagner, by placing his accompanying voices above motive *B*, insures a retention of the proper register until motive *B* crosses over in bar 56 (Examples 12 and 12b). As noted earlier,

185

EXAMPLE 12

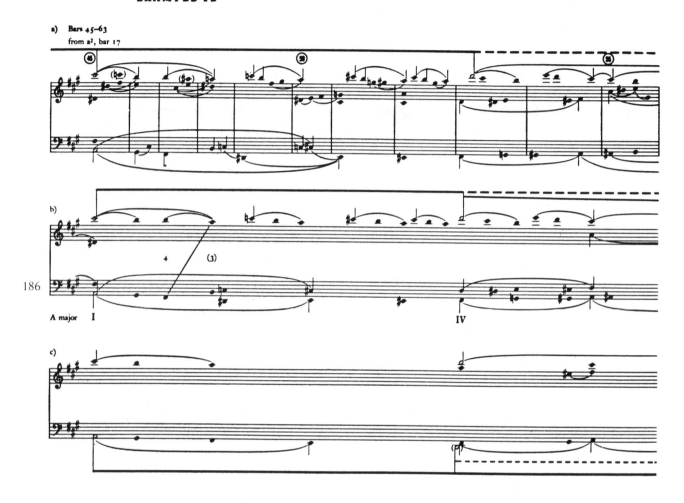

EXAMPLE 12 *(continued)*

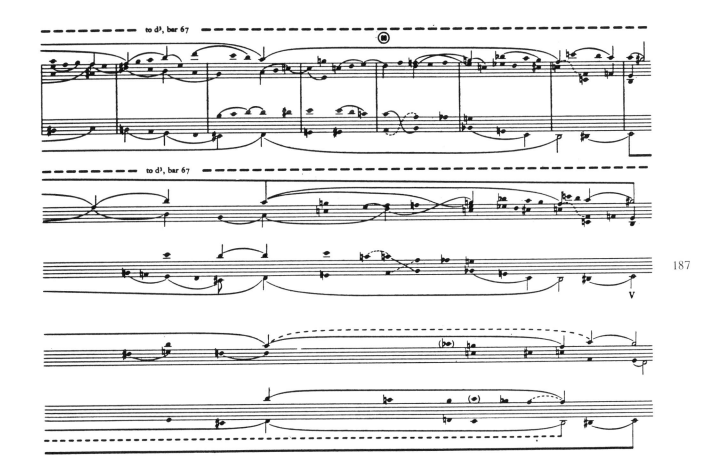

187

most keyboard transcriptions create a false misleading hiatus in these bars by abandoning the register so resourcefully retained by the composer. The same important crossing of motive B and its accompaniment occurs in bars 59–62 and for the same reason. The underlying sense of the entire passage is shown in Example 12c. Observe that the position of the sixth struck in bar 58 is not a "deceptive cadence," but a necessary reaffirmation of the D-chord which continues, as indicated, through bar 62, before giving way to the dominant harmony. It is instructive to compare the reductions of motive B in Examples 12b and 12c with the earlier reductions in Examples 9b and 9c, for the increased chromaticism and complexity of voice leading are reflected in the voice exchanges of Example 12b (bass clef) and in the four-part reduction of Example 12c.

Bars 63–74. Except for bar 74, these bars are property of the dominant harmony. From bars 63–70, it is asserted by a retention of E in the bass. In bars 70–73, however, Wagner uses the same arpeggiation technique that appears in the opening bars of the Prelude.

Above this prolonged harmony, new events occur. As indicated in Example 13a, 13b, and 13c, a stepwise ascent in bars 63–67 connects g$\sharp^2$ with d^3, already asserted in bar 53. The technique whereby Wagner achieves this connection is executed by motive G, a motive that lives its life in two registers (a^2–b^1, b^2–c$\sharp^2$, etc.). Its origin lies in 5–6–5 relationships as indicated in Example 13b. Motive G continues as an accompaniment through bar 72 of the section under examination, and in bars 73–74 it is brought down from its exploration of upper registers by a series of descending transfers, as indicated by slurs in Example 13a.

Once d^3 has been reaffirmed in bar 67, it is retained by the flutes and reiterated by the first and second violins as each of these sweeps upward. Below this, woodwinds and horns in increasing numbers sound motive A^2, carrying it upward, much in the manner of bars 1–17, but less protracted, from g$\sharp^1$ (bar 66) to a^2 in bar 74. Note that *Tr* has been modified in bars 66 and 68 by the necessity of retaining the structurally important d^3, as against the characteristic d$\sharp$. However in its following transpositions (bars 70 and 72), there is no need to modify the sonority, hence its original color remains intact. Specialists in the harmonic analysis of *Tr* would do well to observe and reflect on this modification brought about for structural reasons. However, beware of the run of piano transcriptions which modify the phrasing slurs.[9] Motive A^1 does not enter, except as aspects of it are incorporated into extensions of motive *G* in bars 70 and 72.

Bars 74–84. These bars, the dynamic and emotional climax of the Prelude, are organized around three prolonged harmonies, represented by the following bass tones: (1) f (bars 74–78) arpeggiated in the form of f (bars 74–76), c–A (bar 77), and F (bar 78); (2) B♭ (bars 79–82), the goal of descents from f (bars 80, 81, and 82); (3) e in bar 84, reached immediately from the neighbor f, and the basis of organization in most of the following section. These bass tones, f, B♭, e, representing the vi, ii (Phrygian), v of a minor, shoulder a feverish surge of the music. As noted earlier, the bass of bars 79–82, participating in this delirium, seems about to abandon all pretense of a relationship with the guiding tonality in favour of an excursion into other realms. The arrival of e, and the E-chord in bar 84, however, settles the issue in favour of a. Attention in these bars should be given to *Tr*, for its relation to the B♭-chord (bars 80–82), and its relation to the E-chord (bars 83–84), provide clear evidence that a♭ and the enharmonic g♯ are chordal elements rather than appoggiaturas,[10] as indicated in Example 14.

The prevailing motive in bars 74–78 is motive *B* in its most elaborate setting. Here again the orchestral score must be the analytic referent, for Wagner, as in the preceding instances, places his accompaniment above the motive initially to retain the proper register, as d^3 of bar 67 resolves ultimately to c^3 in bar 77. In essence c^3 is fetched from a^2 of bar 74 as indicated in Examples 14a and 14b. By comparing the present setting of motive *B* with earlier ones (bars 32–36), it can be seen that a new element is needed to carry the motion from a^2 through $b♭^2$ (bar 76) to the desired c^3 of bar 77. Note that in the earlier settings the motion from a^2 has descended by step

9 As in the transcription by Richard Kleinmichel.

10 Dr. Lorenz, who regards g♯[1] as an appoggiatura, writes (p. 20): "The appoggiatura, g♯, is present as a held tone up to the antepenultimate chord (bar 84) [83 according to the usual count] where it finds its normal resolution to a." Quite a feat!

EXAMPLE 13

a)   Bars 63–74

b)

190

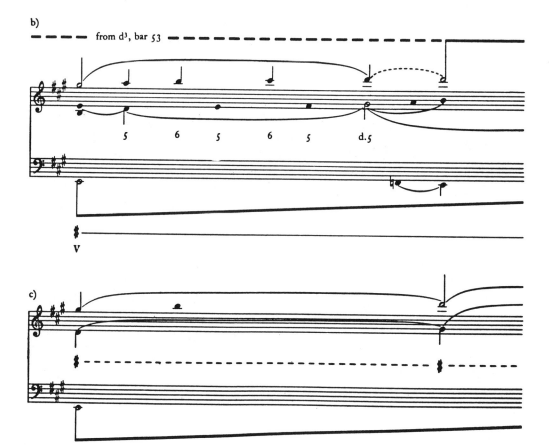

EXAMPLE 13 (*continued*)

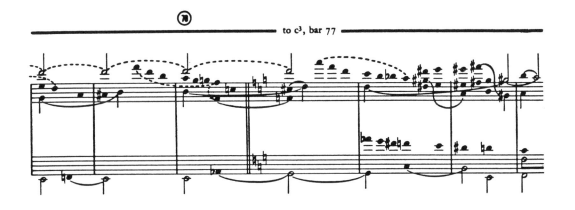

191

EXAMPLE 14

a)   Bars 74–84

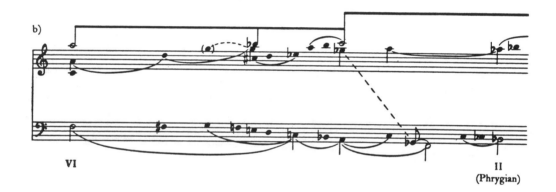

VI   II
                                                                    (Phrygian)

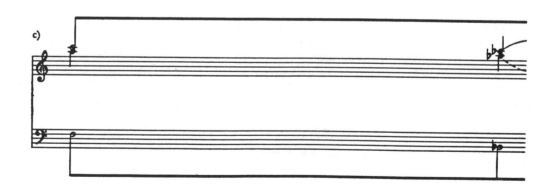

EXAMPLE 14 (*continued*)

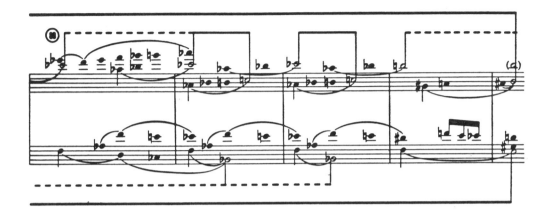

193

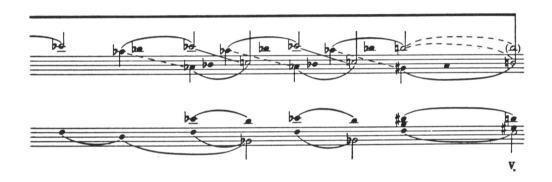

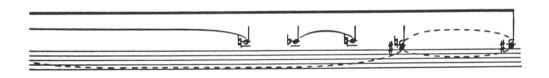

EXAMPLE 15

EXAMPLE 16

to f^2. Actually this earlier motion is still present, but above it Wagner places the new motion. The derivation of this complex passage is shown in Example 15. In 15a the bass moves upward in tenths with the top voice. However, 15b, with its downward motion, opens up new avenues of voice leading which create several additional chromatically inflected chords of detail.

Having reached c^3 in bar 77, the orchestra now spreads out to encompass an imposing range from $B\flat^1$ to $a\flat^3$. Within this vast tonal edifice, woodwinds, brass, and cellos secure the registers pertinent to the overall structure. The complexity of interwoven motives in bars 80 to 84 requires an additional illustration in short score. Example 16 indicates motivic derivations and the distribution of registers. Note that motives A^1, A^2, Tr, and B participate in the action, that motive A^1 is the agency by which the high point, $a\flat^3$, is brought downward to its proper register. The tones of motive A^1, $a\flat$ up to f^1, etc. (bars 79–84), become $a\flat^3$ (bars 81–83) down to f^3 to f^1, e^1, $e\flat^1$, d^1 (bars 83 and 84).

Example 14a incorporates most of the total activity of these bars. In 14b the coupling of $a\flat^2$ and $a\flat^1$, $c\flat^3$ and $c\natural^2$, are stressed. Finally Example 14c indicates the structural frame with the coupling brought into a single register above the broad march of the bass from f to $B\flat$ to e.

Bars 84–96, etc. As noted earlier, the present analysis will end with the beginning of Wagner's concert ending rather than with the transition to Act I, Scene 1. Hence we have been examining a Prelude, that is, a self-enclosed piece, rather than an Introduction leading to other actions. Wagner seems to have used both terms, Vorspiel and Einleitung interchangeably.

The structure of these closing bars is identical with a recurrent closing technique, represented in its generic form at the end of Example 2b. Specifically, b^2 of bars 83–84 connects with a^2 in bar 95, but with the help of a circling extension whereby b^2 moves first through a^2 (bar 92) to $g\sharp^2$ (bar 94) before its termination on the a^2 of bar 95, etc. Below this action, the prevailing structural bass, e, representing the dominant harmony, provides escort for the circling extension in the form of a (bar 90), d^1 (bar 92) and B, e (bars 93–94), before giving way in bar 95 to the terminal A. All of these relationships are shown in Example 17.

EXAMPLE 17

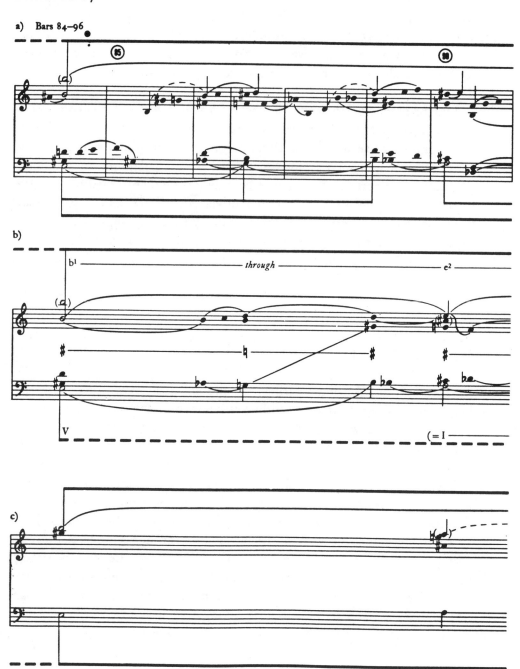

a) Bars 84–96

b)

196

c)

EXAMPLE 17 (*continued*)

197

The motives employed in the section are B, A^1, A^2, and the sonority Tr. Although these bars recall the opening bars of the Prelude as well as bars 36–40, the orientation is quite different. Each bass tone, e, a, and d^1, has its own extension. In bars 84 to 89, e is arpeggiated through the tones e (bar 84), g (bar 87), and b–b♭^{1} (bar 89). Next, a is similarly extended by way of a (bar 90), c and e♭^{1} (bar 91). The bass d in bar 92, however, drops down a third to B (bar 93) before moving on to the concluding and reaffirming e of bars 93–94. Note the quickening harmonic rhythms of these bars as e (six bars) passes on to a (two bars) to d^1 (one and a half bars) and to e (one and a half bars). Above these bass tones, the upper parts engage in an intermediate extension whereby b^1 (bar 84) moves to e^2 (bar 90) to connect with g♯^{2} (bar 92), as pointed out in Example 17b. Note the fine parallelism to the changes of register and the connection between g♯^{2} and a^2 in the concluding ascent (g♯^{1} up to a^2) of bars 92–94.

The beginning of the concert ending is included in the sketches of Example 17. Although its motivic content is related to the concluding bars of Act III, it nevertheless joins with the preceding music of the Prelude in an arresting manner. As indicated in Example 17a, the upper appoggiatura, b^2, has been featured throughout. However the suspension of f♯^{2} from the preceding music forms a strong transitional link. This tone has appeared earlier, in bars 10 to 16, and bar 73, as a prominent feature in the lengthening of g♯^{2}–a^2 into a motivically needed third, f♯^{2}–g♯^{2}–a^2. Its retention in bar 95 is heightened by the plagal support given to it by the bass.

THE FORM

VIEWED as a linear-harmonic entity, the form of the Tristan Prelude is a continuous, uninterrupted whole, subserved by a series of prolonged harmonies and an inclusive, descending melodic structure. The derivation of the broad harmonies and the extension of the prime melodic structure are sketched in the illustrations of Example 18. The purely harmonic elements are, as indicated, i–ii–v–i. The sketches of Example 18a and 18b, portray such a structure in A major, then in A minor, and finally in A minor with a lowered or Phrygian second step. Example 18c unites these modal variants in the manner of the Prelude and indicates the origin of the

EXAMPLE 18

a)

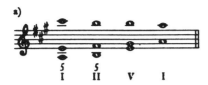

b)

c)

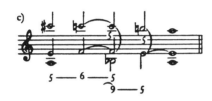

199

d)

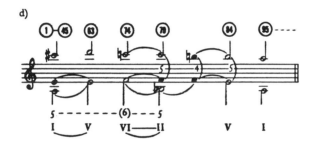

e)

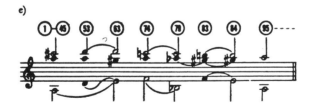

F-chord of bar 74 in an age-old 5–6–5 technique. It also shows the origin of the ninth over b♭ as a suspension. Example 18d illustrates the horizontalizing of I and II as first depicted in Example 18a. Out of this technique grow the v of bar 63 and the vi of bar 74. As a feature of this succession, the prime melodic structure acquires the neighbor d³. Note also the first suggestion of *Tr* between bars 79 and 84 in the working out of the linear technique 5–4–5. Finally, in Example 18e, a significant accompanying voice makes its appearance. It is the intervallic space created by this voice against the prime outer voice that is filled in by so many of the motivic elements, as already shown in Example 2b.

CONCLUSION

THREE POINTS remain to be mentioned as we bring this linear-harmonic analysis to an end. The first is the linking of the Prelude or, better, the Introduction, with the beginning of Act I, which hovers between C minor and E♭ major. The seeds of the modulatory transition are sown in bar 17, for the F-chord, which appears at this point and again in bar 74, becomes eventually the agent for the shift from A to C. Following its final appearance in bar 94 of the piece as usually performed, the music shifts its weight to the dominant of C, employing the F-chord, this time, as a subdominant. Note, in bar 107 and further, the imaginative way in which preparation is made for the ensuing solo of the young sailor. The ascending sixth is, of course, closely related to the similar interval of motive A^1.

The second point is concerned with the extraordinary difficulties that harmonic theorists have had in analyzing the chordal details of the Prelude in terms of one or another system of harmony. At best, chordal analysis provides only a one-dimensional view of a composition. Thus, even when some kind of agreement can be reached about chord names and functions, the resultant values are bound to be limited. However, in the case of the Tristan Prelude, even this kind of agreement over labels has not been reached, as can be discovered by a random sampling of available chord and key analyses.

The reason is not hard to find. There has been a preoccupation with each of the striking sonorities as individual sounds, or at most these have been related only to an immediate environment. This is, of course, not the only chromatic piece that has refused to reveal its harmonic meanings when its techniques are assessed on a chord by chord basis. It is axiomatic that the more intense the chromaticism, the greater the need to relate individual sonorities to a broad context. A simple case in point can be found in bars 32–40, where only a summoning of the inclusive frame provided by the D-chord can illuminate the meaning of the details. Without such a reference the analyst cannot help but record a confusing welter of chord labels and modulatory activities. With it, his problem shifts to one of assessing chords as elements of motion within a clearly marked area. Hence, the possibility of finding an insightful reading of detail becomes real and immediate.

The third and final point, to which the preceding considerations lead, relates to the attempt to find an embracing structure by means of linear-harmonic analytic procedures. Such an aim carries us well beyond the meaning of detail, for its ultimate problem is the relating to each other of the several pervasive frames with their contents. This can be a challenging and sometimes a despairing assignment. In the case of the Tristan Prelude, it has proven to be less formidable than in many another piece. For one thing, the harmonic pilings are strongly marked; for another, the broad contexts are easily found; and for a third, the controlling outer parts are always reasonably in evidence.

This does not mean, however, that there can be only one exemplary linear-harmonic analysis of a work such as this. Clearly, when so many diverse, often competing, factors await evaluation, when a desired objectivity is constantly menaced by the limiting slants of personal musical experience, a resolute effort must be made to reduce arbitrary readings to the zero point, to eliminate purely capricious judgments. When these hampering conditions are overcome, the success of an analysis can be measured by the degree of musical insight that it provides. Some will fall short of the mark; others will approach the heart of the work. It remains idle, however, to speculate on the most viable of all viable analyses, for in the end the analytic conclusions reached are individual judgments, however rarefied, rather than mechanical derivatives. This is a source of strength for linear-harmonic analysis, for it suggests a constant matching of the musical maturity of the analyst with the elusive essence of the work analyzed.

201

THE THEMATIC PLAN
OF THE NINTH SYMPHONY

After an introductory group of sixteen bars (harmonically a long extended dominant), the first theme enters (*a* in the following example). To obtain a basis for later reference, we divide this shape into its four motivic [1] elements (*b*):

Ex. 1

---

[1] We call *motif* any musical element, be it a melodic phrase or fragment or even only a rhythmical or dynamic feature which, by being constantly repeated and varied throughout a work or a section, assumes a role in the

11

We notice that motif II, after its first occurrence in bar **3** of the theme, reappears in bars **5** and **6**, and a third time in bars **7** and **8**, here transposed to a higher pitch.

Turning to the theme of the next movement, the Scherzo, we become aware that its shape surprisingly constitutes an almost perfect replica of the Allegro theme's [2] design. This becomes apparent once we extract, as in the following example, the four motivic parts from the Scherzo theme:

Ex. 2

compositional design somewhat similar to that of a motif in the fine arts.

A *theme,* then, could be defined as a fuller group or "period" which acquires a "motivic" function in a composition's course. Since, however, as this study is about to demonstrate, in a work of higher structural form no group can be entirely outside the motivic unity, the whole conception of a "theme" becomes somewhat problematical. We shall elaborate on this more specifically.

In general, the author does not believe in the possibility or even desirability of enforcing strict musical definitions. Musical phenomena come to existence in the constant fluency and motion of compositional creation. Therefore any descriptions of them must finally prove but approximations. It is for this very reason that in the course of this analysis it was considered more useful to cling as far as possible to the familiar expressions, and to apply them even in instances when their accuracy could be debated, rather than to invent new terms.

[2] For abbreviation's sake the four movements may henceforth be referred to as Allegro, Scherzo, Adagio, and Finale. In this sense the themes also may be quoted as first Allegro theme, second Allegro theme, Scherzo theme, and so on.

Thus we see that all four motivic characters of the Allegro not only reappear but even succeed each other *in exactly the same order as in the Allegro theme*. In other words, not only the motivic fragments but the image of the Allegro's *full theme* are reiterated in the Scherzo.

Specifically speaking, the kernel of motif I reappears almost unchanged, and so does motif II. However, of this latter motif the particles are exchanged: while in the Allegro the first occurrence F, E, D, is later followed by its inversion D, E, F, in the Scherzo the inversion is first and the original shape comes after it.

Motif III has undergone the most visible change: it simply reads E, F, G instead of A, G, E, A, thus assuming simultaneously the shape of a transposed motif II. However, its appearance exactly between the two occurrences of motif II makes it certain that this E, F, G, is nevertheless meant as a corresponding substitute for motif III. For the kernel of these bars reads, as is easily seen,

Ex. 3

Allegro

Scherzo

and the identity is obvious. But in the speed and concentration which the composer wished for the Scherzo, the leap to the A would have torn the design.

The analogy of motif IV (apart from its transposition to another pitch) is complete.

Let us dwell for a moment on the meaning of the features just described. They represent a first illustration of the fact, indicated in our introductory remarks, that the different movements of a classical symphony are built from one identical thought.

However, to comprehend this phenomenon in its true sense, the following should also be understood. It is by no means alleged that this identity implies that a theme from one movement is literally, or even almost literally, repeated in the next. Naturally, such a procedure would be nonsensical and would never lead to any compositional form of higher structure. The composer's endeavor is just the opposite. He strives toward *homogeneity in the inner essence* but at the same time toward *variety in the outer appearance*. Therefore he changes the surface but maintains the substance of his shapes.

Accordingly, we see the Allegro theme transformed in the Scherzo into quite a different theme. Tempo, rhythm, melodic detail, in fact the whole character and mood are altered and adjusted to the form in which the composer conceived them fitting to the new movement. Nevertheless, there can be no doubt, as the examples clearly prove, that it is one common musical idea, *one basic pattern,* from which both themes have been formed.

As for the individual motifs, I, II, and III are even audible at the same pitch in the Scherzo as in the Allegro. Only motif IV appears transposed. However, as the Scherzo develops into a fugato, it is interesting to note that when the theme is taken over by the violas (and later by the first violins), this motif too is heard in the Scherzo at the same pitch as in the Allegro. And this original pitch is maintained when the definitive statement of the theme in fortissimo climaxes the design of the Scherzo:

Ex. 4

Proceeding to the following movement, the Adagio, we realize, incredible as it may seem considering the entirely different picture which this movement presents at first glance, that here again the similarity of the basic substance is not to be questioned. After two introductory bars the main theme of the Adagio enters:

Ex. 5

There is no doubt that the kernel of motif I from the Allegro theme, the descending triad D, A, F, D, also speaks clearly from the Adagio theme. Of course, tempo, rhythm, and the whole character are again changed. Also, in order to adjust the motif to the desired mood of the Adagio, the melodic course had to be expanded and a B-flat and an E-flat included.

Through this a particularly interesting situation arises. The Adagio theme is in B-flat. Yet the old motif from which it is derived, the D-minor triad of the Allegro theme, is not transposed according to the new key but sounds through at original pitch. We hear a theme in B-flat with a D-minor triad, as it were, at its base. This method of *transforming a shape from one theme to another which is in a different key, but at the same time letting it sound at original pitch,* will in many of the later examples become apparent as one of the most effective means of structural transformation.

This same phenomenon is seen immediately in the continuation of the theme. For, of course, we have so far examined only the Adagio theme's beginning. Now considering also the theme's continuation, which in example 6a is given by omitting a few repetitions, and comparing it to the corresponding continuation of the Allegro theme (example 6b),

Ex. 6

it is not difficult to trace the identity in the outline, the contour, of these two groups, in spite of their contrasting surface and key.

Note how motif II plus its inversion (D to F, up and down) is again clearly spelled in the beginning of the Adagio group. Motif III may not seem as obviously identifiable in the Adagio, but the transposition of motif II (up to the B-flat) and the following motif IV are recognizable in full transparency, completing the familiar design.

Thus we have arrived at the symphony's Finale.

After a gigantic introduction, in which fragments of the former movements' openings reappear in striking flashes,[3] the Finale's first theme, the "Ode to Joy," enters:

---

[3] This feature alone, so well known to every musician—that in the Ninth Symphony bits of the preceding movements are quoted in the Finale—should have sufficed to evoke an inquiry among analysts as to whether the different movements of a Beethoven symphony are not, indeed, thematically united. Naturally, the feature is also intended to convey a programmatic idea. Nevertheless, seen from the technical point of view, how could a mind of a structural, a "symphonic," intensity such as Beethoven's ever have thought to include in his work an effect tending seemingly to the sphere of the potpourri rather than to serious music, unless he were convinced that these themes represented three different expressions of one identical idea.

Ex. 7

The kernel of its opening is again motif I from the Allegro, the triad in D, though here transposed to major.

But while in the preceding movements the original triad was still more or less verbally preserved, in the Finale, where the work's architectural and emotional drama drives to its solution, it is filled with bridging notes, thus making it fluent, songlike. The theme has changed to a tune.

Through this, however, the transformation has gone so far that on the surface it is no longer discernible as such. But recognizing the unquestionable analogy in all themes, in the secondary themes no less than in the first ones (as shall presently be demonstrated), and, moreover, adding innumerable proofs of a similar ceaseless homogeneity in all the other works of Beethoven—indeed, of almost all great composers—we must conclude that in this instance, too, the identity of the *underlying* triad suffices to assure us of the basic homogeneity.

The following motifs are easily recognized in the theme of this movement also. The ascending and descending thirds of motif II appear as interwoven subphrases in the melodic course. In fact, they form, transposed and at original pitch, the very bridging notes by which the triad is filled to produce the tune of the "Ode." Motif III is indicated by lifting the theme from D, E, F-sharp (bars 8 and 9) to E, F-sharp, G (bars 10 and 11).[4] Motif IV, finally, the descending seventh, is expressed through bars 11 and 12:

Ex. 8

IV

---

[4] After this chapter was written, the author looked once more through Beethoven's sketches to the Ninth Symphony. He was rewarded by a striking confirmation of his analytic deductions. In our motivic specification above, bars 9 and following of the "Ode" are introduced as repre-

That motif IV is really meant becomes evident when, as the first counterpoint in the following repetition (variation) of the "Ode," the phrase just quoted is immediately imitated, but appears now in the following version, clearly mirroring the motif's appearance in the Allegro:

Ex. 10

Thus we come to realize that the Finale theme is derived from the pattern of the Allegro no less than are the other movements.

With this the cycle of identity in the four first themes of the Ninth Symphony is closed. A symphony, however, is built not only on its first themes but also on its secondary themes. And the true picture, the full intensity of the symphony's amazing architectural planning, will only reveal itself if we include these second themes as well in our examination.

Before the Allegro's second theme is introduced, we hear a few bars which we may term a bridge or intrada to it (*a* in the following example). Motivically this intrada group somewhat echoes motif II, the pair of thirds. Then the actual second theme of the first movement enters (*b* in the following example):

a   *b*

Ex. 11

---

senting motif III. However, we could merely state that the motif is here expressed "in indication." But in the sketches these bars appear in the following version:

Ex. 9

This is an exciting discovery. For it shows that in Beethoven's original conception the bars really and truly represent the motif. The whole shaping is here in exact analogy to the form in which the motif appears in the Scherzo. In the sketchbook version especially, there is no sign of the D which appears in the score and thus complicates the analytic proof. Without the D, as in the sketch, no one can doubt the motivic meaning.

At first glance one would think this shape quite different from the previous ones. And the difference would seem logical, for this is, after all, the movement's second subject, and as such, according to all accepted conceptions, it must not resemble but contrast with the first theme. Yet looking at it closely, we discover that its kernel, the ascending triad D, F, A, is identical with that of the first theme, or, to be precise, it is its inversion.

This fact becomes still more apparent once we notice that these opening bars of the second theme are immediately repeated in a slightly varied version. This version makes the similarity to the triad kernel of the first theme still more obvious, as it begins:

Ex. 12

However, to avoid any misconception, it must be emphasized: It is not averred that this beginning of the second Allegro theme is just a "variant" of the first theme. It should not even be termed a "transformation," such as we would consider the Scherzo theme. No, this opening of the second theme is a new musical idea, with every appearance of a "contrasting" shape. Yet a structural affinity cannot be denied.

That this affinity, although an affinity through inversion, is not merely analytic conjecture is definitely proved by the continuation of the two themes. For, as we recall, the continuation of the first theme is the little figure called motif II (*a* in the following example), to which the continuation of the second theme (*b*) must be compared:

Ex. 13

Startled, we realize that the group from the second theme is none other than an expanded version of the little motif from the first theme. The change from E-natural to E-flat is merely due to the change of key from D to B-flat.

And in the second theme, after the phrase quoted has been repeated in transposition, a further shape follows (*a* in the following example), which—another surprise—is clearly a replica of the subsequent group (motif IV) in the first theme (*b*):

Ex. 14

Thus in its outer appearance, in the gentle mood of its curved line, this second Allegro theme indeed "contrasts" with the energetic first, yet it is a complete reiteration of the latter's inner content and design.

Now the significant question arises: Can an image of this second Allegro theme be discovered *in the second themes of the following movements,* just as the first theme of the Allegro was mirrored in the first themes of the other movements?

This would seem unlikely as far as the next movement, the Scherzo, is concerned, since scherzos usually lack an actual second theme. Nevertheless, if it has no second theme, a scherzo has a trio. And the Trio of the Ninth mirrors the design of the second Allegro theme, as shown in the following examples.

As mentioned above, the second Allegro theme was preceded by a short intrada. Comparing this intrada group, which in the following example is quoted in a transposed key (example 15*a*), with the Trio's opening (example 15*b*),

Ex. 15

it is obvious that the Trio group (*b*), though it is said to have been taken from a Russian folk tune, nevertheless clearly echoes the group quoted above as *a*.

In the first movement the group that follows is the actual second theme (*a* in the following example), which thus should correspond to the group that now enters in the Trio (*b*). Etching out the corners, the contour, from the Trio group (given under *c*), we realize that here too the analogy continues:

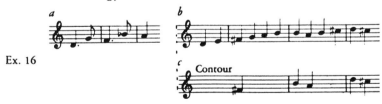

Ex. 16

Contour

211

Proceeding to the Adagio, we must logically turn to its second section to discover whether this "affinity of the second themes" is integrated in this movement also. This second Adagio section enters with the following theme (*a*), from which we extract a contour (*b*):

Ex. 17

Again the analogy to the second Allegro theme cannot be mistaken. Note, by the way, motif IV at the end of the theme (see bracket in the example). Yet with regard to this last example, one might perhaps argue: In this contour, why was D notated as the first note, while in Beethoven's text the soprano clearly shows F-sharp, the D being confined to the bass?

Therefore, at the risk of being repetitious, it must be emphasized again and again that naturally the composer did not feel the slightest compulsion to produce a textbook example for the sake of "thematic identity." But considering that, according to his self-chosen structural plan, the Adagio's second theme had to be derived from the second Allegro theme (*a* in the following example), we must admit that a more transparent transformation than the shape quoted as *b* could hardly be imagined:

Ex. 18

In the Finale this principle of analogy is increased to a fascinatingly wide architectural pattern. We may follow this far-reaching analogy between the first and last movements step by step. It will

212

be seen that in the Finale the single sections are expanded to much larger proportions, but that apart from this, the analogy and symmetry not only of the themes but of the whole architectural plan are indeed astounding.

The Allegro commences with an introductory group of sixteen bars, after which the first theme enters. In the Finale the introduction is extended to a huge section of improvisational passages, after which the "Ode to Joy," as the Finale's first theme, is sounded. The structural analogy of the first Allegro theme to the "Ode" has already been pointed out. In the Finale, however, the design is still further enlarged by expanding the "Ode" to a cycle of variations and by repeating this whole section (Introduction and "Ode") with solo voices and choir.

What comes next?

In the first movement, after the group of the first theme has been developed and before the second theme follows, a second statement of the first theme is introduced. While the original statement was in D-minor, this second statement is in B-flat major:

Ex. 19

213

Does the Finale also carry such a second statement?

In the Finale the group which follows is the section of the tenor solo (*b* in the following example), which at first glance would hardly appear to be a second statement of the "Ode" (*a*). But comparing the two thoroughly,

Ex. 20

we recognize the second example as literally identical to the first, merely with changed rhythm and transposed to B-flat. Thus the section of the tenor solo proves to be a repetition in B-flat (the "seventh variation" of the "Ode"), or, viewed from a wider architectural angle, truly the "Ode's" second statement, to which the later following tenor voice merely forms a contrapuntal enrichment (though naturally from a programmatic view a most important one).

Therefore, only the section which follows after that of the tenor solo would represent the Finale's second theme. This next section is centered on the so-called "Hymn":

Ex. 21

Seid um-schlun-gen, Mil - li - o-nen! Die-sen Kuss der gan-zen Welt!

Here, then, a crucial question presents itself. If the averred architectural analogy is a fact and not merely a casual similarity in the movements' beginnings, this "Hymn" must definitely prove a derivative of the second Allegro theme. However, in this case it would seem no affinity were to be traced.

Yet, probing more deeply into this melodic line, a striking realization emerges. This theme, though not a direct reiteration of the second Allegro theme's idea, is an inversion of it. We must only, as in previous instances, extract a kind of melodic contour from its shape to make this clear:

Ex. 22

It becomes obvious that the second Finale theme of the Ninth Symphony, Beethoven's venerated "Hymn to Mankind," is, technically speaking, none other than an inversion of the Allegro's second subject. This certainly is a structural realization of the first magnitude, and we should investigate the compositional core of the phenomenon.

The author harbors some fear that readers may oppose his deductions, even if at a loss to contradict their validity concretely, for the simple reason that they seem contrary to cherished illusions. "If the shaping of a musical work," they might argue, "really evolves according to the preceding explanations, composing must be regarded as a kind of musical engineering rather than as an emotional art—which we refuse to believe."

Such objections, however, are not founded on reality. With regard to the *harmonic* sphere, for instance, we all know that there are certain basic ideas and cadential progressions that classical composers constantly apply in ever varying combinations when forming the harmonic structure of their works. Yet would anyone for that reason accuse Mozart, Beethoven, or Brahms of composing according to formulas?

In the same way *thematic* shaping evolves from some basic structural methods, even though these have not yet been comprehended in our theoretical system. But creative inspiration and emotional power are by no means hindered by these structural principles directing them—as the great compositional literature proves. For the creative mind structure is a means, not an obstacle, to the manifestation of its inspiration.

Let us try to envision the process of musical formation through which the last example from the Ninth may have evolved. The composer, having in the course of the work reached the point where the last movement's second subject had to be shaped, was aware that according to his own architectural plan this theme somehow had to be built as a kind of structural offspring of the second Allegro theme. However, he seems to have felt that any shape derived from the direct form of this theme would not agree with the concept of character and mood which he wished for the section in question. But the inversion seemed the right thing.

The second Allegro theme (*a*), to which the inversion is added as *b*, reads:

Ex. 23

In modeling the inversion, the E-flat of the theme was replaced by a D (added in parenthesis). This D was inserted as a variant by Beethoven himself in the theme's repetition. (See example 12.)

Adjusting the inversion to the rhythm and spirit of the text as the composer conceived it, it would have appeared in the version quoted below as example 24*a*, which in its melodic course is still the literal inversion.

But we can easily understand that this somewhat dry utterance did not yet please the composer. Hence he inserts some slight changes through which the final form of the theme, as we find it in the score of the symphony, comes to life (example 24*b*):

215

Ex. 24

Seid um-schlun-gen, Mil - li - o-nen! Die-sen Kuss der gan-zen Welt!

In this inconspicuous, minute alteration [5] (apart from the ingenious rhythmical shaping) is centered the actual process of creation. Whether the composer came to it in the flash of a momentary vision or in a lengthy creative struggle, we do not know. We only know the result, which tells us that inspirational *and* structural forces—nobody can deny that it really is an inversion which lies here at the base—must have combined to bring this theme about.

Having thus outlined the architectural affinities of the symphony's main themes, this description would have to be complemented by much further detail if a full insight into this great work's structure were our immediate goal. This, however, would require a separate analytic study which is beyond our present purpose.

Only one specific feature shall be briefly elaborated upon, as it forms a decisive element, a central pillar, as it were, in the work's admirable architectural edifice. It is that *progression from D to B-flat* in which, as demonstrated above, the two statements of the opening theme present themselves both in the first and in the last movement. This step from D to B-flat develops to an ever recurring effect in the symphony's structural course and correspondingly also in its dramatic and emotional evolution.

Already in the opening theme, which climbs from D to its peak on the B-flat, this motivic progression forms its emphatic melodic contour:

Ex. 26

---

[5] From a subtler structural view it will of course be realized that the "change" itself is also a motivic feature, as the phrase thus brought about (*a*) is, as such, a kind of inversion, or transformation, of the original (*b*):

Ex. 25

This motif is still more profoundly rooted in the second Allegro theme. For here it represents the innermost structural idea. It has already been pointed out how the essence of the first theme, the D-minor triad, also sounds through from the second theme. This second theme, however, is actually in the key of B-flat major. Thus, not only the D-minor triad, which is the Allegro theme's first statement, but at the same time the B-flat-major triad, meaning the second statement, is audible from its shape:

Ex. 27

In fact, the combining of the two statements of the first theme is the motivic idea from which the structure of the second theme came to life. Such a procedure, the building of a thematic shape from a blending of two previous ones, is one of the favorite means in the technique of classical composers, one which endows their creations with such astounding logic and consistency. In this instance the motivic progression from D to B-flat, as manifested through the Allegro theme's two statements, forms the core of this impressive structural feature.

This step is also heard in the opening of the Scherzo. Here D to B-flat is transposed to A to F. True, one could say that A to F is in itself a part of the D-minor triad and, therefore, naturally included in any occurrence of the first theme, and in this connection hardly to be understood as a separate feature. Yet in the Scherzo it grows to particular emphasis by means of the instrumentation. For, thus sculptured by a stroke of genius into singular transparency, the step A to F becomes a powerful expression of the described motivic progression:

Ex. 28

No more effective way could have been found to impress this A to F on the listener than thus lifting it from the regular course of the instrumentation by letting the F sound in a melodic thunder from the timpani. Indeed, it is this motivic relation which, once established, echoes in the listener's ear through the whole movement, rendering the later recurrences of these timpani F's (no matter where the soprano has wandered in the meantime) one of the most mysterious effects in all music.

This fundamental motivic third is, in the further course of the Scherzo, reiterated with such almost overemphatic vigor that the composer's conscious intention to impose this effect on the listener cannot be doubted. During the transition between the Scherzo's exposition and the development section, the following group is heard (of which only the bass line is quoted in full):

Ex. 29

In seemingly endless succession the motivic thirds march by. Though harmonic logic compelled the composer in some cases to change major thirds to minor, the continuity of the phenomenon is not to be mistaken. Bar by bar, the harmony progresses over the thirds into new and unknown regions: C, A, F, D, B-flat, G, E-flat, on and on. With each bar, each "modulation," there is a new and exciting surprise, until, in the last few bars, this dynamic as well as thematic crescendo reaches its peak.

It has already been demonstrated how this same relation from D to B-flat emerges in the opening theme of the Adagio, this

"D-minor theme in B-flat" (see example 5).

In the Adagio it is also audible as a concrete utterance, precisely at the summit of the movement's structural and dramatic development, when the horns and trumpets in utter fortissimo fall from the F to the D-flat of the full orchestra:

Ex. 30

However, not until the Finale is this phenomenon led to a climax. The Finale opens with a particular harmony:

Ex. 31

This multiple unprepared suspension, which, moreover, abruptly opens a movement, this combination—in fact, collision—of a D-minor and B-flat-major triad, so often in floundering attempts at explanation quoted as a proof of Beethoven's revolutionary style if not, stupidly, of his deafness, can be understood only from a *thematic* angle. For it is none other than an explosive expression of the D to B-flat motif compressed into a harmony, into one chord.

When later, before the entrance of the human voice, the opening section of the Finale is repeated, the chord is sounded once more, now increased to an utterance of apocalyptic power:

Ex. 32

Again we hear the collision of the D and B-flat harmonies, to which the dominant seventh of D (A, C-sharp, E, G) is added. Here the note B-flat need not even be interpreted as denoting a separate harmony, but it can be regarded as a part of the dominant harmony of D-minor; namely, the dominant ninth, A, C-sharp, E, G, B-flat. Thus any harmonic explanation of the chord must necessarily remain ambiguous and artificial. But from a thematic angle the feature assumes real meaning. For besides the basic motivic step D to B-flat, latent also in this increased harmony, the present chord discloses in its thematic sum total an expression, or rather a compression into one chord, of the full line of the work's main theme. The notes of this second chord read: D, E, F, G, A, B-flat, C-sharp. In other words, the chord consists of the notes of the D-minor scale, the very notes from which the Allegro's main theme (example 1) is formed, which is in turn the source for all the themes of the symphony.

Admittedly, it was a programmatic idea that led the composer to this feature. For the work's dramatic course had reached such a degree of overconcentrated intensity that the composer, wrestling for adequate expression, attempted to force, as it were, the entire thematic content into one chord. But through this the boundaries of the rational were almost burst asunder. Therefore the human voice is introduced, entering with the words, "O friends, no more of these sad tones, but let us intonate more pleasant and more joyous ones." The stimulus for this feature was indeed based on a programmatic vision. But this vision was materialized through musical, that is, structural and, in particular, thematic means.[6]

Through all this the dramatic function of the basic step D to B-flat gained greatly in power. For only when the listener has become accustomed to accepting this step as a fundamental motif, a symbol of one of the work's strongest impulses—no matter whether he

---

[6] The reaction of Hector Berlioz to this feature, which strongly attracted his attention, is extremely interesting. In one of his essays on Beethoven, after having convincingly elaborated on the programmatic idea and the harmonic problem of these discords, Berlioz confesses that though he had searched for Beethoven's reason for introducing them, it remained unknown to him. ("J'ai beaucoup cherché la raison de cette idée, et je suis forcé d'avouer qu'elle m'est inconnue.") Thus, since the programmatic and harmonic function was clear to Berlioz, it is obvious that what puzzled him was the *thematic* mystery.

knows the theoretical implications or grasps the phenomenon by instinct—only then will his ear and mind be responsive to the impact of the subsequent overwhelming appearance of this motivic progression at the peak of the work's architectural and dramatic climax, in the group, "Doch der Cherub steht vor Gott—vor Gott!":

Ex. 33

Seldom in the whole musical literature is a harmonic step to be found striking with a power comparable to that of these last two chords.

Through an example like this, a realization may dawn on us of how great an influence the thematic idea in music can exert. Such a step from D to B-flat (or A to F) is an almost neutral musical event that ordinarily would scarcely be noticed. Only through the motivic role that it gradually assumes in the course of the work as a regular element in the forming of the themes and in the establishing of relations between the themes; only through introducing it at the high points of expression, underlined by the effects of a striking instrumentation, as in the Scherzo or in the fortissimo of the choir masses; and, finally, through its connection with the stimulating text—only through all this, and through the whole web of conscious and instinctive conceptions which the structure spins, does this simple step from D to B-flat assume an almost magical importance and open the door to the highest spiritual and emotional spheres.

Thus, as a result of the symphony's thematic analysis, a picture of the most manifold, most effective, and most logical architectural interconnections has unfolded itself, far beyond that hitherto ascribed to a classical symphony.

Specifically, a far-reaching analogy, in fact a full identity in pattern, was seen between the first themes of the four movements (first Allegro theme, Scherzo theme, first Adagio theme, and "Ode") and also between the second themes (second Allegro theme, Trio theme, second Adagio theme, and "Hymn"). Since, in addition, the first and second Allegro themes themselves proved to be built from one common substance, it can be said in a wider sense that one thematic idea permeates the whole work.

This last must not be misunderstood. A close analogy is seen only between the four first themes on the one side, and between the four second themes on the other. In this twofold symmetry the actual architectural idea of the symphony is centered. Moreover, in the first and last movement this idea is intensified to an impressive, architecturally developed plan.

Finally, a specific architectural feature presented itself in this ever recurring thematic progression from D to B-flat. This motivic step, first expressed through the two statements of the symphony's opening theme, reappeared invariably at the high points of the work's evolution. Now attention may be directed to a most interesting fact. This same motivic progression also forms the keys of the work's movements, which are D, D, B-flat, D. This question of a thematic key relationship between the movements of a musical composition, on which we merely touch at this time, will become the subject of a more detailed investigation in a later section of this study.

Rhythm and Linear Analysis

DURATIONAL REDUCTION

CARL SCHACHTER

O N E O F Beethoven's conversation books for the year 1824 contains the following entry in the hand of Anton Schindler: "The extended rhythms in your works do not result from computation but rather from the nature of the melody and, not infrequently, from the harmony. Am I right?"[1] I have not been able to find out if the entry is genuine or one of Schindler's later insertions.[2] But in either case, the remark holds considerable musical interest. In my first article on this subject,[3] I suggested that musical rhythm has two sources. One is the division of time, measurable by the motion of a physical body in space (clock or metronome)—Schindler's "computation." The other is the complex of periodicities inherent in the tonal system, in such phenomena as octave equivalence, scalar functions, dissonance resolving to consonance, and so on—in other words, "melody and, not infrequently, . . . harmony." I used the terms *durational rhythm* and *tonal rhythm* to refer to these two components. The earlier article

[1] Ludwig van Beethoven, *Konversationshefte*, Vol. V, ed. by Karl-Heinz Köhler, Grita Herre, and Peter Pötschner (Leipzig: VEB Deutscher Verlag für Musik, 1970), Heft 57 (end of February to mid-March 1824), p. 198; also cited in Hans Kann's preface to J.B. Cramer, *21 Etüden für Klavier* (Vienna: Universal Edition, 1974), p. vii. The original German reads as follows: "Die verlängerten Rhythmen in Ihren Werken liegen nicht in der Berechnung, sondern in der Natur der *Melodie* und öfters sogar in der *Harmonie*—habe ich Recht?" At that time, the word "rhythm" was often used to mean a group of measures or, broadly speaking, a phrase; Schindler probably employed it in this sense.

[2] Recent investigation has shown that many of Schindler's entries in the conversation books were added by him after Beethoven's death.

[3] Carl Schachter, "Rhythm and Linear Analysis: A Preliminary Study," *The Music Forum*, Vol. IV (New York: Columbia University Press, 1976), pp. 281–334, hereafter referred to as Rhythm I.

was of a very general, introductory nature with few rhythmic analyses and none treating in detail examples more than eight bars long.

In this second article I shall try to develop further some of the ideas sketched out in the earlier one. I shall do so by demonstrating an analytic notation that can help to reveal connections between durational and tonal organization, at least in some types of music. This notation is based on *durational reduction* applied to and coordinated with significant structural levels of voice leading; in other words, durational reduction combined with a reduction, in Schenker's manner, of the tonal contents. In music with clearly defined measure groups and phrases, the use of durational reduction frequently shows a "higher-level" metrical organization of bars, an organization of "hypermeasures," to use Edward Cone's term.[4] By indicating tonal events in durational proportion and by specifying the larger metrical divisions, such an approach can sometimes clarify aspects of rhythmic organization not directly revealed by graphic analyses that deal mainly with voice leading and harmony.

The examples that I shall discuss are, for the most part, short, relatively simple works. This will help the reader (and the writer!) to verify the analyses by ear, always an important consideration and one of overriding importance when the analytic procedure is, in some respects, a new one. If the analyses presented here are convincing—if, in some significant manner, they are true to the way the music sounds—then the approach will have demonstrated at least a limited utility, even though the pieces analyzed are comparatively short and simple ones.

Durational Reduction in Composition. That one might gain insight into some aspects of rhythmic organization by reducing note values and by grouping measures into larger metrical units is hardly a new idea. First of all, reduced note values and hypermeasures sometimes appear in compositions and in composer's sketches in a way that can clarify the rhythmic shape of an idea. Thus Beethoven's compression of the opening theme in the coda of the "Waldstein" Rondo (Example 1a) makes notationally explicit the theme's strong/weak metrics, though, to be sure, they are clear enough at the

---

[4] Edward Cone, *Musical Form and Musical Performance* (New York: Norton, 1968,) pp. 79–80.

EXAMPLE I   *Sonata, Op. 53, Rondo*   Beethoven

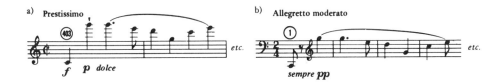

opening of the movement (Example 1b). On the other hand, a sketch of
Beethoven's for the Allegro molto of the Piano Sonata, Op. 110, sheds
light on a passage whose rhythmic shape is anything but obvious, having
eluded some excellent musicians, among them Artur Schnabel.[5] This
sketch does not employ reduced note values, but it is written, in part, in
hypermeasures of 4/4 time instead of the 2/4 meter of the movement. The
position of the bar lines shows that Beethoven heard the rhythm as syncopated; the chords appear off the main beats. Compare Example 2a (the
upper voice of the passage as it appears in the composition) with Example
2b (the sketch).[6]

225

EXAMPLE 2   *Sonata, Op. 110, Allegro molto*   Beethoven

[5] Beethoven, *32 Sonatas for the Pianoforte*, ed. by Artur Schnabel (New York: Simon and Schuster,
1935), Vol. II, p. 804, footnote *a*.

[6] The sketch is transcribed by Karl Michael Komma in Beethoven, *Die Klaviersonate As-Dur
Opus 110: Beiheft zur Faksimile-Ausgabe* (Stuttgart: Ichthys Verlag, 1967), p. 11.

Durational Reduction in Analysis. Recently, some musicians and writers have used reduced note values, hypermeasures, or the two combined as analytic tools; among them are Roy Travis,[7] Grosvenor Cooper and Leonard B. Meyer,[8] and Wallace Berry.[9] Years earlier, Schenker used such tools in a particularly interesting way in one of his *Tonwille* monographs: the study of Beethoven's Piano Sonata, Op. 2, No. 1. At the end of his discussion of the first movement, Schenker presents a rhythmic reduction of the first twenty bars of his graph (*Urlinie-Tafel*) of the movement. Since this is a facet of Schenker's work that hardly anyone knows, I should like to reproduce the rhythmic reduction (Example 3a) together with the first twenty bars of the voice-leading graph (Example 3b).

EXAMPLE 3   *Sonata, Op. 2, No. 1, Allegro, bars 1–20*   Beethoven

a) Schenker's rhythmic reduction

b) Schenker's voice-leading sketch

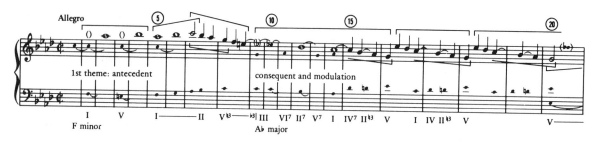

[7] Roy Travis, "Toward a New Concept of Tonality?," *Journal of Music Theory*, Vol. III, No. 2 (November, 1959), pp. 274–75.

[8] Grosvenor Cooper and Leonard B. Meyer, *The Rhythmic Structure of Music* (Chicago: University of Chicago Press, 1960), pp. 83–87.

[9] Wallace Berry, *Structural Functions in Music* (Englewood Cliffs: Prentice-Hall, 1976), Chapter 4, especially pp. 334, 352, and 395–96. Also see his review of Cone's *Musical Form and Musical Performance* in *Perspectives of New Music*, Vol. IX, No. 2–Vol. X, No. 1 (Spring–Fall, 1971), pp. 280–81.

Schenker writes the following about his rhythmic reduction: "To deepen the reader's understanding of the sketch, it is warmly recommended that he picture its contents according to the following reduction of note values. This provides valuable insight, particularly into the reinterpretation of weak bars as strong ones."[10] (The final, normally weak bar of a phrase will be reinterpreted as strong if the beginning of a new phrase overlaps the cadential goal, as in bar 20 of the Beethoven movement.[11]) After showing the rhythmic reduction, Schenker continues: "In addition one might derive a metrical schema from the notes of the reduction:

$$- \smile \mid - \smile \mid - \smile \smile \mid - \smile \smallsmile \text{ etc.}$$

In so doing, one will derive still further insight into the rhythmic freedom of the whole."[12]

As far as I know, Schenker did not continue (or, at least, did not continue to publish) this kind of rhythmic reduction in any of his later analyses, those worked out after he had found clearer ways of indicating the various levels of voice leading than are found in the early *Tonwille* studies. (The reader will note that the durational reduction of Op. 2, No. 1 applies only to the foreground.) And the later writers whom I have cited, even those influenced by Schenker, have not attempted to coordinate their rhythmic reductions with the deeper levels of tonal structure. This, I think, has been a drawback. For one thing, details—rhythmic as well as tonal—often reveal their meaning only when perceived as part of a larger whole; to understand the foreground at all, one must take the middleground into account. In addition, larger considerations of rhythm almost inevitably escape a rhythmic analysis that concentrates upon the foreground alone. The analyses that · I shall present in the remainder of this article (imperfect as they probably are) represent an attempt to understand rhythmic movement in its relation to large as well as to small tonal progression.

[10] Heinrich Schenker, *Der Tonwille*, Heft 2 (Vienna: A. Gutmann Verlag, 1922), p. 30.

[11] Schenker refers to this technique in *Der freie Satz* (Vienna: Universal Edition, 1935); 2d ed., revised by Oswald Jonas (Vienna: Universal Edition, 1956), p. 194, § 298. Page numbers given in subsequent references are those of the 2d ed.; parallel passages in the English ed., *Free Composition*, translated and edited by Ernst Oster (New York: Longman, 1979), may be located by means of section and figure numbers.

[12] Schenker, *Der Tonwille*, Heft 2, p. 30. Each 2/4 bar of Schenker's durational reduction (Example 3a) becomes a strong or weak *beat* in the metrical schema. Thus the first grouping ($- \smile$) represents bars 1–4 of the piece.

ANALYSES

Chopin, Prelude, Op. 28, No. 3
(Example 4)

The Analytic Notation. Example 4 contains four graphs (Examples 4a–4d), vertically aligned, of the first piece that I shall discuss: the G-Major Prelude from Chopin's Op. 28.[13] In these graphs, note-values do not correspond to structural levels. Instead, they have a purely durational meaning: each

EXAMPLE 4   *Prelude, Op. 28, No. 3*   Chopin

228

[13] My analysis of the tonal events of the Prelude is based on Schenker's in *Der freie Satz*, Anhang, p. 36, Figure 76/2. My reading differs from Schenker's in a few details.

quarter note equals a full bar (¢) of the actual composition. Thus, the graph of Example 4d, which represents the foreground, contains thirty-three quarter notes, corresponding exactly to the thirty-three bars of the Prelude. Examples 4a, 4b, and 4c, which show three levels of middleground, contain fewer quarter notes than Example 4d: Example 4a contains sixteen; both Examples 4b and 4c contain twenty-four. These discrepancies do not result from different scales of reduction; the quarter note equals a bar on all four levels. They indicate, rather, that some of the prolongations go together with durational expansions. Thus the two introductory bars of the Prelude, the six bars of coda, and bar 11, which extends a four-bar group to five bars, all belong to the foreground and are represented only in Example 4d. Note that Example 4 does *not* include a graph of the background; more about this omission in the last part of the article.

Bar lines occur in all four graphs; they demarcate measure groups (hypermeasures) in the composition. In these graphs most of the bars contain four quarter notes and, consequently, represent groups of four bars in the original piece. Since the Prelude also contains smaller hypermeasures of two bars—they are particularly clear in the introduction and coda—it might seem possible to place the bar lines after every two quarter notes instead of every four. Such a procedure, however, would give a distorted picture of the piece, for most of the two-bar groups form part of larger, four-bar units. In making durational reductions, it is advisable to show graphically the largest groupings of measures that recur more or less consistently throughout the piece or section. The reasons will be increasingly clear as we proceed. But it should be apparent already that the two-bar groups are easily discernible in Examples 4c and 4d, whereas the four-bar groups would be largely obscured if one doubled the number of bar lines.

In graphic analyses that use durational reduction, the measures in the graphs may represent phrases in the piece. They do not do so here if by "phrase" we understand a unit of tonal motion as well as of duration. Bars 3–6, for example, do not form a phrase, for they contain no tonal progression. The complete phrase includes the succeeding five bars (bars 7–11); it is a phrase of eight bars extended to nine.

Other symbols that occur in Example 4 have the same meanings that they would have in any graphic analysis.

229

Since the analytic technique I am using here is not a familiar one, I shall comment upon the graphs of this first example in rather considerable detail. I believe that the implications of the analysis will be understood most readily if we proceed from Example 4a to Example 4d. The reader should compare each of the four graphs with the actual composition, for each of them views it from a somewhat different perspective.

Example 4a. This graph shows the level of middleground closest to the piece's fundamental structure. In it the background progression ($\hat{3}$–$\hat{2}$–$\hat{1}$ over I–V–I) is divided and extended by the familiar technique of *interruption*, producing the progression $\hat{3}$–$\hat{2}$ ‖ $\hat{3}$–$\hat{2}$–$\hat{1}$ over I–V‖I–V–I.

Whenever an interruption divides the fundamental structure, it is decisive for the piece's form. In our Prelude, the form-making power of interruption is particularly apparent. Like several of the Op. 28 Preludes, this one has a form more usually characteristic of a section than of a whole piece. In essence it consists of a single period of two phrases in antecedent–consequent relation. Of course a piece that was simply a period of, say, sixteen bars would be a virtual impossibility; it would sound incomplete. Chopin avoids this difficulty by modifying the consequent phrase; most often, as in our Prelude, he enlarges it and, by delaying the final tonic, creates a stronger ending. Many of the Preludes—and especially those written in period form—have a character different from almost anything else in the literature: they sound like stylized fragments and, because they are stylized, they are satisfying and complete in themselves. Unlike some of Schumann's fragmentary pieces, which are often true fragments, even the shortest of the Chopin Preludes makes sense when played alone.

In comparing this graph with the piece, two apparent discrepancies immediately stand out. The first has already been mentioned: the graph indicates a total duration of only sixteen bars while the piece contains thirty-three bars. A related discrepancy is that the sixteen beats of the graph divide equally into eight plus eight whereas the piece is divided asymmetrically: even disregarding the introduction, the coda, and the "extra" bar 11, the second part of the piece is considerably longer than the first. By showing the main body of the piece with an equal duration for its two parts, I indicate that its asymmetrical proportions grow out of an underlying symmetry.

I don't believe that all rhythmic and metric irregularities in tonal music necessarily derive from an underlying regularity. But some surely do. And in the case of our Prelude we have excellent grounds for assuming that the tonal organization implies an equal division of time. For in hearing the consequent phrase of a period, we are guided by the expectations created by the antecedent. And one of these expectations is that the consequent will resolve the tonal tension produced by the antecedent *and that it will do so within the same amount of time*. Were this not so, expansions or contractions of the consequent phrase would lose much, if not all, of their effect. (To attempt to explain the grounds for this durational expectation would take us too far afield. I believe that most musicians will agree with me that it exists; besides, most consequent phrases do, in fact, have the same length as their antecedents.)

I should like to call attention to one other feature of this graph: the final tonic (bar 26) enters in the second half of a hypermeasure—in a metrically weaker place, therefore, than the dominant that precedes it. In my earlier article, I discussed the rather prevalent view that phrases are normally end-accented, that the final cadential chord falls on an accent or downbeat.[14] I disagree with this view and follow Schenker in assuming that the final tonic of a phrase does not normally receive a metrical accent.[15] I see no reason to believe that the metrical organization of a group of measures differs in principle from that of a single measure and assume that both are beginning- rather than end-accented. Within a group of measures, just as within a measure, rhythmic organization can contradict the meter and produce a stress on a normally weak place. In the Chopin piece, however, the goal tonic of the soprano line falls at the end of a legato slur—a notation that suggests that it is rhythmically, as well as metrically, weak. The metrical position of the final tonic, incidentally, registers in the graph only if we show groups of four rather than two bars, another reason for barring the graph in fours.

14 Rhythm I, p. 305.
15 Schenker, *Der freie Satz*, pp. 187–88, § 288.

231

Example 4b. The most striking feature of this graph is, of course, the enlargement of the consequent phrase; here it contains sixteen beats (sixteen bars in the piece) as against eight in Example 4a. Part of the added time is filled with an extension of tonic harmony (bars 16 and 17); reference to the score (or to Example 4c) will show that this expanded tonic becomes a V⁷ of IV. A subdominant chord, supporting a neighboring tone in the soprano, occupies the rest of the time. It would be wrong to maintain that the extra bars serve merely to provide space for the IV chord; Chopin could easily have accommodated a IV–V–I cadence within the framework of an eight-bar phrase. By extending (and, consequently, emphasizing) the subdominant for as long as he does, however, Chopin adds immeasurably to the force of the cadence and gives the goal tonic a finality it would altogether lack if it came at the end of a symmetrical, sixteen-bar period. Thus we see an element of durational rhythm—pacing—serving to clarify a tonal function.

Chopin continues to group the measures of the consequent phrase into fours; the expansion does not disturb the larger meter. Note that the I and IV chords (of bars 12–23) occupy six bars apiece. The change of chord, therefore, overlaps the four-bar groupings and helps to prevent an excessive segmentation. Incidentally, the fact that the I becomes an applied dominant to the IV in bars 16 and 17 does not mean that the prolongation of IV begins in bar 16. The contents of bars 16 and 17 are not heard as IV, but as I directed toward IV. Therefore it would be incorrect to assume that the "harmonic rhythm" of six bars (I) plus six (IV) has as its basis the division of four plus eight bars of the larger meter, as in Example 5. Here again, as

EXAMPLE 5   *Prelude, Op. 28, No. 3, bars 12–23*   Chopin

in some of the examples from my previous article, the conflict between tonal and durational groupings is built into the deeper fabric of the composition.[16]

Example 4c. From the point of view of rhythmic implication, this level offers more of interest in the consequent phrase than in the antecedent. A primary question is whether we even ought to regard it as a single phrase expanded to sixteen bars or rather as a group of two phrases of eight bars apiece (bars 12–19 and 20–27). At first hearing, the cadential effect of bars 16–19 (they suggest V^7–I in C major) and the long halt in bars 18–19 on the soprano's e^2 might lead one to hear two phrases. The "C major," however, is the IV of a I–IV–V–I progression; it moves on without a break to the V and I. In a deeper sense, therefore, the sixteen bars contain a single cadential progression, I–IV–V–I, and constitute a single phrase.

This graph sheds light on the contrapuntal meaning—and also, therefore, on the harmonic status—of the $\frac{6}{4}$ chord (apparently a II$\frac{6}{4}$) interpolated in bars 22–23 between the IV and V. (The b^1 in the soprano of bar 22 is a passing tone and does not affect the status of the chord.) In a true II$\frac{6}{4}$, the sixth above the bass $(\hat{2})$ is a consonant tone; it represents the root of the chord. The foreign, dissonant element is the fifth; usually, it is a suspension resolving into the third of V. As the graph indicates, however, the a^1 in the Prelude is not a chord tone; it anticipates the fifth of dominant harmony. The chord, therefore, is not really a II; it is a IV with an anticipation added. Only an awareness of the larger metrical pattern enables us to perceive the a^1 as an anticipation and to hear the chord succession correctly.[17] Here, again, organizing the graph in small hypermeasures of two beats apiece would obscure this larger meter.

One other feature of this graph deserves mention. The main melodic tones b^2 (bars 5 and 14) and a^2 (in the graph, bar 9; in the piece, bars 8 and 10) now fall in the middle of the hypermeasures rather than at the beginning. Such displacements often result from melodic arpeggiations and unfoldings.

---

[16] Rhythm I, pp. 329–34.

[17] In *Der freie Satz*, p. 178, § 280, Schenker cites this passage (in his Figure 76/2) as one where we might hear either a single harmony (IV$^{5–6}$) or two harmonies (IV–II). But if we take the hypermeter into account, we cannot infer a functional II.

233

Here they also help to give the right-hand part the same contours as the ostinato figure of the left hand.

Example 4d. This graph represents the foreground of the piece; only the rapid figuration is omitted. The most obvious "new" features are, of course, the introduction and the coda. But some of the rhythmic implications of the main body of the piece, viewed from this perspective, are just as interesting. In the second half of the antecedent phrase (bars 7–11), the melodic progression e^2–a^2 appears twice, together with its harmonic accompaniment. (A seventh, $c\natural^2$, is added to the second statement of the D chord.) This is a simple example of prolongation by repetition. Its purpose here is twofold. First, it continues the larger metric groups of four bars begun in bars 3–6; the extra, fifth bar is heard so clearly as an extension that it does not at all disturb the hypermeter. Secondly, the repetition fills the four bars without retarding the melodic pace; compare Example 4d, where quarter-note motion prevails, with Example 4c, where half notes appear. In the second part of the consequent phrase, in contrast, the larger melodic progression does in fact slow down (see the half notes in Example 4d). How appropriate that it should do so just at the place where the phrase begins to expand and where the final tonic becomes a more distant goal.

No sooner has Chopin established a hypermeter of four (bars 3–6, 7–10) than he playfully contradicts it with the "extra" bar 11. Here the rhythmic quirk calls attention to a beautiful tonal development: the enlargement of the motivic neighboring-tone figures e^2–d^2 and c^3–b^2 (see Example 6).

EXAMPLE 6   *Prelude, Op. 28, No. 3, bars 10–14*   Chopin

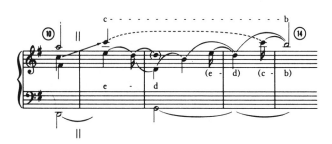

The most remarkable features of the introduction and coda lie in the sixteenth-note figuration—in the most immediate level, therefore, of the foreground—and are not registered in this graph. (For the sake of completeness, and because they are so beautiful, I shall describe them briefly a bit further on). This graph does shed light, however, on the large metric organization of the introduction and coda. Note that the four-bar hypermeter continues into the coda (bars 28–31) and that the piece ends, as it begins, with a two-bar group. I doubt that this symmetry is accidental, though I can't prove that it is not.

Some Features of the Immediate Foreground. Example 7 shows how the right-hand melody grows out of the accompaniment. The connection is so apparent that it hardly requires demonstration. One rhythmic aspect of the relationship, however, is perhaps not so obvious. The emphasized tones of the accompaniment form a rhythmic pattern (as well as a melodic one) very similar to that of the right-hand part; particularly striking is the appearance of the neighboring e^2 on the fourth sixteenth of a weak beat (Example 7a). The right-hand part of bars 3 and 4 has the same rhythmic contour "stretched apart," so to speak (Example 7b). In bars 16 and 20, Chopin uses the rhythm of bar 3 for the reiteration of a single note (Example 7c). Thus we find that the tonal rhythm concealed in the figuration of the opening bar gradually evolves into a purely durational pattern.

235

EXAMPLE 7   *Prelude, Op. 28, No. 3*   Chopin

The progressive shortening of rhythmic groups in the coda (whole bars, half bars, quarter bars) is easy to recognize from the score and does not require an illustrative example. Less easy to see, but immediately apparent to the ear, is the way the two final chords indistinctly echo the accompaniment pattern and, indeed, the opening phase of the melodic line.

Mozart, Symphony No. 35, K.385, Trio of Menuetto
(Example 8)

Graphic Notation. Example 8 contains graphs of the next piece we shall discuss; the Trio of the Menuetto from Mozart's "Haffner" Symphony. In addition to the durational graphs (Examples 8a–8e), there is a voice-leading graph of the foreground, not in rhythmic reduction (Example 8f). As with the Chopin Prelude, each bar of the original becomes a quarter note in the proportional reductions; groups of four bars in the piece become measures of four quarters each in the graphs. I have used an alla breve signature rather than one of 4/4 in order to represent the subdivision of the four-bar groups into smaller hypermeasures of two bars each. The two-bar groupings are even more strongly marked in the Trio than in the Chopin Prelude.

Examples 8a and 8b: Phrase Structure and Form. The Trio has the usual A:‖:BA:‖ form. The two A sections are identical; in the autograph, in fact, the second one is not written out but merely indicated by a da capo.[18] Each main section consists of a single phrase: one of eight bars in the A sections and one of twelve bars in the B section. (As in the Chopin Prelude, the four-bar groups are not complete units of tonal motion; therefore, they are not really phrases.) In Examples 8a and 8b, the twelve bars of the B section are represented by only eight quarter notes. This apparent contradiction indicates that the twelve bars must be regarded as the expansion of an eight-bar phrase. More about this expansion on pp. 214–15 below.

[18] See W. A. Mozart, *Symphony No. 35 in D, K.385, "Haffner" Symphony,* facsimile edition, with an introduction by Sydney Beck (New York: Oxford University Press, 1968).

Like the Chopin Prelude, the Trio is based on interruption; but here the technique leads to a three-part form. The first A section and the B sections make up the first phase of the interrupted progression; the second A section provides the second, closing phase. Three-part forms based on interruption occur frequently, a well-known example being the second song of Schumann's *Dichterliebe*, analyzed by Schenker in *Der freie Satz* and commented upon by Allen Forte in a widely-quoted essay.[19] In such three-part forms, the two A sections function differently within the whole piece even when—as in the Trio—they contain identical material. The difference in function is not "theoretical"; it can be confirmed by direct musical perception. No one with any experience in music would hear the first part of the Trio as a complete piece, despite the strong harmonic cadence and the $\hat{3}$–$\hat{2}$–$\hat{1}$ progression of the top voice. It is too short, too lacking in articulation, development, and contrast. But when the same material recurs after the B section, the tonal resolution creates a definite impression of closure.

In the Trio, a *three*-part form grows out of a tonal structure divided into *two* parts by the technique of interruption. This relationship bears upon the most striking feature of Example 8a: the disproportion in duration between the two segments of the interrupted progression. In particular, the melodic $\hat{2}$ and the harmonic II⁶–V (bar 26) of the second A section seem dwarfed by the long duration of the preceding structural chords and top-voice tones. (In the graph, the duple division of bar 26 is purely a notational convenience.) The disproportion is in marked contrast to the Chopin Prelude, in which the large-scale structure proceeds at a much more even pace (compare Example 8a with Example 4a). It is, perhaps, too early to draw conclusions from the lopsided proportions of Example 8a, but a few ideas suggest themselves:

In *Der freie Satz*, Schenker maintained that the *first* $\hat{3}$–$\hat{2}$ over I–V in an interrupted progression had greater structural weight than the second.[20] At least for pieces like our Trio—those where the first structural V forms the

237

[19] Schenker, *Der freie Satz*, Anhang, p. 8, Figure 22b. Forte's comments are found in "Schenker's Conception of Musical Structure," *Journal of Music Theory*, Vol. III, No. 1 (April, 1959), pp. 9–14; reprinted in Maury Yeston, ed., *Readings in Schenker Analysis and Other Approaches* (New Haven: Yale University Press, 1977), pp. 12–18.

[20] Schenker, *Der freie Satz*, p. 72, §90, and Anhang, p. 8, Figure 21b.

EXAMPLE 8   *Symphony No. 35, K.385, Trio of Menuetto*   Mozart

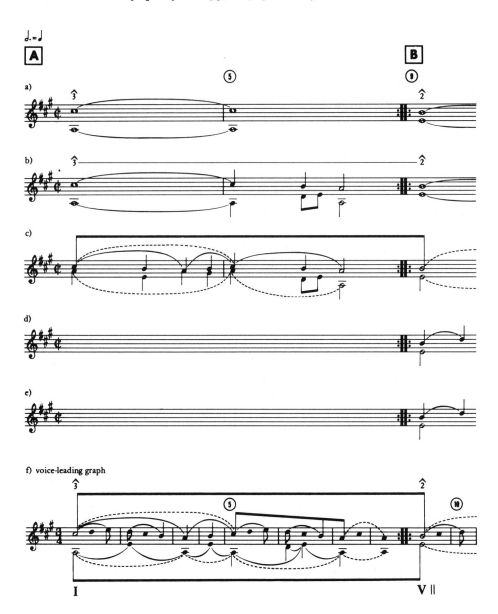

238

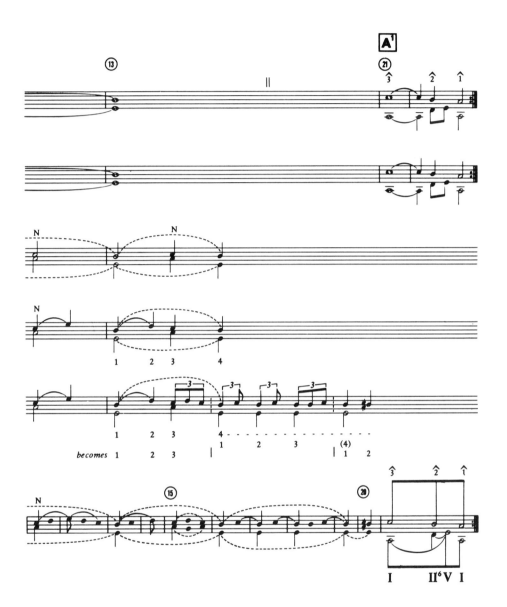

basis for an entire section—Schenker's contention is confirmed by the durational values.

Even within the A sections themselves, however (see Example 8b), there is a marked disproportion between the duration of the extended initial tonic and that of the closing cadential progression—so much so, in fact, that by itself the progression sounds most unconvincing. One is reminded of Schenker's comment that the masters tried to avoid the juxtaposition of sharply contrasting rhythmic values, and that they would adjust the rhythms of a piece so as to prevent such contrasts.[21] A glance at Example 8c will show how the adjustment takes place here; similar adjustments take place in the countless other cases where the opening tonic has a much longer duration than the cadential dominant. As Example 8c shows, the cadence continues the rhythmic values of the prolongational motions within the I rather than the extended duration of the prolonged I itself. Thus the pacing of middleground or background progressions may be partly determined by the rhythms of the foreground—a very frequent possibility, evident in the Trio but not in the Chopin Prelude, where the foreground rhythms of the top voice move at an unusually slow pace.

Examples 8c, 8d, and 8e: The Expansion of the B Section. Without a doubt, the most interesting rhythmic feature of the Trio is the expansion, in bars 16–20, of the B section, an expansion that produces a phrase of twelve bars from an "original" (in the middleground) of only eight. (That the phrase is to be heard as an expanded eight bars seems unquestionable, if only because of the varied repetition, starting in bar 13, of bars 9–12, a four-bar group; one expects the repetition to reach its goal in bar 16.)

This expansion is very different from the one in the second part of the Chopin Prelude. In the Prelude, the expansion coincides with a new harmony (IV) and a new melodic diminution; in the Trio, no new tonal material appears. In the Prelude, the extended phrase divides into regular four-bar groups; in the Trio, the expansion produces a metrically irregular grouping: the twelve bars do not divide evenly into three groups of four. Finally, the

---

[21] *Ibid.*, p. 189, §291.

five-bar expansion in the Trio (bars 16–20) sounds like the enlargement of a single bar of the middleground (bar 16)—a clear and simple example of what Schenker calls a *Dehnung*.[22]

Examples 8d and 8e show very clearly the inner rhythmic organization of bars 13–20, far more clearly than the voice-leading graph (without rhythmic reduction) of the foreground. Note, first of all, that bar 16—in the listener's expectation a weak (fourth) bar—is reinterpreted as a strong (first) one.[23] Mozart emphasizes bar 16 by placing Great E in the second bassoon. The low bass note provides an accent that defines the bar as the beginning of a new rhythmic unit. This new unit would also contain four bars (bars 16–19), except that rhythmic activity stops at the onset of bar 19 (note especially the viola part); once more a weak bar becomes reinterpreted as strong. A brief two-bar group (bars 19–20) restores metrical equilibrium and leads to a normal reprise that begins on a strong bar.

Beethoven, Sonata, Op. 14, No. 1, Allegretto
(Example 9)

241

Graphic Notation. The graphs of Example 9 deal with the second movement of Beethoven's Piano Sonata, Op. 14, No. 1, with the E-minor part only, not with the Maggiore. In these graphs, unlike the earlier ones, I have represented a full bar in the original by an eighth-note. A measure of 4/4 in the graphs, therefore, is equivalent to eight bars of the original, not to four. And in these graphs, the measures coincide with complete phrases in that each of them ends with a clear cadence (except the last one, which closes into the codetta). I have chosen this different scale of reduction for two reasons: In this piece, for the most part, the eight-bar phrases divide much less clearly into two groups of four bars each than in the Chopin Prelude or the Mozart Trio. And, more importantly, the chief rhythmic feature of this piece—syncopation—is not conveyed clearly by a reduction of whole bars to quarter notes.

---

[22] *Ibid* p. 192, §297.

[23] As in bar 20 of Beethoven's Sonata, Op. 2, No. 1, first movement, discussed on p. 201 above.

EXAMPLE 9   *Sonata, Op. 14, No. 1, Allegretto*   Beethoven

243

Overview of the Piece: Some Details of Voice Leading. The Allegretto is written in ABA[1] form and shows simple but effective use of registral contrasts. Each of the three sections contains two phrases in antecedent–consequent relation. In the first A section, the two phrases form a normal sixteen-bar period, all within an extended tonic. The B section also consists of a sixteen-bar period, based harmonically on a prolonged VI that moves (through an augmented sixth chord) to a dividing V. As in the Mozart Trio, the A and B sections together form the first segment of an interrupted structural progression. The final A section is not an exact repetition of the first one; the consequent phrase is changed by the introduction of a strong IV, by new diminutions, and by an expansion from eight to ten bars. There is a codetta of twelve bars on I$^{\sharp 3}$.

Though it is fairly simple in its tonal organization, the Beethoven piece is certainly more difficult to understand than the two other pieces I have analyzed. It would take us too far from our main subject if I were to discuss in detail every aspect of voice leading. However, I feel I must mention three important ones, especially since the rhythmic reductions do not reveal their meaning as clearly as voice-leading graphs would.

1. The entire piece is permeated by the initial neighboring-tone figure and related figures derived from it. Example 10, a voice-leading sketch of the first eight bars, indicates the figure by means of brackets. In bars 17–24 (see Examples 9c and 9d), the right-hand part, a polyphonic melody, contains two neighboring-tone motions, each extended over several bars. The first, e^1–$f\natural^1$–e^1, belongs to the lower "voice" of the implied polyphony; the second, g^1–$f\sharp^1$–g^1, belongs to the upper (and main) "voice." These figures are expansions of the opening motive.

2. Example 10 also clarifies the meaning of the strange descending bass line of bars 1–5. The underlying idea is a downward transfer of the tonic (e–E), achieved by means of an arpeggiation. The unusual feature is that one tone of the arpeggiation, B, is omitted; through this elision, A$\sharp$ (which would normally ascend to B) proceeds directly down to A$\natural$ (compare Example 9d).

3. Bars 41–45 are difficult. As Example 11 indicates, the c^2 of bar 43 is a suspension resolving to b^1. The opening I moves to IV through a passing diminished seventh in $^4_3$ position (bars 43–44). The main top-voice motion is e^1–b^1–a^1; the bass passes from e through d to c.

EXAMPLE 10   *Sonata, Op. 14, No. 1, Allegretto,*   Beethoven
                bars 1–8

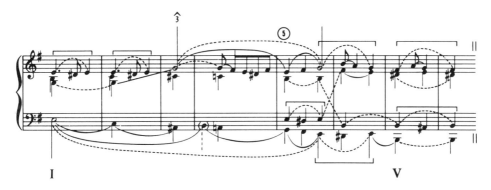

EXAMPLE 11   *Sonata, Op. 14, No. 1, Allegretto,*   Beethoven
                bars 41–45

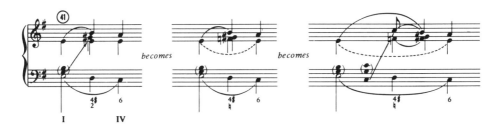

Examples 9a and 9b. As in the Mozart Trio, the disproportion between the rapid structural cadence at the end and the prolonged harmonies earlier on is a striking feature of the first graph. A similar disproportion, involving the intermediate cadence that closes the first A section, can be observed in the second graph. Prolongational motions, on levels closer to the foreground, prepare the cadential rhythms—just as in the Mozart example.

However, this piece differs from the Mozart and Chopin examples in that the final tonic enters in a very strong metrical position—at the beginning of the twelve-bar codetta (bar 51). It is very instructive to compare the rhythmic effect of the final tonic, which falls on a true "downbeat," with that of the tonic that closes the first A section on a metrically weak bar (bar 16). Yet this significant difference would be minimized (or even ignored altogether) by an approach that in principle regards cadential tonics as "downbeats," no matter what the actual metrics might be.

Some readers might perhaps wonder whether bar 51, the beginning of the codetta, ought not to be heard as a weak measure reinterpreted as strong, for the tonic chord that begins there functions both as the goal of the preceding cadence and as the beginning of a new grouping. However, a necessary condition for such a reinterpretation is lacking here: the preceding phrase does not sound metrically incomplete, for it has a final (weak) bar— bar 50. It would, therefore, require a mental contortion to understand bar 51 as weak and as belonging to the preceding group of measures.

One brief further comment about Examples 9a and 9b. In bar 30, I have shown the A♯ in the bass rather than the middle voice (where it occurs in the music) simply to be able to fit the graphs on a single staff. Example 9d shows the actual disposition; in any case, the two versions share more or less the same meaning, so the rearrangement changes nothing fundamental.

Examples 9c and 9d. The character of this Allegretto is, to a great extent, influenced by the numerous sforzandi that occur in bars 3, 18, 45, and parallel places. They produce an unusually powerful effect and, perhaps, might bear out Schindler's otherwise surprising statement that Beethoven performed the piece almost as if it were an Allegro furioso.[24] A study of the music reveals that all of the sforzandi have at least one thing in common: they accentuate weak beats or bars and produce syncopated rhythms.

In the first eight-bar phrase, for example, rhythmic and textural changes produce strongly-marked groupings of two bars. The two-bar hyper-measures, in fact, project so clearly as almost to create the impression of a 6/4 meter. I say "almost" advisedly, for actually writing the piece in six would create a very different (and much weaker) notational picture. There are, of course, four two-bar groups in the phrase; as my graphs indicate, I

[24] Anton Schindler, *Biographie von Ludwig van Beethoven* (2d ed.; Münster: Aschendorff, 1845), p. 234. While it appears in this and the 1st ed. (1840), as well as in Ignaz Moscheles' translation (1841), this statement is absent from the 3d ed. (1860), on which Donald MacArdle based his English ed., *Beethoven as I Knew Him* (Chapel Hill: University of North Carolina Press, 1966; reprinted, New York: Norton, 1972).

hear the phrase as metrically analogous to a bar of 4/4. The third bar of the phrase, therefore, would be equivalent to the second beat of a 4/4 measure; though strong in relation to the immediately preceding and following bars, it counts as weak within the larger metrical scheme (four "beats" of two bars each). In relation to this larger scheme, the sforzando in bar 3 creates a syncopation (see especially Example 9c).

The meaning of this sforzando relates to the tonal organization as well as to the meter. Example 10 indicates that g^1 $(\hat{3})$ of the main top-voice line is shifted away from the tonic chord to which it belongs and into a dissonant relation with the A♯ of the bass. The displacement of g^1, therefore, produces a syncopation that is not only rhythmic, but contrapuntal as well.[25]

The motivic connection of bars 17–24 with bars 1–8 is obvious. As a consequence, we hear the sforzandi of bars 18 and 20 as related to the one in bar 3. Nevertheless, the new sforzandi have a partly different character and meaning. First of all, they produce syncopations within a smaller time span, for they stress the second bar of a two-bar group. This contraction is reflected in the graphs; these syncopations appear at a later level (Example 9d) and stress eighth-notes, not quarters. And secondly, the displaced g^1's now form only rhythmic syncopations, not contrapuntal ones. Reference to the score (or to Example 9e) shows that the shifted tones are consonant with the G chords against which they sound, as well as with the C chord that governs the section.

The sforzandi in bars 45–46 (Example 9d) produce syncopations within a still narrower metrical framework, for they fall on the second beat of a 3/4 bar. These syncopations, too, are purely rhythmic, not contrapuntal. Yet the drastic rhythmic effect results, in part, from the contradiction of a tonal implication. As Example 9d indicates, bars 45–47 (first beat) count as the expansion of a single bar; the expansion arises out of the repetition of the eighth-note figure of bar 44 and of the downbeat chord to which it leads. Now the beginning of the eighth-note figure (in bar 44) contains the resolution of a dissonant suspension; such a resolution, of course, must be played more softly than the preceding dissonance. But when the figure repeats in

[25] In the Chopin Prelude, the $\hat{3}$ is also shifted to the third bar of the phrase. But the effect of syncopation does not arise in the foreground, partly because there is no unusual dynamic stress and partly because tonic harmony continues—the b^2 is a locally consonant tone.

bars 45 and 46, the sforzandi fall on repetitions of the very note that had previously taken the resolution. This sudden reversal in dynamic "gesture" gives these syncopations an almost violent character.

All of these syncopations that we have cited fall on the *second* unit of a metrical group. The syncopation in bar 3 falls on the second of four hyper-measures within an eight-bar phrase. The one in bar 18 falls on the second bar of a two-bar hypermeasure. And the one in bar 45 falls on the second beat of the bar. As the piece moves forward, each "new" syncopation occurs on the same "beat" as the preceding one, only measured against a faster pulse. This compression, if one can call it that, contributes greatly to the developing momentum of the piece.

Schubert, Valse Sentimentale, Op. 50, No. 13 (*Example 12*)

Graphic Notation. The last piece that I shall discuss will be the A-Major Waltz from Schubert's Op. 50 (Example 12). I have used the same scale of reduction for these graphs as for those of the Beethoven example: a 3/4 bar in the piece becomes an eighth-note in the graphs; more important, a hypermeasure of two bars becomes a quarter-note beat. Such hypermeasures occur very prominently in this piece—more so than in any of the other three I have discussed. This is partly because the bass moves almost every two bars, and where it does not (bar 7 and parallel places), a $^6_4$ moves to a V⁷. The most striking rhythmic feature of the piece, the cross-rhythm of the right-hand part, also emphasizes two-bar units: the right-hand sets up a secondary meter of 3/2 against the 3/4 pattern of the left-hand part.

Texture and Form. The right hand plays two melodic lines written in free imitation. The lower of these lines (starting on c♯² in bar 2) carries the main melodic motion and is, in general, more active than the upper one. The upper line, therefore, functions as a secondary part placed over the main one. A curious feature of the upper line is its beginning on f♯², a tone foreign to tonic harmony (the f♯², of course, is the upper neighbor of e²). A glance at the Waltz that precedes this one helps to explain the emphasis on f$\sharp^2$ in our piece; Op. 50, No. 12 is in D major with f$\sharp^2$ as its most prominent melodic tone. The f$\sharp^2$ forms a link between the two Waltzes; such links occur fairly often in a chain of short pieces.

The Waltz is written in ABA form with varied repeats of the A section. Taking the repeats into account, we might represent the form as A^{1}A^2‖:BA^3:‖. The varied repetitions of the A section change it only very slightly, but where so much repetition takes place, even slight changes assume significance. Of these changes, perhaps the most important occur at or near the cadences. Thus, at the first cadence (bars 8–9), the main melodic line settles on its goal, a^1. However, the secondary line above it remains immobilized on e^2. At the second cadence (bars 16–17), both lines lead to the tonic; the cadence, therefore, is stronger. And at the end of the piece (bars 34–37), both lines resume their original registers after a sojourn in the higher octave; again, as at the second cadence, the two lines move to the tonic. The final cadence, therefore, is the strongest of all.

249

Example 12a. The first of the graphs represents a level of middleground very close to the background of the piece. I regard the twelve bars of the B section as resulting from the expansion of an eight-bar phrase, as we shall see when we discuss Example 12d. Therefore, the B section is represented by one bar of 4/4 (eight eighth-notes, equivalent to eight bars of 3/4 in the piece). The first complete phrase begins in bar 3. I have therefore left out of the graph the opening two bars, whose rather special meaning becomes clear only from a perspective slightly closer to the foreground of the piece.

One aspect of the tonal structure must be mentioned here. The B section is based upon a prolonged C$\sharp$-major chord: III$^{\sharp3}$ in A major. As the graph indicates, I hear this chord as passing to the II^6 of bar 29, which belongs to the final A section. Example 13 adds some explanatory detail and shows that the bass tone, C$\sharp$, supports and makes consonant a passing G$\sharp$ in the middle voice. It might seem plausible, at first, to understand the C$\sharp$ chord as the main connection between I and V, thus: I–III$^{\sharp3}$–V; in that case, the II^6 would assume the status of a passing chord. But such a reading would

EXAMPLE 12   *Valse Sentimentale, Op. 50, No. 13*   Schubert

250

251

contradict a chief feature of the Waltz: the fact that the II⁶, most unusually, occurs at the "downbeats" of all three A sections.

EXAMPLE 13

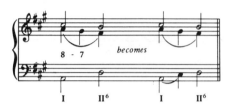

Examples 12b and 12c. At the level of prolongation shown in Example 12b, the meaning of the first two bars begins to become clear. In order to understand them, let us compare the opening of the Waltz with the Chopin Prelude. Both pieces begin with tonic harmony in the left-hand part alone. In the Prelude, the tonic persists beyond the introductory bars and continues through the next four-bar group. To leave out the two introductory bars, therefore, would not change the tonal structure at all, though it would disfigure the Prelude in other ways. In the Waltz, on the other hand, I moves to II⁶ at bar 3. To omit the first two bars would be to suppress the opening tonic altogether; more than that, it would make the whole piece pointless and nonsensical. For a basic premise of the Waltz is a version of the age-old musical paradox, "ma fin est mon commencement." Schubert places the tonic in the two bars before the first strong downbeat; in the light of subsequent events we might say that the tonic falls in bars 7 and 8 of an incomplete phrase. The closing tonics of all three A sections also fall in bars 7 and 8; by analogy with the beginning, therefore, the cadential tonics also function as the initial chords of the subsequent phrases.

The first two measures also determine the end of the B section (bars 29–30), for a convincing reprise requires two introductory measures and the eighth-note upbeat figure of the right hand. But here a problem arises. At the beginning of the piece (and also at bars 9–10) the two measures in question contain a structural tonic. At the reprise, however, this would be an impossibility; the main connection in the bass, C♯ to D, excludes a structural return to I at this point. Luckily, an alternative solution exists.

A 5–6 motion above C♯ (together with a return from E♯ to E♮) produces an A chord (Example 12b). This chord, solely a product of voice leading, takes on more stability if the root, A, occurs in the bass (Example 12c). Even in root position, however, the A chord does not function as a true tonic, as a beginning or goal of motion. It is clearly "on the way" from the C♯ chord to the II⁶. But it is close enough in sound to the beginning, and especially to bars 9–10, to lead convincingly into the reprise. Incidentally, the seventh, G♮, derives from the last eighth-note of bar 10.[26]

Example 12c helps to explain the ⁶₄ chord of bars 5–6 and parallel places. This ⁶₄ seems to be of the familiar cadential type, with V in the bass and normal stepwise motion to tones of V⁷ in the upper parts. Rhythmically, however, the ⁶₄ is anything but normal, for it occurs in a weaker metrical position than the V⁷ to which it resolves. The weak metrical position of the ⁶₄ is not immediately evident from *looking* at the music, for the larger meter is, of course, not notated. But it is easily heard. As the graph indicates, this ⁶₄ arises out of an *anticipation* in the bass that counterpoints the passing fourth in the main melodic part. In the normal cadential ⁶₄, by contrast, the bass tone is stable; the fourth functions as a *suspension* (sometimes an accented passing tone) in one of the upper parts. In the Waltz, the metrically weak ⁶₄ allows the final tonic of the phrase also to fall in a metrically weak position (fourth hypermeasure)—a necessity here, since this tonic represents the two introductory bars. In *Der freie Satz*, Schenker cites a metrically weak ⁶₄ in bar 38 of Chopin's Waltz, Op. 64, No. 2; there, too, the ⁶₄ permits a weak final tonic.[27] Anticipating ⁶₄'s are not frequent, but they occur from time to time, especially in music of the nineteenth century. Schubert and Chopin probably use them more than any other great composers, though examples can also be found in music by Schumann, Mendelssohn, and others. They are hardly ever mentioned in theory books.[28]

Example 12d. This graph shows the foreground of the piece, including the secondary, "covering" voice of the right-hand part and the changes in

253

[26] A similar apparent tonic that results from a 5–6 over III (in this case, ♭III), occurs in Brahms's Waltz, Op. 39, No. 8, bars 21–24.

[27] Schenker, *Der freie Satz*, pp. 187–88, § 288, in a reference to Figure 137/1. Schenker does not call the bass of the ⁶₄ an anticipation; I believe that it is one, just as in the Schubert Waltz.

[28] But see Edward Aldwell and Carl Schachter, *Harmony and Voice Leading*, Vol. I (New York: Harcourt Brace Jovanovich, 1978), p. 275.

register effected by this secondary voice. For the most part, the graph is self-explanatory. However, some explanation must be given of the B section, with its expansion of eight bars to twelve. That the twelve bars do, in fact, grow out of eight bars in the middleground is borne out by examining how they are built. Note that bars 24–27 repeat bars 20–23 and that bar 23 has a double meaning: the goal of the preceding four bars, it is also (exactly like bar 19) the beginning of the next motion. The listener, so to speak, goes over the same ground twice; when he arrives at bar 27, he is visiting bar 23 for the second time. Without this repetition, the section would contain eight bars, as shown in Examples 12a, 12b, and 12c.

Example 12d also points to other interesting features of this section. Note, first of all, that the C♯ triad—the main chord of the section—always appears in a strong metrical position, on an odd-numbered "beat." This is in marked contrast to the A sections, where the tonic chord is always metrically weak. The strong position of the C♯ chord furthers the coherence of the piece, for it permits bars 29–30, which represent the first two bars, to fall in a weak hypermeasure.

A curious feature of the melody accompanies the metrically strong C♯ chord. For the most part, bars 20–23 are an almost exact transposition of bars 14–17, the cadential bars of the A² section. But, as the graph shows, the metrics are reversed: bars 20–23 reach their goal on a strong bar, whereas bar 17, the goal of the A² section, is weak. Because of the rhythmic alteration, the melodic figure becomes almost a new motive. And this at least partly explains the repetition and the consequent expansion of the section. For to present a striking new idea once only would make it sound arbitrary and unconvincing. At least one repetition (exact or disguised) is required to make the idea a "motive," that is, an element in the compositional design. Incidentally, the abrupt tonal contrast between the C♯ triad (bars 27–28) and the seventh-chord on A (bars 29–30) can easily mislead the listener into hearing bar 29 as a downbeat. The performer must take care to project bars 29–30 as an upbeat to the II⁶ in bar 31.

DURATIONAL GRAPHS: SOME IMPLICATIONS

The Fundamental Structure. I should like to conclude with a few general observations about the durational graphs. The first has to do with leaving the fundamental structure out of the graphs; each of the four analyses begins with a level of middleground, specifically with that level of middleground where the form of the piece first becomes apparent. As I explained in my earlier article, I believe that the fundamental structure does have some rhythmic implications, but that these arise out of tonal function only and have nothing to do with duration.[29] To include the fundamental structure in durational graphs, therefore, would make little sense. To be sure, one might show the *pacing* of the structural progression in these graphs. One would first establish a "basic duration" for the piece, that is, the number of bars it would contain without expansions (or elisions) that belong to the middleground or foreground. (If the piece is short and clearly articulated, we do, I think, measure its flow against such a basic duration, though not usually in a fully conscious way.) We could then coordinate the structural progression with this basic duration.

But to do so would be misleading, for the basic duration takes on meaning only in relation to the groupings of bars and to the form. In the Schubert Waltz, for example, the basic duration is 32 bars: four phrases of eight bars each. Example 14 shows the background progression of the Waltz distributed over this duration, using the same scale of reduction as in Example 12. Since the C♯ chord of the B section is not part of the structural framework, I have not included it in the graph. But the omission obliterates any trace of the piece's form. For without the contrast between A and C♯, there is no B section, no ABA (or A¹A²BA³) form, no inner necessity for four phrases or for a basic duration of 32 bars. The graph shows the pacing of the structural progression, but it does so too abstractly to demonstrate a

255

EXAMPLE 14   *Valse Sentimentale, Op. 50, No. 13*   Schubert
              (Fundamental Structure)

---

29 Rhythm I, pp. 317–18.

convincing connection with the 32-bar time span. Only when we take the C♯ chord into account—only with the middleground, therefore—does the basic duration have meaning.

Since the form of a piece always relates to the prolongation, segmentation, or repetition of its structure and never simply to the structure itself, we can safely assume that we would find similar difficulty in applying durational proportion to the background level of any piece.

Larger Metrical Organization. In discussing the rhythmic features of the four pieces that I have analyzed, I have proceeded on the assumption that a *metrical* relation of strong to weak exists between the downbeats of successive measures. And that a similar relation exists between the downbeats of successive hypermeasures, if such hypermeasures are clearly in evidence. I assume that such a relation exists because I hear it in these pieces (and in many others). Some readers may be skeptical about the possibility of metrical organization on so large a scale. If they are, I would ask them to consider the syncopated effect of the sforzando in bar 3 of the Beethoven example, the upbeat character of the first two bars of the Schubert Waltz, as well as the unusual sound of the $^6_4$ chords throughout the Waltz. How are we to understand such phenomena if not in relation to a larger metrical scheme? If we understand "meter" as "measure," then the durational graphs show metrical organization on a scale still larger than that of measures or hypermeasures within a phrase. For each of the pieces analyzed, the level nearest the background (Examples 4a, 8a, 9a, and 12a) shows a division into two, three, or four *equal* segments of time, thus:

Chopin	two segments of eight bars
Mozart	three segments of eight bars
Beethoven	three segments of sixteen bars (plus codetta)
Schubert	four segments of eight bars (perhaps
	two segments of sixteen bars: $A^1 A^2 \| : BA^3 : \|$)

Each of these large segments is, in turn, subdivided into two equal spans of four or eight bars. And the listener "measures" the music's flow quite as much against these large periodicities as against the smaller ones of bars, beats, and fractions of beats. As the graphs approach the foreground of the piece, the smaller metrical units become more and more prominent as do the tonal and durational features that contradict and modify the large symmetries.

When we speak of "meter" we normally mean something more than the division of time into equal (or equivalent) segments; we mean a pattern composed of strong and weak impulses in some kind of regular alternation. That a metrical relation of strong and weak exists over the very large sub-divisions of time seems doubtful to me, for reasons that I explained in my earlier article.[30] And even if we were to assume that, say, bar 33 of the Beethoven example is "weaker" than bar 1, the assumption would lead to no further insights into the music, at least none that I am aware of. But at our present state of knowledge, it would be premature—and, therefore, wrong—to close our minds even to such seemingly doubtful possibilities.[31]

For this article, I selected pieces in which groups of measures exhibit clearly defined metrical organization. To forestall possible misunderstandings, I should perhaps mention that there are pieces—indeed, whole categories of pieces—where the groupings are less regular. I have sometimes found that durational reduction can reveal interesting aspects of the free rhythmic structure of such pieces. But they are more difficult to understand than the ones that I have presented and, therefore, are less suitable for an introductory discussion.

The Utility of Durational Reductions. This article has shown, I hope, that durational graphs can be a useful analytic tool. The analysis of the Chopin Prelude, for example, demonstrated that the "II⁵" of bars 22–23 is not a harmonic entity—a fact that eluded even Schenker. The anticipatory character of the ⁶₄ chords in the Schubert Waltz, the syncopated entrance of the 3̂ in the Beethoven Allegretto, the rhythmic structure of the expanded B section in the Mozart Trio—all these and many other rhythmic features are conveyed by the durational graphs with great clarity. The pacing of tonal events with respect both to phrase structure and to form also emerges more clearly from durational than from voice-leading graphs.

[30] Rhythm I, pp. 308–9.
[31] I hope to discuss meter—including large-scale meter—more fully in a later article.

At the same time, certain inescapable disadvantages limit the usefulness of these graphs. As I mentioned earlier, the rhythmic notation makes it more difficult to show structural levels and, in general, makes the voice leading harder to perceive. This problem is minimized in simple pieces, such as the four analyzed here. With longer and more complicated works, the deficiencies of the notation would soon make themselves felt. In addition, at or near the foreground of the piece, the reduced durations suggest a tempo several times faster than the real one, and, consequently, produce a distorted picture. (This drawback, incidentally, does not exist in Schenker's rhythmic graphs of the foreground, for they use the actual time values of the piece.) And finally, the smaller details of rhythm, those at the most immediate level of foreground, do not show up at all in these reductions.

The solution to these problems seems simple and obvious. It is to use the durational reductions only where they reveal important features of the piece more clearly than other methods would. And, where necessary, to offset their deficiencies by using them together with voice-leading graphs. The rhythmic reductions will probably prove most useful as an adjunct to graphs of the voice leading and harmony, used to clarify some otherwise obscure aspect of the rhythmic organization.

The Largo of J.S. Bach's
Sonata No. 3 for Unaccompanied Violin,
[BWV 1005]

HEINRICH SCHENKER
Translated by John Rothgeb

THE FORM of this Largo is revealed in Example 1a.[1] The fundamental octave-line (*Urlinie-Oktave*)[2] that horizontalizes the F-major chord clearly divides into two segments, $\hat{8}-\hat{5}$ and $\hat{5}-\hat{1}$. As a result the form is binary, the two parts consisting of bars 1–8 and bars 8–18. The piece closes with a coda, bars 18–24, which brings back the $\hat{4}$.

Example 1a also presents the fundamental structure (*Ursatz*) with the harmonic progression I–II$_{\flat3}^{7}$–V in the first section, V–I in the second, and I–IV–V–I in the coda. At the level of the fundamental structure the motion to V in the first section and the return to I in the second cannot be considered modulations. Just as the first melodic unfolding (the horizontal expression of the F-triad in the form of the octave line $\hat{8}-\hat{1}$) defines the F-tonality, so the harmonies that support this melodic unfolding represent steps of the F-major scale. The scope and weight of events in the fundamental structure are still too limited to justify explaining them as keys. The latter arise only in connection with the more richly developed foreground,

[1] This essay has been translated from Heinrich Schenker, *Das Meisterwerk in der Musik*, 3 vols. (Munich: Drei Masken Verlag, 1925, 1926, 1930; reissued as 3 vols. in 1 in slightly reduced facsimile, Hildesheim: Georg Olms, 1974), I, 63–73. Schenker's own annotations are given as footnotes, even though many of them originally appeared as part of the text. Footnotes supplied by the translator have been placed in square brackets. We thank the original publisher for permission to issue this translation.]

[2] See Schenker, *Meisterwerk*, I, 203, "Erläuterungen," Figs. 1–3.

EXAMPLE I

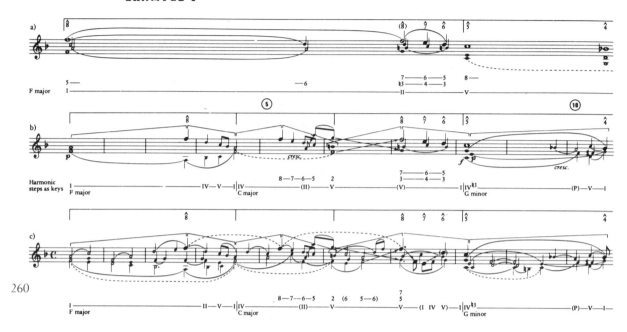

but even there they are basically nothing more than the harmonic steps of the background as shown in the fundamental structure (Example 1a).

The first harmonic progression, I–II$^{\natural3}$, not only poses the threat of parallel fifths (as in any root progression of a second), but also yields the undesirable succession of two major thirds.[3] Bach avoids the parallel fifths through the use of the 5–6 succession, but he is able to counter the effect of the major thirds only in one of the more significant progressions of the diminution (see Example 1b).[4] Above the II$^7_{\natural}$ step the $\hat{8}$–$\hat{7}$–$\hat{6}$ functions as a linear progression through a third over the II$^{\natural3}$; this results in the interval succession 7–6–5.

[3] Cf. Schenker, *Kontrapunkt* (2 vols.; Vienna: Universal Edition, 1910, 1922), I, 202.
[The two volumes of *Kontrapunkt* together comprise Vol. II of *Neue musikalische Theorien und Phantasien*. Vol. I of the series is the *Harmonielehre* (Stuttgart: Cotta, 1906); Vol. III is *Der freie Satz* (Vienna: Universal Edition, 1935), 2d ed., revised by Oswald Jonas (Vienna: Universal Edition, 1956).]
[4 The direct succession of major thirds is eliminated not in the fundamental structure but at the first level of prolongation.]

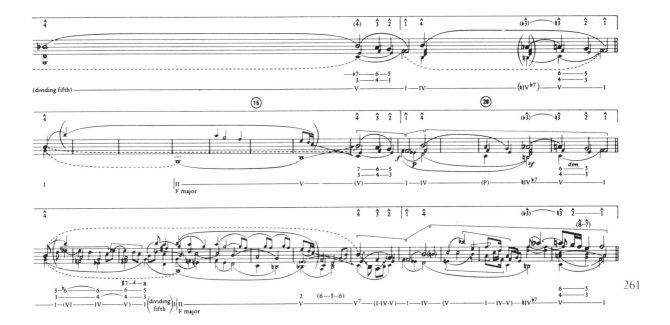

261

In essence the $\hat{4}$ in bar 10 is basically a passing seventh over V; the lower voice, however, transforms the seventh into a consonance[5] by placing under it the supporting root tone G, which then functions as the dividing upper fifth (*Oberquintteiler*) of the C. This interpretation is borne out by the motion of the lower voice in bars 8–17, c^1–g–c^1, which can in no way be understood as V–II–V. In bar 17 the $\hat{4}$–$\hat{3}$–$\hat{2}$, like $\hat{8}$–$\hat{7}$–$\hat{6}$ in bar 7, functions as a linear progression producing the intervals 7–6–5.

In the coda the recurrence of $\hat{4}$ also gives an opportunity for a IV, and thus for the concluding cadence, I–IV–V–I.

Example 1b shows the first stages of the diminution, the motives of the first order: the unfolding of the upper voice into progressions through the sixth, fifth, and fourth, transfers into the lower and higher registers, and so

[5] See Schenker, *Meisterwerk*, I, 204, "Erläuterungen," Fig. 6.

on. All of these motives are produced by the upper voice which, in its constant rise and fall, transforms vertical intervals (see Example 1a) into melodic progressions and leaps, thereby horizontalizing them. In other words, the motives serve as links between the upper and middle voices. The slanting brackets, in pairs, show the rising and falling motions in the melody; these brackets are grouped into higher-level unities by the larger brackets above them.

In bars 1–4 the top voice unfolds a sixth, first upward and then downward. The same sixth is unfolded by the bass, but in contrary motion. On beat four of bar 3, the melodic apex, f^2, is reached and becomes the first tone of the fundamental line. Thus we can see why the first melodic span of the upper voice was of necessity a sixth rather than any other interval. At the midpoint of bar 4, the soprano and bass return to their original position (see bar 1).

In bars 4–6 a progression through a sixth leads upward to f^2, and there follows a downward progression through a fifth to the $b\natural^1$ in the first quarter of bar 6.

If, in bar 6, the lower voice had ascended directly to the bass tone g^1, the seventh-chord that appears in the fundamental structure (Example 1a) would have occurred immediately. The bass, however, must instead remain on f^1 (in the $\frac{4}{2}$ position), in spite of the fully accomplished change of harmony. The reasons for this are twofold. First, it avoids the direct succession of two major thirds (see above) and, second, it makes possible the introduction of the octave [of the root], g^2, in the upper voice before the seventh, f^2. This voice-leading procedure was highly esteemed by the masters because it exposed and intensified the passing nature of the seventh. Thus, in the fourth quarter of bar 5, Bach expressly shifts the a^1 of the middle voice to a higher octave in order to drive more strongly and solidly to the g^2. Only by means of an exchange of voices (see the crossed arrows in Example 1b) do the root and seventh arrive at their proper position (bar 7). It is the ascending fifth, $b\natural^1$–f^2 (bar 6), that places the seventh on top. The $\hat{8}$–$\hat{5}$ progression of the fundamental line (Example 1a) coincides with the descending series of tones of bar 7.

Bars 8–18 are governed entirely by the alternately rising and falling pattern so fundamental to this piece. In bar 8, the diminished fifth, e¹–b♭¹, rises out of the middle voice (cf. bar 1). It brings in the $\hat{4}$ and is answered by a descending succession (signifying $\hat{4}$–$\hat{3}$–$\hat{2}$–$\hat{1}$, cf. bar 7) in bars 17–18. In bars 10–17, the b♭¹ is first transferred up an octave and then restored to its original position. (Note the dotted slur connecting the two b♭¹'s.) The upward motion of the fifth [e¹–b♭¹] draws the bass along with it. The latter now climbs to g², pushing the middle voices upward at the same time. However, if the middle voices were to serve as simple passing tones, voice-leading errors could result (see Example 2). If the dissonant passing tones (Example 2b) were given consonant support by accompanying lower thirds (Example 2c), then a direct succession of two major thirds and perhaps also parallel fifths could occur, depending on the number of passing tones used. Bach circumvents this difficulty (see Examples 2d and 1b) by using two superpositions (*Übergreifzüge*), b♭¹–a¹ and c²–b♭¹[6] which the bass

EXAMPLE 2

263

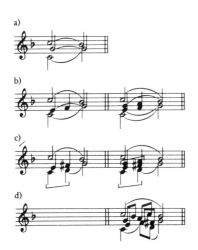

a)

b)

c)

d)

accompanies with two additional inserted roots, producing the effect of V–I progressions (*Quintfälle*). As richly varied as the voice-leading prolongations are in this section, they are all clearly directed toward a single goal,

[⁶ b♭² in the original, a misprint.]

namely to achieve the $\hat{4}$ of the fundamental line (see Example 1a). Bars 16 and 17 repeat the events of bars 6–7.

The pattern of rise and fall, characteristic of the preceding sections, occurs again in the coda—upward to $\hat{4}$ in bar 18 and down to $\hat{1}$ in the last bars. The descending fifth, I–(IV)–♮IV♭⁷, in bars 18–20 is elaborated: at the midpoint of the descent, $\hat{4}$ enters as the top voice of IV⁶; the second descent through a third in the lower voice, d¹–c¹–b♮, is accompanied by a parallel descent in the upper voice, b♭¹–a¹–g¹, which prolongs the b♭¹.

Example 1c, pertaining to the second level of diminution, presents the motives of the second order. The first sixth, in bars 1–3, comprises three smaller arpeggiations, each spanning a third. The ascending sixth in bars 4–5 is accomplished by means of two ascending leaps, each spanning a fourth. These are supported in the bass by an upward arpeggiation of the tonic triad, f¹–a¹–c². The upper voice continues with a descending diminished fifth, which is matched by the falling fifth, c²–f¹, in the bass. Thus, in its entirety, the arpeggiation of the lower voice not only reinforces the unity of the chord, but also demarcates the rising and falling pattern of the upper voice.

In bar 6 the fifth, b¹–f², is divided into two thirds, b¹–d² and d²–f²; at this point the lower voice carries out a neighboring-tone motion [f¹–e¹–f¹] in order to provide consonant support for the passing c² (occupying the second and third beats of the bar) which, as a dissonant fourth, would clash with the G-triad. In bar 7 the segment e²–d² ($\hat{7}$–$\hat{6}$) of the fundamental line is withheld from the upper voice; the seventh [f²] is taken over by the bass as f¹, on which now devolves the obligations of the earlier $\frac{4}{2}$-chord [bar 6]. The lower voice leads this seventh to e¹, but then, instead of continuing to d¹, returns upward to the root tone, g¹. Because, in the fourth quarter of bar 7, the leading tone [b♮], which had already been present in the basic structure for two measures, was still waiting to be resolved, there was no opportunity to state the d². The latter tone, $\hat{6}$, however, is understood from the G-triad, and is implicit in the continuing motion to c², the $\hat{5}$.

In bars 8–9, the neighboring-tone motion 3–4⌢4–3[7] extends the duration of the third [of the C-chord]. Similarly, the voice leading in bars 10–12 is

---

[7] Cf. Schenker, *Kontrapunkt*, II, 251.

to be understood as a neighboring-tone motion, since its basic meaning is as
follows:

EXAMPLE 3

One may easily perceive that the voice leading in Example 3 is the same as
that of bars 10–12 of Example 1c if one thinks of the bass tone, g, as being
sustained in these measures. Since g is the violin's lower limit, the lower
voice could not have descended further. Thus g^1 had to be used, and this,
too, is part of the reason why the lower voice climbed to g^1 in bars 9–10 (see
above). The first two sonorities in Example 3 occur in the third and fourth
quarters of bar 10. The third sonority ($^6_4$) occurs in the second half of
bar 11,[8] while the fourth sonority ($^{\sharp 7}_4$) follows on the downbeat of bar 12.
The next two sonorities occur in the third and fourth quarters of the same
measure, and bring the broad neighboring-tone motion to a conclusion.[9]

The general upward drive in this section results in the register transfer
that brings $b\flat^2$ in place of $b\flat^1$ on the last quarter of bar 10. This facilitates
a second register transfer, $e\flat^2$ for $e\flat^1$, on the same beat. A series of three
progressions of a third (indicated by brackets) follows: the first, $e\flat^2$–c^2,
expresses the content of the second and third sonorities of Example 3; the
second, also $e\flat^2$–c^2, that of the fourth sonority; and the third, d^2–$b\flat^1$, that
of the fifth and sixth sonorities. The correspondence of these measures with
Example 3 is emphatically confirmed by the fact that the $b\flat^2$ serves as a
sustained higher voice above all three of these progressions. (Incidentally,
this gives rise to a foreground impression of G minor: I–VI–IV–V–I.)

[8 The a^2 and f^1 in the first half of bar 11 are regarded as passing tones and are not represented in
Example 3.]

[9 More precisely, the neighboring-tone motion concludes on the first quarter of bar 13; this is what
Schenker has shown in Example 3.]

265

The b♭¹ that enters in the third quarter of bar 12 initiates an ascending arpeggiated third, b♭¹–d², that answers the foregoing descending third; this b♭¹ also calls forth b♭², which connects with the b♭² of bar 10. In retrospect, one realizes that all of the detailed events of bars 10–12 have served primarily to support and extend the duration of b♭².

In bars 13–16, the descending seventh, b♭²–c², is elaborated by a series of descending progressions through thirds, the last of which, in the first quarter of bar 16, is accelerated. The stimulus for these thirds was provided by the b♭²–a²–g² of the upper voice at bars 12/13 and the g¹–f¹–e♭¹ of the lower voice in bars 10–11. Since these progressions move in parallel ⁶₃-chords, the parallel fifths that would have occurred between the upper and middle voices had to be avoided by syncopation. My earlier remarks on the voice leading of bars 6–7 also apply to bars 16–17.

In bars 19–20, b♭¹ is transferred up an octave. The regaining of a¹ in bar 20 may be explained as follows:[10]

EXAMPLE 4

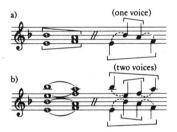

Example 4 shows a certain type of horizontal elaboration of vertical events. We see in Example 4 how it is possible for a¹ to appear in the lower voice in the first quarter of bar 20, before the entrance of the a¹ that follows f² in the upper voice.

A still more advanced stage of diminution, embracing the motives of the third order, is shown in the foreground graph (*Urlinie-Tafel*) [see Example 5].[11] From this vantage point, finally, we see how the composer's imagination creates a foreground, bringing forth motives which, by virtue of their

10 Cf. Schenker, *Meisterwerk* I, 204, "Erläuterungen," Fig. 8.

[11 In the original, the *Urlinie-Tafel* appeared as an unnumbered figure. Thus, in this translation, Schenker's Figure 5 becomes our Example 6. Example 7 was added by the translator.]

EXAMPLE 5
Foreground Graph (*Urlinie-Tafel*)

* All dynamic markings are by the author of the graph.

literal presence in the music, are so readily accepted as "melodies" by the ear incapable of hearing longer spans. But the source of these "melodies" is revealed only through an understanding of the successive stages of voice leading, beginning with the fundamental structure. The specific shapes of such melodies are determined not by the whim of an imagination concerned with nothing more than "melody," but rather by the necessity that the voice-leading process be anchored in a fundamental structure.

The figures in bars 1–3 describe the arc of a sixth. Here one could easily make the mistake of regarding the apex of the new motive, f² on the third eighth note of bar 1, as the definitive high point. We avoid this error only through our feeling for the true motive, the arpeggiated third (see Example 1c), in which f² has no place. This demonstrates the importance of understanding the structural basis for the diminution.

In bars 4–5, at those places where $\frac{6}{3}$-chords occur in the voice leading shown in Example 1c, the lower voice inserts roots, so the tones of the arpeggiation are approached by leaps of a fifth. Here again, it is only our feeling for the broad arpeggiation that guards against a misunderstanding of the inserted tones.

The tones of the ascending fifth in bar 6 are decorated by motives of a sixth which produce a three-voice setting. In bar 7, in the second quarter, the last leap of a sixth, b¹–g², is decorated by a neighboring tone, a²; the resulting melodic progression a²–g² echoes the a²–g² of bars 5/6. This parallelism is part of the reason why the upper voice's progression e²–d² ($\hat{7}$–$\hat{6}$) had to be taken over by the lower voice (see above).

The return in bar 8 of the motive originally stated in bar 1 confirms the significance of the $\hat{3}$ that divides the fundamental line, even though this motive is used here simply to elaborate a neighboring-tone motion. In bar 11, a²–g², which essentially belongs to an inner voice (see Example 1c), provides a continuation for the bb² of bar 10; thus, regaining the bb² in the third quarter of bar 12 is also justified by the parallelism [bb²–a²–g² in bars 12–13] with the bb²–a²–g² in bars 10–11. In bars 13–14 the diminution, with its rising and falling arpeggiations, eliminates the parallel fifths that arise from the succession of $\frac{6}{3}$-chords. From the second half of bar 14 onward the motivic shape of bar 1 returns, although now in the service of a different voice leading. Moreover, in bars 18–19 the motives span intervals of a fifth, sixth, and seventh [f¹–c², bb¹–g², c²–bb²],[12] thereby confirming the unified character of the motives, represented in the foreground graph, of the third level of diminution.

At the final level of compositional elaboration (*Ausführung*), the eighth-note figures of the foreground graph are fleshed out with sixteenth-notes. The comparison of surface diminution with that of the preceding level, as instructive as it is regarding the nature of diminution, must be left to the reader. His attention is directed to two motives of the lowest level of diminution, which might be called "atomic particles" of the diminution (see Example 6). The motive given in Example 6a appears later, in aug-

EXAMPLE 6

a)   bar 1   bar 2   bar 3   bars 3–4   b) bar 1

mentation, in bars 3/4; this will be referred to later. The motive given in Example 6b constitutes a neighboring-tone figure. Integrated into diminution motives of a higher order, it serves to bind these together over longer spans.

It was stated above that the two-part form of the composition is incontrovertibly established by the division of the fundamental line into the segments $\hat{8}$–$\hat{5}$ and $\hat{5}$–$\hat{1}$. The $\hat{4}$, as the fifth below[13] the tonic, cannot be the divider of the tonic harmony, since the latter contains within itself the upper fifth.[14] It appears here as a passing tone (see Example 1a), a fact that is not modified in the least by the foreground effect of G minor (Examples 1b and 1c), since II is even less possible as a dividing harmony than IV.[15]

[12 These are not shown clearly in Schenker's foreground graph.]
[13 The text has *Unterquart*, an error.]
14 See Schenker, *Harmonielehre*, p. 51. [Schenker's meaning here is that the lower fifth would contradict the upper, which has priority by virtue of its function as the boundary tone of the tonic triad.]
15 For the possible divisions of a fundamental octave line, see Schenker, *Der freie Satz* [pp. 67–68].

For a deeper insight into the form, it is fruitful to study the technique of connecting different registers (*Lagen-Koppelung*), or octave coupling. I regard the gradual unfolding of an octave as an extension of the basic idea of octave coupling. Any such octave coupling creates a sense of musical unity and protects the ear from aimless wanderings; that is its value in a consideration of form.

A very high register was proscribed because of the special nature of slow movements; on the other hand, in the low register, the tonic tone, f, was not available. This explains why the Largo contains only one octave coupling in the lower voice (g^1 to g, bars 10–13) and two in the upper (bb^1–bb^2–bb^1, bars 10–17 and 18–19).

Finally, the changing motivic content contributes to the delineation of formal parts. Each structural level carries with it its own motives (see Examples 1b and 1c); the specific organization and growth of these motives parallels the specific organization and growth of the structural level to which they belong. The nearer they are to the foreground, the more developed and varied the motives will be; and those motives that belong to the most detailed level help to define the smallest constituent parts of the form, even the periodic groupings of measures.[16] The Largo shows changes of motivic content at the following points:

1. bars 4/5 at the beginning of the modulation to C major, to speak in terms of keys;
2. bars 5–7 at the cadence in C major;
3. bars 8–9 at the beginning of the second part, where the motive of bar 1 returns for the first time;
4. bars 9/10 at the modulation to G minor;
5. bars 10–11 at the confirmation of the new key, where the motive again exhibits a certain kinship to that of bar 1;
6. bars 13–14 at the transfer to the lower register;[17]
7. bars 14–15 at the preparation for the parallelism of bars 16–17 to bars 6–7, where the motive of bar 1 is expressly used again; and
8. bars 18 ff. at the coda.

[16] See Schenker, *Der freie Satz* [pp. 183 ff.], and *Meisterwerk*, I, 16 and 195.

[17] The *Tieferlegung* referred to here is that completed by the lower voice at the beginning of bar 13 with the arrival of g.]

The piano accompaniments written by Schumann for Bach's sonatas for solo violin [see Example 7][18] are neither obbligato nor accompanimental (in Bach's sense of the terms). The piano part does not constitute an obbligato to the violin part, nor does it limit itself to a more or less free realization of an imagined figured bass. Rather, Schumann's accompaniment may be considered *sui generis*. Its evident purpose was to provide Schumann with an account of all aspects of the compositional procedures. It is a reduction as much as an accompaniment—in short, a work with a didactic purpose. As such, it redounds greatly to Schumann's credit: it demonstrates that, for the most part, he understood Bach's voice leading correctly. The great scope of his understanding will be demonstrated in the critique that follows. If I nevertheless raise objections concerning certain details, I do so without the slightest intention of denigrating Schumann, who has himself contributed so much of perfection to the art of composition. I intend, rather, to treat problems of voice leading that transcend the indisputable superiority of the Bach to Schumann's arrangement, in order to arrive at generally valid solutions.

271

It was shown in Example 6 that Bach bases bars 3/4 on the progression through the third, f^1–g^1–a^1. The upward motion of the lower voice wants to be confirmed by a parallel progression in the upper voice, since passing tones like to go in pairs.[19] The counterpoint of the outer voices is 6–6–5–3; g^1 goes on to a^1 in the third quarter of bar 4. Schumann, however, uses g^1 as a neighboring tone and, at the same time, as the head tone of the falling third, g^1–f^1–e^1.[20] Thus he has to repeat the indispensable g^1 on the fourth eighth-note of the bar. Moreover, he adds the chromatic progression $c\sharp^1$–d^1, causing the first beat of bar 4 to represent, instead of Bach's $\frac{6}{4}$-chord, an appoggiatura to a IV harmony: IV $\frac{6\text{-}5}{\frac{4\text{-}3}{\sharp2\text{-}3}}$.

The arpeggiation that begins on the third quarter note of bar 4 in the lower voice can be expressed by the piano as a continuous ascent, f–a–c^1–f^1,

---

[18 Although today the making of arrangements and/or accompaniments for Baroque compositions is considered by many to be a violation of stylistic ethics, in Schumann's time the practice was widespread and was considered completely acceptable. Schumann composed accompaniments for Bach's sonatas for solo violin in 1853; they were published in the following year by Breitkopf & Härtel of Leipzig. Example 7 is based on the edition published in Leipzig by C.F. Peters, Plate No. 7309.]

19 See Schenker, *Kontrapunkt*, II, 176 and 181.

[20 Schenker's remarks on this passage are mutually contradictory. If the initial harmony of bar 4 in Schumann's accompaniment is a IV, as Schenker implies in a later remark, then the g, as a neighbor, cannot be the initial tone of a falling third.]

EXAMPLE 7
Schumann's Accompaniment to the Largo

272

EXAMPLE 7 (*continued*)

273

thus more clearly than by the violin. In this respect the Schumann setting agrees with the Bach. But the remaining voices in Schumann's version show imbalance, even errors. Since d¹ occurs on the last eighth-note of bar 4, it cannot return on beat two of bar 5 (before the c¹ on beat three); this obscures Bach's inserted fifth-leaps d¹–a¹, f¹–c² (see above). The tones a and c¹ on the first and third quarter notes should by no means be approached by the same tone, d¹, because a parallelism is clearly indicated in Bach's voice leading; the leap of a fifth (fourth), d¹–a, should not be answered by the stepwise progression d¹–c¹. If Schumann wished to go beyond Bach in inserting additional passing sonorities, other possibilities exist that could also have expressed the parallelism. Finally, one should note that the effect of f¹ in bar 5 is preempted by the premature statement of f¹ on the penultimate eighth-note of bar 4.

In bars 6–7 Schumann adds beautiful imitations of Bach's motive. In bar 7, Schumann's deceptive cadence goes beyond the implications of Bach's voice leading. In the Bach, the g² in the fourth eighth of the bar is implicitly tied over into the third quarter, because there is no indication to the contrary, such as the chromatic alteration g♯. Schumann, however, leads the lower voice to VI by way of the chromatic g♯. But at the fourth sixteenth-note of the third quarter of the bar, everything once again moves along Bach's path.

Schumann adds beautiful inner voices in bar 8, and also in bars 14–15. These additions do not in the least obscure Bach's voice leading. But in bars 13/14 the upper part seems to me too angular, because of the consecutive leaps g²–e² and e²–b♭²; specifically, the b♭² in bar 14 lacks an antecedent such as that provided by Bach in bar 13.

Schumann celebrates the beginning of the coda appropriately and excellently by sustaining the tonic as a pedal point.

Once the content of the piece is completely understood, performing it poses no problems. In my forthcoming treatise, "The Art of Performance,"[21] it will be systematically shown for the first time that dynamics, like voice leading and diminution, are organized according to structural

[21 The treatise, "Die Kunst des Vortrags," was never completed.]

levels, genealogically, as it were. For each level of voice leading, background or foreground, and for each diminutional level, there is a corresponding dynamic level of the first order, second order, and so forth. In the foreground graph these various levels are shown separately: the primary dynamic shading, which belongs to the first level of voice leading and diminution (see Example 1b), is given below the staff, while the inner shadings, those that apply to diminutions of the third order that emerge only in the foreground graph, are given above the staff. The results of applying these principles to the Largo are described in the following paragraphs.

The primary dynamic shading of the first section, bars 1–8, begins piano. Then a crescendo begins in bar 5 at the start of the descending progression f^2–b^1. The crescendo begins precisely at the approach to d^2, a tone that represents the 6 of the 5–6 progression of Example 1a and also, to speak in terms of the prolongations indicated in Example 1b, the arrival of II within the new key. This crescendo, in the light of Example 1b, is to be regarded as continuing to a forte, because it must support the modulation to C major and the cadence.

275

To this must be added inner shadings based on the third order of diminution (see the foreground graph). The $^6_4$-chord on the downbeat of bar 4, being a dissonance, should receive a stronger emphasis, thus we have the dynamic motion $<$ $>$ around g^1. But this dynamic intensification must not be executed in such a way that the primary dynamic level, piano, begins to change noticeably, for it is too soon to begin the increase in dynamic level specified in Example 1b. In the third quarter of bar 4, at the conclusion of the first rise and fall through a sixth and at the beginning of the second one, the inner shading has reached an end and the piano of the primary dynamic level is reinstated.

The second inner shading commences in bar 6 at the beginning of the new rising progression, b^1–f^2. This progression, standing as it does in the service of a voice exchange (see Example 1b), requires special treatment. The crescendo ends with the forte of bar 7. The $^4_2$-chord at the beginning of bar 6, like that in bar 4, should have more emphasis than the consonant final quarter of bar 5, and for that reason the piano in bar 6 is displaced by an eighth-note. Near the end of the trill in bar 7 a barely noticeable diminuendo leads to piano at bar 8.

In the second section, bars 8–18, the primary dynamic level changes as it did in the first section: piano–crescendo–forte (see Example 1b). In bars 8–9, the piano remains in effect for the duration of the neighboring-tone motion around the third. The crescendo, which continues to forte as in the first section, commences just where the passing tones begin to undermine C major in order to express the modulation (to speak in terms of Example 1b) toward G minor.

And now to the inner shadings. At the last eighth of bar 11, the renewed motion from $e\flat^2$ should be underscored by a piano–crescendo. The crescendo, however, leads only to a mezzo forte in bar 13 because, in the second section, in terms of the fundamental structure (see Example 1a), the G [-minor] triad functions only as a dividing fifth of V. In other words, the events of bars 10–13 must not be equated with the two cadences of a higher order that occur in bars 6–7 and 16–17, for no other cadences have as much weight as these. Decisive for this reading is the broader elaboration of the V in bars 6–7, with its voice exchange and its rising and falling fifths (see above). By contrast, in the modulation to G minor (see Example 1b), the V that occurs on the second beat of bar 10 is not prolonged by a $\hat{7}$–$\hat{6}$–$\hat{5}$ motion or anything comparable: it is merely a chord with an added chromatic tone! The two cadential progressions expressed by the ensuing prolongation have no bearing on the modulation, which is already completed. This prolongation, characterized by its octave couplings in the upper and lower voice, remains only a compositional elaboration of the G-triad, without influence on the large-scale formal articulation.

Immediately after the mezzo forte in bar 13 there is a return to piano, a prerequisite for beginning a new crescendo. This piano lasts until the third quarter of bar 14. The goal of the voice leading—to introduce the chromatically raised third of II (see the $b\natural$ in bar 15)—must be expressed appropriately by means of a crescendo.

The coda, too, begins piano. At the $\natural IV^{\flat 7}$ a sforzato is necessitated by the chromatic tones, whereupon the piece closes with a diminuendo. The inner dynamic shading $<$ $>$ serves to unify the progression of a third, $b\flat^1$–a^1–g^1.

Beyond all these shadings, still further, more delicate nuances come into consideration. They serve the motives of the lowest level of diminution—

the suspensions and neighboring tones, the 7–6 progressions, and so forth. But they must all be integrated into the primary dynamic scheme and the inner shadings of a higher structural order.[22]

[22] The literature pertaining to this Largo is discussed in *Meisterwerk*, I, 85 ff.

BEETHOVEN

XLIII. NINTH SYMPHONY IN D MINOR, OP. 125
—ITS PLACE IN MUSICAL ART

It is well known that Beethoven had in his earliest period the ambition to set Schiller's 'Ode to Joy'. This project had in itself nothing to do with the idea of a choral symphony. At the time he was sketching his Seventh and Eighth Symphonies, he had already made up his mind that the next symphony should be in D minor, though he did not jot down any themes for it. This project again had nothing to do with Schiller's 'Ode'. Years later, after the Choral Symphony had been produced, Beethoven, no doubt in a moment of depression, said to some friends that the choral finale was a mistake, and that perhaps he might some day write an instrumental finale. This, in fact, had been his first intention, and the early sketches of the Ninth Symphony give the theme of the finale of the great A minor Quartet in D minor as the finale of the symphony. Beethoven had not hitherto written much choral music; and the study of that stagnant backwater of musical history, the choral art as practised by composers for the church and the stage in Vienna at the beginning of the ninteenth century, does not reveal the existence of anything like a 'good school' in this branch of composition. Nobody cares for the choral works of Beethoven's contemporaries, and so the extravagant compass Beethoven assigns to his voices looks like some enormous violence of Beethoven's genius; whereas it is but little worse than the habits of contemporaries of his who were under no excitement whatever. Other difficulties more enormous and less effective in Beethoven's choral writing arise from the fact that his two great choral works, the Ninth Symphony and the Mass in D, are for him, morally speaking, early works in this art. The Mass in D is longer than the whole of the Ninth Symphony, and is choral from beginning to end; yet, enormously difficult as is the Mass, the finale of the Choral Symphony is more exhausting in twenty minutes than the whole Mass in an hour and a quarter.

Beethoven was only fifty-seven when he died of a complication of disorders aggravated by a neglected chill. Constitutionally, in spite of his deafness and the moodiness it naturally engendered, he was on the whole a healthier and stronger man than, say, Samuel Johnson; and there is nothing but accident that deprived the art of music of a fourth period in Beethoven's development, which should have been distinguished by a body of choral work fully

II   B

equal in power and perfection to the symphonies and string
quartets.[1]

The arguments which would persuade us that the chorale finale
of the Ninth Symphony is the outcome of a discontent with instrumental music are by this time discredited. Wagner committed
some indiscretions on these lines, but they were too obviously grist
to the official Wagnerian mill to survive in a musical civilization
which recognizes Wagner as one among the greatest composers
instead of putting him into a category which excludes all the rest
of music. On the other hand, those arguments are equally futile
which would persuade us that the choral finale was a 'mistake',
because of some fundamental fallacy in the introduction of voices
and words into a symphony. Contemporary performances, and
contemporary judgements of the work, gave Beethoven abundant
cause for moments of depression. At Aachen not only did the
choral parts not arrive in time for performance, but the conductor,
Beethoven's favourite pupil Ries, had to make large cuts in the
slow movement simply because the orchestra could not master its
difficulties. The only way to understand, not only the choral finale,
but the other three movements of the symphony, is to attend
strictly to the music from its own point of view as Beethoven
wrote it; and not to be distracted by what he may have said about
it when he was thinking of writing something else. We have no
right to dismiss it as a mistake until we have thoroughly followed
its meaning, whether we like it or not. The more we study it,
from whatever point of view, the more obvious do its real mistakes
become; and the more obvious they become, the more readily, and
even impatiently, will the music-lover with a sense of proportion
dismiss them from his mind as trivial accidents. The question as
to the 'legitimacy' of bringing voices and words into a symphony
is an exploded unreality. Professor Andrew Bradley, without
saying a word about music, exploded it for all time when, in his
inaugural lecture in the Chair of Poetry at Oxford in 1901, he
discussed 'Poetry for Poetry's sake', and showed the fundamental
fallacy in theories of artistic 'absoluteness', viz. the fallacy of
separating form from matter at all. In the case of a choral symphony the essential facts are these; first, that all instruments and all
harmonic and contrapuntal arts imitate, on the one hand, voices,

280

[1] This view has been hotly challenged by critics who urge, as a fatal
objection to it, that Beethoven shows no appreciation of the beauty of
the unaccompanied chorus. Such critics must extend their objection to the
whole of classical choral music between the death of Palestrina and the
maturity of Brahms. Bach, Handel, Mozart, and Haydn wrote not a line
of unaccompanied choral music, unless you count canons scribbled on
menu cards. Bach's so-called 'unaccompanied' motets all require instrumental support.

and on the other hand, dance rhythms or pulse rhythms: secondly, and consequently, the voice is the most natural as well as the most perfect of instruments as far as it goes; so that its introduction into instrumental music arrests the attention as nothing else will ever do, and hence must not be admitted without the intention of putting it permanently in the foreground: thirdly, that the introduction of the voice normally means the introduction of words, since that is how the human race uses its voice: and lastly, that it follows from this that the music must concern itself (conventionally or realistically or how you please) with the fit expression of the sense of the words. The correct application of Professor Andrew Bradley's philosophy (a classical statement of the case which, though not addressed to musicians, every musician should know) will show that there is no inherent impossibility in thus reconciling the claims of absolute music with those of the intelligent and intelligible setting of words. There is no part of Beethoven's Choral Symphony which does not become clearer to us when we assume that the choral finale is right; and there is hardly a point that does not become difficult and obscure as soon as we fall into the habit which assumes that the choral finale is wrong. I am not arguing that it is necessary to prove that it or any other work of art is perfect. That is never necessary, and most people would rashly say that it is never possible. All that is required is a point of view which assumes that Beethoven is not an inattentive artist who cannot keep his own plan in mind, until we have clear evidence to the contrary. If Beethoven were a Berlioz, a Bruckner, or a Mahler, we should find him out all the sooner by assuming that he is nothing of the kind. Hot-headed enthusiasts for these three composers fail to realize the gravity of their inconsistencies, because they assume that Beethoven was no better. The criticism which discovers the inconsistencies starts by assuming that these composers are as consistent as Beethoven. They break down under the test; but the critic who has applied it admires them more than the blind enthusiasts, because he sees more in the art of music wherever he finds it.

If a great work of art could be made responsible for all subsequent failures to imitate it, then Beethoven might have had cause for doubting whether the opening of his Ninth Symphony was worth the risk. It is a privilege of the greatest works of art that they can, if they will, reveal something gigantic in their scale, their range, and their proportions at the very first glimpse or moment. This power is quite independent of the possibility that other works may be larger; it is primarily a matter of proportion, and the actual size enters into the question only when the work of art is brought by some unavoidable accident into relation with the actual size of the spectator. Thus Macaulay once shrewdly observed that the size of the Great Pyramid was essential to its sublimity, 'for what could be more vile than a pyramid thirty feet high?' And thus the faithful reproduction of the noblest proportions will not give sublimity to an architectural model that you can put under a glass case. The truth is that in architecture the size of the human frame is one of the terms, perhaps the principal term, of the art. In pictures this is not so, or rather it is so with a more elastic relativity: you can give any proportions you like to your pictures by introducing human figures or other known objects on whatever scale you please. Music has, like architecture, a fixed element to deal with, the subtlest and most implacable of all. It is no use comparing the dimensions of music for a few instruments with those of music for vast masses: the string quartets of Beethoven are in the most important of all their dimensions fully as large as the symphonies. It is no use saying that the string quartet is a pencil drawing, and the symphony an oil painting or a fresco: pencil drawings are not executed on the scale of frescoes. It is no use saying that the string quartet is monochrome, while the symphony has all the tone colours of the orchestra: people who seriously talk of string-quartet style as monochromatic are probably tone-deaf, and certainly incapable of recognizing anything short of the grossest contrasts in orchestral music. Yet there is what you may call a dimensional difference between a string quartet and an orchestra; and the difference is hardly greater in volume of tone than in range of tone colour. These differences, again, cannot fail to have some effect on the architecture of the works designed for few or for many instruments, but such effects on the designs are not less subtle than profound; and the composer himself is so far from recognizing them until his plans are matured that, as we have already seen, Beethoven for a long time thought that what eventually became the finale of his A minor Quartet was to be the finale of the Ninth Symphony.

The all-pervading, constant element in musical designs is time. Beethoven's chamber music (extending the term so as to include everything from one to eight instruments) is for the most part on the same time-scale as his symphonies. That scale was from the outset so large that his First Symphony, a masterly little comedy, shows him taking the precaution to design his first independent orchestral work on a smaller scale than much that he had already written for solo instruments. But while it was obvious from the outset that his compositions were on the largest known scale, it only gradually became evident that that scale was growing beyond all precedent. Beethoven himself did not avow this fact until he recommended that the Eroica Symphony, being longer than usual, should be placed nearer the beginning than the end of the concert.[1] And the Eroica does not from the outset promise to be larger than the Second Symphony, nor indeed in its first sketches did it show any signs of being so large. Contemporary critics throughout Beethoven's career were continually deceived about the scale of his designs, or they would not so constantly have considered Beethoven inferior to Mozart in power of construction. With the rarest exceptions they always listened to a work of Beethoven in the expectation that its proportions would be those of a work of Mozart; and the mere measurement of the actual length of the work as a whole would not suffice to correct that assumption, for several very perfect works of Mozart may be found which are considerably longer than some characteristic great works of Beethoven. The enlargement of the time-scale is not a matter of total length; it is a matter of contrasts in movement. Mozart's aesthetic system does not admit of such broad expanses side by side with such abrupt and explosive actions as are perfectly natural in Beethoven's art. The first signs of intelligence in this matter came from those contemporary critics of Beethoven who had the sense to be bewildered by many things which are now accepted inattentively. Two of Weber's notorious gibes will clear up the matter once for all. He regarded the introduction to the Fourth Symphony as a monstrous and empty attempt to spread some four or five notes over a quarter of an hour. This shows that he had a sense of something new in Beethoven's time-scale. The other case was that of the sustained note five octaves deep towards the end of the first movement of the Seventh Symphony; a feature which he declared showed that Beethoven was now ripe for the madhouse. This shows that he perceived something unprecedented in Beethoven's scale of tone. Now the scale of tone is a very much more difficult matter to discuss than the scale of time, and I must be content, for the present, to leave all statements about it in the form of dogmatic assertion. It naturally is more easily measured in orchestral works than in works where there is less volume of tone to deal with; but again, as with the time elements, it is not a question of the actual volume, but of the range of contrast. In Beethoven's string quartets it is not less manifest than in his orchestra. In short, just as it is possible in the very first notes of a work to convey to the listener the conviction that this is going to be something on a large scale of time, so is it possible, however small the instrumental means employed, to arouse in the listener a confident expectation of an extraordinary depth and range of tone.

[1] His notion of 'nearer the beginning than the end' was 'after, perhaps, an overture, an aria, and a concerto'. When he produced his next symphony, the Fourth, he preceded it with the First, the Second, and the Eroica. Four hours was short for a concert in those days.

283

The opening of the Ninth Symphony is an immediate revelation of Beethoven's full power in both of these ways. Of all passages in a work of art, the first subject of the first movement of Beethoven's Ninth Symphony has had the deepest and widest influence on later music. Even with an ordinary instrumental finale, the Ninth Symphony would have remained the most gigantic instrumental work extant; its gigantic proportions are only the more wonderful from the fact that the forms are still the purest outcome of the sonata style. The choral finale itself is perfect in form. We must insist on this, because vast masses of idle criticism are still nowadays directed against the Ninth Symphony and others of Beethoven's later works in point of form; and these criticisms rest upon uncultured and unclassical text-book criteria as to musical form; mere statements of the average procedure warranted to produce tolerable effect if carefully carried out. We shall never make head or tail of the Ninth Symphony until we treat it as a law unto itself. That is the very treatment under which Berlioz and Bruckner break down; and it is also the treatment under which a Mozart symphony proves itself to be a living individual, though he wrote so many other symphonies externally similar in form.

The opening of the Ninth Symphony is, then, obviously gigantic. It is gigantic in relation to the sonata style of which it is still a perfect specimen. But its gigantic quality is so obvious in itself that it has been the actual and individual inspiring source of almost all the vast stream of modern music that has departed from the sonata style altogether. The normal opening for a sonata movement is a good, clear, pregnant theme. Whatever happens before the statement of such a theme is evidently introductory, and the introduction is generally so separable that it is in an obviously different tempo, whether or not it does itself consist largely of something broadly melodious. But it would hardly do to call the opening of the Ninth Symphony an introduction: it is impossible to imagine anything that more definitely plunges us into the midst of things. No later composer has escaped its influence. Nearly all modern music not on sonata lines, and a great deal that is on sonata lines, assumes that the best way to indicate a large scale of design is to begin with some mysteriously attractive humming sounds, from which rhythmic fragments gradually detach themselves and combine to build up a climax. When the climax is a mighty theme in unison for the whole orchestra, and the key is D minor, the resemblance to Beethoven's Ninth Symphony becomes almost absurd. And this is actually the case in Bruckner's third and ninth symphonies; while he hardly knows how to begin a first movement or finale without a long tremolo. It is no exaggeration to say that the typical opening of a modern orchestral work has become as thoroughly conventionalized on these lines as any tonic-and-dominant sonata formula of the eighteenth century. There is no objection to this, so long as the composer can draw the rest of his work to scale. Only through lifelong mastery of the sonata style could such an opening be continued in anything resembling sonata form; and the crushing objection to the forms of Berlioz and Bruckner is not their departure from sonata principles, but their desperate recourse to them in just the most irrelevant particulars. Another set of difficulties arises when the composer continues such an opening without relying upon sonata forms. The orthodox reproach that is levelled against 'symphonic poems' is that of form-lessness: it is generally a foolish reproach because it is based on some foolish text-book notion of form as the average classical procedure. The real trouble with an unsuccessful symphonic poem is generally that it either fails to maintain the scale set up by its ninth-symphony type of opening, or makes an even more radical failure to come to a definite beginning on any scale at all; as, for instance, in the extreme case of Liszt's *Ce qu'on entend sur la montagne.* This work consists of an introduction to an intro-duction to a connecting link to another introduction to a rhapsodic interlude, leading to a free development of the third introduction, leading to a series of still more introductory developments of the previous introduction, leading to a solemn slow theme (which, after these twenty minutes, no mortal power will persuade any listener to regard as a real beginning), and so eventually leading backwards to the original mysterious opening by way of conclusion.

The whole difference between Wagner and such interesting but unconvincing pioneers is that Wagner, when he abandoned the sonata time-scale, thoroughly mastered his own new proportions. He talked partisan nonsense about Beethoven's attitude to 'abso-lute' musical forms, but he made no mistakes in maturing his own musical style; and the fact that his medium was music-drama must not mislead us into denying the validity of his mature sense of musical form as a factor in the purely instrumental music of later times.

This opening of the Ninth Symphony has, then, been a radiating point for all subsequent experiments for enlarging the time-scale of music; and the simplest way to learn its lessons is to set our mind free to expect to find in the Ninth Symphony the broadest and most spacious processes side by side with the tersest and most sharply contrasted statements and actions. There are listeners (indeed their complaint is one of the intellectual fashions of the day) to whom it is a cause of nervous irritability that the Ninth Symphony is recognized by orthodoxy as the most sublime musical composi-tion known. Orthodoxy happens to be perfectly right here, and

285

for the same reason that it is right about Handel's *Messiah*, and Bach's *Matthew Passion* and Mass in B minor. These things do not rest upon fashion: they rest upon the solid fact that these works deal truthfully with sublime subjects. As a modern poet has remarked, 'All is not false that's taught at public schools'; and if there are large numbers of contemporary music lovers who are in heated revolt against the aesthetics of Beethoven's music, that is a nervous condition which concerns nobody but themselves.[1] There will always be still larger numbers of music lovers who have not yet heard anything like as much classical music as they wish to hear. It is just as well that they should realize that there is nothing more than an irritated condition of nerves behind the talk that still goes on about the need of a revolt against Beethoven. No artist of such a range as Beethoven has ever set up a tyranny from which revolt is possible. We hear a great deal about the way in which English Music was 'crushed by the ponderous genius of Handel'. It was crushed by nothing of the sort; it was crushed simply by the fact that the rank and fashion of English music patrons would for centuries listen only to Italian singers and Italian composers. Handel's methods were Italian, and he benefited accordingly. The real objection that is felt against Beethoven's aesthetics is the eternal dread felt by the artist of *genre* in the presence of the sublime. Modern British music has derived much stimulus from highly specialized *genres* of French music, and these *genres* do not aim at the sublime. They thus do not blend well with the Ninth Symphony, though they are conspicuously free from the false sublime that would blend infinitely worse.

We have seen that there are two factors which cause the impression of the enormous size in the opening of the Ninth Symphony. The one factor, that of proportion in time, we have already dealt with, and on that head all that remains is to explain how the actual length of the opening is not exceptional. Indeed, the whole first movement, as Sir George Grove has pointed out, is, though the greatest of Beethoven's compositions in this form, by no means the longest. And this does not mean that it is more terse than longer movements such as the first movement of the Eroica Symphony. Those longer movements are not diffuse; but the compression of Beethoven's later style is balanced by a still wider power of expansion. What happens is that, as we have already

[1] The quaintest manifestations of the revolt were those of the writers who at the centenary of Beethoven's death told us that the 'humanism' of Beethoven's slow movements was antiquated. From time to time the Superman *may* seem to be as fashionable as all that: but nevertheless he does not exist as yet.

pointed out, the range of contrasts in phrase-length is greater; and the result is that more space is gained by compression than will ever be filled up by expansion. Sir George Grove pointed out how, already as soon as the first mysterious sounds begin to make their crescendo, the rhythmic fragments are compressed and hurried. So much, then, for the rhythmic side of this opening.

The rest of its enormous effect is the result of the scale of tone. And here again the Ninth Symphony, like the Fifth and the *Leonora* Overtures, teaches us that there is for the massive treatment of the orchestra a criterion which many modern orchestral composers have entirely forgotten. Orchestral music since Beethoven has undergone its greatest developments chiefly at the hands of composers who contemplated music from the standpoint of the theatre. It is true that Liszt wrote nothing for the theatre, and that Berlioz's operas were brilliant failures; but the fact remains that nearly everything that marks an advance in nineteenth-century orchestral technique since Beethoven is an advance in essentially dramatic orchestration; and this in the narrow sense, that the characteristic orchestral discoveries would be even more useful in an opera than in a purely symphonic work. Finally, it is universally admitted, even by partisans, that Liszt and Berlioz did not often achieve complete mastery of their art problems, and that if we are to find a style for the post-Beethoven orchestra which we can always confidently expect to say what it means and mean what it says, we must turn to the later music-dramas of Wagner. It is no more necessary to prove that these are perfect works of art than to prove the perfection of ethics, theology, science, and sentiment throughout *Paradise Lost*. But you can, on the whole, find mastery wherever you look in the later works of Wagner, just as you can in Milton, without taking any precaution to select specially inspired passages; whereas with Liszt and Berlioz you will find mastery about as sporadically as you will find it in Walt Whitman. Wagner is, in short, the most authoritative classic of the orchestral technique of the age after Beethoven; and Wagner's life's work is for the stage.

Now there are two far-reaching consequences of this that we must take into account before we adopt Wagner as a criterion for the symphonic orchestra. The composer for the stage (like the composer of symphonic poems on the basis of Liszt and Berlioz) is constantly occupied by illustrating something outside the music. This *may* tend to limit his capacity for inventing sounds which do not obviously illustrate something external; and it *must* limit his opportunities for developing such sounds. The purely symphonic composer has no use for illustrative sounds unless they are also useful to a purely musical design; and as soon as they are so useful, their imitative aspect ceases to attract notice. There is a very large class of orchestral procedure which is thus common to the symphonic orchestra and the stage; and so long as music confined itself to Mozart's range of expression the distinction between symphonic and dramatic orchestration remained a subtlety. In music of his period you might perhaps be able to distinguish between first-rate and second-rate mastery of the orchestra in this way, that with second-rate composers the dramatic orchestral devices lacked musical point, while the musical devices lacked dramatic point. But the divergence of interests did not as yet amount to this, that a composer could write symphonic orchestration which would be impossible in stage music. All that had happened was that much which was tolerable or even effective on the stage, would be too thin and commonplace for the symphonic orchestra. The mature works of Wagner are far too highly organized in all respects for this to be crudely manifest; but it is self-evident that the orchestration of Wagnerian opera contains much that is not only out of place but inadequate for symphonic writing. And practically this is a more important truth to the modern composer than the converse truth, that the mastery of a symphonic style for full modern orchestra is in itself no qualification for the handling of operatic orchestration. There are far more composers who can write a good modern opera than there are composers of good modern symphonies.

But the subtle aesthetic distinction between the dramatic and symphonic in orchestration is not more important than the very much simpler practical fact which determines the opera-writer's orchestral outlook. Nine-tenths of the opera-writer's orchestration is designed for the accompanying of voices. It does not matter whether, like Wagner, he puts all his invention into the orchestra and gets the voice to declaim through the orchestral design as it best can, or whether, like Mozart, he puts his primary invention into the voice. Whatever he does, he knows that the voice must be heard somehow; and his orchestral climaxes are severely restricted to situations in which there is either no solo singing, or the voices are able actually to interrupt the full orchestra, and so to convey an ingenious illusion of dominating the storm when all the time the orchestra gives way to the singer with the readiest tact. The imagination of the public and of students is impressed by the extent to which Wagner enlarged the orchestra; and Wagner is one of the greatest composers in the handling of massive orchestration; but massive orchestration seems such a simple thing, and the immense majority of Wagner's interesting orchestral devices are so closely associated with the singer on the stage (even where they are not actually accompanying the voice) that very few critics and students pay much attention to Wagner's handling of an orchestral tutti. Hence there arises a conception of the modern orchestra as an organization which on the one hand can make an alarmingly loud noise, and on the other hand can indulge in astounding complexities of musical spider-lines. The attempts of ordinary go-ahead composers to handle the tutti of a modern orchestra with no technique at all, or perhaps with a humdrum military bandmaster's technique, can hardly fail to produce a noisy impression; 'noisiness' being a popular term for bad balance of tone. The position, then, with commonplace exploitations of the modern orchestra is that the tuttis are apt to be scored with no technique to speak of, and that the rest of the writing, though often very interesting and clever, is unwittingly based upon a conception which reduces itself to the art of accompanying a voice. Again and again the inner history of an ambitious piece of contemporary orchestration has been that it was scored in some complicated and interesting way; and that, after the usual disheartening experiences of inadequate rehearsals, the composer has found that the full passages had better be expressed in the old scrubbing-brush of tremolo, with the theme entrusted to the trumpet as the only person capable of carrying it through.

The real method for scoring a tutti will be found in Wagner, in Richard Strauss, and Elgar, and a very few other composers since Beethoven; and it will be found to be in all essentials surprisingly like Beethoven's method. Now the clue to the whole orchestration of the Ninth Symphony is to be found in the statement of I forget what French authority that the whole work, or at all events a great part of it, is one grand tutti. This must not be taken to mean that it is full of useless doublings, or that it does not contain numberless passages in which single instruments weave delicate threads. What it does mean is that the composition is for a whole orchestra employed for its own sake, and that no part of its aesthetic system is concerned with the accompaniment of anything else—until, of course, the voices enter in the finale. And there we find proof of how curiously irrelevant that present-day style of criticism is which patronizes Beethoven for having 'attempted' in the Ninth Symphony an orchestration which only the resources of Wagner could have enabled him to carry out successfully. No such criticism can tackle the choral part of the symphony at all; for, whatever may be said against Beethoven's choral writing (and choral technique is no strong feature in modern musical progress), Beethoven is completely at his ease in *accompanying* the voice. There is, in fact, very little trouble with the orchestration of the choral finale; nor is there much difficulty in getting the slow movement to sound clear, although there is a prevalent and very gross misunderstanding of a certain horn passage therein, which we will discuss in its place. The whole set of difficulties of the orchestration of the Ninth

289

Symphony is confined to the first movement and to one famous theme in the scherzo. Wagner adjusted these matters easily; Weingartner adjusts them more accurately: with a large orchestra such as that of Dresden, with 150 players and triple wind (six flutes, six oboes, and so on), the adjustment becomes purely the business of the conductor, and of some one's marking the extra wind parts according to his directions.[1] The first movement of the Ninth Symphony is no doubt the most troublesome of all Beethoven's scores; but no virtuoso has ever written a work for the pianoforte which does not, in proportion to its size, throw far more responsibility upon the player for adjusting its balance of tone.

The first thing, then, to realize about the Ninth Symphony is that it is a work for the orchestral tutti; and that nine-tenths of the patronizing criticism that is nowadays directed against it is based on a judgement that is frankly incapable of following any genuine orchestral tutti whatever. If your ear is accustomed entirely to the pianoforte, the clearest organ-playing in the world will be a chaos of echoes to you. If you know nothing but music for the full orchestra, your first impressions of the finest string quartet will consist mainly of squeak and scrape. And if your only conception of the orchestra is fundamentally operatic, it is no use to argue that Beethoven's symphonies are so often performed that you have nothing to learn from them; a cathedral choir-boy may have sung in the church services every day, and yet have escaped understanding the English of the Bible and Prayer Book. I have noticed that any truly symphonic orchestration sounds to me, for the moment, impenetrably thick after I have got my ears into focus for operatic or otherwise illustrative modern orchestration. Of course the impression is only momentary, because I know by experience that such impressions are mere physiological effects of contrast; the mind learns its accommodations just as the eye or the ear. But it will not learn its accommodations if it is told that there is no moon because the first step out of a brilliantly lighted room seems to be a step into pitch darkness.

ANALYSIS

1 *Allegro ma non troppo, un poco maestoso.*
2 Scherzo: *Molto vivace* alternating with *Presto.*
3 *Adagio molto e cantabile* alternating with *Andante moderato.*

[1] It has been objected that all bad scoring can be defended and rectified on these lines. This is not so. Errors of calculation are not defects of imagination. Beethoven's imagination never fails; and there is no master of modern instrumentation who could trust himself to publish fewer miscalculated passages than Beethoven, if he were, like Beethoven, deprived of the opportunity for correcting his scoring at rehearsals.

4 FINALE: *Presto* alternating with quotations from previous movements, and leading to *Allegro assai*; leading to recapitulation
of *Presto* with a Baritone solo followed by the Choral Finale,
which consists of variations and developments of the theme of
the *Allegro assai* as follows:

Allegro assai: theme and two variations (quartet and chorus),
Allegro assai vivace alla marcia: variation with tenor solo and
male chorus; fugal episode; variation with full chorus.

Andante maestoso: new theme with full chorus.

Allegro energico, sempre ben marcato: double fugue on the two
themes.

Allegro ma non tanto (with changes of tempo) leading to *Prestissimo*: coda with quartet and chorus.

FIRST MOVEMENT

When we compare the opening of the Ninth Symphony with
many of those imitations of it that have almost become a normal
procedure in later music, two characteristic features reveal themselves. First that, as has already been indicated, Beethoven
achieves his evidences of gigantic size in a passage which is, as a
matter of fact, not very long; and secondly that this moderate
length is filled with clearly marked gradations, which succeed one
another more rapidly as the intensity increases. It is interesting to
see how few composers have ever by any refinement of technique
and apparatus mastered the natural aesthetics of climax as shown
in any of Beethoven's crescendos and most simply of all in this
opening. External details have been echoed by later composers
with excellent though sometimes obviously borrowed effect.
Bruckner's Ninth Symphony even gets in Beethoven's characteristic anticipation of the tonic chord on an outlying bassoon under
the dominant chord before the full orchestra bursts in with the
mighty unison theme.

Ex. 1.

But such resemblances are fatal; there is only one ninth-symphony
opening, and that is Beethoven's. If anybody else could get
those proportions right, he would arrive at Beethoven's Ninth
Symphony and not his own. If his own is going to be different
enough to justify its existence, it will not adopt, long after its
harmonies have moved into all manner of foreign keys and emotional tones, a characteristic external detail the whole point of
which was that the harmony had not yet begun to move at all.
And the real sublimity of Beethoven's conception has not yet fully
appeared with the entry of the mighty unison theme in the tonic

after this mysterious crescendo on the dominant (mysterious, by
the way, because, as the harmony was nothing but bare fifths and
octaves, that characteristic anticipation by the bassoon was the first
indication that it was not the tonic chord of either A major or
A minor). This opening is indeed gigantic, but its full power
begins to manifest itself in the fact that it is not unwieldy. The
mighty unison theme leads to a variety of short melodic and
harmonic sequences, no two phrases being of easily predictable
length; and it comes to a kind of full close very characteristic of
Beethoven's latest work, a close in which the tonic chord has been
arrived at without the intervention of the dominant as a penultimate. And so the theme, as Weingartner says, disappears into the
ground like some Afrit vanishing in a column of smoke. And now
we find ourselves on the tonic, with the same mysterious bare fifth
quivering and growing until it pervades the whole orchestra.
Immediately before the climax the bass changes the harmony, this
time in the unexpected direction of B flat; and in this key the
unison theme bursts out again, soon to make its way back to the
dominant chord, where another new and terse theme appears.

This new theme leads, by a movement of its last three notes downward in a very few further steps, to the famous pathetic introduction to the second subject; a passage which attracted the eager
attention of the musical symbolists who surrounded Liszt, on
account of its superficial and entirely accidental resemblance to
the theme of the *Ode to Joy*.

It cannot be too often or too strongly urged that no such thematic
resemblances are of the slightest importance unless the composer
himself establishes the connexion on the spot by the most unmistakable formal methods.[1] We shall find plenty of such methods
in the Ninth Symphony and in any late work of Beethoven; which
will conclusively prove that what is said about Beethoven's revolutionary tendencies in musical form is, for the most part, nonsense
which it would be a mistaken courtesy to treat as anything but

[1] Strange to say, no English musician has been more strongly bitten
by the Lisztian view than Stanford, who always upheld Liszt as the awful
example of lack of musical logic; in spite of the fact that Liszt was a
fanatic pioneer of music on a single leitmotif.

ignorance. Here it will suffice to say that Beethoven's forms become more and more precise in his later works; and that if thereby they become less and less like each other, this is what anybody who understands the nature of artistic forms as compared to living forms ought to expect. I am obliged to leave these general statements dogmatic where I am dealing with only one work; if proof is required I am ready for it with any work and any part of a work in Beethoven's third period; no very large field of survey, comprising, as it does, only thirteen works in sonata form, and not half a dozen other important compositions.

The second subject, at which we have now arrived, consists of a large number of different themes grouped into paragraphs of every imaginable size and shape. Of these I quote five: the consolatory opening cantabile divided between wind instruments of contrasted tone—

the stormy figure of scales in contrary motion—

the energetic theme with its contrast between sharp rhythm and cantabile, leading to the famous modulation into a distant key (flat supertonic)—

which in its turn leads to the most flowing and elaborate paragraph in this exposition where all is so flowing and rich; and so to the complicated and expressive dialogue between wind and strings (a difficult passage where Wagner's and Weingartner's suggestions are valuable in the interests of clearness)—

293

and the final triumphant tutti on the tonic chord of B flat—

294

which ends the exposition and collapses dramatically onto the dominant of D and back to the cloudy opening.

In discussing the first subject we saw the advantage of terseness in the very act of establishing an impression of immense size, for we noted that Beethoven was enabled thereby to give two great waves rising from mystery to their sublime crash. It might be argued that these two great waves are perhaps not so enormous as the longer passages often achieved by later composers, where it is inconceivable that the passage should be given twice over in its entirety. Very well then; Beethoven can do this greater type of passage also. The mysterious opening is now going to develop; it remains intensely quiet without crescendo, its periods marked by a distant boom of drums and flashes of red light from the trumpets, an extraordinarily solemn resource in the primitive classical treatment of these instruments already well known to Mozart and often used by him with sublime effect. The novelty in the present instance consists in the very low pitch of the trumpets. The harmonies drift through a major chord to the subdominant. The passage still remains intensely quiet, but in the subdominant the articulate main theme gathers shape in dialogue between the wind instruments. Suddenly on a fierce discord the energetic rhythmic figure of Ex. 8 bursts out on the full orchestra. The following plaintive treatment of figure (*b*) then makes, with the addition of four closing chords, a six-bar phrase.

This closes into G minor, and the dialogue on figure (*a*) is resumed. Now it leads to C minor, and again Ex. 8 intervenes on the full

orchestra and yields to the six-bar phrase. This time the last two bars are repeated with a crescendo, and the orchestra plunges into a vigorous triple fugue with figure (b) (Ex. 1) for its main subject and a pair of admirably clear and contrasted counterpoints. This drifts with the grandest and simplest breadth straight through from C minor to G minor, D minor, and so to A minor. On reaching this key its energy abates until it subsides into a famous and exquisitely plaintive passage, which Sir George Grove was fond of quoting as an example of Beethoven's peculiar use of the word *cantabile*. Grove indicates that Beethoven applies the term rather specially to passages of a simplicity which makes them liable to be overlooked. To this we may add that as long as Beethoven refrains from using the German language he can hardly find any word that will give the player the chance of putting what the Germans call *Innigkeit* into his rendering. Beethoven does not want to prescribe what he calls *intissimo sentimento* here: his best chance of getting what he wants is to tell the player to sing, and as the passage is too quiet to lend itself to obvious swellings of tone, the mere action of getting a singing quality into its calm will go far to express its inwardness.[1]

This A minor cantabile develops itself almost happily in its own touching way (notice, for example, the place where the whole mass of wood-wind gathers itself together in a staccato crescendo). Suddenly, with childlike pathos the main theme of the second subject (Ex. 4) appears. The basses take it up in F major, and in that consolatory key the dialogue on figure (b) is resumed. Nothing indicates that the situation is going to change in any near future. The development has in fact been on fully as large a scale as the rest of the movement, but the present passage has every appearance of being in the middle of its flow. If Beethoven had left the movement unfinished here, no mortal could have made a better guess at the sequel than that somehow or other Beethoven would climb to another climax, and from it build a passage of anticipation of return which should surpass in length and excitement any of the famous returns he had achieved before; such as the return to the tonic in the Eroica Symphony, or the return three times anticipated in the first movement of the First Rasoumovsky Quartet. It would,

---

[1] I know of no more crushing evidence of racial incompatibility of temper than is furnished by Debussy's beautiful arrangement of Schumann's pedal pianoforte studies. The French composer shows all his exquisite sensibility for pianoforte tone and his scrupulous scholarship in every note of these arrangements, yet where Schumann writes *innig* Debussy translates it *très expressif*, which is as flatly the opposite term as any two languages could supply between them. This leaves open the question whether Debussy has not after all correctly interpreted Schumann's sentiments, which hardly reach Beethoven's *Innigkeit*.

II   C

however, be difficult to know exactly what a long and exciting preparation of a return is to prepare for in this case; for the opening of the Ninth Symphony is itself a long and exciting passage of preparation. There are people who talk *a priori* nonsense about the sonata forms, as if these forms were stereotyped moulds into which you shovel your music in the hope that it may set there like a jelly. The real facts of sonata form seem complicated only because we have to describe them in purely musical terms, just as the facts of pictorial forms would seem enormously complicated if we had to describe them in geometrical terms. In reality such a fact of sonata form as this matter of 'return to the tonic for the first subject', is the barest definition of the capacity of the music to make us expect to return to anything whatever.

Beethoven's conduct of this great development has so far contrived the course of events as to make us feel thoroughly in the swing of an almost happy conversational episode, when suddenly, with a change of harmony, four abrupt bars carry us roughly into the tonic major, and the whole development is at once a thing of the past, a tale that is told.

This return to the recapitulation is utterly unlike any other in Beethoven's works; and we shall always find that in these cardinal features of form, no two works of Beethoven are really alike. In this matter of return to the first subject Beethoven achieved every conceivable gradation, from famous record-breaking lengths of anticipation to not less record-breaking abruptness; nor did he neglect the possibilities of bringing about the return with all Mozart's quiet formal beauty and symmetry. The present catastrophic return now reveals fresh evidence of the gigantic size of the opening. Hitherto we have known the opening as a pianissimo, and only the subtlety of Beethoven's feeling for tone has enabled us to feel that it was vast in sound as well as in spaciousness. Now we are brought into the midst of it, and instead of a distant nebula we see the heavens on fire. There is something very terrible about this triumphant major tonic, and it is almost a relief when it turns into the minor as the orchestra crashes into the main theme, no longer in unison, but with a bass rising in answer to the fall of the melody. Each phrase given out by the strings is now echoed by the wood-wind (it is ridiculous to complain of Beethoven's orchestration here, when the whole difficulty of such passages might easily be remedied by simply doubling and trebling certain of the wind parts—a purely financial question). The whole first subject is thus on the one hand amplified by this dialogue treatment, while on the other it is mightily compressed by being gathered up in one single storm from the outset of its introduction down to its abrupt subsidence into the consolatory preparation for the second subject.

From this point the recapitulation follows bar for bar the course of the exposition, but there are new details of far-reaching significance. There is an interesting historic process in the expression of pathos in sonata form. The first great master in whose hands sonata forms became definitely dramatic is Haydn. When Haydn writes a sonata movement in the minor mode, his second subject will certainly be in the relative major key. What will happen to it in the recapitulation? If the work is of Haydn's maturity and the character of the movement is blustering and impetuous, Haydn's sunny temperament is almost certain to impel him to recapitulate his second subject in the major, and so to end with childlike happiness. Not so Mozart, who rises to his highest pathos by translating the second subject from the relative major to the tonic minor, and translating it by no means literally, but in every way heightening the pathos in both harmony and melody. Beethoven has further resources at his command, and his practice in such a case depends upon his power to design a coda equal in importance to the whole development of a movement. Accordingly, if Beethoven chooses to recapitulate the whole of his second subject in the tonic major, this does not commit him to a happy ending; on the contrary it is, for him, a powerful expression of tragic irony. Nowhere since Greek tragedy do we so forcibly feel the pathos of the messenger who comes with what has the appearance of good news but which really brings about the catastrophe, as when we have in a tragic work of Beethoven the comfort of the recapitulation of the second subject in the tonic major. In the Ninth Symphony, however, Beethoven has achieved a yet more powerful pathos; he can get both major and minor wherever he pleases. For six bars the second subject proceeds happily in the major, and then, sorrowfully repeating the fifth and sixth bars in the minor, continues in minor, with the exception of the pleading second phrase of Ex. 6. The wonderful modulation to the flat supertonic in this passage looks much simpler as a modulation from D minor to E flat than it did when it was written as a modulation from B flat, not to C flat, but to B natural. Gevaert and other eminent writers on music have argued from this that it actually sounds less remarkable here; but with all respect I submit that they are misled by appearances. The modulation was, in the first instance as in the second, a simple modulation to the flat supertonic; and if Beethoven chose in the first instance to spell it in an extraordinary fashion, that is no reason for playing it out of tune. Classical and modern music from the time of Mozart onwards is constantly offering us passages in which the notation is enharmonic while the sense is diatonic. On the other hand, many real enharmonic changes are not visible in the notation at all. The real difficulty here between the first and the

297

second passages is that in the first instance the whole context is in a major key, whereas now in the recapitulation we are in the minor tonic, and so to this extent it is true that the modulation to the flat supertonic is less remote. On the other hand it is more pathetic, and Beethoven contrives to heighten the pathos by a subtle change in the position of the loud figure. From the following crescendo onwards, all the rest of the recapitulation is in the minor, including the once triumphant energetic close (Ex. 8).

What is going to happen next? Put this into technical language, and ask how Beethoven is going to begin his coda. The superior person who assumes that everything is silly as soon as it can be designated by a technical term will hereupon quote the gentleman who asked the painter where he was going to put his brown tree. But this is not a true parallel to our question. A fair parallel would be, what are you going to put in the middle distance on the left-hand side of your picture? or what form of dome, tower, or spire are you going to have in the middle of your cathedral roof? These technical terms for the sonata forms describe no more than the points of the compass, and there is no more resemblance between the standard examples of even the most particularized of these forms than there is between them and works in totally different forms. If we once more imagine that the movement be left unfinished at this point, we should find it just as difficult to guess the next event as we did at the end of the development. The coda of the first movement of the Eroica Symphony began with an astounding and mysterious modulation which carried it off into distant keys. Other codas of Beethoven begin as if to lead into the development again in the same way as the close of the exposition did; others bring the main theme or some other theme out in a great climax; others settle down at once to a comfortable tonic-and-dominant swinging passage on some important figure. Nearly every great coda will contain some such passage as its most natural means of expressing finality in the action of the piece. I suppose that if we did not know how Beethoven's coda was to begin here, our first guess would be some dramatic stroke of genius. Bruckner's most enthusiastic admirers are the first to deplore the fatal ease with which their master strikes his dramatic stroke whenever his huge creations try to lift their acreage of limbs without muscles to work them   One of the reasons why the first movement of the Ninth Symphony dwarfs every other first movement, long or short, that has been written before or since, is that, more evidently than in other compositions, it shows that no member of its organization is so large as to lose freedom in its function as part of a larger whole. The whole, when it has been heard, proves greater than the sum of its parts. In works of art which take time instead of space, it is inevitable that the highest organization should be concentrated towards the beginning; thus the first movement of a great classical work is normally the most highly organized. What has just been said of the first movement of the Ninth Symphony is true of every other mature work of Beethoven. It is only more easily seen here, and more profitably pointed out, because of the enormous influence this particular movement has had upon later music dealing with totally different forms. The technicalities or points of the compass of sonata form are merely relative; the principles of form are universal. As every part of the Ninth Symphony presents us with a constantly increasing impression of greatness in due proportion to a whole which is still greater than the sum of its parts, so does this movement stand towards the rest of the symphony. It matters not that the other movements are all simpler in organization; or rather, it is necessary that they should be. The simplicity means increase of breadth, and it is so organized that the mind is always fully occupied with the right actions and reactions.

And now for Beethoven's coda. We have just heard the end of the exposition, an emphatic close to one of the most flowing and elaborate paragraphs ever written in music or words. And instead of any abrupt modulation, Beethoven quietly and in a gentle vein of melancholy continues a flowing dialogue with the figures of the mighty first subject (Ex. 1), as if mysterious introductions and stormy outbursts were but old ancestral memories. The form of the dialogue is that which arose out of the mysterious introduction at the beginning of the development, but the tone-colour is not mysterious now; it is a grey noonday. Gradually and without change of key, the dialogue rises in an impassioned crescendo and bursts into a storm paragraph developing Ex. 5, which is followed up by a sequence based on Ex. 8. Suddenly the whole mass of strings stands hushed and overawed while the horns, softly in the full major tonic, are heard developing figure (*b*) of the main theme. This moment of distant happiness has never been surpassed for tragic irony. It is very characteristic of Beethoven, and many parallel passages can be found, besides what has been adduced above as to his habit of finding room for the major tonic in recapitulations where his main key was minor. Here it is evident that his translating most of his second subject into the minor was done as much for the sake of throwing this passage into relief as for its own pathos at the moment. Soon the whole mass of strings takes the theme up in four octaves, while isolated wood-wind instruments give out the semiquaver countersubject of the big fugue passage in the development. The strings carry on their quaver figure in a menacing crescendo. Neither in numbers nor in tone do the wood-wind make the slightest effort to be heard

299

through this crescendo; but as Weingartner points out, there is something peculiarly fascinating in the very effect of their disappearance behind this rising granite mass of sound, and their quiet emergence again as the mass subsides. No sooner has it subsided than Ex. 5 bursts out again with the utmost passion. (In the score the entry of the first violin of this theme shows a capricious change of octave which looks exactly like an accidental omission of the *ottava* sign[1]; it is always corrected accordingly in performance, perhaps rightly. Other cases of the kind are frequent throughout the symphony, but are sometimes much more difficult to deal with, as Beethoven purposely made capricious changes of octave a feature of his later style.) This passage suddenly ends with the pathetic ritardando phrase (Ex. 9) which preceded the triple fugue passage in the development. It now leads to the final tragic passion. We have noted that a great symphonic coda is pretty sure to contain a passage that swings from tonic to dominant on some important figure. One such passage we had when those horns entered so suddenly in the tonic major. We now have the most famous of all tonic-and-dominant passages, in the minor; the famous dramatic muttering in semitones of the whole mass of strings, beginning with the basses and rising until it is five octaves deep in the violins. Next to the opening of the symphony this passage has been more imitated by ambitious later composers than any other in music, classical or modern. As Beethoven has it, the universal quality in it is its normal truth of emotional tone and musical form; its unique quality is that the melody that is sung above it is to all intents and purposes quite new.

EX. 10.

Of course the rhythm in dotted notes vaguely recalls the figure of the opening, which is more clearly alluded to by the trumpets and drums; but the fact remains that Beethoven here shows himself capable (as he has done elsewhere though never in a movement on so colossal a scale) of introducing at the very last moment a theme that has never been heard before. The procedure is perfectly logical. This melodic expression is external and emotional; the logic is no more to be looked for in melodic connexions of figure here than it is to be relied upon where such connexions are abundant. Like all musical logic, it lies in the proportions of

[1] The autograph, and the corrected MS. sent to the publishers, and every other authentic document, are in absolute agreement on this and almost every other disconcerting detail!

the rhythms and paragraphs. And so it is the most natural thing
in the world that the paragraph should finally burst into the mighty
unison of the main theme, and thus end the tragedy abruptly, yet
in the fullness of time, with its own most pregnant motto.

SCHERZO

After tragedy comes the satiric drama. The next movement is,
as Sir George Grove remarks, at once the greatest and the longest
of Beethoven's scherzos. The chord of D minor is thrown at us by
the strings in a rhythmic figure which pervades the whole; the
drums tuned in octaves supply the minor third of the chord, and
it is only as the work proceeds that we realize how this grotesque
introduction makes an eight-bar phrase.

EX. 11.

Then the strings begin a very regular five-part fugue on the following subject, the wood-wind marking the first of every bar—

EX. 12.

until almost the whole orchestra is mysteriously alive and busy.
Soon there is a short crescendo, and the theme bursts out in a tutti.
Suddenly the key swings round towards C major, the flat seventh
(a relationship, by the way, which Beethoven had only once before
brought into prominence, and that in one of his most mysterious
imaginations, the ghostly slow movement of the D major trio,
op. 70, no. 1). On the dominant of this key there is an exquisitely
harmonious passage of preparation, after which nothing less than a
broad second subject bursts out in the wood-wind which the
strings furiously accompany with the octave figure.

EX. 13.

With Beethoven's scoring the theme cannot be heard with less than
double wind; and even triple wind would be better (as at Dresden,
for instance, where there are six flutes and six oboes, &c.), for they

can divide the parts among themselves according to their importance. For less well-endowed orchestras the measures indicated by Wagner and Weingartner are absolutely necessary. They have this disadvantage that the horns, to which Beethoven could not give the melody because of their imperfect scale, now have the effect of throwing the weight of tone into the lower octaves. The trouble about all difficulties of balance with Beethoven is that his feeling for tone-colour is invariably poetical and Beethovenish, while the obvious ways of getting correct balance are apt to produce tone which is neither.

So far the scherzo, including its grotesque opening, has proceeded in clear four-bar periods. Beethoven's scherzos, however, will never permanently settle down to the spin of a sleeping top: before the swing of the rhythm can cease to stimulate us it will be enlivened by some momentary change of period. Here in the first lull we have a six-bar period.

Ex. 14.

302

The wood-wind echo its last four bars, and then the exposition is brought to a tonic-and-dominant end in an even number of two-bar phrases with a new figure.

Ex. 15.

The initial figure now moves down a series of thirds in a harmonious pianissimo dialogue between strings and wind. Having thus reached a D minor chord it stops abruptly, and the exposition is repeated from the beginning of the fugue theme. After the repeat the development begins by carrying on the dialogue in descending steps of thirds which are so managed as to lead crescendo through an enormous range of key until the dialogue ends angrily on the dominant of E minor, a key entirely alien to D minor. And now comes the famous passage in three-bar rhythm, *ritmo di tre battute*, which has drawn the attention of commentators to this scherzo as containing an interesting rhythmic effect presumably not to be found elsewhere. The truth is that this passage differs from incidents such as that quoted (Ex. 14) only in being extended over a wide region systematically enough for the special mention of three-bar periods to save trouble in construing it. It is carried out in great simplicity and breadth through E minor and A minor.

Suddenly the drums burst in with their figure on F, and the whole passage continues perfectly happily in F major. The entry of the drums has often been described as throwing the three-bar periods out again. It does nothing of the kind; it goes on making three-bar periods, giving figure (*a*), while the wind continue with figure (*b*). The key shifts in a leisurely way round to D minor. Now that we are in the tonic again, suddenly without the slightest break the rhythm relapses into four-bar periods, various instruments taking the theme up bar by bar.

Ex. 16.

The harmony drifts towards E flat (the flat supertonic), on the dominant of which the drums and horns mysteriously build up figure (*a*) into a chord. At last there is a crescendo, the chord suddenly changes to D minor, and the whole orchestra bursts out with the main theme in a tutti which stands for a recapitulation of the first subject. The key changes to B flat, where we have the harmonious transition passage. Again two odd bars are inserted bringing the passage on to the dominant of D; it is now expanded, with suggestions of the minor mode; and the second subject then bursts out, at first in D major; but from the ninth bar onwards it is translated into D minor. Otherwise this recapitulation is quite regular. The dialogue on figure (*a*) leads back to the development which is marked to be repeated, an injunction not often followed in these days of hustle. Afterwards this dialogue leads very simply to a short imitative coda. The tempo is hurried until the octave figure is compressed into duple time as follows—

Ex. 17.

303

And here a great confusion has arisen from the history of a certain change in Beethoven's way of writing the ensuing trio. The autograph shows that the bars of the trio were originally half their present length, and that the time was 2/4. With this notation it would have been impossible to conduct the trio too fast; and it is quite certain, from the very nature of the connecting passage, that Beethoven's intention is that two crotchets of the trio should correspond roughly to three (that is, one bar) of the scherzo. I say roughly, because a stringendo has intervened, and if the half-bar corresponds too exactly to the original tempo the effect will be heavy and stiff. Beethoven has given metronome marks throughout the symphony, and they have been much studied; with the general effect of confirming Beethoven's own recorded dissatisfaction with efforts so to fix the tempi. They do serve, however, to prove what tempo corresponds to what other tempo; and in general they prove *relative* tempi. Unfortunately, through the aid perhaps of a misprint, the trio, now that the notation is changed, still has a metronome mark indicating that its bars correspond to the bars of the scherzo; with the result that for the best part of a century violent efforts were made to take it twice as fast as it has any business to go. There is no possible doubt of Beethoven's real intentions; and the best tradition has no more been misled by the metronome mark than scholars would be misled by the reading *mumpsimus* instead of *sumpsimus*.[1]

The trio thus violently brought into being out of the stretto of the scherzo, proceeds with heavenly happiness on the following combination of themes.

Ex. 18.

The upper melody is as old as the art of music. Beethoven had already written something very like the whole combination, bass and all, long ago in the trio of the scherzo of his Second Symphony. Moreover, in some of the earlier sketches for the Ninth Symphony he reverts very nearly to the exact terms of this passage in the Second Symphony. The difference between the mature final idea and

[1] After this analysis was in the press, Sir Charles Stanford wrote to *The Times* (March 4th, 1922) conclusively proving, by a photograph of the page in question in the original edition, that the original metronome mark was for a minim and not a semibreve.

these earlier versions is that the final conception makes a point of its simplicity. The idea in the Second Symphony is childlike only in so far as it is without affectation and without introspection. A child-prodigy like Mozart or Mendelssohn might have invented it quite spontaneously as regards infant mental activity, but without any more understanding than is employed in the child's special faculty of mimicry. In the Ninth Symphony the meaning is very different: this naïve self-repetition with delicate differences (see the notes marked *) that carry more weight than they seem aware of; this swarm of fresh themes all ending in full closes; this piling up of the primitive little theme into a climax of mere tonic-and-dominant and merely square rhythms, but of grandiose proportions: all this is true of the child as seen by the poet who recognizes that the outward semblance belies the soul's immensity.

If Beethoven had read Wordsworth he would never have forgiven him for speaking of 'fading into the light of common day'. Nowhere is Beethoven's power more characteristically shown than when his ordinary daylight bursts in upon the trailing clouds of glory; as the mere formal da capo of the scherzo bursts in when the climax of the trio dies romantically away.

If this scherzo had been on a less gigantic scale, Beethoven would unquestionably have done as he did with his earlier great scherzos, and caused the alternating cycle of scherzo and trio to go at least twice round; that is to say, the scherzo would again lead to the trio, the trio would again be given in full, the scherzo would come round yet again and show every sign of again drifting into the trio, whereupon some drastic stroke would cut the process short. This double recurrence is possible only where the main body of the scherzo is worked out on a scale not greatly transcending what we may call the melodic forms, at least in its first strain. We have seen that the present scherzo, quite apart from the trio, is a fully differentiated and developed sonata movement; and the miracle therein is that it has never lost the whirling uniform dance-movement character essential to the classical scherzo. Amid all the variety of Beethoven's works you will always thus find each individual movement true to type. The minuet had already come to be regarded by Haydn and many of his contemporary critics as too slight an art-form longer to retain its place in the growing scheme of classical symphonies. Haydn's own minuets tend more and more to foreshadow the Beethoven scherzo, while Mozart's minuets never show what we may call the scherzo temperament; yet Mozart's are sometimes capable in their own calm way of being quite as big as the other movements of the work to which they belong. The most significant thing about the Beethoven scherzo is that it becomes worthy of its position in Beethoven's most gigantic works, not by abandoning the dance

305

character, but by emphasizing it. There are people who apply to music certain eighteenth-century methods of criticising poetry; methods which simply measure the amount of information that would be conveyed if the art in question were reduced to prose. To such critics the double repetitions of Beethoven's scherzos are an idiotic mystery. Why should Beethoven say the same thing three times over in the same words? Why should dancers dance three times round the same ball-room? That depends upon the size of the ball-room, not upon the interest of its decorations. The size of the scherzo of the Ninth Symphony makes double repetitions out of the question; but an adequate expression of the characteristic perpetual circle is attained when for the second time the scherzo leads into the trio, and the first phrase (Ex. 18) starts on its course surrounded in a blaze from the whole orchestra, breaks off abruptly, and is closured by the two bars which have just led to it for the second time.

ADAGIO

In the slow movement Beethoven explores melody to its inmost depths. All musical form is melody 'writ large'; but there are forms in which the composition is felt not primarily as a single whole but as a series or colony of identical melodic schemes. The obvious case of this is the form of a theme with variations. The external form of the whole set of variations can tell us little about the composition except the number of variations, and the points, if any, at which they cease to confine themselves within the bounds of the theme. We are forced from the outset to attend to the emotional and other contrasts produced by their grouping; so that the analysis of a set of variations becomes instantly and automatically an analysis of style. The primitive simplicity of the external quasi-collective organism leaves us with nothing else to understand except the structure of the theme. Now when a great set of variations exists as a composition by itself, there is full scope for the variations to explore many aspects of the theme beyond the melody. Some of the greatest works in variation form have been based on themes of which melody was by far the least significant aspect. In these cases, at least the phrase rhythm of the theme will be found to be specially distinctive, so that its identity may be recognized in a totally different melody with totally different harmonies and totally different metric rhythm. In fact, this condition of things, which Sir Hubert Parry called rhythmic variation, is the highest type of independent variation form. If the phrase rhythm is not strong enough to support entirely new harmonies and melodies, then the harmonic scheme must be strong enough to support new melodies: the phrase rhythm, strong or weak, is prior to everything else, and cannot be altered without dissolving the sense of variation form. (Most modern sets of variations do thus dissolve the classical conception of the form, and compensate for the loss by retaining the melody far more constantly than Beethoven and Brahms think worth while.)

Now all this may seem a digression, inasmuch as the variations in the Ninth Symphony, both in the slow movement and the choral finale, are purely melodic. But it is worth while drawing attention to the fundamental importance of phrase rhythm in all classical variations; because until this is grasped the vaguest ideas are apt to prevail as to the value of purely melodic variations; and cases have been known where composers have introduced most interesting variations into works in sonata form, and wondered why procedures perfectly justifiable in an independent variation work somehow did not prove satisfactory in the sonata environment. We must not lose grasp of the principle that all sonata form works through external melody. It follows from this that variations must stick to the melody of their theme if they are to form part of a sonata scheme. It is also certain that a variation which is faithful to the melody is also faithful to the phrase rhythm. It is not good criticism to dismiss with contempt a merely ornamental variation as a poor thing; it is a simple thing, but it is also safe. If it is stupid, that is because the composer has a bad style. In the hands of the great composers the ornamental variation reaches the sublime just because of its utter simplicity and dependence upon the melody of the theme. In other words, the theme is pre-eminently sublime, and the variations are its glory. Some of the critics who have sneered at melodic variations should be more careful to make sure that they can recognize them.[1] I have seen more than one of the strictest of Beethoven's late slow movements in variation form described as 'a group of detached episodes with no discoverable connexion' by writers who are very full of 'the progress that has been made in the variation form since Beethoven's time'. And this is not a matter of speculative opinion; speaking generally I may say that no statement is made in any analysis of mine which the reader cannot verify for himself by following it in the score.

The slow movement of the Ninth Symphony is a set of variations on two alternating themes; at least, we could say so, if the second theme had more than one variation. On strict formal principles it does not matter whether the theme is actually varied at all so long as it is repeated: for instance, most of the slow movement of Beet-

[1] I have often been told that all good musicians deplore the disgraceful poverty of the first vocal variations in the choral finale. This does not represent a very advanced professional point of view. Good musicians do not estimate variations only as models for a student's exercises.

hoven's Seventh Symphony is aesthetically a set of variations, though the very essence of its variations is the cumulative effect of their repeating the same combination of melodies with no change except growing fullness of orchestration. In the Ninth Symphony Beethoven carries to its highest development a scheme for which he has given us only one exact counterpart, the Lydian Hymn of Thanks in the A minor Quartet; though he had written two earlier variation movements depending upon a pair of alternating themes, the slow movement of the Fifth Symphony, and the first allegretto which does duty for slow movement of the great E flat Trio, op. 70, no. 2. For all purposes except that of the antiquarian, it was Haydn who invented the idea of making variations on two alternating themes. Whichever theme was in the major, the other is in the minor; both themes are complete binary melodies with repeats, and the first impression on the listener is that the second theme is a contrasting episode like the trio of a minuet. Then the first theme returns, perhaps unvaried in its first strain, which however is repeated with ornamental variation, the rest of the theme continuing in the varied state. Then, just as Beethoven's most characteristic scherzos go twice through their cycle of repeating their trio, Haydn goes on to a variation of his second theme, and his scheme often goes far enough to include a third variation of the second theme, before the fourth variation of the first expands into a coda. Beethoven in his great E flat Trio adopts Haydn's form exactly, with the mock-tragic difference that, his first theme being in the major, he makes his coda end in pathetic childish wrath with a development of the minor theme. In the Fifth Symphony the two themes grow one out of the other in a more subtle way than Haydn's; and the second theme, though starting in the tonic, makes its point in the famous triumphant outburst in a bright foreign key. This is the only recorded sign of preparation for the bold and subtle art-form invented by Beethoven in his slow movements of the Ninth Symphony and the A minor Quartet. In these cases the two alternating themes are in brilliantly contrasted keys and tempi. In the Ninth Symphony the formal effect is enriched by the fact that the second theme is, on its second reappearance, in another contrasted key, so to speak twin, but not identical twin, with its first key. The scheme is as follows:

(1) First theme B flat major, 4/4.
(2) Second theme (*andante moderato*) D major, 3/4.
(3) Variation of first theme in tonic.
(4) Second theme in G major almost unvaried except for new scoring. As D major led back to B flat, so G major leads back to E flat as if to resume the first theme therein. This involves

(5) a modulating episode which will be described in due course
The episode leads suddenly back to the tonic where

(6) a complete second variation is given. At the point where the second theme should appear, the change of harmony which led back to it is replaced by a modulation to the sub-dominant, such as is typical of the last phase of a design that is to end quietly.

(7) The rest of the movement is coda, and the strong backbone of the most complicated parts of this coda consists of repetitions of melodic figures of the first theme, as will be shown in our musical illustrations.

Now let us look at the themes. I need not quote the two bars of introduction, famous as they are for their profound pathos. I write the melody on one stave, numbering its phrases; and on the upper stave I write the echoes of each phrase given out by the wood-wind

Ex. 19.

It will be seen that at first these echoes punctuate a melody that without them would be in symmetrical square phrases; but at last the wind instruments tend to develop something independently complete out of them, and end by taking over the climax of the main melody itself. They hesitate however at its close, and, while so hesitating, faint in the bright light of a change to a remote key.[1] The second theme is a single strain swinging along with glorious tenderness and warmth in its new key and rhythm.

Ex. 20.

The small notes in the musical illustration indicate the fragmentary counterpoint which enhances the effect of its immediate repetition. Its last bar is echoed with a change of harmony which plunges us back into the rich shadows of the main theme. Nowhere is the art of florid ornament more consummate than in the first violin part of the two complete variations in this slow movement. I say the first violin part, because the point of these variations is that, while the melody is given in Beethoven's finest florid ornament, the echoes of the wood-wind remain unvaried. If we had been given the theme, echoes and all, as the subject for a work in variation form, we might have felt at a loss to see what sort of variation could be made of it. To preserve the echoes as an unvaried background is a stroke of genius self-evident only because Beethoven has accomplished it. (He could not have accomplished it at once; for the first sketches of the theme show that at one time he seriously thought of making the wind instruments repeat regular whole sections instead of fragmentary echoes.) Now when the wood-wind take over the climax of the theme they still keep their part unvaried; and the

---

[1] I was not prepared, when I wrote this essay, to find that the slow movement of the Ninth Symphony was so out of fashion that an eminent critic could ask, apropos of this change, 'Where is the skill in abandoning your idea as soon as you have stated it?' To which the only fit answer is to ask, 'Where is the sense in supposing that the "idea" has been completely expressed before the first change of key or time that catches the eye by its appearance on paper?' People whose attention is not roused by that first modulation must be tone-deaf: people who don't see the point of its leading to an analogous but different key next time can have no memory. People who have noted it clearly both times will be wondering what will happen when the music approaches it for the third time; and when they hear the grand burst into the subdominant, they will have heard the complete statement of Beethoven's 'idea'. If critics are then going to argue that an idea cannot thus be spread over ten minutes, they must abandon any claim to understand Wagner, who spreads them over four whole evenings.

great change of harmony leads without effort to G major instead
of D major. The melody of the second theme is not varied, but
the scoring is now bright instead of deep, and the counterpoint
added by the first violins is lighter. At the end, the change of
harmony leads to E flat, and the clarinets give out the first two bars
of the main theme unvaried. This is taken up by a horn, the
clarinets giving a syncopated counterpoint. The slow figure of
the theme descends into the depths and the key shifts to C flat
major. The syncopated counterpoint is now given to the horn,
the notes in this distant key being such as the player on the
ordinary horn of Beethoven's time could produce only as closed
notes by skilful use of his hand in the bell of the instrument.
These notes are all very muffled and mysterious; they are not easy
to produce in this way, and they therefore occurred so rarely in
orchestral music that conductors used to need some experience and
decision to protect themselves and Beethoven against the round
assertion of the average player that the passage was impossible. It
was, indeed, extremely difficult, but Berlioz (in the chapter which
Strauss declares, in editing the *Grand Traité d'instrumentation*, to
be of merely historic interest) quotes the very bar that culminates
the difficulty, and demonstrates that it is skilfully written for the
hand-horn. Now it has been discovered that Beethoven gave all
these passages in this movement to the fourth horn, because he
knew a fourth-horn player who possessed a pioneer two-valved
specimen of the ventil-horn! The moral is not that we ought to
play these passages with a boastful confidence to show that modern
instruments make them child's-play, but that we ought to admire
the sense of style and practical wisdom with which Beethoven uses
the pioneer new instrument in the way best calculated to graft its
resources on to the old stock.

The whole character of the passage is profoundly reflective,
tender, and remote. Its dying fall seems about to be echoed; but
instead of an echo the tone becomes rich and full, and the harmony
brightens into a full daylight of the tonic. The second and last
variation bursts in with the richest ornament achieved in music
since Bach; and now we may appreciate fully the deep simplicity
of Beethoven's most elaborate conceptions, inasmuch as throughout this variation the wood-wind have the theme without ornament
except in so far as it is adapted to the prevailing triplet rhythm.
The violins are silent while the wind instruments finish each phrase
with its unadorned echo. In due course the point is reached where
the wood-wind are dwelling upon the final cadence before breaking
into one or other of the distant keys in which the second theme
appeared. Instead of the exquisite soft foreign chord, there is now
a sudden resolute modulation to the subdominant and an outburst

311

of solemn triumph in which the trumpets enter for the first time.
The drums also have their first forte; the drum-part being elsewhere throughout this movement remarkable for mysterious, soft
rhythmic figures. The solemn outburst of triumph yields to a
pleading development of the first two notes of the theme without
ornament.

312

Mark well its four distinct entries within two bars, and note that the
calm continuation in the tonic with what has the freshness of a new
melody is simply an ornamental version of figure (*a*). As it proceeds, listen to the bass and you will find that the whole first phrase
of the theme is moving upwards two bars at a time, each pair of
bars being repeated.

Again the solemn triumph bursts out on the subdominant. Now
see what becomes of the two bars of modulating sequence on
figure (*a*). The magnificent plunge into the sombre key of D flat,
with the four bars in which its consequences are worked out—these
are the magnified version of those last two bars of Ex. 21, twice as
slow and with richer harmonic detail.

They lead back to the new version of figure (*a*), which now continues happily, echoed bar by bar, with another new figure (note the dialogue between the drums and the basses).

Ex. 24.
Cantabile.

Drums.

Then the second phrase of the theme is taken up and treated in the same way; at first two bars at a time, then its last bar alone, until it expands into a final broad melodious climax. At last nothing is left but the solemn rhythmic figure of the drums and the basses, the dying sigh of the clarinets, and the throbbing of the strings, from which last arises one final majestic crescendo. And hereupon the movement, like most of Beethoven's late slow movements, closes with subtle allusions to figures of the principal melody, in such a way as to fill the last bar with articulate musical speech up to its last quarter.

FINALE

The great problem for Beethoven in the composition of the Ninth Symphony was obviously that of providing a motive for the appearance of the chorus. The general scheme of the whole symphony as a setting for Schiller's 'Ode to Joy' is simple and satisfactory enough. The first movement gives us the tragedy of life. The second movement gives us the reaction from tragedy to a humour that cannot be purely joyful, except in a childhood which is itself pathetic when contemplated from that distance of time at which alone it can be appreciated. The slow movement is beauty of an order too sublime for a world of action; it has no action, and its motion is that of the stars in their courses—concerning which, however, Beethoven has surprising things to tell us later on. But it is a fundamental principle in Beethoven's art that triumph is to be won in the light of common day. Only twice in all his works (Sonatas, opp. 109 and 111) has Beethoven allowed the conclusion of the whole matter to rest in a slow movement of this type—a paradise like that of Dante, in which the only action and the only movement are the ascent from Heaven to higher Heaven as measured by the enhanced glory in Beatrice's eyes.

Now we shall find that this account of the first three movements of the Ninth Symphony is Beethoven's own; and the Ninth Symphony is not the first work in which he had attempted something of the kind, a search for a theme on which the mind could rest as a final solution of typical human doubts and difficulties. The Fantasia, op. 77, adumbrates a search for happiness through a storm of conflicting emotions and humours: so bold is the sketch and so violent the contrasts during the conflict, that the work is hardly to be understood except in the light of the Ninth Symphony. Again in the Choral Fantasia a solo pianoforte executes a massive and cloudy introduction (which at the first performance Beethoven extemporized); the orchestra enters group by group, exchanging rhetorical questions with the pianoforte; and then the pianoforte settles down to a placid melody not unlike a childish foreshadowing of the great choral melody in the Ninth Symphony; a set of variations ensues which passes through various tempi and keys with developing episodes; until a dramatic crisis is reached, giving rise to further questions which are answered by the entry of voices, bringing the matter to a conclusion with a short ode in praise of music.

In the Ninth Symphony Beethoven's plan is to remind us of the first three movements just as they have been described above; and to reject them one by one as failing to attain the joy in which he believes. After all three have been rejected, a new theme is to appear, and that theme shall be hailed and sung as the Hymn of Joy. Beethoven's first idea was that a baritone should express all this process in words, from the outset, in an impassioned recitative. The orchestra was to start with a confused din expressing terror and violence; the singer was to rebuke it; whereupon the orchestra was to give out the opening of the first three movements, after each of which the singer was to point out why it was not to the purpose; until, on the appearance of the new theme, the singer was to accept it with triumph and set it to Schiller's Ode. Beethoven sketched all the recitatives with the necessary words, very sensibly making no effort to achieve a literary style in such a sketch, but writing the flattest prose to indicate what was going on. In any case it would have been a mistake to aim at poetic diction when *ex hypothesi* not only is the poem not yet begun, but the music of it has not been found. Plain prose is absolutely necessary to this scheme, if such a recitative is to be sung at all; that being so, Beethoven soon saw that he had better commit himself to the smallest amount of plain prose that could possibly suffice. Moreover, words without metre may be prose, but music without metre is recitative; and recitative, especially in a symphony, is by all historic association either the most lofty symbolism, or it is pretentious rubbish. Away, then, with these paragraphs of amateur prose attempting to describe emotions which only music can express. Let the basses of the orchestra seem on the point of articulate speech with their passionate recitative. Everything is there without words; nor could any words do justice to the pathos with which the recitative, after

furiously rejecting the tragic solemnity of the first movement,
seems to hope wistfully for something better, only to be stung into
indignation by the playful theme of the scherzo. At the appearance
of the slow movement the pathos touches perhaps the greatest
height ever attained in recitative; fully as great as Bach and Handel
achieved in accompanied recitative with voice and with Bible words.
A few wind instruments give a halo of mysteriously luminous
harmony above the basses so long as these remain softened. Then
for a moment the passion breaks out again in despair; and now
comes the new theme.

Ex. 25.

At once the situation is changed; the recitative of the orchestral
basses greets the new theme with exultation. The wind-band
closes the recitative with the old conventional final chords, and
instantly the basses take up the theme and give it out in full. (It
is customary to make an impressive pause before this definite entry
of the theme; but Beethoven's notation of the final chords of the
recitative is against this reading. There is no meaning in his
putting the last chord at the end of a triple-time bar, unless it is
to have the special rhythmic effect of leading straight into the next
bar. It may be argued that this effect is not convincing; but
whether it convinces us or not, it is thoroughly characteristic of
Beethoven's later style and, like all such features, is the only
possible alternative to an effect which, if convincing, is also the
kind of commonplace Beethoven studiously avoids.)

Here now is the great theme which is to carry the stanzas Beethoven has collected from Schiller's 'Ode to Joy'. The melody is in
two parts, of which the second is always repeated.

Ex. 26.

When the basses have given out the whole melody unharmcnized, with its repeat, the violas in unison with the violoncellos go through it again in a higher octave also with the repeat. The double-basses have a melodious counterpoint, forming with the melody a very interesting two-part harmonic framework, to which the first bassoon adds an inner part melting occasionally into unison with the melody in a very subtle way.[1] The first violins enter in the soprano octave, and the theme is now in transparent widespread four-part harmony, to which the interior bassoon adds a more symphonic colour by doubling the melody at every odd pair of bars (see bars 3–4, 7–8, &c.). With the repeat there is now a crescendo: then the theme bursts out in the full wind-band, the trumpets blazing at high pitch with the melody, which is so simple that they can play every note of it in spite of the imperfect scale the trumpet had in Beethoven's time. (And yet such is Beethoven's delicate feeling that in one place in the eleventh bar he avoids a note which the trumpet has already played, because at this moment it is so harmonized as to suggest something beyond the natural character of the instrument.)

After the repeat the last four notes (*a*) of the theme are taken up and turned into a neat codetta, which henceforth becomes an integral part of the theme as treated in future variations.

EX. 27.

I give it here as it occurs in the choral statements.

This codetta is developed in energetic sequences, rising to a climax in which fine detail is crowded together in short phrases such as we find in the most elaborate paragraphs in the first movement or in Beethoven's latest sonatas and quartets. A quite new phrase with a ritardando now appears, sounding a reflective note

[1] The second bassoon should play with the double-basses.
After this analysis was printed Sir Charles Stanford wrote to me, 'There is no question that the 2nd bassoon is *col Basso* in the Finale of the Ninth Symphony. It is in the autograph; it is written in *by himself* in the copy made for the King of Prussia in Berlin (I've seen it); and in the copy he sent to the Philharmonic of London (ditto) he always writes it thus / / / (I think) for about 30 bars'.
The autograph, now published in facsimile, is perfectly clear. How, then, did Beethoven's intentions come to be so contradicted in the first edition? It happened thus. In the fair copy revised by Beethoven and sent to the publishers, the contra-fagotto had no separate stave, but was indicated as playing *col. fag. 2do*. Beethoven suddenly saw a disastrous possibility at this point, and, forgetting about the second bassoon, scrawled 'contra-fagotto tacet', adding rests to make sure.

which becomes mysterious in a change to an extremely remote key (*poco adagio*).

This is brushed cheerfully aside; but the doubt which it suggested receives tragic justification in the renewal of the panic of the introduction, which bursts out with greater violence than ever.

And now comes the revelation. The human voice is heard, summing up the beginning and the end of those instrumental recitatives. Beethoven's one piece of verbal prose is, after all, as fine as any master of style could make it. The situation demands a careful abstention from any diction that encroaches on poetry. Critics may cavil at the word *angenehm*, which the dictionary tells us means 'agreeable' or 'pleasant': but a German ear would be accustomed to it as a Biblical word without losing its familiar prosaic sense. Beethoven says 'Oh, friends, not these sounds; but let us attune our voices more acceptably and more joyfully'.[1]

The wood-wind give their first foreshadowing of the theme, the singer cries 'Freude' and is answered by the chorus basses; and then the singer gives out the great theme as a setting of the first stanza of Schiller's Ode. The repeat of the second half is given by the chorus in octaves without the sopranos, and then the orchestra concludes with the codetta.

> Praise to Joy, the god-descended[2]
> Daughter of Elysium,
> Ray of mirth and rapture blended,
> Goddess, to thy shrine we come.
> By thy magic is united
> What stern Custom parted wide:
> All mankind are brothers plighted
> Where thy gentle wings abide.

The next stanza is given by the vocal quartet, and the second part of it repeated by the full chorus in four-part harmony, the orchestra again concluding with the codetta.

> Ye to whom the boon is measured,
> Friend to be to faithful friend,
> Who a wife has won and treasured,
> To our strain your voices lend.

---

[1] Bülow wickedly used the phrase by way of prelude on the pianoforte when he had to play immediately after a dismally bad singer.

[2] Lady Macfarren's translation is reprinted here in revised version by permission of Novello & Co.

317

Yea, if any hold in keeping
Only one heart all his own,
Let him join us, or else weeping,
Steal from out our midst, unknown.

The third stanza is given in an ornamental variation by the quartet (probably the most difficult passage ever written for voices).

Draughts of joy, from cup o'erflowing
Bounteous Nature freely gives,
Grace to just and unjust showing,
Blessing ev'rything that lives.
Wine she gave to us and kisses,
Loyal friend on life's steep road:
E'en the worm can feel life's blisses,
And the Seraph dwells with God.

Again the full chorus repeats the second part with the utmost triumph, and this time the codetta is accompanied by massive vocal harmonies dwelling upon the last line—'und der Cherub steht vor Gott'. This is expanded with a modulation which suddenly plunges to the dominant of a darker key, B flat.

The blaze of glory vanishes. The solemn silence is broken by grotesque sounds in the depths of darkness. These sounds gather into rhythm, and take shape as the melody transformed into a military march, mysteriously distant, and filling a vast harmonic interval between deep bass and its shrill treble. Ruskin has finely described the Grotesque-Ideal as a veil covering the terror of things too sublime for human understanding; and that is unquestionably one of Beethoven's reasons for this treatment of the stanza in which the poet exhorts mankind to run their course as joyfully as the stars in the heavens.

But there was another motive which impelled Beethoven towards the Grotesque Ideal here. He had dismissed all illusions about Napoleon as soon as Napoleon made himself Emperor, but he had not dismissed the poet's ideals of war and victory. No artist, certainly no musician, has more forcibly sounded the true note of military music than Beethoven. He did not often write or wish to write a military march, but whenever he did, he struck with unerring accuracy the formidable note which should underlie the strains which are to inspire those who march to them. Nowhere has the terror of war been so simply and so adequately presented as in the *Dona nobis pacem* of the Mass in D. Beethoven indulges in no silly realism (we may ignore his pot-boiler, the Battle Symphony): he tells us no details about war; but he unfailingly gives the note of terror wherever war is symbolized. In this light we must read the military character of his setting of Schiller's stanza about the stars in their courses. Thomas Hardy has said of the facts of astronomy that when we come to such dimensions the sublime ceases and ghastliness begins. Beethoven is not afraid of the depths of the starry spaces—not more afraid than he was of Napoleon's armies; and so it is his military note that he sounds when Schiller compares heroes with the stars in their courses.

> Glad as suns His will sent flying
> Through the vast abyss of space,
> Brothers, run your joyous race,
> Hero-like to conquest flying.

A solo tenor declaims the stanza triumphantly, but in broken phrases which seem to stagger dizzily across the rhythms of the variation. A male-voice chorus joins in on the repetition of the second part, which is concluded with the codetta. Then the orchestra breaks into a double fugue, of which the first subject is derived from the original melody, and the second subject from its transformation into march rhythm.

Ex. 29.

This double fugue is worked out with great energy, passing through various keys, and aiming at the dominant of B, on which there is a mighty unison climax. As this dies away, three notes of the main melody appear softly in B major, then again in B minor. The bass drops from B to A in an impressive way which we shall recognize again later—

Ex. 30.

and then the full chorus bursts out with the first stanza of the poem set to the unvaried original theme, while the whole string band accompanies with a running bass in the triplet rhythm. After the repeat the orchestra begins the codetta but breaks off abruptly at its second bar. A mighty new theme appears, sung by the tenors

319

and basses and supported by the bass trombone, the first entry of
the trombone since the scherzo. This is the song of the universal
brotherhood of man, well-placed in harmonious reaction from that
military note associated with the stars in their courses.

Ex. 31.

O   ye   mil - lions   I . . .   em - brace   ye!

Here's   a   Joy - ful   kiss   for   all!

The sopranos take up the new theme; and then the basses answer
with another and yet more solemn note, 'Brothers above the starry
vault there surely dwells a loving Father'. This, again, is repeated
in full harmony by all the voices. To strike these solemn notes is
only too easy for a small artist; but great artists, when they strike
them, do as Beethoven does; they show by instinct, not by antiquarian knowledge, that these are the oldest harmonies in the
world. Beethoven had opportunities for understanding the church
modes as used by Palestrina; he was not as completely cut off from
them by temperament and training as was, for instance, Mendelssohn. On the other hand, he had nothing like the scholarship in
such matters shown in modern times by Sir Charles Stanford and
Mr. Gustav Holst. Yet here, as in the 'Incarnatus' of the Mass
in D and in the Lydian slow movement of the A minor Quartet,
he shows exactly the Palestrina instinct for the expression of awe,
mystery, and infinity, in terms of pure concord and subtle inter-
mixture of key.

And now comes the stupendous claim that Joy is meant to raise
us from our prostrate awe to the starry heights where the Godhead
dwells. I give a literal translation, as here the printed English
versions fail:[1]

> Ye millions, why fall prostrate?
> Dost thou, oh World, feel the presence of the Creator?
> Seek Him beyond the starry vault!
> Above the stars He surely dwells.

This is the central thought of the Ninth Symphony, and it also
underlies Beethoven's whole treatment of the liturgical text of his
Mass in D, where we have, throughout the Gloria, the Credo, and

---

[1] Lady Macfarren's translation, though skilfully designed for singing,
here reverses Schiller's and Beethoven's conception, the point of which
is *not* to fall prostrate, but to rise from prostration and look upwards to
the Father above the starry vault.

the Sanctus, three conceptions continually emphasized; first the divine glory; secondly, and always in immediate contrast, the awe-struck prostration of mankind; and thirdly the human divinity of Christ ('Qui propter nos homines'; 'et homo factus est').

As in the Mass in D so here in the Ninth Symphony, the thought of divine glory overawes at first, only to inspire action. The chorus breaks into a torrential double fugue on the two main themes, the invocation to Joy, and the appeal to the brotherhood of mankind.

Ex. 32.

This fugue (the standard example of Beethoven's extreme demands on the voices, justified in this instance by convincing effect) rises to its notorious climax in which the sopranos hold a high A for twelve bars. After this terrific outburst there is an abrupt plunge into the deepest prostration, from which again mankind raises itself in contemplation of the Father above the starry vault. And now, before the final climax, comes that full revelation of Beethoven's range which is seldom absent from his greatest works; the note which only the greatest poets can master, and which lesser artists avoid because it offends their pride. The main theme has been given several complete variations for the orchestra and for the voices; it has been developed in episodes and interludes; the second theme has been stated; and the two themes have been combined in a double fugue. Now comes the coda. And the note of the coda is the purest happiness of childhood; nothing like it had been sounded in music since Mozart's *Magic Flute*; and if we are shocked at the notion of comparing Beethoven's endless round-canon (Ex. 33) with the happiness of Papageno and Papagena, why, then the poet and the composer may twit us with our slavery to fashion which sternly separates what the magic of joy reunites! Beethoven regards this childlike note as the very consummation of joy in *Gloria Dei Patris*. There is only one way to understand an artist of Beethoven's range, and that is to assume that he means what he says and that he has ample experience of the best way to say it.

321

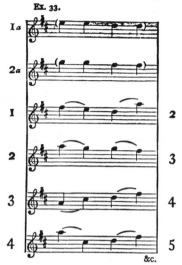

It is not necessary to assume that he is infallible; but it is quite idle to compare his range of style with something narrower, and to rule out as in bad taste whatever exceeds those limits. It is strange but true also of other artists besides Beethoven that the very points which give most offence to superior persons are just those in which the great artist most whole-heartedly echoes his predecessors. Not only does the round just quoted recall Papageno and Papagena, but when it suddenly drops into a slow tempo (*poco adagio*) as Papageno and Papagena did, it rises to one of Mozart's most characteristic forms of medial cadence.

Indeed we confidently expect the notes I have put in brackets; but here the round intervenes again, gathering itself up as before into the full chorus; and so leading again to the *poco adagio*. And then a miracle happens. The solo voices enter in a bright new key, B major, and turn the Mozartian medial cadence into a wonderful florid cadenza that expands grandly and ends on the heights in this distant region. It is the same region to which, after the military variation of the stars in their courses, the energetic instrumental fugue led; and now the same thing happens that happened then (Ex. 30), but in a much more subtle and simple form. The key of B major becomes minor, and while its upper notes are still being held, the bass drops down to A. It is as if the four solo voices had ascended into the heavens, and had then expressed by their change of harmony the link between heaven and earth. The orchestra at first hesitating but with growing confidence, repeats the message (that is to say, this mysterious step in the bass)—

and in a moment the whole mass of singers and voices is ablaze with the wildest outburst of joy. In all this final fury, with the big drum, cymbals, and triangle marking time with frenzied persistence, Beethoven maintains his Greek simplicity and subtlety of proportion. It is only in externals that the music seems to break all bounds; the substance and form are as exactly measured as the most statuesque coda of any string quartet, and most of all in that supreme stroke of genius, the sudden drop into a slow triple time (*maestoso*) with a lyric turn of melody, on the words 'Daughter of Elysium'.

In this solemn tempo the chorus finishes, and then the orchestra rushes headlong to the end. Even here there is no waste of energy, no chaos nor anything perfunctory. The very last bars are a final uprush of melody which happens to be quite new and might easily have been an important theme.

323

X. A PRÉCIS OF BEETHOVEN'S NINTH SYMPHONY, OP. 125

Supplementary to the larger Analytical Essay in Vol. II

The following analysis represents, without use of abbreviations and technicalities, the kind of précis-writing which I was taught by Sir Hubert Parry. As any diplomatic official on an interesting frontier knows, it is essential to good précis-writing that events should be narrated as they were known at the time by the persons concerned, and not as they appeared in the light of wider or later knowledge; human ignorance of the future and of the round-the-corner being an essential element in the shaping of the events. This is nowhere more true than in the case of music. Half the musical miseducation in the world comes from people who know that the Ninth Symphony begins on the dominant of D minor, when the fact is that its opening bare fifth may mean anything within D major, D minor, A major, A minor, E major, E minor, C sharp minor, G major, C major, and F major, until the bass descends to D and settles most (but not all) of the question. A true analysis takes the standpoint of a listener who knows nothing beforehand, but hears and remembers everything.

Whether this précis prove more, or less, unreadable than frontier official documents, a glance at it will show several useful points. For instance, it will make it evident that a full account of any exposition section enormously simplifies the task of analysing developments. The result almost seems as if the analysis grew more perfunctory as it continued. This is not so; though in the finale I have not thought fit to give that detailed phrase-analysis of the fugues and of the final prestissimo that I should require in a class-room. But on the whole the account of the whole choral finale is as complete as that of the first movement. You will find the same appearance of growing simplicity in the analysis of a Wagner opera or of a pure drama.

FIRST MOVEMENT

Allegro ma non troppo, un poco maestoso

Bars

1–16   Bare 5th on A sustained through 14 bars, and deepening to 5th on D at bars 15–16. Rhythmic fragments descend through it in gradually accelerating rhythm, foreshadowing and culminating in—

17–35   Main theme, beginning with figures (*a*) and (*b*) (the first two notes of (*a*) were the substance of the opening);

Ex. 1.

continued in long paragraph with several other figures; closing into tonic (with characteristic late-Beethoven overlapping of tonic chord upon dominant bass).

35–50   Counter-statement of bars 1–16 on tonic bare 5th, changing at 14th bar to B flat, and so leading to

Bars
51–63

Counter-statement of main theme, Ex. 1 in B flat for 4 bars, upon which figure (*b*) is developed in rising sequence and tapering rhythm for 8 more bars, leading to new theme.

Ex. 2.

TRANSITION

64–73

This, repeated in canon, leads in 3 extra bars to the dominant of B flat, where 6 bars of a new dialogue-theme by way of dominant preparation—

74–79

Ex. 3.

lead to the

SECOND GROUP (or 'Second Subject'), B flat major. Four-bar melody in dialogue—

Ex. 4.

80–92

repeated with variation and continued in a paragraph ending with new figure—

Ex. 5. *cres.*

92–101

which is developed for 6 more bars, leading to another theme—

Ex. 6.

102–119

which modulates to the flat supertonic (C flat = B natural), from which it returns in a pianissimo rising sequence leading to

120–137

12 bars of tonic and dominant dialogue in tapering rhythm, crescendo, with rhythm of Ex. 6 in drums. Further energetic

Bars   rising sequences lead to a 12-bar paragraph of dialogue
138–149   beginning thus—

and closing into a final outburst, in the main rhythm of
150–158   Ex. 6, on the tonic chord for 8 bars.

DEVELOPMENT

158–161   Two more bars collapse from B flat to A, and so to the
             opening bare 5th on A.
162–179   Introduction resumed and extended without compressing
             the rhythm; moving to dominant of G minor, always
             pianissimo.
180–187   Ex. 1 (a), treated in dialogue (pp), for 8 bars.
188–191   Outburst of Ex. 8 on dominant chord leads, in 4 bars, to the
192–197   following treatment of (b)—

198–217   The process of these 28 bars is repeated, leading in 2 more
218–252   bars to a free triple fugue with (b) as its main subject.
             Starting in C minor, it proceeds for 34 bars through G
             minor and B flat, and thence drifts towards A minor, where
253–274   it subsides into cantabile dialogue on its first figure, piano.
275–296   After 22 bars of this quiet passage Ex. 4 appears, and, pass-
             ing through F major, leads again to the cantabile dialogue in
             that key. Suddenly the dominant of D minor is suggested,
297–300   and in 4 more bars the development is violently ended with
             a plunge on to the D major 6th.

Bars	
	RECAPITULATION.—FIRST GROUP
301–314	The introduction is transformed to a fortissimo on a D major chord with the F sharp in the bass. This turns to the
315–338	minor in the 12th bar, and so to B flat: thence to Ex. 1, which, with its sequels, is expanded, each item being echoed by the wind in dialogue with the strings; all on a tonic pedal in the drums.
339–344	Suddenly Ex. 3 appears quietly in D major.

SECOND GROUP

345–426	Ex. 4 begins in D major, but 2 bars (351–352) added to its continuation transform the whole sequel into the minor mode, into which everything is accordingly translated. (See Ex. 4 to Ex. 8).

CODA

427–452	Following immediately upon Ex. 8, the coda begins with a quiet dialogue on Ex. 1. In a slow crescendo this culmi-
453–462	nates, after 25 bars, in 10 bars of Ex. 5, which lead to 6 bars
463–468	in the rhythm of Ex. 6.
469–494	Suddenly, through a sustained dominant 5 octaves deep, figure (*b*) is treated in D major for 8 bars by the horns and wood-wind; and then taken up in the minor (4 octaves deep) by the strings in the style of the fugato in the development (bars 218 foll.). This, with a crescendo and diminuendo, leads in 25 bars again to Ex. 5, which after 10 bars ends
495–512	with the close of Ex. 9, twice (making 8 bars). This closes
513–538	into the final tonic-and-dominant peroration, which is on a new theme, punctuated by rhythm (*a*) in trumpets and drums.

Ex. 10.

539–547	closing, after 26 bars, into Ex. 1 expanded into an 8-bar phrase ending with figure (*b*).

SCHERZO. (A) The Scherzo Proper.

FIRST SUBJECT

1–8	First figure (*a*) of main theme dispersed, through 8 bars, down the chord of D minor—

Ex. 11.

329

Bars   exposition of 5-part fugue on main theme—
9-32

Ex. 12.

33-56   continuation leading with a crescendo to
57-76   tutti restatement of theme modulating to dominant of C
            major (the flat 7th).
77-92   Passage of dominant preparation (8 bars, repeated).

SECOND SUBJECT. C major

93-108   8-bar theme (4+4) repeated with variation—

Ex. 13.

109-126   and followed by shorter phrases (on (a)+(b)) including one
            in 6-bar rhythm (2+4)—

Ex. 14.

127-142   an echo of the last 4 bars of which leads to a cadence-theme—

Ex. 15.

            the sequel of which closes into a passage of 8 bars (the
143-150   last three silent) in which chords of (a) descend in 3rds from
            C to D minor.
            Exposition repeated from Ex. 12 onwards.

DEVELOPMENT

151-174   Descent in 3rds continues, at first with the 3-bar pause,
            then steadily for fifteen steps round a wide circle of keys
            landing on A which is screwed up through A sharp to B
            natural, where there is a pause.
177-194   In 3-bar rhythm (a)+(b) is treated in dialogue between

Bars   bassoons and oboes; first for 9 bars in E minor, then for 9 in A minor.

195–233   The drums, in F, suddenly force the music into F major, where it develops, passing into D minor (the tonic). The 3-bar rhythm is retained steadily for 48 bars from the entry of the drums; when suddenly the music drops back into 4-bar rhythm as shown here—

Ex. 16.

234–240   (Figure (*a*) is present in every bar now till the recapitulation begins.) Quiet preparation ensues on the unexpected dominant of E flat (the flat supertonic) reached in 2 bars

241–271   through C minor, and held for 18 bars; then resolved into D minor, the chord of which is built up on figure (*a*) by drums and brass.

RECAPITULATION

FIRST SUBJECT

272–295   First theme (Ex. 12) tutti, with its second 4-bar phrase insisted on, passes from D minor through G minor to B flat where the passage of dominant preparation (bars 77–84)

296–329   appears. A pause of two extra bars on B flat brings it on to the dominant of D where it is repeated and expanded with a third repetition and new harmonies, leading to—

SECOND SUBJECT

330–387 (399)   This, mostly changed to the minor mode, is recapitulated in full, right down to the descending 3rds, which are here so placed as to lead, in the first instance, back to the beginning of the development. [This repeat is never observed in performance, and Beethoven at first erased it in the autograph. But he afterwards changed his mind and wrote over it 'bleibt Alles' or *stet*.]

388–413   In the second instance, it leads to a coda based on a new

331

Bars   imitative treatment of (*a*) (*b*) which, quickening in pace, arrives at a presto in duple time, thus—

Ex. 17.

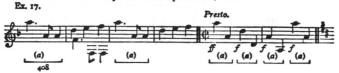

TRIO. D major. *Alla breve*

First strain—

414–421   Self-repeating melody in double counterpoint [note distinctions drawn by the bass at the asterisks]—

Ex. 18.

Second and other strains—

422–437 New 8-bar melody, repeated with fresh counterpoint, and
438–453 closing into Ex. 18 with bass put into treble (i.e. inverted in double counterpoint)—without the distinctions marked by asterisks. This, given twice (or four times), with the counterpoint in lower octaves, leads to a further development on the
454–474 dominant; the theme and its counterpoint leaving their primitive lines and rising in a crescendo, which suddenly subsiding and passing through F major (on a rising bass) leads back to Ex. 18 on the nearly full orchestra. This is
475–491 brought (in 16 bars) to a tonic close; and the second strain (with its sequels) is repeated.

491–530 A coda ensues, on the tonic, working up Ex. 18 by the full orchestra in a 16-bar crescendo, closing into its repetition (inverted in double counterpoint). Eight more bars of plagal cadence lead, with a diminuendo and a G minor chord at the last moment, to the da capo of the scherzo. This extends to the lead into the trio, and to 7 bars of the trio itself fully scored, broken off, and concluded with the last bars of Ex. 17.

ADAGIO. Theme with Alternative and Variations.

FIRST THEME. B flat major

1–24   Two bars of introduction lead to a theme containing three phrases, punctuated by echoes and expanded by repetitions in the following way.

ALTERNATIVE THEME.   D major

The foreign chord at the end leads to a second theme in D major, the major mediant, and in another measure—

Bars
25-42

It is 8 bars long and is repeated with a counterpoint (given in small notes in the quotation). Its last bar is then repeated with a turn back to B flat.

FIRST VARIATION

43-64

The violins vary the melody of Ex. 19; the winds preserve the echoes and the last 6 bars unvaried. The foreign chord

333

Bars
65–82

now leads to G, the major submediant, where Ex. 20 re-appears with fresh scoring. Its close now leads to E flat, in which key, the subdominant, there is an—

INTERLUDE

83–98

This interlude takes the first 2 bars of Ex. 19 as if to begin a variation or plain repetition of them, but drifts in dialogue into C flat (the flat supertonic) and, meditating there for a while, suddenly resolves into B flat and so into the second variation.

SECOND VARIATION

99–120

The violins, in 12/8 time, vary the melody, while the wood-wind give it unvaried, and reveal the unvaried echoes. When the last bar is reached, the foreign chord does not appear—

CODA

121–124

but the coda begins with an emphatic assertion of the sub-dominant, followed by imitations on the first 2 notes (*a*) of the theme.

Ex. 21.

125–130

This leads to a beginning of a new free variation of the first strain passing into the bass thus—

Ex. 22.

131–136

and leading again to the subdominant and to Ex. 21, the latter part of which is plunged into D flat (the flat mediant,

Bars   the dark key thus balancing the bright keys of the alternative theme)—with the following augmentation.

Ex. 23.

137–140   The first part of Ex. 22 returns and is continued, in echoing dialogue, with a new figure—

Ex. 24.
Cantabile.

141–157   leading to a similar cumulative development of strain II of Ex. 19, which leads, in another 16 bars, to the end.

FINALE

INTRODUCTION. *Presto* 3/4

1–29   Seven (8 including pause) bars of confused agitation in D minor lead to 8 bars of indignant recitative in the basses. The agitation, resumed on dominant of G minor, is again, after 8 bars, interrupted by the basses, who in 6 more bars

30–37   call up the ghost of the first movement, of which the first (introductory) 8 bars appear—with C sharp in bass.

38–47   The basses protest again, and lead in 10 bars to A minor,
48–55   where the ghost of the scherzo (8 bars on the fugato theme)
56–62   appears. Still more indignantly the basses reject this, lead-
63–64   ing in 7 bars to B flat. Two bars of the adagio (Ex. 19) greatly soften the anger of the basses, who modulate to a
65–76   distant key, but in the course of 11 bars break into despair. From their half-close in C sharp minor a modulation reaches
77–91   A as dominant of D major, where a new theme appears which they receive with acclamation.

Ex. 25.

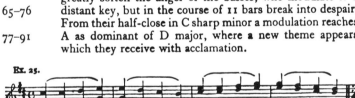

INSTRUMENTAL EXPOSITION. *Allegro assai*

Bars 1–24   The theme.

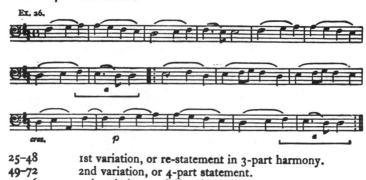

25–48   1st variation, or re-statement in 3-part harmony.
49–72   2nd variation, or 4-part statement.
73–96   3rd variation, or full orchestral statement.
97–111   From the last notes of this arises a codetta—

336

the last bar of which, instead of taking the shape here given,
leads through seven bars of rising sequence ending in A
major, the dominant; where a new figure—

112–116   asks a plaintive question with a vastly remote modulation,
which is cheerfully brushed aside in two more bars of A
major.

CHORAL EXPOSITION AND FINALE

1–9   But the chaotic storm of the introduction bursts out again.
This time a human voice answers with the beginning and
10–29   end of the double-bass recitative—

(Literal translation.) Oh friends, not these sounds;
rather, let us attune our voices more acceptably and more
joyfully.

THE VOCAL VARIATIONS

1–4   Baritone solo and chorus basses having joined in the
5–28   introductory bars of Ex. 25, the first vocal statement (or

Bars   4th variation) is sung by the baritone to the following words
(Lady Macfarren's translation, revised version),[1] the chorus
(without sopranos) repeating the second strain—

Stanza I. Praise to Joy, the god-descended
   Daughter of Elysium,
   Ray of mirth and rapture blended,
   Goddess, to thy shrine we come.
   By thy magic is united
   What stern[2] Custom parted wide:
   All mankind are brothers plighted
   Where thy gentle wings abide.

29–32   The orchestra gives the codetta as in Ex. 27, but in the
bass.

FIFTH VARIATION

Solo quartet; the second strain repeated by full chorus—

33–56 Stanza II. Ye to whom the boon is measur'd,
   Friend to be of faithful friend,
   Who a wife has won and treasur'd,
   To our strain your voices lend.
   Yea, if any hold in keeping
   Only one heart all his own,
   Let him join us,[3] or else weeping,
   Steal from out our midst, unknown.

57–60   The orchestra gives the codetta as in Ex. 27.

SIXTH VARIATION

61–84   Solo quartet in florid ornamentation, the second strain
repeated by full chorus—

Stanza III. Draughts of joy, from cup o'erflowing
   Bounteous Nature freely gives,
   Grace to just and unjust showing,
   Blessing ev'rything that lives.
   Wine she gave to us and kisses,
   Loyal friend on life's steep road;
   E'en the worm can feel life's blisses,
   And the Seraph dwells with God.

85–94   The codetta, given in due course by the wood-wind, is
accompanied by massive choral chords, repeating the words
'and the Seraph dwells with God'. In 7 extra bars the
music, passing on to A, plunges on to the dominant of B
flat (as events prove), and pauses there.

[1] Lady Macfarren's translation is published in revised version here by
permission of Novello & Co.
[2] Reading 'Was die Mode streng getheilt', as in the printed versions.
Beethoven's autograph reads, more Beethovenishly, *frech* getheilt', 'im-
pudently parted'.
[3] Should be 'He who cannot, let him weeping', &c.; i.e. if there be any
that could never make friends.

337

VARIATION 7 (*a*) and (*b*). *Alla Marcia, allegro assai*

Bars   *vivace*, B flat major (flat submediant) 6/8.

(1–12)   After 12 bars of rhythmic fragments building up the chord

13–44   of B flat (without the 5th) and arriving at a march-rhythm,
the 7th variation treats the theme in a syncopated form.
The second strain is not given twice, but the whole variation
is restated with a tenor solo in stammering counterpoint to
the following words—

45–92 Stanza IV.   Glad as suns His will sent plying
Through the vast abyss of space,
Brothers, run your joyous race,
Hero-like to conquest flying.

(Here Beethoven has reversed the order of the third and
fourth lines, in order to get a climax on 'Siegen'.)

Now the second strain is repeated, the male-voice chorus

93–100   joining in and singing throughout the codetta, which follows
in due course.

INTERLUDE

101–187   The orchestra breaks into a double fugue, in which a quaver
derivative of the main theme is combined with another
theme in the syncopated rhythm of the march, thus—

Ex. 29. (2)

Six entries of this, with varying spaces between, and closer
developments of the individual figures, pass through F,
C minor, G minor, E flat, B flat minor, and G flat to B minor
(= C flat), in which region there ensues much dominant
preparation, until finally the fugue is abandoned and only

187–212   the syncopated rhythm is left, on F sharp, with a diminuendo
back to D major, as follows—

Ex. 30.

(Note the fall of the bass from B to A.)

VARIATION 8

213–260   The chorus bursts out with Stanza I, with a running accompaniment in the strings. As usual, it repeats the second

Bars

261–264   strain. Four bars of the codetta are given, and it is cut short on the subdominant, with a silent pause.

NEW THEME. *Andante maestoso.* G major (subdominant), 3/2

Ex. 31.

O   ye   mil - lions   I . . .   em - brace   ye !

Here 's   a   joy - ful   kiss   for   all !

Stanza V.

1–16   This theme, marked by the first entry of trombones since the scherzo, is given out by the choral basses in unison, and repeated in harmony by the full chorus.

17–32   The next lines—

> Brothers, o'er yon starry sphere
> Sure there dwells a loving Father

do not reveal their key (beyond the fact that it is south of the subdominant) when given in unison by the basses; but the full chorus harmonizes them boldly in F major. Having thus obliterated the key of G major, they proceed in a kind of Dorian mode to utter words of which I give a literal

33–52   translation, as the singing versions miss the point—

> (*Adagio ma non troppo*). Ye fall prostrate, ye millions? World, dost thou feel the Creator present? Seek Him beyond the firmament of stars. Above the stars He surely dwells.

53–60   The climax on a chord of E flat is echoed on the dominant of D.

DOUBLE FUGUE

The two themes (Ex. 26 and Ex. 31) are combined as

1–65   follows, each to their original text—

Ex. 32.

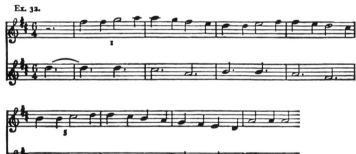

G

339

Bars
66–75

Five entries and several shorter developments of this 8-bar combination suffice to carry this fugue to its final climax where the sopranos hold a high A for 10 bars above the combination in the lower voices.

76–108

Then all themes vanish: there is an awestruck hush at the thought of falling prostrate; from which the thought of the loving Father beyond the stars brings calm, as the music passes in simple chords through the dominant to the sub-dominant, where there is a pause.

CODA. *Allegro ma non tanto.* Alla breve

1–20

The strings, with a diminution of the main figure of the Joy-theme, introduce a childlike new strain for the solo voices, which leads in 20 bars to the following free round, in which the chorus gradually joins, to the words—

21–43

'By thy magic,' &c.

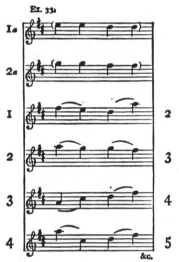

This culminates in the following outburst on—

'All mankind are brothers plighted.'

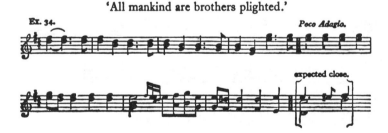

340

Bars
51–57
68–81

The expected Mozartean close is evaded and the round resumed. When it again reaches Ex. 34, the solo voices suddenly divert the poco adagio into B major (the major submediant), in which bright key they expand in a cadenza and finally vanish; the return to D being made by the drop in the bass that was already significant in Ex. 30.

Ex. 35.

Poco allegro, stringendo.

&c.

That drop from B to A is now taken up by the orchestra in 8 bars (*poco allegro, stringendo il tempo*) leading to the final stretto.

FINAL STRETTO. *Prestissimo*

Beginning with a diminution of Ex. 31, the chorus concludes with lines from the three main ideas of Schiller's poem—

'O ye millions I embrace ye!' 'Brothers, o'er yon starry sphere Sure there dwells a loving Father'—

and lastly—

'Praise to Joy, the God-descended.'

At the height of the climax the words

'Daughter of Elysium'

inspire the chorus to fall into a slow *maestoso* time in which they conclude—

Ex. 36.

leaving the orchestra to finish in due proportion with the diminished first figure in 20 bars of prestissimo, the very last five of which contain a new idea.

Key Relations in
Verdi's *Un Ballo in Maschera*

SIEGMUND LEVARIE

Key relations in an opera serve at least two functions. They help build and clarify the overall structure, and they contribute toward characterization and identification of people and issues.

Structuring a long composition like an opera is a particular task. All of Mozart's operas (after *Mitridate,* 1770) begin and end in the same key which, by assuming the role of tonic, determines the harmonic functions of all other keys. The tonic of *Così fan tutte* is C major; of *Die Zauberflöte,* E♭ major. The history of Beethoven's *Fidelio* exemplifies a trend, typical of the nineteenth century, toward a less obvious but always tonal orientation. The original version begins and ends in C major. The final revision, without abandoning the tonic C, opens in E major, which is sub-

sequently understood as a dominant substitute (i.e., the dominant of the tonic relative). This tonal flow across an entire work may properly be called *cadential*. A special case of this kind is Wagner's *Tristan und Isolde.* Withholding the fulfillment of the tonic E major throughout most of the opera (thus paralleling the continuous yearning told in the story), the music begins in A minor and ends in B major—a decisive subdominant-dominant cadence without final resolution. Some other Wagner operas nevertheless define the tonic by clear and identical tonal statements at beginning and end: thus *Lohengrin* (A major) and *Die Meistersinger von Nürnberg* (C major). Verdi's practice is similar. *Falstaff* begins and ends in C major; but *Il Trovatore* begins in E major and ends in E♭ minor, so that the tonal flow of the entire work amounts to an enharmonically reinterpreted Neapolitan cadence.

Characterization by keys is a subtle pro-

0148-2076/78/1100—0143 $0.25 © 1978 by the Regents of the University of California.

cedure, for one must not naively try to equate keys and people on a one-to-one basis. What prevails is tendencies. In Mozart's *Le Nozze di Figaro*, the aristocratic couple generally moves in sharp keys; the servant couple, in flat keys.[1] But the lines are not always sharply drawn; by overlapping, key areas occasionally illuminate each other. Wagner's leimotivs become significantly reinterpreted precisely by reappearing in various keys.

Verdi's technique in *Un Ballo in maschera*, the focus of this investigation, seems representative of most of his operas and of Romantic harmonic practice in general. While tonal direction remains a paramount force, specific keys often serve several functions. Thus the same key may appear as subdominant (F, for instance, in relation to C), Neapolitan (in relation to E), parallel or relative substitute (D minor, F minor, and A♭ major), or enharmonic counterpart (E♯ major). The enharmonic reinterpretation in particular may close the gap between two distant keys and thereby reconcile them.

Un Ballo in maschera opens in B major with five sharps and ends in B♭ minor with five flats. The following table shows the tonal frames of each act:

Act I		Act II	Act III	
Scene i	Scene ii		Scene i	Scene ii
B—A♭	c—A	d—B♭	f—B♭	A♭—b♭

In any cadential flow—whether in a long opera or a Bach chorale—the arrival points serve as guideposts. We may safely stipulate B♭, major or minor, as the tonic key of *Un Ballo in maschera*. The reiterated emphasis on B♭ at the curtains of the second and third acts settles that key in the listeners' ears. The sound of A major at the end of the first act may be interpreted as a tonicized leading tone. In any case, it functions as a dominant of the immediately following key that opens the

second act. Because D minor is the relative of F major—the key in which Amelia's aria "Ma dall'arrido stelo" actually ends—A major may also be understood as a substitute second dominant. The two readings do not at all contradict each other, for both point cadentially toward the tonic. As if to clarify any possible misunderstanding of the role of D minor, the progression d–B♭ of the second act is promptly rectified by the equivalent but more obvious progression of f–B♭ in the third act.

The signal placement of A♭ major widens the overall cadence. In purely melodic terms, the five curtains spell out the chromatic progression A♭–A–B♭, the tonic occupying three —and the last three—of the five places. The wide arch from A♭ in the first scene to B♭ in the last scene is briefly recapitulated by a shorter identical span within the last scene itself. Harmonically, A♭ is the second subdominant of the tonic B♭. Heard in context, the cadential progression A♭–A–B♭ can thus be understood as a well-balanced widened full cadence: second subdominant to (substitute) second dominant to tonic.

The role of B♭ as tonic is moreover confirmed by the many signal recurrences of this key throughout the opera. They serve to remind the listener where he is heading. In Act I, scene i, both Renato's and Oscar's arias are in B♭ major; in Act I, ii, the quintet; in Act II, the finale; in Act III, i, again the finale; and in Act III, ii, the ball and, turned to the parallel minor, the tragic end. In these pieces, the growing participation of the conspirators is noteworthy. One first hears B♭ in Act I in the aria of Renato, who later becomes a conspirator. In the quintet, the situation is more threatening, but the conspirators are still outnumbered or at best—if one assigns a neutral role to Ulrica—balanced against the others. The Act II finale belongs to them. At the next curtain, they have become reinforced by Renato and outdo Riccardo's sympathizers. At the ball, finally, they reach their goal and triumph. Oscar, too, is involved in the tonic key but innocently so. His first aria makes him responsible for the fateful visit to Ulrica. In the three ensembles of which he is part, his high bright line provides contrast to the underlying dramatic tension. From all these pieces

[1] For a detailed analysis of key relations in opera, see this author's *Mozart's "Le nozze di Figaro"* (Chicago, 1952; rpt. New York, Da Capo Press, 1977), pp. 233–57.

in B♭ Riccardo and Amelia, in their role as lovers, are excluded. Their keys belong to a different realm.

The framework set up by the opening and closing keys helps us find our bearings. Five sharps and five flats lie symmetrically around C major, and indeed at the very center of the work stands the great love duet in C major, "O qual soave brivido." It is the divider between the ascending and descending parts of the dramatic action. It is also the musical fulcrum about which the sharps and flats turn. The C-major scene is the only one in which the lovers are happily "in balance," so to speak, and not torn between two irreconcilable and opposed attitudes.

The role of C major as a neutral respite amidst the divergent key tensions is confirmed by the structural placement of the two other pieces in this key: Ulrica's *invocazione* and Riccardo's *romanza*. They lie symmetrically on either side of the C-major center so that these three pieces in C act like fixed piers—two smaller ones around the one in the middle—supporting the wide total span. Their symmetrical position contributes toward shaping the entire opera, for each appearance is surrounded by about the same amount of music. Some other details reinforce the effect of the correspondences:

Act I	Act II	Act III
Invocazione	Duetto	Romanza
c–C	C	c–C
Beginning of Scene 2	Central	Beginning of Scene 2
Middle of Act Solo	Middle of Act Duet	Middle of Act Solo
Minor–Major	Major	Minor–Major
Prophecy	Fulfillment	Reminiscence

The harmonic behavior of C major toward the extremes of B major and B♭ minor is equally neutral. In relation to the opening key, C is the Neapolitan; toward the closing key, the dominant of the dominant. Both these functions are inherently subdominant.

Of the two tonal realms on either side of the central C major, the one with sharps is appropriated by the lovers. Amelia's identification with the key of E is particularly clear and free of ambiguities. Her big entrance scene with Ulrica in the first act is in E minor, turning to E major after Riccardo joins in to form the closing trio. Her ecstatic declaration of love to Riccardo, "Sì, t'amo," fills an E-major section in the middle of the C-major duet (p. 155).[2] She has a comparable E-major island, this time in the middle of threatening flats, when asking her outraged husband for a moment's grace before submitting to his vengeance (p. 203). Characteristically Renato soon thereafter creates his own E-major island amidst flats when deciding to spare Amelia's *"fragile petto"* and kill Riccardo instead (p. 210).

In relation to Amelia's E major, Riccardo's opening reception in B major has an exalted tone which turns rapturous in his F♯-major daydreaming of Amelia ("La rivedrà"). Afterwards, when reality sets in, no key ever again ventures so far up. This F♯-major is enharmonically related to Amelia's dolorous aria ("Morrò") and her acceptance of the invitation to the ball at the other end of the opera ("Qual tristezza," p. 226). The spelling with six flats rather than six sharps is significant, for at this moment it relates her not only to the distant Riccardo but also to her immediate home situation. Here the key circle, which could be ideally closed, actually breaks.

The successful part of Riccardo's life, established by the courtiers' initial chorus of homage in B major, continues to be projected by sharps. Silvano learns of his luck in A major (p. 59) and later initiates the Act I finale, which praises and extols Riccardo's leadership, in the same key. Amelia uses this key in the next act for her first tentative declaration of love (p. 149), at which moment it serves as a subdominant for her more definitive subsequent outbreak in her own key of E major. The Judge, another testifier to Riccardo's political supremacy, appropriates D major. This is also the key in which we first hear, in the orchestral prelude, Riccardo's "daydreaming" melody. A D-major chord also explodes at the dramatic turning-point of the

---

[2] Page references are to the Ricordi and Kalmus vocal scores.

plot when Renato identifies the veiled lady as Amelia, his own wife. The turn to sharps is momentary, amidst flats. Without any particular modulation, an ensemble in B♭ major follows. The psychological insight conveyed by D major here is considerable: at the moment of discovering the shocking relationship of Amelia and Riccardo, Renato pronounces her name in a key belonging to the realm of the lovers rather than to his own. He makes a similar very brief but marked excursion into Amelia's key area of E major when he pulls her toward the urn from which she is to draw the name of her lover's assassin (p. 227).

The only other key with sharps, G major, appears in Oscar's strophic *canzone* in the last scene, "Saper vorreste." Completely surrounded by the tonic B♭, this key seems related more to the ballroom atmosphere than to the lovers. In terms of B♭ major, G major is the relative key reversed from minor to major (TR instead of Tr). In this form it provides some light relief in a tense situation.

The key of B minor associated with the conspirators in the prelude and the first scene projects a negative image, as it were, of the general homage in B major.

These aggregate sharp keys hold their own against the flat keys, which contain the tonic B♭. Thus the real center of gravity lies below the neutral middle, understandably so in the context of a tragic plot. We have already pointed out the dramatic role of B♭ throughout the opera. The final appearance in minor must be interpreted as the parallel mode of the tonic rather than a new concentration of flats. It relates back to, and partly explains, the preceding duet in D♭ major in which the lovers bid each other farewell. In this sense, D♭ major functions as a romantically reinterpreted tonic—the relative major of the minor tonic (tR).

This double version of the tonic justifies the prominence—actually a kind of monopoly—of both F major and A♭ major (both with their relative minors) among the remaining flat keys. Both serve a dominant function and—given the tonal style of the opera—therefore prevail. Of the two, A♭ seems more closely connected with the conspiracy. The dominant function of A♭ major

ties in with our earlier identification of this key (in the course of the overall cadential progression from curtain to curtain) as the second subdominant, of which the basic dominant quality is well established by harmonic theory. The vicariousness of F and A♭ in the context of *Un Ballo in maschera* is noticeable in various places. The finale of the first scene, after a great deal of emphasis on B♭ major, turns directly to A♭ major, which renders a dominant impression. In the third act, the vengeance trio "Dunque l'onta di tutti" and subsequent quartet are in A♭ major, preceded by Renato's aria in F major and followed by the finale of the scene in B♭ major. Standing between F and B♭, A♭ here plays the role of a dominant surrogate. The band at the ball, too, first sounds off in A♭ major (p. 255) and then reaches the desired key of B♭ major via a short stretch in F major.

Because these keys functioning as dominants of the tonic belong primarily to the conspiracy, Riccardo's share in them becomes noticeable and calls for an explanation. The little *canzone* in which he asks Ulrica to "sing his future" ("Di' tu se fedele") moves from A♭ minor to A♭ major, which again acts as a vicarious dominant to the following tonic quintet in which he derides the fatal prophecy. In spite of the light tone, the key of A♭ here points to the inevitable disaster. Similarly at the first curtain it prepares the visit to Ulrica's hut and thus marks the first direct step toward the tragic development.

The real dominant, F major, begins to assert itself from the second act on. It becomes the legitimate meeting point for all the various currents, the musical as well as the dramatic focus of the opera. It first appears in Amelia's solo scene and aria "Ma dall'arrido stelo," gradually established by way of first the relative D minor and then the parallel F minor. Against Amelia's basic key of E, F major functions as the Neapolitan version of the subdominant. Very skillfully Riccardo approaches Amelia through a comparable sequence of keys: D minor, D major, and—in his lyrical appeal "Non sai tu" (p. 145)—finally F major. In relation to the following grand C-major love duet, F major functions again as the subdominant, now in its pure form. With Renato's entrance, this key area experiences one more reinterpretation, this time in reverse order. He sings first in F major, but the following trio ends in the relative D minor. F major, in any case, has acted as a pivot in the overall plan of both the dramatic and the musical structures. Introduced as a subdominant function—surreptitiously, as it were, by the lovers—it asserts itself through Renato as the real dominant of the main key.

This role of F is thoroughly confirmed by the next scene which opens the third act. Renato's big aria "Eri tu" is in F, reached by way of D minor and, at the opening of the curtain, of F minor. This is the moment at which Renato decides to kill his friend. The tonal arch is at its clearest, for this F major is the real dominant to both his entrance aria in the first scene and the assassination in the last scene.

The Act III finale summarizes these diverse interpretations of F. Riccardo's enthusiastic F-major outburst at the end of his solo scene in C (p. 258) harks back to the second-act situation. But this subdominant reminiscence is quickly turned into a dominant reality by immediately pivoting into the final tonic ballroom scene. Here it builds the closing dominant cadence (p. 281) by resolving first to the tender relative major of the tonic (Db major, pp. 283f.) and ultimately to the tragic minor tonic itself (Bb minor, p. 298).

These findings, which (one hopes) may prove persuasive by themselves, will gain support and strength from comparable investigations of other Verdi operas by other musical scholars.[3] A question which remains to be pursued is how Verdi's sense of tonality as a structural force developed throughout his career. *Un Ballo in maschera* is characteristic of his brilliant middle period. How much of the tonal technique uncovered here can be found in his early works? What usages, if any, anticipate the strong and open tonal cohesion of his last opera? Whatever the answers to such and similar questions, there need be no doubt as to Verdi's regard for tonal organization in the service of operatic form and characterization.

347

---

[3]The grapevine tells of such studies in progress.

Viewpoint

JOSEPH KERMAN

Professor Levarie's grapevine[1] tells him true: there are indeed other studies in progress dealing with key relations and drama in the operas of Verdi. And Verdi is not the only composer whose operas are being looked at from the same point of view. Over the short lifespan of this journal we have already received our fair share of contributions along these lines, and have published several. In the present climate of musical scholarship such investigations would seem to be both inevitable and salutory, as I shall suggest later; but they also seem to have a tendency to turn into scholarly minefields. Such, I believe, is the concise study of key relations in *Un Ballo in maschera* by Professor Levarie, who is a veteran—indeed a pioneer—in work of this kind. We are grateful to him for letting his article serve to initiate a general discussion of relevant research problems, a discussion in which we very much hope readers will engage by writing us letters.

It would be a good thing if everyone who writes on key relations felt impelled to explain what he or she means by *tonality*. People use the same terms but mean different things by them. Current concepts of tonality, in fact, can be ranged along a scale between two extreme positions. What is at issue is something more than the interpretation of certain details of harmonic theory—whether the major supertonic is to be regarded as "inherently subdominant" or not, and so on, despite the obvious importance of such questions. The issue that divides the house of theory is more fundamental and touches the phenomenological status of key relations. To what extent are these directly perceived as aesthetic phenomena, and to what extent are they schematic elements in an abstract system of musical organization?

Occupying the right wing in this division (as in so many others) is Donald Tovey, brilliant, contentious, garrulous, sometimes elliptical, but also resolutely common-sensical, a sort of good-old-boy of music theory who has to be handled gingerly even now, seventy-five years after he started writing his famous analytical essays.

The first condition for a correct analysis of any piece of music is that the composition must be regarded as a process in time. There is no such thing as a simultaneous musical *coup d'oeil* . . .

---

[1]See "Tonal Relations in Verdi's *Un Ballo in maschera*," this journal, p. 147, fn. 3.

0148-2076/78/1100—0186 $0.25 © 1978 by The Regents of the University of California.

Some students begin their analysis of a sonata by glancing through it to see "where the Second Subject comes" and where other less unfortunately named sections begin. This is evidently not the way to read a story.[2]

For Tovey key relations were severely limited to what his precocious "naïve listener" might reasonably be presumed to hear:

In classical music no two keys are related through the medium of a third tonic, and . . . no sense of key-relation arises except between keys that are in immediate juxtaposition. Most musicians probably have enough sense of absolute pitch to recognize that two widely separated passages are in the same key, but when they imagine that this recognition is a genuine aesthetic experience they are like persons who, having been told what masterpieces of painting are admirable in proportion and composition, practise measuring the details of such pictures with a foot-rule until they have acquired a skill in estimating the distances to a millimetre by eye.[3]

There is much characteristic Tovey in these quotations—the oblique slap at solfège training in the Conservatoire tradition, the tell-tale analogy between a sonata and a "story," the insistence that key relations must be perceived and perceived directly if they are to be taken seriously, and of course the sharp distinction between mere perception and "aesthetic experience." Tovey's views still have force today, not only because of their logical consistency, which is considerable, if not perfect, but also because they are so handsomely reflected in a body of living criticism. No one has ever cared so deeply about how tonality *feels*, and no one has ever worked so steadily to convey this in the context of music-analytical writing.

Almost all theorists today stand some way to the left of Tovey, if for no other reason than that like Schenker he was reduced to talking reactionary nonsense about twentieth-century music. As far as Tovey was concerned, the proper use of key relations (and with it, proper music) stopped with Brahms. If Tovey's posi-

tion as a theorist of tonality could be called strict contextualism, perhaps Professor Levarie's could be called radical absolutism. For in this view, keys are regarded as absolutes, independent both of their modulatory surroundings and also of any sense of time.

The timeless quality of keys, as Professor Levarie sees them, results in what many will find to be the most questionable of his analyses or judgments. Thus the B- and F♯-major key areas of the very first two numbers in *Un Ballo in maschera* can have an "exalted" and "rapturous" quality in relation to Amelia's prayer in E major, even though she has not yet sung in that key (or in any other) at this early point in the action. Renato's B♭ aria in the same scene can be linked to the ultimate tonic of the opera, and hence to the conspiracy, even though that tonic is not recognized as such until "the reiterated emphasis on B♭ at the curtains of the second and third acts settles that key in the listeners' ears," as Professor Levarie puts it. (Indeed it would take all of Ulrica's Boston voodoo to divine the opera's B♭ tonic in Act I, the main numbers of which come in B, F♯, B♭, B♭, C, A, E, A♭ minor, B♭, and A.) Even "Eri tu," Renato's aria in Act III, is stated confidently to be in F, though the piece starts out just as confidently in D minor and turns to F only at about the halfway mark. Professor Levarie sees no problem in any of this, apparently because he conceives of tonality as a sort of non-temporal spatial field generated by a timeless tonic. And indeed such statements cause problems only if one believes, with Tovey, that a sense of key relationship is established by actually hearing one sound after another, one sound in temporal relation with another.

The immediate context of key areas—how they are reached, how they are established—also counts for very little in the absolutist view of tonality. For Professor Levarie, keys are rather like great mountain peaks which loom up above the mist and which he can admire and speculate upon from afar. Anyone who really wants to know the mountains, however, also knows that he has to get up them; and so for him it is a matter of importance whether he is going to have to proceed

[2] D. F. Tovey, *A Companion to Beethoven's Pianoforte Sonatas* (London, 1931), p. 1.
[3] Tovey, *Beethoven* (London, 1945), p. 28.

349

by road, by funicular, or by axe and rope. What Tovey wrote of Beethoven—

It is a most vital distinction ... whether the modulation asserts a key-relation directly, explains it circumstantially, digresses at large, or deliberately mystifies[4]

—is certainly also true of Verdi. We need to understand and gauge the different local dramatic effects when he juxtaposes key areas without any modulatory explanation, when he moves smoothly from one to another, and when he works things so as to mystify, thrill, or chill. (This he does often; he is working, after all, in a tradition of melodrama. The force of such modulations, Tovey reminds us, is often to disjoin rather than to provide continuity and relation.)

To take some cases in point, the local situation is different with each of Professor Levarie's three C-minor/major plateaus. Ulrica's *invocazione* in Act I, scene ii, opens that scene after an orchestral prelude elaborating C with a variety of diminished chords. The lovers' duet in Act II (more properly the *cabaletta* of their duet) is approached from A major by means of an axe-and-rope modulation to G minor, so that the C major sounds like a surprisingly harsh subdominant. Riccardo's *romanza* in Act III, scene ii, is inserted without true modulation (either before it or after it) into a scene holding with unusual solidity to A♭. So each C-minor/major area sits very differently in its immediate context, and the only way one can hear a "relation" among the three—hear them, that is, as congruent— is by tuning out their local connotations. The absolutist concept of tonality, in short, depends upon the sense of absolute pitch. So much the worse for those unfortunate aural cripples who lack it.

An even more radical form of tonal absolutism seems to underlie Professor Levarie's discussion of the symmetrical balance of the five sharps of the opera's beginning and the five flats of its ending, and their "fulcrum" around the "neutral respite" of a sharpless and flatless C major. For Tovey this would be sheer *vaneggio*; the relation between keys

would stay the same even if the opera were to be transposed up a semitone and the symmetrical tally of sharps and flats completely wrecked. There is only one further stage of tonal absolutism that can be imagined, the assigning to keys of particular characteristics which hold from work to work across an entire repertory. I must not—I cannot—say that Professor Levarie carries things to this stage; yet I fancy I catch a whiff of it, just a whiff, in his remark about the aristocratic couple in *Figaro* "generally moving in sharp keys"—like Count (or rather Earl) Riccardo and Amelia, who take over the "sharp" side in *Ballo.*

In fact Riccardo and Amelia do a pretty poor job of appropriating those sharp keys. Amelia may sing an important trio in E minor/major, but her two actual arias come in F minor/major and E♭ minor. Riccardo's social position may be celebrated in B and D major, but *his* arias are if anything flatter, coming in C minor/major, A♭ minor/major, B♭, and G♭ (though notated in F♯, "La rivedrà" emerges directly as the Neapolitan of F). Indeed, it may be in the general area of the association of dramatic elements with keys that Professor Levarie's analyses will be judged most eccentric. He insists, for example, that B♭ is the key of the conspirators when the only people who initiate music in that key are premature or innocent conspirators like Renato and Oscar (and Riccardo himself). The actual conspirators mutter in B minor, bellow in A♭, and choose B♭ only for the Act II finale, which is the one place in the opera where they take a rest from conspiring and have a bit of heavy fun at Renato's expense. And he claims that when Riccardo in Ulrica's hut sings his light-hearted *canzone* "Di' tu se fedele" in A♭ minor/major, this conspiratorial key "points to the inevitable disaster." Even in Act I of *Tristan und Isolde* such arcane ironies would not be a possibility, let alone in Act I of *Un Ballo in maschera.*

II

Dramatic analysis of this kind is almost too vulnerable, in my view. I should rather return to Professor Levarie's more strictly musical analysis, which (again in my view) seems to raise more significant questions. One of

---

[4]*Beethoven,* p. 40.

these is *not* whether he is "wrong" in an absolute sense, and Tovey right. Almost every article of music theory has arisen in legitimate response to some music or other, and the historian must keep insisting that music theory is not an absolute, but something controlled by a historical context. The operative question is how tonality was conceived by Verdi, by the Verdi of 1859. This we do not know, and we will not find out by simply assuming it was the same as Beethoven's conception, or Tovey's, or Wagner's, or our own, whoever we are.

But surely it is clear that Verdi was less interested in tonal absolutes (or absolutes of any other kind) than in what could impress *his* naïve listener, the man who bought his ticket at the Teatro Apollo, the San Carlo, and La Scala. Verdi was a composer who wrote for a specific audience. Like all great composers, no doubt, he was always at least a little ahead of his listeners—always leading them by the ear, as it were, into new and strange artistic territories. No doubt. But in *Simon Boccanegra*, two years before *Ballo*, he had moved so far ahead of his listeners that he had a near fiasco on his hands. There is every indication that *Ballo* represents a determined effort to win his audience back.

This was in 1859, the year of *Tristan und Isolde*. What a difference between these two works in sophistication of musical technique and dramatic psychology! In the nineteenth century Wagner was the standard against which Verdi was found wanting. In the twentieth, it seems, he is the standard against which Verdi establishes his tonal credentials. For of course it is Wagner, as expounded by Lorenz, who provides us with the model of an opera organized into a fully articulated tonal-dramatic whole. Professor Levarie, in his book on *Le Nozze di Figaro*, leans heavily on Lorenz. However sharply the details of Lorenz's theory have been attacked, his basic insight as to the tonal nature of opera—of Wagner's operas, but also of other people's—continues to provide inspiration for a wide complexion of opera scholars today.

Lorenz has finally gone under after withstanding a fantastic pounding, like the *Admiral Graf Spee*, but his support vessels are still ploughing full steam ahead through dangerous waters. It is a dangerous thing to take Wagner as a model for anyone else, when his dramatic conception and his musical style were both so highly idiosyncratic. Considering his dramatic conception, first of all, we should never forget that Wagner dealt in myth. In myth everything was, is, and will be the same. Time exists in a special dimension, and Tovey's way of reading a story does not necessarily apply. With *Tristan* we are supposed to know the story when we enter the theater; with *Ballo* the fiction is that we do not, just as when we listen to a Beethoven sonata the fiction is that we do not know where the second subject is going to come, how the development will proceed, and so on. In a post-Wagnerian opera like *Wozzeck* the last bars of the epilogue can hook into the opening scene with the Captain because time is circular and the child is beginning a new incarnation as Wozzeck. *"C'est le tour de la pauvre petite"* at the end of *Pelléas et Mélisande*, too, and it has even been suggested that one can tune in to *Pelléas* at any point without it making too much difference. But this is not the case with *Ernani* and *Il Trovatore* and *Un Ballo in maschera*. At the end of the action in these operas things are different than they were at the beginning—terribly, astonishingly different. Why *should* these pieces be organized in the same way as a Wagner opera? A myth is not a melodrama, any more than a diamond is a sunset.

And in considering musical technique, let us not forget Wagner's complex thematic web and let us not forget his large sectional recapitulations. For Tovey, it was by such means and only by such means that Wagner was able to maintain clear key relations over a larger time span than that of any earlier music. Certain categories of leitmotivs are associated with particular keys and even—for greater clarity yet—with particular on-stage instruments.[5] In this regard Verdi's practice in *Ballo* is scarcely encouraging. There are a number of recurring themes, but none associated with a particular key. "La rivedrà" is

---

[5] See the lucid summary by Robert Bailey, "The Structure of the *Ring* and its Evolution," *19th-Century Music* 1 (1977), 48–61.

heard in D and A (in the prelude), F#, Ab, and F, Amelia's prayer in E and D, the Tom-and-Sam fugato in B minor and F minor. On the face of it, it does not look as though the composer who dealt this mess expects to win many contracts in the great game of key relations.

Yet on a more local level Verdi does fine things with tonality—things which are only obscured by absolutist system-making. Take, for example, the love-duet in Act II. The *cantabile* of this begins with Riccardo's long, powerful outpouring in F major. When Amelia resists his advances, she starts singing in Db without any true modulation, but her second phrase moves back ("collapses," I think we are permitted to say) to F, where Riccardo can and does renew his seduction. And when a moment later she actually capitulates, her rich, intimate key of A major has been smoothly prepared. The next time they meet is at the masked ball, with that curious little F-major dance played by the on-stage orchestra providing an accompaniment for their *parlante*. At the instant Amelia is recognized by Riccardo, the music shunts again without true modulation to Db, Professor Levarie's "romantically reinterpreted tonic," in which key she pleads with him to escape from the assassins. The echo of the previous scene is unmistakable—and for Tovey's naïve listener would be just as unmistakable if the dance were in E and the recognition in C. It would not be, though, if the modulation were arranged in some conspicuously different fashion.

Since the A minor of the brief *Presto agitato* which marks the actual assassination follows not from F but from Db, and follows not by means of a smooth modulation but by another jolt, there is nothing to be made of the coincidence between this key and the A major of Amelia's original capitulation. But when the E dominant of the assassination scene resolves deceptively to F, of course we hear this as the same key as that of the opening dance—because it is not only the F-major tonality that comes back, but also the on-stage dance tune. In this scene (let us not speak of the opera as a whole) there is indeed a strong sense of long-range "cadential flow" as this drawn-out F major resolves gently to the Bb

minor of Riccardo's death agony. Here Verdi picks up the progression E–F as a mournful appoggiatura in the low clarinet, and even expands this into an F–Gb appoggiatura in preparation for the Gb of the *sotto voce* hymn "Cor si grande e generoso" just before Riccardo expires.

These are elegant details of tonal organization which it is hard to think carry any particular dramatic message. On the other hand, Verdi's treatment of Db in the two duets helps to project and then magnify the poignant blend of love, distress, and helplessness in Amelia's relationship to Riccardo—a quality achieved more truly with Amelia, I believe, than with any other of Verdi's anguished heroines. I believe also that effects of this kind fall safely within the range of Verdi's musical technique and dramatic psychology in the late 1850s.

III

It would be silly to decry or discourage studies of key relations and drama in the operas of Verdi or any other composer. Until the current mania for finding "unity" in musical compositions runs its course, it is clear not only that such studies will continue, but that they will continue to be in the mainstream (and damn the torpedos). They can and they will produce exciting results. One must only ask that they be conducted with tact, common sense, an awareness of history, and respect for the integrity of each individual composer. One's instinct is to applaud the generous motive behind the effort to show that Verdi was privy all along to the secrets that made Beethoven, Brahms, and Wagner great. But generosity can sometimes be misguided, and we will stifle him in kisses if we succeed, finally, in turning him into a sort of melodious Richard-come-lately.

I see opera studies of this kind as a natural part of a larger scholarly movement in our field, a movement dogged by revealing ironies which are worth bringing to the surface and thinking about. For Tovey and his generation, as for Adorno and his, there was a clear hierarchy of musical value culminating in Brahms or Wagner—or in the case of the subtlest musical minds, both Brahms and Wagner. Italian and French music lacked the intellectual and moral character of the great German tradition, and the music of outlying regions was simply not in the picture. This critical monism was linked to the prevailing evolutionary view of music history—the view manifest both in Schoenberg's insistence on his own link to the tradition and in everyone else's hysterical rejection of his art. It is true that the evolutionary scheme of values caused problems, so that a somewhat hazy exception was made for Mozart and Bach. Sooner or later, though, as one went back in history there came a point beyond which music became "primitive," beyond which one entered the successively more primitive worlds of Cavalli, Byrd, Josquin, and Machaut.

Today, as Richard Crawford has remarked in another connection, musicians, listeners, and musical academics exist in a much more ecumenical climate. We know a great deal more about Cavalli and Byrd and Josquin and Machaut. We listen to Lester Young records when we are home and go to huge Ali Akbar Khan spectaculars when we are at musicological conferences. In the limited area of nineteenth-century repertory, Verdi and Berlioz, Rossini and Massenet, even Alkan, Berwald and Sullivan come into the sights of our constantly twirling periscope. Yet many scholars seem to be so firmly set in the old monism that they can only validate these new sightings by accommodating them to the guidelines set by the old establishment. So the *Dichterliebe* and the *Fantastic Symphony* and the Verdi operas must be shown to be constructed according to the same principles as those manifest in a Beethoven symphony or a Wagner music-drama. The effort is difficult, but evidently not so difficult as seeing that other composers have a life of their own and principles of their own of parallel integrity.

This is a state of affairs that we accept in regard to composers of earlier centuries, and we certainly accept it in regard to the early and late twentieth-century masters. Among the latter the basic, shattering diversity is scarcely to be ignored, even by minds rotted by reductionism. Is it only, then, in studies of nineteenth-century music that we are still bound to the nineteenth-century monism? That would be a final irony worth thinking about.

Viewpoint

On Key Relations in Opera

GUY A. MARCO

After half a century of "tonal analysis" we still have no usable general theory of operatic structure based either entirely or partly on key relations.[1] The exciting and controversial analyses of Wagnerian music dramas by Alfred Lorenz[2] are applications of largely unstated principles. His method is to find and describe "poetic-musical periods" (as mentioned all too briefly by Wagner in *Oper und Drama*) and then to look for patterns which relate them. It is all impressive enough, but pervaded by a romantic instability and stained with infelicities—in particular the announcement

that *Tristan* ends in the dominant, although Lorenz does acknowledge that "to the musical sense" the final B major is the tonic terminus of a gigantic Phrygian cadence beginning with the A minor of the *Vorspiel*. Siegmund Levarie, in his scrutiny of the structure of *Le Nozze de Figaro*,[3] has given us a most elegant explication, but again the critical principles are stated only in the broadest of terms. A recent attempt by Graham George to shape a theory of key relations[4] seems to falter on what is undoubtedly a formidable difficulty: the fact that a number of great operas end in a key other than what would be—by traditional criteria— the tonic. George's conclusion, that such works actually have two "interlocking" tonics, cannot easily be reconciled with the nature of tonicization itself—the central focus of relations and of repose. If there could be two tonics, there could be any number, but they could not in fact be centers. Other studies of key effects in opera and dramatic music have tended to be personal and descriptive, quite unable to account for the non-symmetrical elements except by labeling them as dramatic

---

[1]These remarks, outlining some points of departure for a general theory of key relations in opera, are in response to Siegmund Levarie's article "Key Relations in Verdi's *Un Ballo in maschera*," this journal 2 (1978–79), 143–47, and Joseph Kerman's "Viewpoint" in the same issue, 186–91. Later references to Levarie and Kerman are to these articles, unless otherwise indicated.

[2]*Das Geheimnis der Form bei Richard Wagner* (Berlin, 1924–33; facsimile edn. in 4 vols.: Tutzing, 1966). It seems to me that Kerman exaggerates in declaring Lorenz to have "gone under after withstanding a fantastic pounding," but certainly the torpedo damage has been significant and will call for reconsideration in dry dock. Robert Bailey is one who has pierced the hull: "The Structure of the *Ring* and its Evolution" (this journal 1, [1977–78], 48–61), but even he seems to realize that the vessel has something basically sound about it. In *Opera as Drama* (New York, 1952), Kerman had made some negative remarks about Lorenz, without going into detail; but details are the power of Lorenzian analysis, despite the way in which they are sometimes manipulated.

[3]*Mozart's Le Nozze di Figaro: a Critical Analysis* (Chicago, 1952).

[4]*Tonality and Musical Structure* (London, 1970).

contrasts or the like.[5] Even Donald Francis Tovey ran into trouble over tonal structure, finding himself more than a little off balance with Haydn's decision to end *The Creation* in B♭ instead of in C.[6]

Opera composers have been no more helpful than critics in articulating such a theory, but of course it is not their task to do so. Wagner did not say how his poetical-musical periods were joined into patterns, nor even how to tell where one started and ended. Verdi's letters are a useful source of his ideas on relevant points, but they never speak to the details of large-scale structure. What he did mention was that each work did have its proper structure: "It is best that artists sing not their way but mine ... that ultimately everything depends on me; that one will dominates all, my own. This may seem tyrannical to you, and perhaps it is. But if the opera is cast from one mold, the idea is one, and everything must concur to form this One" (letter to DuLocle, 7 December 1869). The reader of the *Macbeth* or *Aida* correspondences will be struck by the control which the composer exerted in the shaping of his libretti, always striving for artistic form and dramatic effect. He objected to Scribe's libretto for *I Vespri siciliani* because three acts showed the same pattern; he labored to put the *Aida* libretto into a satisfying form.[7] It is of interest to find, in one 1870 letter to Ghislanzoni, evidence of Verdi's new awareness of the Wagner prose works which DuLocle had sent earlier in the year. He writes at one point that the form of a piece was good "and I believe I shall be able to make of it a good poetical-musical period" (*squarcio poetico-musicale*).

Reflection on what composers and scholars have produced on the topic of operatic structure with special reference to key relations has only reconfirmed the need for a general theory. It would be well to begin with the definition of key as a formal element; I fully agree with Kerman that writers are all too flexible in their application of the terminology. Keys must be clearly identified, and just as clearly located in the design. Identification should distinguish among keys that are firmly established (capable of generating their own substructures of related keys) and those which are merely signalled by a chord or two, and there should be intermediate categories as well. In locating keys, the analyst should address the participation of a key in the micro-structure, the mid-structure, and the macro-structure,[8] and it should be aware that crossover affinities from one structural level to another are likely to be suspect. Without a certain degree of clarity on this sort of issue, binary oppositions and the other symmetries may be illusory. But now let us consider the nature of opera itself.

Opera must operate in accord with laws of musical structure and also in accord with laws of drama; indeed it must also observe the laws of other art forms to the extent that they are involved. If we consider only the primary ingredients of opera—music and drama—we may suppose that the "laws" of each, i.e., their norms and conventions, may either be treated as separate domains or else be treated as a single union of those domains. Even in the case of separate treatment, there must be a sense in which the one domain absorbs the other. A play within a play, for example, may develop its own plot and characterization, but it will invariably have to accept its final meaning from the place it has within the larger work.

---

[5]For instance, Hugo Leichentritt: "In addition to making use of the emotional and expressive meaning of various keys, Handel builds entire acts of his operas and oratorios of four hours' length according to an ingeniously devised architectural plan of tonalities, making use of the relationship of the various keys and grouping them in symmetrical order, or, when necessary, destroying this symmetry by a striking contrast." *Music, History, and Ideas* (Cambridge, Mass., 1938), pp. 143–44.

[6]*Essays in Musical Analysis* (London, 1937), V, 114–46. Graham George simply designates both B♭ and C as tonics (*Tonality and Musical Structure*, pp. 31–33).

[7]See Edgar Istel, "A Genetic Study of the *Aida* Libretto," *Musical Quarterly* 17 (1931), 34–52.

---

[8]These concepts are lucidly articulated in John D. White, *The Analysis of Music* (Englewood Cliffs, 1976).

Taking Erving Goffman's term, the overall experience is "framed" by the play, but the inner play is a viable layer within it.[9]

But this is not the mode of opera. Drama does not exist in a distinct compartment, but flows simultaneously with the music; its own laws of time and diction are set aside in favor of musical norms and demands. As Suzanne Langer says, the music swallows the other arts of the opera.[10] Still, in this assimilation there is a certain accommodation. Music with drama is not the same structurally as pure instrumental music—consider the very matter of key relations: its patterns are different and connected differently. Its meaning, in short, is different. When two arts are combined, one becomes the patterngiver for both, and it is on the basis of those patterns that the work's value may be judged. In the combination of music and text, the music gives the patterns; the combiner— the finder and user of an extant work from another medium—always gives the patterns and takes the credit or blame for the result.

So a model of the artistic union between music and drama will be distinct from the models of either art taken singly. It will partake of the laws of both, but with final reliance on music as "the primary apparition" and with an outgrowth which is a dialectic blending at a higher level of creation. To describe this model, at least in outline, is a basic task for anyone who wishes to propose a general theory of operatic structure.

Fortunately there are some suggestive analogies available in other fields of thought which may prove useful as stepping stones. And above all we have a seminal concept to guide us: the Jungian view of arts as the symbolic language of the collective unconscious. The collective unconscious contains the archetypes of human experience, archetypes which are beyond the reach of language and approachable only through symbol and myth. The collective unconscious "provides categories of phantasy-activity, ideas *a priori* as it were, the existence of which cannot be ascertained except by experience. In finished or shaped material they appear only as the regulative principle of its shaping, i.e., only through the conclusion derived *a posteriori* from the perfected work of art are we able to reconstruct the primitive foundation of its primordial image."[11] Art translates the archetype "that repeats itself in the course of history. . . . It is a mythological figure."

Northrup Frye and his followers have fleshed out this theory with descriptions of mythic models which underlie legends and narrative fiction. Frye identifies four *mythoi*, named for the four seasons, which mold the generic or "canonical" plots: Spring is the comedy/romance; Autumn the tragedy; Summer the successful quest; Winter the unsuccessful quest.[12]

Such models do not explain a work of art, but they prepare it for explanation by setting it into a credible frame; i.e., they establish some of its basic laws and norms. These laws are in fact so basic that they may be rooted in the way the human brain functions.[13]

So let us inquire: what is the ultimate form of opera, the cluster of effects which calls out for explanation? We need to explain how opera

357

---

[9]The notion of a frame which limits and informs experiential situations is pervasive in Goffman's writings, but see especially his *Frame Analysis* (New York, 1974), chapter 5. For a brilliant example of another sort of frame we have Vladimir Nabokov's *Pale Fire* (New York, 1962), a novel which encloses an intriguing poem.
[10]*Problems of Art: Ten Philosophical Lectures* (New York, 1957), pp. 84–85.

[11]Carl G. Jung, "On the Relation of Analytical Psychology to Poetic Art," in *Contributions to Analytical Psychology*, trans. H. G. and Cary F. Baynes (London, 1928), pp. 225–49.
[12]Northrup Frye, *Anatomy of Criticism* (New York, 1957), pp. 158–239.
[13]Structural linguistics has looked for these fundamental patterns of brain activity in the way languages develop, and recently linguistic principles have been applied to the literary arts in an effort to find elemental patterns and models of meaning. For a lucid, critical summation of American and European structural and "post-structural" thought, see Jonathan Culler, *Structuralist Poetics: Structuralism, Linguistics, and the Study of Literature* (Ithaca, 1975). I am much indebted to Culler's book for much of what follows in this paper.

can hold in firm unity, over a time period of considerable magnitude, the diverse systems of norms which constitute dramatic and musical laws.

What interplay of patterns, what mix of building blocks and mortars, gives this great edifice its strength? I would like to suggest one line of thought which may prove fruitful, while recognizing that many others may be devised· and indeed be preferable. What I have in mind is that opera is a system of musico-dramatic symbols which represent the comic and tragic *mythoi*, the highest refinements of those Aristotelian binary opposites, comedy and tragedy. These are clearly the modes, in their extreme forms at that, which have dominated opera libretti since the Camerata. Opera plots have typically been peopled with fun-loving peasants and servants or dying heroines, and one is hard put to imagine a repertoire made up of ordinary plays: romances, mysteries, family chronicles, quest stories, and character studies. The reasons may be that comedy and tragedy, in their purest manifestations, are the most suitable structures for the amalgamation of the diverse systems which comprise the operatic effect. This is the common ground shared by drama and music; these are the pattern types susceptible to manipulation by both arts.

To be brief, let us set comedy aside for another day and look only at tragedy. The original definition is still the best one: "Tragedy is an imitation of an action that is serious, complete, and of a certain magnitude; in language embellished with each kind of artistic ornament, the several kinds being found in separate parts of the play; in the form of action, not of narrative; through pity and fear effecting the proper katharsis, or purgation, of these emotions."[14] One does have to tread softly in approaching this definition, mindful of Butcher's remark: "It would be a curious study to collect the many and strange translations that have been given of this definition in the last three hundred years. Almost every word of it has been misinterpreted in one way or another." But those errors may have been correct as responses to the ambiguities in the sentence, which have made it a fit subject for centuries of speculations and interpretation.[15]

In any case I do wish to grasp some thorny terms—pity, fear, and catharsis—and try to apply them to our task. I also need the concept of "reversal" which Aristotle explains later in the *Poetics* as the point in a so-called complex plot where the situation changes direction to the detriment of the tragic protagonist. For our purposes the most valuable engagement with pity and fear (he calls it terror) has been made by I. A. Richards: "Pity, the impulse to approach, and Terror, the impulse to retreat, are brought in Tragedy to a reconciliation which they find nowhere else. . . . Their union in an ordered single response is the catharsis by which Tragedy is recognized, whether Aristotle meant anything of this kind or not. This is the explanation of that sense of release, or repose in the midst of stress, of balance, and composure given by Tragedy."[16] The tragic law of drama vivifies the impulses to approach and retreat in a plot enacted by characters; the tragic law of music expresses approach and retreat with respect to the melodic, harmonic, and rhythmic organizing centers.

Our immediate concern is with key relations, so let me suggest how tonal patterns might help to enact these impulses and also that of reversal. Pity and fear, as binary oppositions, may be symbolized by opposed keys (with the nature of "opposed" being drawn from the musical style at hand), but the binarism of tonalities must correspond to that of the piteous and fearsome phases of the dramatic plot. At the same time, directions of tonal movement may correspond to directions of plot movement: drawing near and backing away. At the reversal scene of the plot (if it is "complex"), tonality ought to reflect greatest tension; at the end of the drama it ought to embody response and reconciliation, the

[14]Aristotle, *Poetics* 6. 2. Translated in S. H. Butcher, *Aristotle's Theory of Poetry and Fine Art* (Edinburgh, 1894; New York, 1951).

[15]One fine anthology is *Aristotle's Poetics and English Literature: A Collection of Critical Essays*, ed. Elder Olson (Chicago, 1965).
[16]*Principles of Literary Criticism* (New York, 1925), pp. 245–46.

dialectic catharsis. In an opera of the eighteenth or nineteenth century we would expect the tension-release cycle to sound like an authentic or possibly a plagal cadence, so the end of a tragic opera could only be in the tonic key (with reversal scene in the dominant or perhaps the subdominant domain). And since there is really no other point of high tension and release in the tragic plot, there ought to be no other macrolevel cadence formed by operatic key relations.[17]

If I am on the right track here, we have some basis for understanding several puzzles about Verdian operatic procedures. One puzzle is the lack of emphasis on the tonic (i.e., the closing, reposeful key) in the body of a work; this lack has led some critics to discover alternate tonics.[18] But tragedy's tonic, unlike that of a sonata, needs to be reserved, in its full flowering, for the catharsis. *Aida* demonstrates this. The closing tonic of Gb signals the only possible "ordered response" to the pity-fear opposition of the plot, the union in death of the lovers. Their fate was tonally announced in the reversal scene (the betrayal of Radames, the unmasking of Amonasro) by the dominant, Db. There is no other establishment of Gb in the opera.

We cannot pursue here details of application and method in the Verdi canon. It should be observed though that Verdi's "tragic" operas end in keys other than those in which they began, while *Falstaff* rings of C major all the way. And Mozart's mature works—all comedies—hew to a single tonal center throughout.

Another puzzle is the choice of specific keys within a work, for binary and other symmetries could theoretically be shaped from various possible tonalities.[19] In a tragic opera, however, built on the symmetry of the piteous (reaching toward, unifying, joining) and fearful (leaving, running away, separation, disunity) domains, keys ought to express these states and finally ought to conjoin them in the key of tonic resolution. How keys may be conjoined is a topic too complicated for this introductory essay. But one approach is suggested in Levarie's identification of C major in *Un Ballo* as "the musical fulcrum about which the sharps and flats turn ... a neutral respite amidst the divergent key tensions."[20]

The brief discussion above has perhaps suggested points of departure in the direction of a general theory. In summary, it seems to me that the basis of that theory may be found in the way a composer perceives a particular literary/dramatic action, associates it through a symbolic transfer with his own collective unconscious, and restates it in musical symbols which both transform and affirm the original literary patterns. The unique macrostructure of opera, and its remarkable dependence on key relations, stems from the artist's struggle with a unique and substantive problem.

A Postscript on the Listener: Kerman labels Levarie's method as "absolutist," and observes that "the absolutist concept of tonality, in short, depends upon the sense of absolute pitch. So much the worse for those unfortunate aural cripples who lack it." His point is

359

---

[17]Macro-level cadences—movements whose keys fall into authentic or plagal relationships—are rare in the instrumental works of the common-practice period. Schenker and Salzer find their grand cadences only within movements, not between them. A symphony finale concludes, but does not resolve.

[18]Graham George, in *Tonality and Musical Structure*, gives several specimens. An imaginative approach to the search for an alternate, non-terminal tonic is found in Bruce Archibald, "Tonality in Otello," *Music Review* 35 (1974), 23–28. The tonal center of Act I is said to be F major, from which prior and later keys are seen to "radiate" in the form of a star. Even this pattern depends, however, on various symmetries between established keys and transitory effects; it fails, in my opinion, to unseat the closing key of Db as the rightful tonic.

[19]The fact that certain composers had favorite keys for this or that situation has been a popular subject of description, if not of explication. A sensible review, with bibliography, is given by Martin Chusid, "Significance of D Minor in Mozart's Dramatic Music," *Mozart Jahrbuch* 1965/66, pp. 87–93. The most appealing explanation of key preferences is that of Hans Keller, "Key Characteristics," *Tempo* 3 (1956), 5–16; he attributes choices to the way instruments sound in particular keys, e.g., violins on open strings.

[20]Kerman's objection, that the nature of C major as a fulcrum would vanish if the opera were transposed up a semitone, strikes me as dubious. Whatever C major might become, in a transposed version, it would remain in a central "neutral" position with respect to the tonalities on either side in the circle of fifths.

compelling; and it raises the larger question of what the listener can actually perceive of structural patterns and relationships, tonal and otherwise. Let me offer a few comments. A popular view places a good deal of trust in the intuition of the aesthetic observer (musical listener, viewer of the visual arts, reader of poetry, and so on). "Artistic perception . . . always starts with an intuition of total import, and increases by contemplation as the expressive articulations of the form become apparent."[21] Or, as Nikolaus Pevsner puts it in his study of Brunelleschi's Santo Spirito church in Florence, "The nave is just twice as high as it is wide. Ground floor and clerestory are of equal height. The aisles have square bays, again half as wide as they are high. . . . Walking through the church, one may not at once consciously register all these proportions, but they contribute all the same decisively to the effect of serene order which the interior produces."[22]

Well, I find the intuiting observer to be a troubling construct. Let us grant that he may form an agreeable impression of an unfamiliar artwork, and that the intricate patterning of the work is at the heart of that impression. But what can we say of the possibility that he will, through "contemplation," in due time "register all these proportions"? Are not the most subtle proportions—of Chartres, of *Finnegan's Wake*, or *Tristan*—beyond the power of any observer to grasp while he experiences them? Does he not have to halt the experience and approach the proportions analytically, in cold blood? While some few gifted persons may carry out this dissection unaided, most of us will need plenty of help.

The serious audience for an art work is made up of two types: the ideal observer, and the teachable observer. Only the first type is indispensable. The group of ideal observers may consist of one person, the artist who creates the work and observes the product, but it may be enlarged with the presence of others who have acute critical gifts and stylistic competence. In the teachable group are persons of sufficient competence to comprehend an interpretation, an analysis of proportions and

structure, when it is explained to them. Such persons—and they are numerous in the musical world—can, with guidance, meet the most formidable work on its own terms.

Even gifted critics learn from one another, over time; significant truths about familiar masterworks are often undiscovered for centuries. (For example, it is only within the past twenty years that critical imagination disclosed the structural-psychoanalytic subtleties of the father surrogates in *Oedipus Rex*[23] and the thematic unfoldings in the Appassionata Sonata.[24]) In the end, what matters for the observer/listener is the achievement of a level of understanding. It does not count for much whether that level is reached instantly or slowly, in the concert hall or at the desk, alone or with assistance. We find our artistic meanings however we can, and gratefully. In some respects the long search is superior to the immediate discovery. *Zur Wahrheit gehört nicht nur das Resultat, sondern auch der Weg.*

---

[21]Langer, *Problems of Art*, p. 68.
[22]*An Outline of European Architecture*, 4th edn. (London, 1953), p. 117.

[23]James Schroeter, "The Four Fathers: Symbolism in 'Oedipus Rex'," *Criticism* 3 (1961), 186–200.
[24]Rudolph Réti, *Thematic Patterns in Sonatas of Beethoven* (New York, 1967).

360

On Key Relations in Opera

SIEGMUND LEVARIE

The best an article can accomplish is to evoke a discussion. Hence I quickly consented when the editors of *19th-Century Music* suggested that my comments on "Tonal Relations in Verdi's *Un Ballo in maschera*" (this journal 2, 143–47) be used to initiate an experimental controversy. Thought, as Plato stated, is provoked by opposite opinions.

Mr. Kerman has made a correct observation: in a study of key relations, everything depends on one's definition of tonality. His definition is obviously not mine. He and I are talking about different things. Thus there is no real discussion. Yet while he is rather impatient with people who do not share his viewpoint, I think that the difference in approach deserves a few comments.

Every phenomenon can be considered in

two different manners. The terms *ontic* and *gignetic* (from the Greek roots for, respectively, "being" and "becoming") have been profitably used to mark the antinomy. I can do no better than to quote from a recent essay on different interpretations of music history:

In an ontic position, we abstract from time; we consider things *sub specie aeternitatis*, under their typical permanent aspect, not subject to change. In a gignetic position, on the contrary, we consider phenomena according to their temporal nature, changing and fugitive. When we speak of a baby, of an old man, a river, a musical scale, a chord, we speak of the being of things. When we speak of development, of getting old, of erosion, of a scale rising or falling, of a chord progression, we speak of the becoming of things. When you swim fighting against the waves, you experience gignetism. Rise high enough to perceive the contours of the lake or the sea, and you will discover that the movement of the water was, after all, no more than an agitation within an immobility. Thus one will have experienced successively the gignetism and the ontism of the same phenomenon.

Now these two modes of apprehending phenomena are reflected in the things themselves according to whether their nature participates more or less in the one or in the other. Music offers revealing examples. A consonance is by its nature ontic whereas a dissonance is naturally **gignetic**. Yet if one employs a perfect major triad as a dominant, one thereby confers a gignetic aspect to a consonance. Inversely, by ending a piece on a dissonant chord, one thereby confers on it an ontic aspect.[1]

In reality, all music presents at the same time both aspects. We can think of a composition as a definitive entity isolated from the notion of time, or as an evolutionary entity experienced in time. Even Mr. Kerman, whose entire argument is wholeheartedly gignetic, must have his moments of ontic orientation whenever, for instance, he refers to a composition as a whole. Donald Tovey, whom Mr. Kerman uses a bit as a colonel uses a footsoldier, was also dogmatically gignetic: "The composition must be regarded as a process in time. There is no such thing as a simultaneous musical *coup d'œil*." *Must* be? There *is* no such thing? He misses half the experience and, if he really means it, half the pleasure.

Following an exclusively gignetic orien-

tation, Mr. Kerman, as anyone knowing him may safely assume, proceeds logically and intelligently (if not always gracefully). His thoughts have their own validity. In brief moments when he seems to sense the possibility of a mode of thinking other than his own, his terminology and imagery strike me as not fortunate. "Radical absolutism" (not necessarily a pejorative) explains little in the context; and the poetic reference to mountain peaks can easily be turned around and work both ways. The intelligent reader of *19th-Century Music* will discover by himself the distance between my position and that of various straw men Mr. Kerman has skillfully put up throughout his discourse in order to be able to knock them down conveniently. His own intelligence may have led him to recognize (and perhaps regret?) his indefensible exaggeration in calling critical concern for artistic unity a "current mania."

Having granted Mr. Kerman his gignetic approach, I maintain, of course, the validity of my ontic conclusions. By coincidence, there appeared almost simultaneously with my article a critical journal (the editorial board of which includes Mr. Kerman) with several contributions which, in different terms, deal with the question of ontism.[2] Against Tovey's "must be," I need here only posit René Wellek's: "Although the process of reading [hearing] is inevitably temporal in criticism, we must try to see a work as a totality, a configuration, a gestalt, a whole." In my consideration of an entire work, I found the ontic approach appropriate and fertile.

Contrary to Mr. Kerman's claim, absolute pitch has nothing to do with it, nor does the artificial Verdi-Wagner confrontation. Our present civilization, in music and elsewhere, has completely sold out to gignetism. The wish to be "dynamic" (a real "current mania") has removed restraint from most activities and aspirations. Ontism is needed to maintain a proper balance in the dangerous play of forces. For—so ends Ernst Lévy's essay quoted above—"if ontism without gignetism lacks life, gignetism without ontism is self-destructive."

---

[1] Ernst Lévy, "Aperçu sur un arrière-plan de l'histoire de la musique," *Revue musicale de Suisse Romande* 31 (1978), 72–82. The translation is mine.

[2] *Critical Inquiry* IV/4 (Summer 1978). See the essays by Wellek, Arnheim, and Subotnik.

Motivic and Tonal Interaction in Verdi's
*Un ballo in maschera**

By ROGER PARKER and MATTHEW BROWN

V ERDI'S *Un ballo in maschera*, first performed in Rome on 17
February 1859, not only remains one of the most popular works
in the operatic repertory, but is also one of the most written-about. A
brief chronological review of the literature reveals a predictable
progression of subject matter and orientation, which could be repeated with many other operas. Initially, studies focused for the most part
on biographical and documentary matters, charting the painful progress of the opera through a maze of southern Italian censorship, from
Antonio Somma's Scribe adaptation, *Gustavo III di Svezia*, to *Una
vendetta in domino*, to the abortive *Adelia degli Adimari* (or, as Verdi
scornfully dubbed it, *degli Animali*), to the unlikely and much-
criticized Bostonian setting of the definitive version.[1] Much of this
early work was reviewed, and much new material added, when *Un
ballo* became the subject of the first three *Bollettini* of the Istituto di
studi verdiani, volumes that collectively run to well over 1,500 pages.[2]
In the meantime, musical studies had begun to appear. Massimo
Mila's 1933 monograph is an important early landmark; his thoughts
were enlarged upon by several later writers, notably Guido Salvetti

363

---

* Material for this article, first conceived in London, was elaborated upon and
discussed during the Fall 1982 Seminar in Romantic Music at Cornell University.

[1] The three most important studies are: Alessandro Pascolato, ed., *Re Lear e Ballo
in maschera* (Città di Castello, 1902); Gaetano Cesari and Alessandro Luzio, eds., *I
copialettere di Giuseppe Verdi* (Milan, 1913), pp. 561–76; and Alessandro Luzio, ed.,
Carteggi verdiani, 4 vols. (Rome, 1935, 1947), I, 217–40. The best modern survey is in
Julian Budden's *The Operas of Verdi*, 3 vols. (London, 1973, 1978, 1981), II, 360–76.

[2] *Verdi. Bollettino dell'Istituto di studi verdiani. "Un ballo in maschera,"* Vol. I, Nos. 1–
3 (Parma-Busseto, 1960). Among the most interesting contributions are: Frank
Walker, "Unpublished Letters: A Contribution to the History of *Un ballo in
maschera*," No. 1, pp. 28–43; Francesco Flora, "Il libretto," No. 1, pp. 44–72, No. 2,
pp. 662–78; Andrea Della Corte, "Saggio di bibliografia delle critiche al *Ballo in
maschera*," No. 3, pp. 1165–97; and Fedele D'Amico, "Il *Ballo in maschera* prima di
Verdi," No. 3, pp. 1251–1326. All articles appear in English, Italian, and German.

and Julian Budden.[3] In recent years, selected passages from the opera have stimulated more thoroughgoing analysis. Luigi Dallapiccola's account of the Act II trio "Odi tu come fremono cupi" has been highly influential; less well-known but nevertheless of interest is Robert Moreen's analysis of the relationship between words and music in the preceding trio, "Per salvarti da lor."[4] In 1970 the Italian literary critic Gabriele Baldini roundly declared *Un ballo* to be Verdi's masterpiece, and supported his argument with a detailed discussion of the dramatic structure.[5] Finally *Un ballo*, in the last few years, has become the forum (one might almost say battleground) of a lively debate on the problems of large-scale tonal organization in Verdi's operas.[6]

One reason why the opera has received such attention is that, in at least two respects, it holds a special place in Verdi's œuvre. (Both of these have been noted and discussed often enough, but, possibly because they call into question basic preconceptions about the composer, neither seems to have gained popular currency.) The first concerns musical style: *Un ballo* represents Verdi's most consistent attempt to blend comedy with tragedy. In earlier and later works we can find comic *scenes*—the opening scene of *Rigoletto* (which resembles

[3] Massimo Mila, *Il melodramma di Verdi* (Bari, 1933), pp. 77–85, an expanded version of which appears in his *Giuseppe Verdi* (Bari, 1958), pp. 224–36. Guido Salvetti, ed., *Un ballo in maschera*, in *Opera. Collana di guide musicali*, Serie Prima, No. 2 (Turin, 1973), pp. 63–184. (This volume also contains a "critical" edition of the libretto, though not one that preserves the lineation or precise verse structure of the original.) Budden, *Verdi*, II, 376–423.

[4] Luigi Dallapiccola, "Parole e musica nel melodramma," *Appunti. Incontri. Meditazioni* (Milan, 1970), pp. 5–28; translated into English as "Words and Music in Nineteenth-Century Italian Opera," in *The Verdi Companion*, ed. William Weaver and Martin Chusid (New York, 1979), pp. 193–215. Robert Moreen, "Integration of Text Forms and Musical Forms in Verdi's Early Operas" (Ph.D. diss., Princeton Univ., 1975), pp. 112–27. One small point concerning Dallapiccola's analysis has, surprisingly in the light of the number of citations it receives, gone unnoticed: in his computation of the length of the trio, he counts measure 88 twice (as the end of his fourth section and the beginning of the coda). Thus, with the doubling of the final measure, the piece comes out as 113 measures long rather than 112. This in fact makes the symmetry all the more startling, as the precise midpoint now emerges as exactly on Riccardo's high *a*—halfway through measure 56.

[5] Gabriele Baldini, *Abitare la battaglia. La storia di Giuseppe Verdi* (Milan, 1970), pp. 277–308; English version, *The Story of Giuseppe Verdi*, ed. and trans. Roger Parker (Cambridge, 1980), pp. 245–71.

[6] The debate opened with Siegmund Levarie, "Key Relations in Verdi's *Un ballo in maschera*," *19th-Century Music*, II (1978–79), 143–47; comments on this in Joseph Kerman's "Viewpoint" (same issue, pp. 186–91) stimulated further replies from Guy A. Marco and Levarie in *19th-Century Music*, III (1979–80), 83–89. Levarie has since published a further article on the opera: "A Pitch Cell in Verdi's *Un ballo in maschera*," *Journal of Musicological Research*, III (1981), 399–409.

that of *Un ballo* in more than one respect), or the Fra Melitone episodes of *La forza del destino*—but in *Un ballo* the comic genre invades even the most serious scenes of the opera, vigorously challenging Verdi's reputation as one obsessed with the gloomy and melodramatic. Vital to this "comic flow" is the fact that the protagonist, Riccardo, is intimately associated with this side of the drama. In the opening scene, for example, his comic persona precedes our view of him as the impassioned lover; in Act I, scene 2 it is primarily his presence that provides comic relief from Ulrica's somber incantations. Riccardo's relationship with the young page Oscar is, in this respect, of particular importance. As Baldini points out, Oscar is in one sense merely an extension and exaggeration of Riccardo's musical personality—an ironic intensification of his tendency towards the language of comic opera. Thus, when Riccardo becomes too enmeshed in the tragic elements of the plot to continue his comic voice (in the third act), Oscar can quite naturally assume this role.[7]

The second reason for our particular "placing" of *Un ballo in maschera* lies in what we might term its emotional center of gravity: in this, as in no other Verdi opera, physical love is central to the musical action. Of course, nearly all Verdi's works have some love interest— some "tenor-soprano relationship"—but other matters are invariably of greater importance, especially if musical weight is (as it should be) the final arbiter. In *La traviata*, for instance, the love music between Alfredo and Violetta is pale and conventional beside the passionate exchanges of Violetta and Germont *père*. There are extreme cases, such as *La forza del destino*, in which the two lovers around whom the plot mechanism ostensibly revolves spend almost the entire opera physically apart. The importance of physical love in *Un ballo* is, on the other hand, essentially a matter of musical structure: the duet between Riccardo and Amelia is placed at the center of the score, midway through the second act; it is, furthermore, one of Verdi's longest and most complex set pieces, moving through a series of different phases as it follows Amelia's gradual weakening and final capitulation. In its length, centrality, and developmental nature, the duet presents us with a pair of lovers unique in the Verdian literature.

Nevertheless, despite widespread recognition of these stylistic and structural novelties, it is striking (perhaps symptomatic of Verdi studies in general) that the large-scale issues have tended to obscure particular instances: with the exception of the Dallapiccola and

---

[7] Baldini, *Abitare*, pp. 284–86; English translation, pp. 251–53.

Moreen pieces cited above,[8] there has been little detailed analysis of the score. The present article attempts to fill part of this gap by reviewing a single scene (Act I, scene 1) from several analytic perspectives; from this foundation we will consider certain aspects of the entire score and, ultimately, attempt to engage some general questions about the analysis of Verdi opera.

There are several reasons why Act I, scene 1 presents a particularly interesting case study, apart from its obvious advantage in carrying no weight of previous reminiscence. The "fusion of genres" (to borrow Piero Weiss's term[9]) inherent in *Un ballo* is clearly set forth: the basic mode of discourse is that of comic opera, but the scene also introduces (albeit obliquely, and with one of the principals absent) the tragic element of the plot—the "fatal triangle" of Riccardo, Amelia, and Renato—and the agents through whom this element will be activated—the conspirators. But tragedy is clearly subsumed under a traditional, long-standing form of comic opera: that of the *introduzione*.[10] Even very early in his career, with the *dramma giocoso Un giorno di regno* (1840), Verdi can be seen experimenting with this form, expanding and altering its conventional layout, as well as supplying motivic cross references that serve to support and articulate its dramatic structure.[11] The opening scenes of *Rigoletto* and *La traviata* had proved how fruitful this line of experiment was to be; Act I, scene 1 of *Un ballo* is, in this sense, the culmination of an important area of formal development.

A sense of conscious motivic working is nowhere more obvious than in the Preludio, where two rhythmic figures, first presented side by side in the opening bars of the opera, undergo a series of augmentations and diminutions (Example 1). Both figures are, of course, basic elements of the rhythmic language, and need (as here) a high degree of repetition and emphasis in order to be perceived as unifying features of some significance. It is not surprising, therefore,

[8] See n. 4.

[9] See Piero Weiss, "Verdi and the Fusion of Genres," this JOURNAL, XXXV (1982), 138–56. Weiss concentrates for the most part on comic elements in the operas up to and including *Rigoletto* (1851).

[10] For further information on the standard Rossinian *introduzione*, see Philip Gossett, "Gioachino Rossini and the Conventions of Composition," *Acta musicologica*, XLII (1970), 48–58.

[11] For a full account of Verdi's treatment of this scene, see Roger Parker, "Studies in Early Verdi (1832–1844); New Information and Perspectives on the Milanese Musical Milieu and the Operas from *Oberto* to *Ernani*" (Ph.D. diss., Univ. of London, 1981), pp. 88–91. The chapter on *Un giorno di regno* will be published in *Studi verdiani*, II (forthcoming).

Example 1

Two rhythmic figures from the Preludio

that they have no such prominence in the ensuing scene, or that their use here is too pervasive to allow any precise sense of semantic identification. The anapest rhythm (left-hand column) does perhaps become loosely identified with Riccardo and Oscar through the accompaniment of "Volta la terrea" (28/3ff.)[12] and the opening theme

[12] In this and all subsequent musical citations, references are to the page/system/measure of the current Ricordi piano-vocal score, Plate No. 48180.

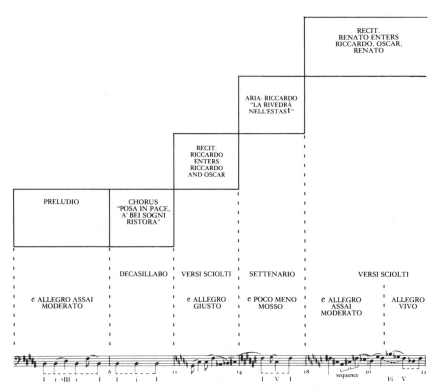

368

Figure 1. Schematic diagram and

of "Ogni cura si doni al diletto" (36/4); on the other hand, in Act 1, scene 2 it is the four-note figure (right-hand column) that consistently acts as Riccardo's *carte de visite*.

Noticeable as such features are on the local level, however, the most distinctive aspect of the entire opening scene is its classical balance—what Budden describes as its "subtly varied symmetry."[13] Though it fulfills the traditional task of the *introduzione* of presenting major characters, Act I, scene 1 is remarkable for its economy, pace, and equilibrium: unusually brief solo pieces are given to no less than three of the five principals, this trio of arias being flanked by a pair of choral numbers which are themselves "multi-character" in that each juxtaposes contrasting groups. The entire scene lasts only about

[13] Budden, *Verdi*, II, 383.

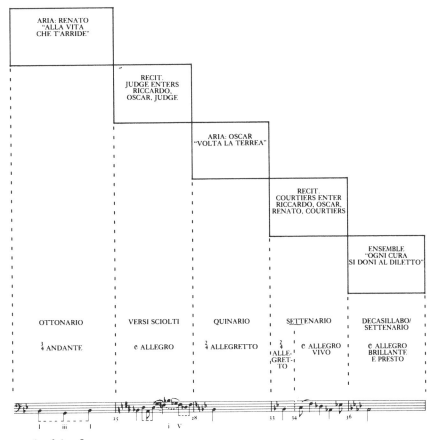

graph of Act I, scene I

twenty minutes in performance.[14] As we can see from Figure 1, the five-part structure forms an arch: the outer choral movements enclose arias for Riccardo and Oscar, characters who, as we mentioned earlier, are intimately related both musically and dramatically; at the center of the scene—the apex of the arch—comes Renato's cantabile "Alla vita che t'arride."

This central placing of Renato's solo in fact turns out to be of crucial importance to the structure of the scene, as "Alla vita" is set apart both musically and dramatically from the surrounding action, creating a hiatus that ultimately serves to emphasize unifying elements within the rest of the music. This sense of isolation is, of

[14] By comparison, the corresponding section of Auber's *Gustave III ou Le Bal masqué* (the original setting of Scribe's text) is noticeably dilated.

course, quite appropriate so far as the drama is concerned—Renato casts a brief but telling shadow over the predominantly comic atmosphere; but his presence is critical to the denouement, hence the aptness of his central position in the scene.[15] On the simplest level, the nature of this disjunction is easy to demonstrate. While the arias of Riccardo and Oscar contain interpolations from others on stage—a suggestion (no more than that in Riccardo's case) of conversation or at least interaction—Renato sings uninterrupted, heard only by Riccardo. His aria, furthermore, is surrounded by musical and dramatic non-sequiturs: musically, its clear B-flat tonality is preceded by an emphatic cadential progression in D flat (22/1/1–3), and followed, without preparation, by a section in D (25/1/1–3); dramatically, Renato responds only obliquely (and with considerable circumlocution) to Riccardo's self-confident assertions, and, when his aria concludes, other characters immediately appear, moving the focus of attention briskly on to fresh matters.

These "surface" procedures for isolating Renato's aria are certainly effective; but they are of less interest to the analyst than a number of other means whereby, while still serving his dramatic ends, Verdi adds to the unity and precise balance of the entire scene. The first of these concerns the sequence of verse forms noted in Figure 1.[16] As we would expect, passages of *versi sciolti* (the unrhymed, seven- and eleven-syllable verses standard in recitative) alternate with *versi lirici* (rhymed verses of fixed line length). The two choral numbers are related by their use of *decasillabi* (ten-syllable lines) with their tendency towards anapest rhythms (Example 2).

Example 2

Anapest rhythms in Act I, scene 1

(a) Po - sa in pa - ce_a' bei so - gni ri - sto - ra

(b) O - gni cu - ra si do - ni al di - let - to

---

[15] As Julian Budden remarks in connection with this scene: "Renato is the pivot on whom the drama turns" (*Verdi*, II, 383).

[16] We can be reasonably sure that the precise nature of these verse forms was chosen by Verdi rather than his librettist. In an early letter to the composer, Somma, evidently nervous about his inexperience, asks Verdi to "note down in the margin [of the scenario] the form of the verses, and the type and length of line for each verse, because then I can more easily provide you with suitable poetry" (Luzio, *Carteggi*, I, 219).

Both Riccardo's and Oscar's arias, on the other hand, have lines of odd-number syllable length, in which the initial stress is variable: "La rivedrà nell'estasi" is in *settenari* (seven syllables); "Volta la terrea" in *quinari* (five syllables). The resulting link is strengthened by the shared use of *sdruccioli* (in which final words are stressed on the antepenultimate syllable: "*esta*si," "*ter*rea"). Verdi's unusually free use of word repetition in these two arias, taken to an extreme in the opening quatrain of "La rivedrà," shows the flexibility with which verse structure and musical phrase interact. By contrast, the regular stress on the third and penultimate syllables in the *ottonari* of Renato's *cantabile* ("Alla *vi*ta che t'ar*ri*de") displays a uniformity that is exploited by Verdi's setting, which places each stressed syllable at the beginning of a measure. The correlation between word stress and musical accent produces a sense of rhythmic formality that is perfectly in keeping with Renato's rather conventional discourse, and is further highlighted by the triple meter of the aria—(the rest of the scene shows a progression from ¢, to 2/4, to ¢).

Various other features contribute to the unity, atmosphere, or, to use a notoriously untranslatable Verdian word, the *tinta* of this opening scene.[17] Perhaps most immediately striking is a continuing tendency to juxtapose tonic major and minor mode (Example 3). The first chromatic note of the entire opera, in the opening bars of the Preludio, suggests such a juxtaposition (Example 3a), although the tonality at that moment is not precisely defined, and the gesture can only be understood as a B-major/minor alternation retrospectively.[18] No such ambiguity is present in the opening chorus, where the "uffiziali e gentiluomini"—supporters of Riccardo—hymn his praises in B major (Example 3b), to be interrupted (or, rather, counterbalanced) by Sam, Tom, and their "aderenti"—the conspirators—whose

371

[17] For a thorough discussion of the word *tinta*, and an attempt to interpret it in semiotic terms, see Frits Noske, *The Signifier and the Signified* (The Hague, 1977), pp. 294–308.

[18] Siegmund Levarie's "Pitch Cell" article (referred to above, in n. 6) isolates the d♯–c♯ progression in measure 2 of the opera as "the pitch cell that influences, unites, and gives character to the whole opera" (p. 401). Many of his specific examples seem bizarrely out of context (for example, his submission [p. 401] that the pitch cell, "enharmonically reinterpreted as *e*♭ to *d*♭ . . . dominates the closing ten measures of the opera after Riccardo's death"). Later in the article, Levarie perhaps betrays an awareness that his cell is rather cramped. On p. 403 we read: "The occurrence of *d* as both sharp and natural admits of a modification of the basic cell (a technique I have also found in other works)." Elliott Antokoletz follows Levarie's methodology (with perhaps more significant results) in "Verdi's Dramatic Use of Harmony and Tonality in *Macbeth*," *In Theory Only*, IV, No. 6 (1978–79), 17–28.

Example 3

Major-minor juxtapositions in Act I, scene 1

muttered threats are in B minor (Example 3c). The musico-dramatic intention (one might almost say semantic equivalence) is clear, and this simple equation is reinforced in the coda of "La rivedrà" (16/2/1–2), in which Sam and Tom drag the music flatwards with a reminiscence of Example 3c. The final number of the scene, "Ogni cura si doni al diletto," offers another case in point: Renato's repeated injunctions towards vigilance against the conspirators inflect the music towards the minor mode (37/2/1ff.). But such clear equivalences should not deflect attention from the broader significance of modal mixture in this scene. Far from depicting exclusively one area of dialectic tension (loyal courtiers versus conspirators), its function is rather to highlight different levels of duality and, by the resulting musical cross reference, to suggest parallels between them. In Riccardo's case, the turn to the tonic minor in "La rivedrà" (Example 3d) adumbrates the inevitable tragic consequences of his passion for Amelia, just as the sudden move from F major to minor had done in the measures immediately preceding (13/2–3). Parallel moments in Oscar's "Volta la terrea" then fall easily into place: it is perfectly in accord with the intimate dramatic relationship between Riccardo and Oscar (mentioned earlier) that the latter's aria has a passage whose turn to the minor complements Riccardo's in exaggerated, mock serious fashion (Example 3e). The fact that Oscar's words could easily apply to Amelia and Riccardo is yet another level of ironic cross reference.[19] We are left again with Renato's *cantabile*, alone among the five set pieces in *not* featuring prominent tonic minor inflections. As if in deliberate contrast, the secondary key area of "Alla vita" is the more conventional relative minor; the occasional but potentially disturbing $g^\flat$ is thus far less important than its enharmonic equivalent—clearly directed $f\sharp$ leading tones in G minor. The tonal structure of Renato's aria thus represents a further level on which his musical conventionality serves to isolate him from the flow of the drama.

Another, perhaps contingent feature that contributes both to the *tinta* of the scene and to its internal dramatic articulation is the use of dominant harmony over tonic pedals. The frequency of this device may well derive in part from Verdi's often-stated desire to imbue the score with a "Gallic" atmosphere.[20] Auber's setting of the original Scribe libretto (*Gustave III, ou Le Bal masqué*, [Paris, 1833]) is certainly bestrewn with examples, many of them employed with (to use Budden's phrase) "a persistency worthy of Sullivan,"[21] although the device can just as clearly (and perhaps more pertinently) be found in the later scores of Donizetti. Again, all the set pieces *except* Renato's make use of the device (6/1/1–2; 14/1/1–2; 28/3/4–5; 39/1/2–5: inclusion of the opening bars of "La rivedrà" may seem to stretch the point, but the unusual placing of leading tone against tonic harmony is perhaps sufficient to allow it within the family grouping); and again, as with the replacement of tonic minor with relative minor, we find a conventional analogue in "Alla vita"—its noticeably prolonged *dominant* pedal at the outset (22/2/2–4).

373

---

[19] In the first verse, his lines are: "Quando alle belle/Il fin predice/Mesto o felice/Dei loro amor!" ("When she [i.e. Ulrica] predicts to the beautiful girls the sad or the happy end to their love!") In the second: "Le sue vicende/Soavi, amare/Da questa apprende/Nel dubbio cor." ("From her these doubting hearts [i.e. those of young men] learn of their fortunes, whether bitter or sweet.")

[20] Take, for example, the following passage, in which Verdi responds to suggestions that the venue of *Un ballo* be changed: "I really think that the twelfth century is too distant for our Gustavo. It's such a rough and brutal time especially in those countries that I find it sheer nonsense to have characters sculpted in the French manner like Gustavo and Oscar" (quoted in Budden, *Verdi*, II, 368).

[21] Budden, *Verdi*, II, 381.

It is interesting, certainly significant in terms of any search for unity within the entire opera, that the musical devices we have isolated here are never again so prominent as in this scene. Act I, scene 2 is characterized by quite different material: chromatic passages in parallel thirds; open tritones; a tendency to cadence vocally around the diminished third. All these are associated with Ulrica, whose musical presence dominates this scene almost as much as did Riccardo's the first. The major-minor alternations of Act I, scene 1 are typically reversed into the more conventional minor-major progression, as in Ulrica's opening double aria (50–58), or Riccardo's "Di' tu se fedele" (83–89). The creation of a particular ambience for each scene, the setting of each in musical relief, as it were, does of course allow for striking cross references—meaningful incursions of a set of devices from one scene into the territory of another. The atmosphere of sinister repression that surrounds Ulrica is briefly and tellingly referred to in scene 1, when Riccardo's "Segreta, acerba cura m'opprime" ("A secret, bitter care oppresses me") is preceded by a cadence in which the vocal line describes a diminished third and is underpinned by a bare tritone in the orchestra (19/2–3). Similarly, Silvano's injection of Riccardo-influenced opera buffa language into scene 2 features tonic minor inflections (59/3/1–2) and dominant harmony over tonic pedals (59/4/1–3).

Act I, scene 1 is, then, a discrete section of the opera in which words, music, and drama combine to form a coherent, symmetrical structure. Needless to say, the effect of equipoise is not total—nor could it conceivably be at this stage of the drama. We noted earlier a sense of rhythmic acceleration that carries the scene to its well-nigh frenetic conclusion. But, to return to an earlier image, the overall impression is one of "classical balance." It is now time to turn to the one important musical area in which, at least on the surface, this balance seems not at all in evidence, an area that is frequently ignored even by the most thorough commentators: we refer to the overall tonal motion.

As a starting point we might return to Figure I, and to the bass graph of the scene offered there.[22] It is immediately clear that the tonal flow does not underpin our previously-identified dramatic

---

[22] Graphs such as this, which derive in part from Schenkerian concepts and terminology, have rarely been used in Verdi analysis. The most significant exception is David Lawton, "Tonality and Drama in Verdi's Early Operas" (Ph.D. diss., Univ. of California, Berkeley, 1973). Readers might also like to consult Daniel Sabbeth,

symmetry in any obvious manner. The scene is tonally open-ended, with the progression of B major to A-flat major suggesting no clear goal direction. The arch-form structure and subsequent isolation of Renato's *cantabile* is hardly supported: Oscar's and Riccardo's arias are in keys only distantly related; but Oscar and Renato are seemingly drawn together by their shared use of B-flat major, which causes (at least so far as the set pieces are concerned) a kind of tonal plateau following the midpoint of the scene.[23] If tonality and drama interact, it is clearly in a manner either more subtle, or more random, than has been the case with musical features discussed earlier. Before considering the implications of this, it will be useful to examine some of the harmonic details sketched in Figure I.

Just as the libretto alternates *versi lirici* and *versi sciolti*, so the music alternates sections of tonal stability and instability. The five set pieces (in *versi lirici*) are all closed forms in the major mode. In each number, the harmonic motion is restricted to closely-related keys: the opening chorus has an episode in the parallel minor; "La rivedrà" moves to a cadence on the dominant in its central section; "Alla vita" modulates to the relative minor; Oscar's *ballata* remains in the tonic, as does (with a brief excursion to V of V) the final ensemble. But within this narrow tonal orbit, Verdi achieves considerable harmonic variety. Two particular techniques stand out: modal mixture (previously identified as a prime contributor to the *tinta* of the scene); and a tendency—often found in Verdi—towards chromatic substitution of pre-dominants. These two features subtly interact in the Preludio (Example 4).

375

Example 4

Modal mixture and chromatic pre-dominants in the Preludio

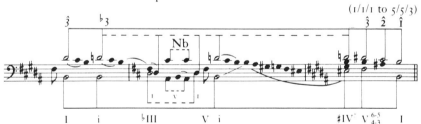

"Dramatic and Musical Organization in *Falstaff*," *Atti del III° congresso di studi verdiani* (Parma, 1974), pp. 415–42. Schenker himself wrote a number of pieces on Verdi and other Italian opera composers for the periodical *Die Zukunft*. Two of these discuss *Falstaff*: "Notizen zu Verdis Falstaff" (June, 1893), pp. 474–76; and "Verdis Falstaff" (May, 1894), pp. 230–33.

[23] One tonal feature that supports the arch form is the pair of prolonged dominant pedals, the first introducing the opening recitative (11/1–4), the second preceding the final ensemble (34/1–4). But in both cases, it seems that the *scenic* function—the

The modulations to B minor, D major, and back to B minor prolong the minor third (d♮), thus raising modal mixture to a higher level of structure in the opening, purely instrumental part of the scene; d♯ is eventually restored, and is preceded (and emphasized) by an unusual ♯IV⁷ pre-dominant (5/2/3).[24] As we know, the following chorus also juxtapose B major and minor but, in contrast to the earlier situation, here B minor does not generate the secondary key area of D major. Modal mixture is thus of far less structural significance.

The progress of the five set pieces, from B major via F-sharp major and B-flat major to A-flat major, necessitates transition passages, and these occur in the recitatives. Each recitative describes a different tonal motion and, naturally, underpins different stage events, but they have various links that contribute to the unity of the scene (though again without clear reference to our previously-established symmetrical structure). The most obvious of these is thematic recall. In the recitative immediately following "La rivedrà," the stage clears to leave Riccardo alone with Renato. The opening bars of "La rivedrà" are juxtaposed with a theme earlier identified with the conspirators (Example 3c); and the resulting dissonances are clearly intended as a musical illustration of the sharp contrast between (and incompatibility of) the two characters' inner preoccupations (18/1–4).

Moments such as these (there are others in the opera) have clear significance, are easily "decoded" in terms of the plot. Other linking devices are at once more basic to the structure and more difficult to interpret. Consider, for example, the parallels between the second and third recitatives (18/1/1 to 22/1/5; 25/2/3 to 28/3/2). Both employ pedal *d*s in their first halves and, though one is a dominant and the other a tonic, both pedals serve to inflect the music towards G minor (20/1–3; 26/4/2ff.). However, it is in the final measures that they are drawn most strikingly together. Both quickly reach an *f* pedal after leaving the repeated *d*s, but then indulge in an unusual tonal excursion via B-flat minor and D-flat major before finally moving back to *f* and relaxing on the B-flat major tonic of the ensuing set piece. In both cases there is a dramatic reason for the tonal digression: in the first recitative, it coincides with Riccardo's attempt to divert Renato from

---

provision of a generic sense of musical expectation to accompany an important entrance (Riccardo's) or a necessarily protracted one (the courtiers')—outweighs the tonal, as neither pedal heralds a long-lasting key center.

[24] Schenker examines the concept of mixture for first-level middleground in *Free Composition (Der freie Satz)*, trans. Ernst Oster (New York, 1979), pp. 40–41 (figs. 28–30). A precedent for the bass progression I-♯IV⁷-V-I may be found in Schenker's graph of Handel's B-flat Prelude (*Free Composition*, Fig. 73/ii).

his self-appointed stance as prophet of doom; in the second, with the Judge's attempt to inject a note of seriousness into Oscar's presentation of Ulrica. But the generic similarity of situation cannot convincingly account for this close musical relationship, which is further strengthened by the fact that the passages approach *f* via an identical unison ascent of *d♭-e♭-f* (21/3/3–5; 28/1/3–4) and share prominent vocal sonorities: Riccardo's high *g♭* falling to *f*, which emphasizes the function of *g♭* as an upper neighbor of V of B-flat major. For convenience, we have aligned the two recitatives vertically (Example 5).

Example 5

Comparison of recitative passages from Act I, scene 1

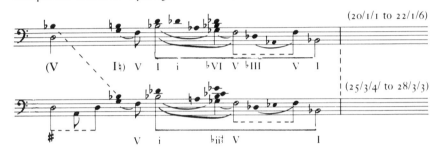

Once identified and accepted, the presence of such a "model" suggests parallels with other sections of the scene. One might, for example, say that the important role of B-flat minor is foreshadowed in the moments immediately preceding "La rivedrà," where the move to F-sharp major is made via a B-flat minor triad (13/3/4); certainly the manner in which *f♯* is approached *vocally* at this point (through *f♮*) must link the passage to the recurring *g♭-f* "vocal sonority" mentioned in the previous paragraph, and suggests that, on this level, G-flat major might be a more appropriate key signature for the aria.[25] Later in the scene, Oscar's *ballata* touches momentarily on D-flat major, demonstrating that set pieces are not necessarily excluded from this particular web of cross references. The final recitative is a particularly interesting case: F major again gives way to D-flat major (34/5/3ff.), and it is perhaps not until Riccardo's final statement ("E tu m'appronta un abito/Da pescator"), with its emphatic high *g♮* and (not uncharacteristic) disruption of the four-bar units, that we become aware of a tonal goal different from that of the previous two recitatives.

---

[25] This passage will be referred to in more detail later.

This tendency to prolong the dominant of B-flat major with excursions to D-flat major, though a recurring feature of Act I, scene 1, is not one to which we can attach any immediate significance in terms of the drama. For clarification, we must now consider the role of D flat in the remainder of the opera.[26] First, the key is plainly associated with a dramatic event; so plainly that it is surprising to find no mention of the fact in the existing literature. In Act I, scene 2, Ulrica's prediction of Riccardo's assassination is prepared in F major (91/1–2) but then begins in D-flat major (91/2/4); as the tension increases, we move to D-flat minor (92/2/3) in which the flat sixth ($b\flat\flat$) is prominent in the bass. This progression comes to a climax as Ulrica mentions death ("Ebben, presto morrai"), at which point the flat sixth is unexpectedly reinterpreted as an A-major chord (92/1/2). From there we move briefly to E major, the *e* then being prolonged as part of a diminished chord before rising to *f*, which becomes the dominant of the next ensemble, "È scherzo od è follia." This singular chromatic elaboration is reproduced almost exactly when the event itself occurs, in the final scene of the opera. Again, D-flat major emerges without preparation from F major (291/2–3), turns to D-flat minor (or turns in that direction: at any rate, the flat sixths in the bass—291/3 or 292/1—are unmistakable), and then, as the fatal blow is struck, moves to an A-major chord (292/3/2). A (changed to the minor mode) is prolonged as the bystanders react, but eventually comes to a pause on an E-major dominant chord; this then rises to F major (297/1/1), which in turn acts as the dominant of the concluding set piece. Again, vertically aligned bass graphs will serve to clarify and summarize the relationship (Example 6).

Example 6

Comparison of passages from Act I, scene 2 and the finale to Act III

[26] Kerman, "Viewpoint," p. 90, mentions certain occurrences of this key in Acts II and III. As will become obvious, we cannot entirely agree with his conclusion that "these are elegant details of tonal organization which it is hard to think carry any particular dramatic message."

Two supplementary points are worth noting, First, as with the matched recitatives in Act I, scene 1, the shared tonal progression is strengthened by shared vocal sonorities, notably at the climactic moment of enharmonic shift, at which Ulrica and Renato declaim on *d♭/c♯* (Example 7). Second, the sense in which these progressions may be understood as prolongations of an F-major dominant is put to magnificent dramatic effect in the assassination scene. The initial F-major section is a stage-band mazurka, which then returns, intact and at the same pitch, after the murder, giving the impression that it has continued unaware of the violence of the onstage events. There could be no better illustration of the subtle manner in which tonality and drama can interact in mature Verdi.

Example 7

Shared vocal sonorities from Act I, scene 2 and the finale to Act III

As with the repeated progressions of Act I, scene 1, this "double cycle"[27] places in a more coherent context other noteworthy aspects of the harmonic syntax of *Un ballo in maschera*, allowing us to see a complex network of cross references. Moving backwards from the assassination scene, we come to Riccardo's *romanza* "Ma se m'è forza perderti" (251–54). Much could be written about this curious, elliptical piece, in particular about its symbiotic relationship with Ulrica's double aria in Act I, scene 2; here we can refer only to the section in which Riccardo unconsciously predicts his own end:

> Ed or qual reo presagio
> Lo spirito m'assale,
> Che il rivederti annunzia
> Quasi un desìo fatale . . .[28]

[27] A term borrowed from Lawton, "Tonality and Drama."

[28] "And now what dark misgivings assail my spirit, because to see you again seems like a fatal desire." It is surely significant that, after painting "fatale" so obviously, Verdi omits it from the coda when this quatrain is repeated.

As if to confirm the accuracy of his prediction, the word "fatale" (253/2/1–2) coincides with a firmly-prepared authentic cadence in D-flat major, a key whose distance from the overall tonality of the aria (C minor/major) is emphasized by Verdi's refusal to resolve it through the usual Neapolitan channel. Further references to D flat in Act III strengthen its identification as an "accordo della sventura" in *Un ballo*, but none is more telling than that in the scene where the conspirators draw lots for the opportunity to murder Riccardo. The stage directions run as follows:

> Amelia si avvicina lentamente e tremante al tavolo su cui vi è il vaso, Renato fulminandola sempre dello sguardo: finalmente sul ppp (*) d'orchestra, Amelia con mano tremante estrae un viglietto che suo marito passa a Samuel. (228)[29]

making it quite clear that the moment in which Amelia draws forth her husband's name coincides precisely with the moment the accompanying orchestral sequence reaches a chord of D-flat major.

It would be at best prosaic, at worst belittling and distorting, to attempt to foist such a clear equivalence of tonality and plot mechanism on the remainder of the opera; Verdi had early enough (certainly after the experiments of *I due Foscari* in 1844) realized the limitations of such obvious equations. Perhaps the conspirators' "E ci vedrai" (194/2–3) is a solitary exception from Act II—but it occurs very near the end and belongs more to the atmosphere and events of Act III. Yet the second act is by no means irrelevant so far as this aspect of the tonal working of the opera is concerned: during the love duet and subsequent trios, it is primarily the *context* of D flat that is explored, in particular the varying ways in which it may be linked to F major and A major. The two most interesting examples are best represented graphically (Example 8).

Example 8

Excursions to D-flat major in Act II   (145/3/1 to 151/2/1)

[29] "Trembling, Amelia slowly approaches the table on which lies the vase. Renato continues to stare angrily at her: finally, on the orchestra's ppp (*), Amelia with a trembling hand takes out a piece of paper, which her husband passes to Samuel."

Both turns to D flat from an F-major context have immediate dramatic justification: Amelia's attempt to avoid the implications of Riccardo's love song in Example 8(a); Renato's turning of the conversation towards Amelia in Example 8(b). In the longer term, though, both also serve to strengthen the tonal coherence of the opera by repeating in different contexts an important feature of harmonic syntax.

Moving back still further, we come to Ulrica's prophecy in Act I, scene 2, and would seem to have completed a full circle. But in fact the connecting strands continue to stretch back. Compare, for example, Ulrica's prediction of Riccardo's fate (the "model" for the final scene) with her previous divinations concerning the sailor Silvano. The two men are linked together (at least so far as operatic etiquette will allow—Riccardo is *primo tenore*, Silvano merely *secondo basso*): both are sailors (Riccardo only for the nonce, of course); both introduce themselves by way of "characteristic" arias;[30] both have their fortunes told by Ulrica to an identical orchestral pattern (60/1/4ff.; 91/2/4ff.). But of course their fates are quite different: Silvano gets promotion and a sack of gold; Riccardo gets murdered by his best friend. The moment of prediction at once identifies and distinguishes between them. In Silvano's case, Ulrica, departing from a C-sharp major chord, intones on $c\sharp$ before moving purposefully to a cadence in E major. With Riccardo, she again intones on $c\sharp$ (initially notated, and understood, as $d\flat$), but then drops the octave to the accompaniment of an A-major chord, which (in *this* context) is disturbing. Riccardo, in an attempt to put a happy (i.e., Silvano-like) face on the prediction, echoes the latter half of Ulrica's Silvano prediction (Example 9).

381

Example 9

Comparison of passages from Act I, scene 2

[30] In Silvano's "Su, fatemi largo" the D-flat major/A-major relationship is explored from another angle: the aria is in A major with a middle section (59/3–5) in C-sharp major.

Needless to say, his attempted modulation away from danger is immediately countered by Ulrica.

And so we return to Act I, scene 1, with the realization that its seemingly anomalous excursions to D-flat major are in fact just links in a chain of related tonal explorations which, as the opera progresses to its tragic end, become increasingly complex and increasingly related to the dramatic events. In this sense, the first scene might be compared with the early scenes of a Shakespearean drama, in which a central theme may invade the poetic level—primarily by means of metaphor—before it emerges as a dramatic issue: certain harmonic relationships are explored in the basic fabric of the music—as "neutral" underpinning of stage actions—long before they appropriate specific dramatic connotations. One possible exception lies in the recitative passage that accompanies Renato's first entrance, mentioned earlier in connection with thematic recall (18/2–3). As Oscar leaves, he "hands over" Riccardo to Renato with the words "Libero è il varco a voi" ("The way is open to you"); it is the first moment in the opera in which attention is focused on the future assassin, and the music, which has previously been left hovering on the dominant of C-sharp minor, moves unexpectedly to A major to state, with a "characteristic" sonority (borrowed from the Preludio) of 4^a corda first violins, a complete statement of the first phrase of "La rivedrà." Renato then sings for the first time, with precisely the repeated ♯s on which he will conclude his role in the drama (cf. 292/3/1). But this fleeting reference, a last thin strand stretching back from the tragic denouement, should not be overstressed; as we have seen, the recitatives of Act I, scene 1 have larger-scale and more significant harmonic preparations for what is to come.

In conclusion, we should discuss briefly some general implications of our specific inquiry. Our isolation of D flat, and exploration of its relationships with A, F, and B flat, albeit seen as a major feature of the opera, by no means suggest that any (or all) of these keys may be regarded as "tonics" in the largest context. And we have made no mention of other keys (notably C and A flat) that figure prominently, and that set up further networks of cross reference and syntactic pattern. We should also mention that, far from defining the structure, the tonal models we found in Act I, scene 1 tended to cut across more obvious and immediate connections between dramatic and motivic elements. In short, it seems clear that the musical structure of the opera, whether geared to motivic or harmonic matters, or to both, lies essentially in an accumulation of detail rather than in any abstract pattern. Verdi's treatment of tonality and motive is best expressed metaphorically as a complex web of interlocking relationships. It may at times be tempting to cut through this web, to shape an empyrean path along which *all* details can be neatly arranged: but the unity of purpose thus achieved can only be chimerical, and will be attained only by ignoring or distorting contradictory evidence.

The metaphorical orientation suggested above allows one to accept, even to rejoice in, a rich vein of ambiguity: something that arises quite naturally out of a medium in which elements governed by different structural laws are combined. For example, any attempt to discuss the role of tonality in opera in "absolute" terms is bound to give rise to distortions, to ignore this deep ambiguity. Take Guy Marco's advice towards forming a definition of "key" in operatic terms:

> Keys must be clearly identified, and just as clearly located in the design. Identification should distinguish among keys that are firmly established (capable of generating their own substructures of related keys) and those which are merely signalled by a chord or two, and there should be intermediate categories as well. In locating keys, the analyst should address the participation of a key in the micro-structure, the mid-structure, and the macro-structure, and it [*sic*] should be aware that crossover affinities from one structural level to another are likely to be suspect. Without a certain degree of clarity on this sort of issue, binary oppositions and other symmetries may be illusory.[31]

On the surface, a sensible, middle-of-the-road approach; but as soon as one considers the practical implications, doubts arise. "Crossover affinities from one structural level to another," far from being "suspect," seem on the basis of the present analysis to be the very stuff of flexible operatic working. Depending on the dramatic situation, related musico-dramatic events may be articulated by a fully worked-out key, generating its own substructure, or perhaps merely by a gesture or chord, backed up by a vocal or orchestral sonority. We have mentioned such moments: the A-major chord in Act I, scene 1 that is the more-or-less ignored prediction of an aging sibyl (92/1/2), becomes in the final scene an extended section in A minor, the necessary reaction to a political assassination-cum-*crime passionnel* enacted in public view.

---

[31] Guy Marco, *19th-Century Music*, III, 84.

To take this argument a stage further, are we justified in regarding it as axiomatic that the set pieces of an opera such as *Un ballo* govern in some fundamental way its tonal structure? Set pieces are often perceived as "frozen time"—as an interruption of external events; could not their tonality on occasions also be regarded as such, as an expanded moment of interruption rather than a goal? Riccardo's "La rivedrà" is a good case in point. Reading his beloved's name on the guest list for the *ballo in maschera*, Riccardo goes into an extended aside; the music plunges from F major to F minor (13/2–3) as he calls her name—"Amelia!"; still in his reverie, he sings an aria in F-sharp major—an F sharp that, as we have said, is introduced vocally as a Neapolitan relation of *f*; after the aria, his private thoughts continue (in the orchestra), and he calls her name a final time—"Amelia!"—immediately before being "awakened" by Renato; and, at the moment of awakening, as if coming back to land, the music reverses its modulatory pattern, moving from F minor back to F major (18/4 to 19/1); all in all, a perfect sense of tonal interruption. The fact that Riccardo's aria is nothing more than an "expanded moment"—a momentary thought given idealized vocal expression—was evidently something stressed in the original production, which took place under Verdi's supervision: in the official production book—the so-called *disposizione scenica*—we are informed that "While Riccardo sings his cavatina at the footlights, Oscar should be seen exchanging compliments with the bystanders."[32] If this F-sharp major aria is seen as a massive interruption of F, then, in *one* sense, the opening of the opera might be seen as "in" B-flat major: the B of the opening chorus as a tonicized leading note (which, incidentally, conforms rather well with its eventual turn to C major in 11/1–4); then II-V-interruption!-V-I in B-flat major. And, of course, this would be a gross simplification—a *Hamlet*-without-the-Prince analysis. The strong relationship of B major and F-sharp major is backed up by prominent thematic recall, and can hardly be fortuitous; furthermore, this concentration on sharp keys at the beginning of the scene makes the recitative after "La rivedrà," which is so interesting in other respects, a true turning point in the structure, the sequential move from F sharp to A to C sharp to F marking the renunciation of sharp keys in favor of flat. What all this proves is that any *one* explanation of the tonal or motivic structure of a piece as complex as *Un ballo in maschera* is bound to be unsatisfactory.

---

[32] *Disposizione scenica per l'opera* Un ballo in maschera *di G. Verdi sulla messa in scena del Teatro Apollo in Roma il carnevale del 1859, del direttore del medesimo, Giuseppe Cencetti* (Milan, 1859), p. 8 (quoted in Budden, *Verdi*, II, 379).

That those irremediably wedded to organicism are doomed to distort this repertory. That the web may have less attraction than the empyrean path, but that healthy entanglement is more likely to produce results than sublime disregard.

Cornell University